T0122912

Get the eBooks FREE!

(PDF, ePub, Kindle, and liveBook all included)

We believe that once you buy a book from us, you should be
able to read it in any format we have available. To get electronic
versions of this book at no additional cost to you, purchase and
then register this book at the Manning website.

Go to https://www.manning.com/freebook and follow the
instructions to complete your pBook registration.

That's it!
Thanks from Manning!

RxJS in Action

RxJS in Action

COVERS RxJS 5

PAUL P. DANIELS
LUIS ATENCIO

FOREWORD BY BEN LESH

MANNING
SHELTER ISLAND

For online information and ordering of this and other Manning books, please visit
www.manning.com. The publisher offers discounts on this book when ordered in quantity.
For more information, please contact

> Special Sales Department
> Manning Publications Co.
> 20 Baldwin Road
> PO Box 761
> Shelter Island, NY 11964
> Email: orders@manning.com

Manning Publications Co.
20 Baldwin Road
PO Box 761
Shelter Island, NY 11964

Development editor:	Frances Lefkowitz
Technical development editor:	Dean Iverson
Project editor:	Janet Vail
Copyeditor:	Linda Recktenwald
Proofreader:	Katie Tennant
Technical proofreader:	Cody Sand
Typesetter:	Dottie Marsico
Cover designer:	Marija Tudor

ISBN 9781617293412
Printed in the United States of America

brief contents

PART 1   UNDERSTANDING STREAMS 1

    1 ▪ Thinking reactively   3
    2 ▪ Reacting with RxJS   28
    3 ▪ Core operators   61
    4 ▪ It's about time you used RxJS   85

PART 2   OBSERVABLES IN PRACTICE 119

    5 ▪ Applied reactive streams   121
    6 ▪ Coordinating business processes   151
    7 ▪ Error handling with RxJS   182

PART 3   MASTERING RxJS 209

    8 ▪ Heating up observables   211
    9 ▪ Toward testable, reactive programs   245
   10 ▪ RxJS in the wild   271

contents

foreword   xiii
preface   xv
acknowledgments   xvii
about this book   xix
about the authors   xxiv
about the cover   xxv

PART 1   UNDERSTANDING STREAMS.................................1

1   **Thinking reactively   3**

 1.1   Synchronous vs. asynchronous computing   5

  Issues with blocking code   5 ▪ Non-blocking code with
callback functions   6 ▪ Understanding time and space   7
Are callbacks out of the picture?   9 ▪ Event emitters   11

 1.2   Better callbacks with Promises   12

 1.3   The need for a different paradigm   14

 1.4   The Reactive Extensions for JavaScript   17

  Thinking in streams: data flows and propagation   17
Introducing the RxJS project   18 ▪ Everything is a
stream   19 ▪ Abstracting the notion of time from your
programs   21 ▪ Components of an Rx stream   23

 1.5   Reactive and other programming paradigms   26

 1.6   Summary   27

2 **Reacting with RxJS   28**

   2.1 Functional programming as the pillar of reactive
        programming   29
        Functional programming   30 • The iterator pattern   38

   2.2 Stream's data-driven approach   41

   2.3 Wrapping data sources with Rx.Observable   43
        *Identifying different sources of data   43 • Creating RxJS
        observables   44 • When and where to use RxJS   46
        To push or not to push   49*

   2.4 Consuming data with observers   53
        *The Observer API   53 • Creating bare observables   55
        Observable modules   57*

   2.5 Summary   60

3 **Core operators   61**

   3.1 Evaluating and cancelling streams   62
        *Downside of eager allocation   62 • Lazy allocation and
        subscribing to observables   64 • Disposing of subscriptions:
        explicit cancellation   65 • Cancellation mismatch between
        RxJS and other APIs   67*

   3.2 Popular RxJS observable operators   69
        Introducing the core operators   70

   3.3 Sequencing operator pipelines with aggregates   77
        *Self-contained pipelines and referential transparency   77
        Performance advantages of sequencing with RxJS   80*

   3.4 Summary   83

4 **It's about time you used RxJS   85**

   4.1 Why worry about time?   87

   4.2 Understanding asynchronous timing with JavaScript   88
        *Implicit timing   88 • Explicit timing   88 • The JavaScript
        timing interfaces   90*

   4.3 Back to the future with RxJS   94
        Propagation   98 • Sequential time   99

   4.4 Handling user input   101
        Debouncing   101 • Throttling   108

   4.5 Buffering in RxJS   111

   4.6 Summary   116

PART 2   OBSERVABLES IN PRACTICE 119

5   *Applied reactive streams   121*

5.1   One for all, and all for one!   122
       *Interleave events by merging streams   124 ▪ Preserve order
       of events by concatenating streams   130 ▪ Switch to the
       latest observable data   133*

5.2   Unwinding nested observables: the case of
       mergeMap   135

5.3   Mastering asynchronous streams   141

5.4   Drag and drop with concatMap   146

5.5   Summary   150

6   *Coordinating business processes   151*

6.1   Hooking into the observable lifecycle   152
       *Web hooks and the observer pattern   153
       Hooked on observables   154*

6.2   Joining parallel streams with combineLatest and
       forkJoin   159
       *Limitations of using Promises   162 ▪ Combining
       parallel streams   163 ▪ More coordination with
       forkJoin   168*

6.3   Building a reactive database   170
       *Populating a database reactively   172 ▪ Writing
       bulk data   175 ▪ Joining related database
       operations   177 ▪ Reactive databases   180*

6.4   Summary   181

7   *Error handling with RxJS   182*

7.1   Common error-handling techniques   183
       *Error handling with try/catch   183 ▪ Delegating errors
       to callbacks   184 ▪ Errors and Promises   186*

7.2   Incompatibilities between imperative error-handling
       techniques and functional and reactive code bases   188

7.3   Understanding the functional error-handling
       approach   189

7.4   The RxJS way of dealing with failure   193
       *Errors propagated downstream to observers   193
       Catching and reacting to errors   195 ▪ Retrying failed*

streams for a fixed number of times 197 ▪ *Reacting to
failed retries 199*

7.5   Summary 208

PART 3   MASTERING RxJS 209

8   *Heating up observables   211*

8.1   Introducing hot and cold observables   212
Cold observables   212 ▪ *Hot observables   215*

8.2   A new type of data source: WebSockets   217
A brief look at WebSocket   218 ▪ *A simple WebSocket
server in Node.js   219* ▪ *WebSocket client   220*

8.3   The impact of side effects on a resubscribe or a
replay   221
Replay vs. resubscribe   222 ▪ *Replaying the logic
of a stream   222* ▪ *Resubscribing to a stream   224*

8.4   Changing the temperature of an observable   226
Producers as thermometers   227 ▪ *Making a hot
observable cold   228* ▪ *Making a cold observable
hot   230* ▪ *Creating hot-by-operator streams   232*

8.5   Connecting one observable to many observers   237
Publish   237 ▪ *Publish with replay   240*
Publish last   242

8.6   Summary   243

9   *Toward testable, reactive programs   245*

9.1   Testing is inherently built into functional programs   246

9.2   Testing asynchronous code and promises   250
Testing AJAX requests   250 ▪ *Working with Promises   253*

9.3   Testing reactive streams   255

9.4   Making streams testable   258

9.5   Scheduling values in RxJS   260

9.6   Augmenting virtual reality   263
Playing with marbles   264 ▪ *Fake it 'til you make it   266*
Refactoring your search stream for testability   267

9.7   Summary   270

10   *RxJS in the wild*   *271*

     10.1   Building a basic banking application   273

     10.2   Introduction to React and Redux   274

         Rendering UI components with React   274
         State management with Redux   284

     10.3   Redux-ing application state   286

         Actions and reducers   286 ▪ Redux store   287

     10.4   Building a hot RxJS and Redux store adapter   290

     10.5   Asynchronous middleware with RxJS Subject   291

         RxJS subjects   294 ▪ Building epic, reactive middleware   296

     10.6   Bringing it all home   302

     10.7   Parting words   304

     10.8   Summary   304

appendix A   *Installation of libraries used in this book   305*
appendix B   *Choosing an operator   310*

         index   315

foreword

It's no secret that the web has grown dramatically in popularity as a platform for building large-scale, high-traffic applications. Modern web applications are somewhat unique in the computing world, however, because they require a great deal of asynchrony, ranging from AJAX requests to animations to lazy-loaded client resources and multiplexed web sockets. And all this asynchrony comes with a complexity cost.

A simple drag and drop, for example, is actually a coordination of three or more different events: wait for a mouse-down and then listen to all mouse movements until the next mouse-up. Current imperative approaches to implement this sort of thing are not always straightforward; they're difficult to maintain, and they're rarely bug free.

RxJS is an ideal tool to help you manage asynchronous complexity in your applications in a declarative, easy-to-maintain, and fun way. So how do you learn Rx?

This book, *RxJS in Action*, is to date the only resource of its type to cover the latest version, RxJS 5. As the project lead for RxJS, I'm very happy to see this book reach the masses with important information you need to know about this library in order to be an effective reactive programmer.

—Ben Lesh
Project lead, RxJS 5

preface

We wrote this book to help you understand the power and significance of reactive programming in JavaScript and develop the skills to put RxJS to work.

FROM PAUL: Like many skills, RxJS was not something I had originally set out to learn but instead something I stumbled on and continued in, only because of a confluence of events. Earlier in my programming career, I had been working on a new UI system for an internal tool in which the project owner had given me a large degree of latitude regarding what technologies I employed. Because the only constraint was that it be written in .NET, I was introduced to Rx.NET first while trying to build out various UI interactions. During and after my college years, my experience had been primarily of an object-oriented nature. I understood the singleton pattern, the decorator, the adapter, and others, and I had heard of a fabled programming paradigm that focused—seemingly counterintuitively—on functions. But to me, that seemed entirely backward. Ignoring the larger context involved, I happily plugged the new library into my application, thinking it a simple substitute for the existing .NET event system.

On a later project, where I was first starting to really cut my teeth with JavaScript, I thought back to the library I had used that made my event management so much easier, and I went looking for a parallel in JavaScript. Lo and behold, RxJS entered my life! At first, I happily plugged it in wherever I could, seeing it simply as a way to replace the ugliness of event callbacks. The full breadth of what could be accomplished with RxJS and the benefits of reactive, functional programming dawned slowly. It started with the gift of a book from a family member on Clojure, which gave me some insight into this mystical functional world. It expanded as I looked more into asynchronous patterns and saw the parallels in other asynchronous structures like promises.

It was around this time, as I became more involved in the community of RxJS (primarily through contributions to the open source library back in the old days of RxJS 2!), that Manning approached me about the possibility of writing a book on RxJS. It was to be a rather large undertaking, especially for me as a first-time author. But it presented me with the ability to give back to the overall community in a way that hadn't been available when I started learning Rx, because most of the resources focused primarily on Rx.NET. And I was lucky enough to have Luis join me on the project, making it less daunting.

FROM LUIS: I came across RxJS a couple of years ago, while studying monads in functional programming. The realization that the two were intimately related opened my eyes to new and different ways of designing APIs. I instantly fell in love with it. So I began using RxJS as an orchestration layer to consume information from different remote services and feed user interfaces an object, easy to digest, containing all the information that needed to be displayed.

I wanted others to learn about RxJS, so I decided to end my first book, *Functional Programming in JavaScript*, with a section on reactive programming and RxJS observables. But my passion didn't stop there. A couple of months later, Manning approached me and I was privileged to pair up with Paul, who I found to be an incredibly talented engineer, to coauthor this book. And just like that, I was again writing about my two favorite topics—JavaScript and functional programming.

acknowledgments

Writing a book is no simple task. It isn't a straightforward data dump of knowledge onto paper (or e-ink). Building a book that's accurate, well paced, and sufficiently difficult yet not overly abstract takes many people working through the countless revisions to bring you a book like the one you're reading now.

The staff at Manning were instrumental in getting this book from a loosely related set of lessons into a quality resource of learning material. Special thanks to Mike Stephens and Erin Twohey for originally approaching me about writing a book about RxJS; to Frances Lefkowitz for being the best editor out there and herding the cats otherwise known as us authors through to the finish line; to Bert Bates for never settling for less, passing on his wisdom on teaching technical topics, and always trying to help elevate us as writers; and to everyone on the editorial and production teams, including Kevin Sullivan, Linda Recktenwald, Dottie Marsico, Katie Tennant, and all the other people who worked behind the scenes.

We owe a huge thanks to Aleksandar Dragosavljevic and his amazing team of technical peer reviewers—Álvaro Falquina, Bachir Chihani, Carlos Curotto, Clinton Campbell, Corinna Cohn, Damian Esteban, James Anaipakos, Kamal Raj, Matteo Gildone, Osama Khan, Rod Monk, Sai Ram Kota, Thomas Peklak, Tim Thornton, and Zachary Lysobey—and, of course, all the wonderful insights and suggestions from the forum contributors.

For the technical side of things, we'd like to thank Dean Iverson for being a fantastic technical editor, whose attention to detail was frankly incredible. Also, we'd like to thank Cody Sand for his quick and thorough edits; he was really the best technical proofer one could ask for with tight deadlines. In addition, we'd like to especially thank Ben Lesh for writing the foreword to the book.

FROM PAUL: I would like to thank foremost my family—mother, father, brothers, and all the aunts, uncles, and grandparents who inspired me to grow up reading, writing, and playing with computers. Also, I thank my friends for supporting me through this long process and not being too disappointed when I had to choose writing over you. And finally, I thank my coworkers for being willing guinea pigs as I learned how to teach this topic. And to everyone who asked what the book was about and followed up by asking what JavaScript was—seriously, love you guys ☺— thank you.

FROM LUIS: I would like to thank my wife for being my inspiration and my family for always supporting me, pushing me to become better every day, and not questioning why I decided to do this all over again ☺; also, my friends and colleagues at work for your support in purchasing early releases of the chapters.

Finally, we both would like to thank the JavaScript community at large for adopting RxJS through this book and giving us feedback.

about this book

Asynchronous code is something the human brain never seems quite able to understand. Its behavior is, at best, difficult to synthesize and, at worst, completely nondeterministic.

We, as programmers, have been to the dark side and seen what happens when code is written with a series of timeouts and callbacks. We've tried to keep up with all the possible outcomes and implications of a block of code where asynchronous execution is involved. We've handled new failure cases because we now have to face cases where our code exccutes out of order. And we've seen the type of chaos that nested callbacks and global state bring to code that can execute out of order.

Moreover, the amount of data that we're processing these days, both on the client side and on the server side, means that we can't spend our time sweating the small stuff. We shouldn't reinvent the wheel every time we have data coming over the wire. And the paradigm that we use should include the necessary constructs for free so that we can simply layer our business logic on top.

Reactive programming, and RxJS in particular, gives us the tools to build pipelines to move our data through without worrying about the boilerplate underneath. And it does so using concepts distilled from functional programming to give us clean, readable syntax that will be useful six months from now.

Road map

This book has 10 chapters split over three parts that will take you from a basic introduction to RxJS and the functional concepts underlying it all the way to more-advanced practical examples of using RxJS in the real world.

Part 1 is all about getting your feet wet with reactive programming. We know that, for many readers, this is a new topic, but fortunately, if you've been using JavaScript for any amount of time, chances are you've already been exposed to some of the concepts that RxJS uses:

- Chapter 1 introduces the idea of thinking reactively. We compare asynchronous versus synchronous paradigms and point out where existing patterns fall short. This chapter explains why you need reactive programming and how it fits in with your existing models of computing.
- Chapter 2 introduces the primitives of RxJS: the `Observable` and the `Observer`. We look at RxJS's data-driven model and how the consistent computational model of streams allows you to see all data sources as `Observables`.
- Chapter 3 opens the RxJS toolbox to look at the operators that make building functional pipelines possible. Here, you'll see how streams are built and expanded through the use of these operators.
- Chapter 4 adds time as a new layer of complexity for building pipelines. We examine how time can be recorded and even manipulated by RxJS operators.

Part 2 zeroes in on more-practical aspects of RxJS, such as nesting and combining multiple streams and handling exceptions in Rx:

- Chapter 5 looks at nesting `Observables` and the functional technique of flattening streams. This chapter walks through the process of converting multiple streams into a single stream.
- Chapter 6 covers combining the output of streams to build unions or intersections out of their respective events. In particular, this chapter looks at a few of the possibilities when combining the outputs of multiple observables.
- Chapter 7 is all about exceptions—or, more specifically, how to handle them in a stream without having messy boilerplate logic everywhere. This chapter starts with a foundation in functional error handling through a `Try` object and builds up to an understanding of how exceptions can be handled gracefully in an `Observable`.

Part 3 is about the more complex tasks in RxJS. In this section, we look at practical examples of handling the temperature of `Observables` and unit testing with virtual time, and finally we put together all we've discussed to build a reactive application by integrating RxJS with other frameworks. Note: we decided to wait until chapter 8 to discuss `Subjects` because we think they're often a beginner's crutch that allows you to use patterns that are more familiar to you, while seemingly "Rx-ified." Although this isn't *wrong*, our view is that this isn't in following with the spirit of Rx and it tends to rob developers of many of the benefits of using RxJS. Thus, we focus first and primarily on `Observables` and `Observers`, in order to show the multitude of solutions available before you resort to using `Subjects`.

- Chapter 8 explores how to manage the temperature of Observables. This involves not just a discussion about whether certain data sources are hot or cold but also how you can change the temperature of such data sources to fit your needs.

- Chapter 9 handles reactive testing. We cover topics that are important for testing your Observables and address techniques for building modular and testable applications. Finally, we show how you can control the flow of time explicitly while testing, to avoid making tests dependent on real-world time.

- Chapter 10 puts RxJS to use in the real world by integrating it into a functional banking application with React and Redux. This app is both modular and reactive, and we show how you can easily test and extend this application.

Finally, there are two appendixes at the end of the book:

- Appendix A, "Installation of libraries used in this book"
  Our goal was to use external libraries only as necessary and helpful, while also being as inclusive as possible. So, for instance, we don't use TypeScript, because it's still a sore spot for many developers, with ongoing transpiler wars (with PureScript, CoffeeScript, Dart, or Flow + JavaScript, and others). Eliminating the need to explain TypeScript and its many evolving language features—or worse, assuming all our readers know it—allowed us to focus on the meat of RxJS and avoid alienating developers who haven't, can't, or don't want to join the transpiler bandwagon. Along the same lines, we wanted to go with the simplest route of installation, so we decided not to include the install for other frameworks, even those commonly associated with RxJS. Most frameworks have several steps for installing, and likely those steps will have changed by the time of publication. So we leave it to the library maintainers and Stack Overflow for troubleshooting RxJS integrations with your favorite framework.

- Appendix B, "Choosing an operator"
  This is a list of all the operators that we use in the book. There are plenty more operators, but there is not one standard set that everyone agrees on, and the list is still growing and changing. Purists may wish we included fewer operators, whereas kitchen-sinkers will want operators for a use case they came up with for a pet project no one else may ever see. We decided it would be most helpful if we stuck to the operators that we show you how to use throughout the book, so you can be assured that you'll know how to put all operators on our list to work. A more complete list of operators can be found at http://reactivex.io/rxjs/manual/overview.html#choose-an-operator.

Who should read this book

RxJS in Action is for JavaScript developers who are aware of the current asynchronous challenges facing modern applications. We expect that, for beginners, this book will be quite the crash course because we assume that the reader is already familiar with JavaScript syntax and conventions.

Intermediate developers improve their development chops by adding a new set of tools to their JavaScript toolkit. Reactive programming standardizes the push-based event model to allow the consolidation of many of the familiar patterns of event emission under one roof. Advanced developers or developers who are coming from Rx in other languages will benefit from learning some of the gotchas and pitfalls involved in using RxJS as well as understanding some of the common patterns for using RxJS in practice. Also, although this book covers some functional concepts, it shouldn't be considered an introduction to functional programming. For a better resource on that, see *Functional Programming in JavaScript* (Manning, 2016).

How to use this book

For your best reading experience, it's important to understand that the first three chapters will be new for some readers but review for others. We had to strike a balance between addressing readers who need a more gentle introduction to what is in some ways a large paradigm shift and those who are already "thinking in streams" and coming to this book strictly to learn the RxJS approach. We erred on the side of providing more introduction, and we encourage more-advanced readers to skip ahead to the topics they're ready to learn.

So our recommendations for how to use this book depend on who you are. If you're a beginner or intermediate developer or are just curious about the foundational aspects that led to the development of RxJS, start with chapter 1. If you're a strong programmer already familiar with the reactive paradigm, you can skim chapters 1 and 2 and then jump in at chapter 3, where we really start diving into code samples with RxJS. More-advanced developers, those who are strong JavaScript developers with functional backgrounds or who are coming from Rx in a different language, can probably do a quick review of chapter 3 for JavaScript-specific fundamentals and then start reading in earnest with chapter 4.

Examples and source code

The code examples in this book use ECMAScript 6 JavaScript (aka ES6, aka ES2015), which run equally well on either the server side, aka Node.js, or in the browser. Some examples show network I/O operations or browser DOM APIs but don't include any remarks about browser incompatibilities, nor do we use any browser-specific JavaScript. We assume a basic level of competence with HTML pages and the console. During the course of our examples, this book makes use of third-party libraries like Ramda.js and PouchDB. You can find the documentation and installation information for these libraries in appendix A. This book contains extensive code listings that showcase reactive patterns and compare promises and callbacks to their Rx counterparts. You can find all the code samples at the publisher's website, www.manning.com/books/rxjs-in-action, and on GitHub, https://github.com/ RxJSinAction/.

The sample code project and the final banking application project are both available under the root GitHub at https://github.com/RxJSinAction/rxjs-in-action and https://github.com/RxJSinAction/banking-in-action, respectively. You can find installation details for both projects in appendix A.

Author Online

Purchase of *RxJS in Action* includes free access to a private web forum run by Manning Publications where you can make comments about the book, ask technical questions, and receive help from the authors and from other users. To access the forum and subscribe to it, point your web browser to www.manning.com/books/rxjs-in-action. This page provides information on how to get on the forum once you are registered, what kind of help is available, and the rules of conduct on the forum.

Manning's commitment to our readers is to provide a venue where a meaningful dialog between individual readers and between readers and authors can take place. It is not a commitment to any specific amount of participation on the part of the authors, whose contribution to the Author Online forum remains voluntary (and unpaid). We suggest you try asking them some challenging questions lest their interest stray! The Author Online forum and the archives of previous discussions will be accessible from the publisher's website as long as the book is in print.

about the authors

PAUL P. DANIELS (@paulpdaniels) is a professional software developer with over 6 years of industry experience as a full stack engineer working in various fields from augmented reality to embedded systems to cloud platforms. A long-time user and contributor to the Rx community, he enjoys evangelizing and teaching reactive programming. When not behind a computer screen, Paul is in the dance studio, where he teaches and trains as a competitive Latin dancer.

LUIS ATENCIO (@luijar) is a Staff Software Engineer for Citrix Systems in Fort Lauderdale, Florida. He has a BS and an MS in Computer Science and now works full-time developing and architecting cloud web applications using JavaScript, Java, and PHP. Luis is also very involved in the community and has presented at conferences and local meet-ups. When he isn't coding, Luis writes a developer blog (http://luisatencio.net) focused on software engineering, and has written several magazine articles for *php[architect]* and *DZone*. Luis is also the author of *Functional Programming in JavaScript* (Manning 2016), and *Functional PHP* (Leanpub).

Part 1

Understanding streams

In this first part of the book, you'll get your feet wet with streams by discovering the stream as the missing data contemporary to the iterable.

Chapter 1 lays out the problem with the state of asynchrony in JavaScript and where other solutions don't quite reach your ideal. In chapter 2, you'll get an introduction to functional programming as the foundation for reactive programming. Here, you'll walk through the basic parts of producing and consuming a stream. (If you're already on board with streaming, you may wish to skim or skip these first two chapters.) In chapter 3, you'll start to see some real RxJS usage as you explore your first operators and how you use them to create fluent streaming applications. Finally, in chapter 4, you'll start looking at some more-complex operators and introduce a new dimension of streams: time. With this new dimension, you'll see the real power of using Rx for your asynchronous data.

Thinking reactively

Right now, somewhere in the world, someone just created a tweet, a stock price just dropped, and, most certainly, a mouse just moved. These tiny pinpricks of data light up the internet and pass ubiquitously through semiconductors scattered across the planet. A deluge of data propagates from any connected device. What does this have to do with you? As you push your code to production, this fire hose of events is pointed squarely at your JavaScript application, which needs to be prepared to handle it effectively. This creates two important challenges: scalability and latency.

As more and more data is received, the amount of memory that your application consumes or requires will grow linearly or, in worst cases, exponentially; this is

3

the classic problem of *scalability*, and trying to process it all at once will certainly cause the user interface (UI) to become unresponsive. Buttons may no longer appear to work, fancy animations will lag, and the browser may even flag the page to terminate, which is an unacceptable notion for modern web users.

This problem is not new, though in recent years there has been exponential growth in the sheer scale of the number of events and data that JavaScript applications are required to process. This quantity of data is too big to be held readily available and stored in memory for use. Instead, we must create ways to fetch it from remote locations asynchronously, resulting in another big challenge of interconnected software systems: *latency*, which can be difficult to express in code.

Although modern system architectures have improved dramatically to include faster network devices and highly concurrent processing, the libraries and methods for dealing with the added complexity of remote data haven't made the same strides. For example, when it comes to fetching data from a server or running any deferred computation, most of us still rely on the use of callbacks, a pattern that quickly breaks down when business rules evolve and change or the problem we're trying to solve involves data that lives not in one but in several different remote locations.

The solution lies not only in which library to use but which paradigm best suits these types of problems. In this book, you'll first learn about the fundamental principles of two emerging paradigms: functional programming (FP) and reactive programming (RP). This exhilarating composition is what gives rise to functional reactive programming (FRP), encoded in a library called RxJS (or rx.js), which is the best prescription to deal with asynchronous and event-based data sources effectively.

Our prescriptive roadmap has multiple parts. First, you'll learn about the principles that lead to thinking reactively as well as the current solutions, their drawbacks, and how RxJS improves on them. With this new-found mindset, you'll dive into RxJS specifics and learn about the core operators that will allow you to express complex data flows of bounded or unbounded data in a succinct and elegant manner. You'll learn why RxJS is ideal for applications of any size that are event driven in nature. So, along the way, you'll find real-world examples that demonstrate using this library to combine multiple pieces of remote data, autocompleting input fields, drag and drop, processing user input, creating responsive UIs, parallel processing, and many others. These examples are intended to be narrow in scope as you work through the most important features of RxJS. Finally, all these new techniques will come together to end your journey with a full-scale web application using a hybrid React/Rx architecture.

The goal of this chapter is to give a broad view of the topics you'll be learning about in this book. We'll focus on looking at the limitations of the current solutions and point you to the chapters that show how RxJS addresses them. Furthermore, you'll learn how to shift your mindset to think in terms of *streams*, also known as *functional sequences of events*, which RxJS implements under the hood through the use of familiar patterns such as iterator and observer. Finally, we'll explore the advantages of RxJS to write asynchronous code, minus the entanglement caused by using callbacks, which also scales to any amount of data. Understanding the differences between these two worlds is crucial, so let's begin there.

1.1 Synchronous vs. asynchronous computing

In simple terms, the main factor that separates the runtime of synchronous and asynchronous code is latency, also known as *wait time*. Coding explicitly for time is difficult to wrap your head around; it's much easier to reason about solutions when you're able to see the execution occur synchronously in the same order as you're writing it: "Do this; then immediately do that."

But the world of computing doesn't grant such luxuries. In this world of highly networked computing, the time it takes to send a message and receive a response represents critical time in which an application can be doing other things, such as responding to user inputs, crunching numbers, or updating the UI. It's more like "Do this (wait for an indeterminate period of time); then do that." The traditional approach of having applications sit idle waiting for a database query to return, a network to respond, or a user action to complete is not acceptable, so you need to take advantage of asynchronous execution so that the application is always responsive. The main issue here is whether it's acceptable to block the user on long-running processes.

1.1.1 Issues with blocking code

Synchronous execution occurs when each block of code must wait for the previous block to complete before running. Without a doubt, this is by far the easiest way to implement code because you put the burden on your users to wait for their processes to complete. Many systems still work this way today, such as ATMs, point of sale systems, and other dumb terminals. Writing code this way is much easier to grasp, maintain, and debug; unfortunately, because of JavaScript's single-threaded nature, any long-running tasks such as waiting for an AJAX call to return or a database operation to complete shouldn't be done synchronously. Doing so creates an awful experience for your users because it causes the entire application to sit idle waiting for the data to be loaded and wasting precious computing cycles that could easily be executing other code. This will block further progress on any other tasks that you might want to execute, which in turn leads to artificially long load times, as shown in figure 1.1.

In this case, the program makes a blocking call to process 1, which means it must wait for it to return control to the caller, so that it can proceed with process 2. This might work well for kiosks and dumb terminals, but browser UIs should never be implemented this way. Not only would it create a terrible user experience (UX), but also browsers may deem your scripts unresponsive after a certain period of inactivity and terminate them. Here's an example of making an HTTP call that will cause your application to block, waiting on the server to respond:

```
let items = blockingHttpCall('/data');
items.forEach(item => {
  // process each item
});
```

Loading server-side data synchronously halts program execution. The nature of the data isn't important right now; it's some generic sample data pertaining to your application.

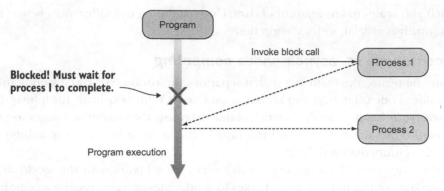

Figure 1.1   A program that invokes two processes synchronously. A process in this case can be as simple as a function call, an I/O process, or a network transaction. When process 1 runs, it blocks anything else from running.

A better approach would be to invoke the HTTP call and perform other actions while you're waiting on the response. Long-running tasks aren't the only problem; as we said earlier, mouse movement generates a rapid succession of very quick, fine-grained events. Waiting to process each of these synchronously will cause the entire application to become unresponsive, whether it's long wait times or handling hundreds of smaller waits quickly. So what can you do to handle these types of events in a non-blocking manner? Luckily, JavaScript provides callback functions.

1.1.2   *Non-blocking code with callback functions*

Using functions as callbacks has been a staple of JavaScript development for years. They're used in everything from mouse clicks and key presses to handling remote HTTP requests or file I/O. JavaScript, being a single-threaded language, requires such a construct in order to maintain any level of usability. Callback functions were created to tackle the problem of blocking for long-running operations to complete by allowing you to provide a handler function that the JavaScript runtime will invoke once the data is ready for use. In the meantime, your application can continue carrying out any other task, as shown in figure 1.2.

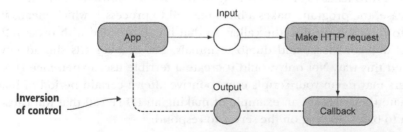

Figure 1.2   Callback functions in JavaScript create an inversion of control where functions call the application back, instead of the other way around.

Unlike the previous code that makes a blocking HTTP call that you must wait for, using callbacks with asynchronous (AJAX) requests creates an *inversion of control* that permits your application to continue executing the next lines of code. Inversion of control in this sense refers to the way in which certain parts of your code receive the flow of control back from the runtime system. In this case, the runtime calls you (or returns control to you) via the function handler when the data is ready to be processed; hence, the term *callback*. Look at this alternative:

```
ajax('/data',                <──── No explicit return value
  items => {                  <──── Declaration of callback function
    items.forEach(item -> {
      // process each item    <──┐  All processing is carried out within the callback body
    });                          │  after the data has been fetched from the server.
});
beginUiRendering();          <──── This function begins immediately after AJAX is called.
```

Callback functions allow you to invoke code asynchronously, so that the application can return control to you later. This allows the program to continue with any other task in the meantime. In this code sample, the HTTP function runs in the background and immediately returns control to the caller to begin rendering the UI; it handles the contents of the items only *after* it has completely loaded. This behavior is ideal because it frees up the application to make progress on other tasks such as loading the rest of a web page, as in this case. As you'll see throughout this book, asynchronous code is a good design for I/O-bound work like fetching data from the web or a database. The reason this works is that I/O processes are typically much slower than any other type of instruction, so we allow them to run in the background because they're not dependent on processor cycles to complete.

> **SYNTAX CHECK** In the code sample in section 1.1.2, the second parameter of ajax() is the callback function. In that code, as in many parts of the book, we use the ECMAScript 6 lambda expression syntax,[1] which offers a terser and more succinct way of invoking functions. Also called *arrow functions*, lambda expressions behave somewhat similarly to an anonymous function call, which you're probably familiar with. The subtle difference has to do with what the keyword this refers to. On rare occasions, when the value of this is important, we'll call it out in the text and switch to using an anonymous function expression.

1.1.3 *Understanding time and space*

Certainly, asynchronous functions allow us to stay responsive, but they come at a price. Where synchronous programs allow us to reason directly about the state of the application, asynchronous code forces us to reason about its *future* state. What does this mean? State can be understood simply as a snapshot of all the information stored into

---

[1] https://developer.mozilla.org/en-US/docs/Web/JavaScript/Reference/Functions/Arrow_functions.

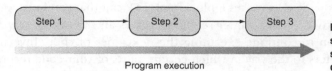

Figure 1.3 Synchronous code is a step-by-step sequential execution of statements where each step depends on the previous one to run.

variables at any point in time. This information is created and manipulated via sequences of statements. Synchronous code can be thought of as an ordered, step-by-step execution of statements, as shown in figure 1.3.

In this model, it's easy to determine at any point what the states of the variables are and what will occur next, which is why it's easy to write and debug. But when tasks have different wait times or complete at different times, it's difficult to guarantee how they'll behave together. Functions that terminate at unpredictable times are typically harder to deal with without the proper methods and practices. When this happens, the mental model of our application needs to shift to compensate for this additional dimension. Compare figure 1.3 to the model in figure 1.4, which grows not only vertically but also horizontally.

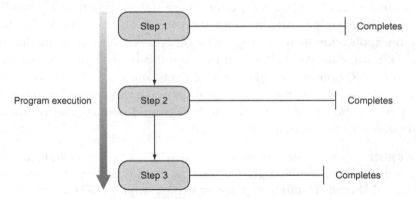

Figure 1.4 In asynchronous execution, steps that are invoked in sequence need not terminate all at the same time. So there's absolutely no guarantee that you can rely on the data from step 1 to be available in step 2, for example.

As of now, if steps 1, 2, and 3 were independent tasks, then executing them in any order wouldn't be a problem. But if these were functions that shared any global state, then their behavior would be determined by the order in which they were called or by the global state of the system. These conditions we refer to as *side effects*, which you'll learn more about in chapter 2; they involve situations where you need to read or modify an external resource like a database, the DOM, the console, and others. Functions with side effects can perform unreliably when run in any arbitrary order. In functional and reactive programming, you'll learn to minimize them by using *pure functions*, and you'll learn in this book that this is extremely advantageous when dealing with asynchronous code.

So, assuming that our functions were side effect free, we still have another important issue—*time*. Steps 1, 2, and 3 might complete instantly or might not complete depending on the nature of the work. The main issue is how we can guarantee that these steps run in the correct order. As you've probably done many times before, the proper way to achieve this is by *composing* these functions together, so that the output of one becomes the input to the next, and therefore a chain of steps is created. The traditional approach that ensures the proper sequence of steps takes place is to nest a sequence of callbacks, and the model of the application's runtime resembles figure 1.5.

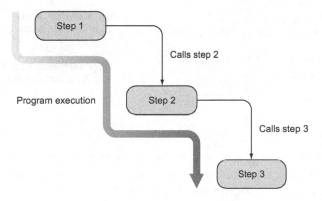

Figure 1.5 **In order to guarantee the proper order of steps and asynchronous invocation takes place, we use callback functions to transfer control of the application once a long-running operation terminates.**

Undoubtedly, this nested control flow is much harder to reason about than the synchronous, straight-line model of figure 1.4. In figure 1.5, step 1 runs first, which then calls step 2 as soon as it completes; then step 3 executes, and so on for the rest of the steps. This suggests the presence of a *temporal dependency* or time coupling between these steps, which means that one can begin as soon as the previous finishes—it's a chain of commands. In this scenario, the callback functions are used to respond to the asynchronous request that happened before them and begin processing its data. This happens typically when making sequential AJAX requests, but it can also happen when mixing in any other event-based system, whether it be key presses, mouse movements, database reads and writes, and others; all these systems rely on callbacks.

1.1.4   *Are callbacks out of the picture?*

The short answer is no. Using a paradigm to tackle event-based or asynchronous code isn't necessary when you're dealing with simple interactions with users or external services. If you're writing a simple script that issues a single remote HTTP request, RxJS is a bit of overkill, and callbacks remain the perfect solution. On the other hand, a library that mixes functional and reactive paradigms really begins to shine when implementing state machines of moderate-to-advanced complexity such as dynamic UIs or service orchestration. Some examples of this can be the need to orchestrate the execution of several business processes that consume several microservices, data mashups, or perhaps the implementation of features of a rich UI made up of several widgets on the page that interact with each other.

Consider the task of loading data from the client originating from different remote server-side endpoints. To coordinate among them, you'd need several nested AJAX requests where each step wraps the processing of the data residing within each callback body in the logic of invoking the next step, as you saw previously in figure 1.5. Following is a possible solution for this, which requires the use of three composed callback functions to load datasets that potentially live in the same host or different hosts, together with its related meta-information and files:

```
ajax('<host1>/items',                    <────── Loads all items you want to display
   items => {
      for (let item of items) {                         For each item, loads
      ajax(`<host2>/items/${item.getId()}/info`,  <──┘  additional meta-information
         dataInfo => {
         ajax(`<host3>/files/${dataInfo.files}`,  <──┐
            processFiles);                           │  For each meta record,
         });                                         │  loads associated files
      }
});
beginUiRendering();
```

Now although you might think this code looks trivial, if continuing this pattern, we'll begin to sink into horizontally nested calls—our model starts to grow horizontally. This trend is informally known in the JavaScript world as callback hell, a design that you'll want to avoid at all costs if you want to create maintainable and easy-to-reason-about programs. It isn't simply aesthetics—making sure that separate asynchronous operations are synchronized is hard enough without also having difficult-to-read code. There's another hidden problem with this code. Can you guess what it is? It occurs when you mix a synchronous artifact like a `for..of` imperative block invoking asynchronous functions. Loops aren't aware that there's latency in those calls, so they'll always march ahead no matter what, which can cause some really unpredictable and hard-to-diagnose bugs. In these situations, you can improve matters by creating closures around your asynchronous functions, managed by using `forEach()` instead of the loop:

```
ajax('<host1>/items',                    The forEach() method of arrays will
   items => {                            properly scope each item object
      items.forEach(item => {      <──┐  into the nested HTTP call.
         ajax(`<host2>/items/${item.getId()}/info`,
         dataInfo => {
         ajax(`<host3>/files/${dataInfo.files}`,
         processFiles);
      });
   });
});
```

This is why in RxJS—and FP in general, for that matter—all loops are virtually eliminated! Instead, in chapters 4 and 5 you'll learn about operators that allow you to spawn sequences of asynchronous requests taking advantage of pure functions to keep all of the information properly scoped. Another good use of callbacks is to implement APIs based on Node.js event emitters. Let's jump into this next.

1.1.5 Event emitters

Event emitters are popular mechanisms for asynchronous event-based architectures. The DOM, for instance, is probably one of the most widely known event emitters. On a server like Node.js, certain kinds of objects periodically produce events that cause functions to be called. In Node.js, the EventEmitter class is used to implement APIs for things like WebSocket I/O or file reading/writing so that if you're iterating through directories and you find a file of interest, an object can emit an event referencing this file for you to execute any additional code.

Let's implement a simple object to show this API a bit. Consider a simple calculator object that can emit events like add and subtract, which you can hook any custom logic into; see figure 1.6.

When an emitter fires the event, it executes the logic associated to that event.

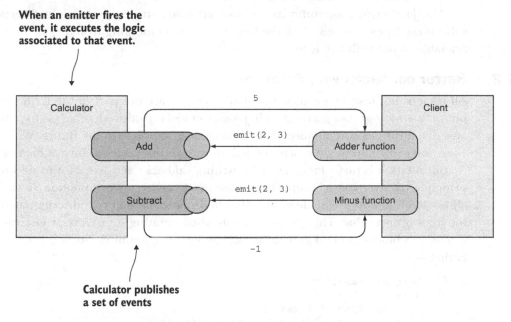

Calculator publishes a set of events

Figure 1.6 Node emitter object representing a simple calculator, which exposes two events: add and subtract

Here's some code for the calculator add and subtract events:

```
const EventEmitter = require('events');          ⟵──── Loads the events module

class Calculator extends EventEmitter {}          ⟵──── Creates a custom emitter

const calc = new Calculator();
calc.addListener('add', (a, b) => {
  calc.emit('result',  a + b);
});
calc.addListener('subtract', (a, b) => {
  calc.emit('result', a - b);
```

Handles the add event

```
});

calc.addListener('result', (result) => {
 console.log('Result: ' + result);
});

calc.emit('add', 2, 3);         //-> Prints 'Result: 5'
calc.emit('subtract', 2, 3); //-> Prints 'Result: 1'
```

Subscribing to an event emitter is done through the addListener() method, which allows you to provide the callback that will be called when an event of interest is fired. Unfortunately, event emitters have all of the same problems associated with using callbacks to handle emitted data coming from multiple composed resources. Overall, composing nested asynchronous flow is difficult.

The JavaScript community as a whole has made strides in the right direction to solve these types of issues. With the help of patterns emerging from FP, an alternative available to you with ES6 is to use Promises.

1.2   Better callbacks with Promises

All hope is not lost; we promise you that. Promises are not part of the RxJS solution, but they work together perfectly well. JavaScript ES6 introduced Promises to represent any asynchronous computation that's expected to complete in the future. With Promises, you can chain together a set of actions with future values to form a *continuation*.[2] A continuation is just a fancy term for writing callbacks and has a lot to do with the principle of Inversion of Control we referenced earlier. A continuation (a callback) allows the function to decide what it should do next, instead of indiscriminately waiting for a return value. They're used heavily when iterating over arrays, tree structures, try/catch blocks, and, of course, asynchronous programming. So, the code you saw earlier—

```
ajax('<host1>/items',
    items => {
        for (let item of items) {
            ajax(`<host2>/items/${item.getId()}/info`,
            dataInfo => {
            ajax(`<host3>/files/${dataInfo.files}`,
            processFiles);
        });
    }
});
```

—is known to be continuation-passing style (CPS), because none of the functions are explicitly waiting for a return value. But as we mentioned, abusing this makes code hard to reason about. What you can do is to make continuations first-class citizens and actually define a concrete interpretation of what it means to "continue." So, we introduce the notion of then: "Do X, then do Y," to create code that reads like this:

---

[2] http://www.2ality.com/2012/06/continuation-passing-style.html.

```
Fetch all items, then                    | The key term "then" suggests
   For-each item fetch all files, then   | time and sequence.
      Process each file                  |
```

This is where `Promises` come in. A `Promise` is a data type that wraps an asynchronous or long-running operation, a future value, with the ability for you to *subscribe* to its result or its error. A `Promise` is considered to be fulfilled when its underlying operation completes, at which point subscribers will receive the computed result. Because we can't alter the value of a `Promise` once it's been executed, it's actually an immutable type, which is a functional quality we seek in our programs. Different `Promise` implementations exist based on the Promises/A+ protocol (see https://promisesaplus.com/), and it's designed to provide some level of error handling and continuations via the `then()` methods. Here's how you can tackle the same example if you assume that `ajax()` returns `Promises`:

```
ajax('<host1>/items')
  .then(items =>
    items.forEach(item =>
      ajax(`<host2>/data/${item.getId()}/info`)
        .then(dataInfo =>
          ajax(`<host3>/data/files/${dataInfo.files}`)
        )
        .then(processFiles);
    )
  );
```

This looks similar to the previous statement! Being a more recent addition to the language with ES6 and inspired in FP design, `Promises` are more versatile and idiomatic than callbacks. Applying these functions declaratively—meaning your code expresses the *what* and not the *how* of what you're trying to accomplish—into then blocks allows you to express side effects in a pure manner. We can refactor this to be more declarative by pulling out each function independently

```
let getItems = () => ajax('<host1>/items');
let getInfo  = item => ajax(`<host2>/data/${item.getId()}/info`);
let getFiles = dataInfo => ajax(`<host3>/data/files/${dataInfo.files}`);
```

and then use `Promises` to stitch together our asynchronous flow. We use the `Promise` `.all()` function to map an array of separate `Promises` into a single one containing an array of results:

```
getItems()
  .then(items => items.map(getInfo))
  .then(promises => Promise.all(promises))
  .then(infos => infos.map(getFiles))
  .then(promises => Promise.all(promises))
  .then(processFiles);
```

The use of `then()` explicitly implies that there's time involved among these calls, which is a really good thing. If any step fails, we can also have matching `catch()` blocks to handle errors and potentially continue the chain of command if necessary, as shown in figure 1.7.

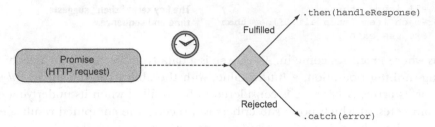

Figure 1.7 `Promises` create a flow of calls chained by `then` methods. If the `Promise` is fulfilled, the chain of functions continues; otherwise, the error is delegated to the `Promise` `catch` block.

Of course, `Promises` also have shortcomings, or else we wouldn't be talking about Rx. The drawback of using `Promises` is that they're unable to handle data sources that produce more than one value, like mouse movements or sequences of bytes in a file stream. Also, they lack the ability to retry from failure—all present in RxJS. The most important downside, moreover, is that because `Promises` are immutable, they can't be cancelled. So, for instance, if you use a `Promise` to wrap the value of a remote HTTP call, there's no hook or mechanism for you to cancel that work. This is unfortunate because HTTP calls, based on the `XmlHttpRequest` object, can be aborted,[3] but this feature isn't honored through the `Promise` interface. These limitations reduce their usefulness and force developers to write some of the cancellation logic themselves or seek other libraries.

Collectively, `Promises` and event emitters solve what are essentially the same problems in slightly different ways. They have different use cases (`Promises` for single-value returns like HTTP requests and event emitters for multiple-value returns like mouse click handlers), mostly because of their own implementation constraints, not because the use cases are so different. The result is that in many scenarios a developer must use both in order to accomplish their goal, which can often lead to disjointed and confusing code.

The problems of readability; hard-to-reason-about code; and the downsides of current technology that we've discussed so far aren't the only reasons that we, as developers, need to worry about asynchronous code. In this next section, we'll outline more concretely why we need to switch to a different paradigm altogether to tackle these issues head on.

1.3   *The need for a different paradigm*

For many years now, we've learned to use many JavaScript async libraries; everyone has their own preference, whether it be JQuery, Async.js, Q.js, or others, yet they all fall short one way or another. We believe that it's not a matter of just choosing a library,

---

[3]   https://developer.mozilla.org/en-US/docs/Web/API/XMLHttpRequest/abort.

but choosing the right paradigm for the job. By combining functional and reactive programming paradigms, RxJS will help you address the following issues:

- Familiar control flow structures (like `for` and `while` loops) with asynchronous functions don't work well together because they're not async aware; that is, they're oblivious of wait time or latency between iterations.

- Error-handling strategies become easily convoluted when you begin nesting `try`/`catch` blocks within each callback. In chapter 7, we'll approach error handling from a functional perspective. Also, if you want to implement some level of retry logic at every step, this will be incredibly difficult even with the help of other libraries.

- Business logic is tightly coupled within the nested callback structure you need to support. It's plain to see that the more nested your code is, the harder it is to reason about. Functions that are deeply nested become entangled with other variables and functions, which is problematic in terms of readability and complexity. It would be ideal to be able to create reusable and modular components in order to have loosely coupled business logic that can be maintained and unit tested independently. We'll cover unit testing with RxJS in chapter 9.

- You want to avoid excessive use of closures, but functions in JavaScript create a closure around the scope in which they're declared. Nesting them means that you need to be concerned about not just the state of the variables passed in as arguments but also the state of all external variables surrounding each function declaration, causing side effects to occur. In the next chapter, you'll learn how detrimental side effects can be and how FP addresses this problem. Side effects increase the cognitive load of the state of your application, making it virtually impossible to keep track of what's going on in your programs. Throw a few loops and conditional `if-else` statements into the mix, and you'll regret the day a bug occurs that impacts this functionality.

- It's difficult to detect when events or long-running operations go rogue and need to be cancelled. Consider the case of a remote HTTP request that's taking too long to process. Is the script unresponsive or is the server just slow? It would be ideal to have an easy mechanism to cancel events cleanly after some predetermined amount of time. Implementing your own cancellation mechanism can be very challenging and error prone even with the help of third-party libraries.

- One good quality of responsive design is to always throttle a user's interaction with any UI components, so that the system isn't unnecessarily overloaded. In chapter 4, you'll learn how to use *throttling* and *debouncing* to your advantage. Manual solutions for achieving this are typically very hard to get right and involve functions that access data outside their local scope, which breaks the stability of your entire program.

- It's rare to be concerned about memory management in JavaScript applications, especially client-side code. After all, the browser takes care of most of these low-level details. But as UIs become larger and richer, we can begin to see that lingering event listeners may cause memory leaks and cause the size of the browser process to grow. It's true that this was more prevalent in older browsers; nevertheless, the complexity of today's JavaScript applications is no match for the applications of years past.

This long list of problems can certainly overwhelm even the brightest developers. The truth of the matter is that the very paradigms that help us tackle these problems are hard to express in code, which is why a tool like RxJS is necessary to redefine our approach.

You learned that Promises certainly move the needle in the right direction (and RxJS integrates with Promises seamlessly if you feel the need to do so). But what you really need is a solution that abstracts out the notion of latency away from your code while allowing you to model your solutions using a linear sequence of steps through which data can flow over time, as shown in figure 1.8.

In essence, you need to combine the ability to decouple functionality like event emitters with the fluent design pattern of Promises, all into a single abstraction. Moreover, you need to work with both synchronous and asynchronous code, handle errors, discourage side effects, and scale out from one to a deluge of events. This is certainly a long laundry list of things to take care of.

As you think about this, ask yourself these questions: How can you write code as a linear sequence of steps that acts only after some event has occurred in the future? How do you combine it with other code that might have its own set of constraints? Your desire for synchronicity isn't just about convenience; it's what you're used to. Unfortunately, most of the common language constructs that you use in synchronous code aren't well suited for asynchronous execution. This lack of language support for things like async try/catch, async loops, and async conditionals means that developers must often roll their own. It's not surprising that in the past few years, other people have asked the same questions and come together with the community at large to address these challenges, emerging as what's known as the *Reactive Extensions*—we have arrived!

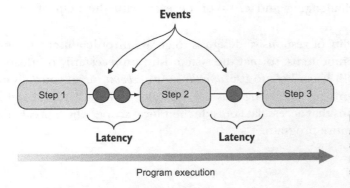

Figure 1.8 **RxJS can treat asynchronous data flows with a programming model that resembles a simple chain of sequential steps.**

1.4   *The Reactive Extensions for JavaScript*

Reactive Extensions for JavaScript (RxJS) is an elegant replacement for callback or `Promise`-based libraries, using a single programming model that treats any ubiquitous source of events—whether it be reading a file, making an HTTP call, clicking a button, or moving the mouse—in the exact same manner. For example, instead of handling each mouse event independently with a callback, with RxJS you handle all of them combined.

As you'll learn in chapter 9, RxJS is also inherently robust and easy to test with a vibrant community to support it. The power of RxJS derives from being built on top of the pillars of functional and reactive programming, as well as a few popular design patterns such as observer and iterator that have been used successfully for years. Certainly, RxJS didn't invent these patterns, but it found ways to use them within the context of FP. We'll discuss FP and its role in RxJS further in the next chapter; in order to take full advantage of this framework, the key takeaway from this section is that you must learn to think in terms of *streams*.

1.4.1   *Thinking in streams: data flows and propagation*

Whether you deal with thousands of key presses, movement events, touch gestures, remote HTTP calls, or single integers, RxJS treats all of these data sources in exactly the same way, which we'll refer to as *data streams* from now on.

> **STREAMS**   Traditionally, the term *stream* was used in programming languages as an abstract object related to I/O operations such as reading a file, reading a socket, or requesting data from an HTTP server. For instance, Node.js implements readable, writable, and duplex streams for doing just this. In the RP world, we expand the definition of a stream to mean *any* data source that can be consumed.

Reactive programming entails a mental shift in the way you reason about your program's behavior, especially if you come from an imperative background. We'll illustrate this shift in mindset with a simple exercise:

```
let a = 20;
let b = 22;
let c = a + b; //-> 42

a = 100;
c = ?
```

You can easily predict the value of c in this case: 42. The fact that we changed a didn't have any influence on the value of c. In other words, there's no *propagation of change*. This is the most important concept to understand in reactive programming. Now we'll show you a pseudo JavaScript implementation of this:

Creates a stream initialized with the value 20

```
A$ = [20];                              Creates a stream initialized
B$ = [22];                              with the value 22
```

```
C$ = A$.concat(B$).reduce(adder); //-> [42]
A$.push(100);        <—— Pushes a new value into A$
C$ = ?
```

> Concatenates both streams
> and applies an adder function
> to get a new container with 42

First, we'll explain some of the notation we use here. Streams are containers or wrappers of data very similar to arrays, so we used the array literal notation [] to symbolize this. Also, it's common to use the $ suffix to qualify variables that point to streams. In the RxJS community, this is known as Finnish Notation, attributed to Andre Staltz, who is one of the main contributors of RxJS and Finnish.

We created two streams, A$ and B$, with one numerical value inside each. Because they're not primitive objects in JavaScript or have a plus (+) overloaded operator, we need to symbolize addition by concatenating both streams and applying an *operator method* like reduce with an adder function (this should be somewhat familiar to you if you've worked with these array methods). This is represented by C$.

> **ARRAY EXTRAS**   JavaScript ES5 introduced new array methods, known as the array extras, which enable some level of native support for FP. These include map, reduce, filter, some, every, and others.

What happens to C$ if the value 100 is pushed onto A$? In an imperative program, nothing will actually happen except that A$ will have an extra value. But in the world of streams, where there's change propagation, if A$ receives a new value (a new event), this state is pushed through any streams that it's a part of. In this case, C$ gets the value 122. Confused yet? *Reactive programming is oriented around data flows and propagation.* In this case, you can think of C$ as an always-on variable that *reacts* to any change and causes actions to ripple through it when any constituent part changes. Now let's see how RxJS implements this concept.

1.4.2   *Introducing the RxJS project*

RxJS is the result of many efforts to manage the myriad of problems that manifest in asynchronous programming, outlined earlier. It's an open source framework ported by Matthew Podwysocki from Rx.Net (Reactive Extensions for .Net), itself open source and created by Microsoft. RxJS has now evolved as a community-driven project owned by Ben Lesh from Netflix, sanctioned by Microsoft as RxJS 5. This latest version is a complete overhaul of the previous version with a brand-new architecture, a laser focus on performance, and drastic simplification of the API surface. It offers several distinct advantages over other JavaScript solutions, because it provides idiomatic abstractions to treat asynchronous data similar to how you would treat any source of synchronous data, like a simple array. You can obtain installation details in appendix A.

If you were to visit the main website for the Reactive Extensions project (http://reactivex.io/), you'd find it defined as "an API for asynchronous programming with observable streams." By the end of this chapter, you'll be able to parse out exactly what this means. We'll demystify this concept and put you on the right path to tackle the problems presented in this book.

Let's see what thinking in streams looks like more concretely in RxJS. In figure 1.9, we show a simple breakdown of a stream (or pipeline) approach to handling data. A pipeline is a series of logic blocks that will be executed, in order, when data becomes available.[4] On the left side of figure 1.9 are the data sources, which produce various forms of data to be consumed by an application. And on the right are the data consumers, the entities that subscribe to (or listen for) these events and will do something with data they receive, such as present it on a chart or save it to a file. In the middle is the data pipeline. During this middle step, data that's coming from any of the data sources that are being observed is filtered and processed in different ways so that it can be more easily consumed by the consumers.

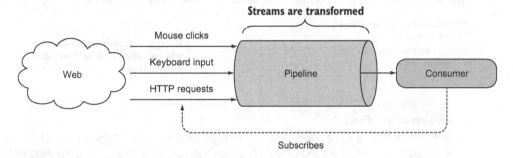

Figure 1.9   A generic data-processing pipeline deals with a constant stream of asynchronous data, moving it from a producer (for example, a user clicking the mouse) to a consumer (code that reacts to the click). The pipeline will process data before it's passed to the consumer for consumption.

You can subscribe to streams and implement functions within the pipeline that will be called (therefore react) when an event occurs (it's this pipeline component where the principles of FP will come into play, as you'll learn about in chapter 2).

DEFINITION   A stream is nothing more than a sequence of events over time.

A popular example that you can relate to would be an Excel spreadsheet. You can easily bind functions onto cells that subscribe to the values of other cells and respond in real time as soon as any of the bounded cells change. A stream is an abstract concept that works exactly like this, so we'll slowly wind up to it and break it down starting with some popular constructs you're familiar with.

1.4.3   Everything is a stream

The concept of a stream can be applied to any data point that holds a value; this ranges from a single integer to bytes of data received from a remote HTTP call. RxJS provides lightweight data types to subscribe to and manage streams as a whole that can be passed around as first-class objects and combined with other streams. Learning how to manipulate and use streams is one of the central topics of this book. At this

---

[4]   You can relate this to the popular pipes and filter design pattern.

point, we haven't talked about any specific RxJS objects; for now, we'll assume that an abstract data type, a container called `Stream`, exists. You can create one from a single value as such:

```
Stream(42);
```

At this point, this stream remains dormant and nothing has actually happened, until there's a subscriber (or observer) that listens for it. This is very different from `Promises`, which execute their operations as soon as they're created. Instead, streams are *lazy* data types, which means that they execute only after a subscriber is attached. In this case, the value 42, which was lifted into the stream context, navigates or propagates out to at least one subscriber. After it receives the value, the stream is completed:

```
Stream(42).subscribe(
   val => {
      console.log(val); //-> prints 42
   }
);
```

> Using a simple function that will be called with each event in the stream

Observer pattern

Behind RxJS is a fine-tuned observer design pattern. It involves an object (the subject), which maintains a list of subscribers (each an observer) that are notified of any state changes. This pattern has had many applications, especially as an integral part of the model-view-controller (MVC) architecture where the view layer is constantly listening for model changes. But the rudimentary observer pattern has its drawbacks because of memory leaks related to improper disposal of observers. You can learn more about this in the famous book *Design Patterns: Elements of Reusable Object-Oriented Software*, known casually as the Gang of Four book.

RxJS draws inspiration from this pattern for its publish-subscribe methodology targeted at asynchronous programs but adds a few extra features out of the box, like signals that indicate when a stream has completed, lazy initialization, cancellation, resource management, and disposal. Later on, we'll talk about the components of an RxJS stream.

---

a. Gamma, Helm, Johnson, and Vlissides (Addison-Wesley, 1977, Oxford University Press).

Furthermore, you can extend this example to a sequence of numbers

```
Stream(1, 2, 3, 4, 5).subscribe (
   val => {
      console.log(val);
   }
);
//-> 1
    2
    3
    4
    5
```

or even arrays:

```
Stream([1, 2, 3, 4, 5])
  .filter(num => (num % 2) === 0)
  .map(num => num * num)
  .subscribe(
     val => {
        console.log(val);
     }
);
//-> 4
    16
```

> Streams also support the Array.map() and Array.filter() functions introduced in ES5 to process the contents within the array.

In this example, the set of operations that occurs between the creation of the producer of the stream (in this case, the array) and the consumer (the function that logs to the console) is what we'll refer to as the pipeline (we'll expand on these concepts shortly). The pipeline is what we'll study thoroughly in this book and is what allows you to transform a given input into the desired output. In essence, it's where your business logic will be executed, as outlined in figure 1.10.

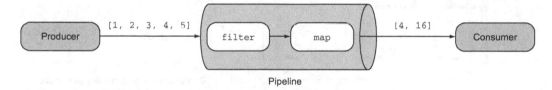

Pipeline

Figure 1.10   A simple producer (an array of numbers) that emits events linearly. These events are submitted through the pipeline and transformed. The final data is then sent to all subscribers to be consumed.

Up until now, we've created streams from *static* data sources: numbers (or strings), sequences, and arrays. But the power of RxJS extends beyond that with the ability to treat *dynamic* data sources in exactly the same way, as if *time* didn't factor into the equation.

1.4.4   *Abstracting the notion of time from your programs*

Indeed, time is of the essence. The hardest part of asynchronous code is dealing with latency and wait time. You saw earlier how callbacks and Promises can be used to cope with these concerns, each with their own limitations. RxJS brings this notion of continuous sequences of events over time as a first-class citizen of the language—finally, a true event subsystem for JavaScript. In essence, this means that RxJS *abstracts over time under the same programming model regardless of source*, so that you can transform your data as if your code was completely linear and synchronous. This is brilliant because you now can process a sequence of mouse events just as easily as processing an array of numbers.

Looking at figure 1.11, you can see that streams are analogous to a real-world monthly magazine subscription. Your subscription to the magazine is actually a collection of magazines that are separated by time; that is, there are 12 magazines annually, but you receive only one every month. Upon receiving a magazine, you usually perform an action on it (read it or throw it away). There are additional cases that you can also consider, such as the time between magazine deliveries being zero, whereby you would receive all the magazines at once, or there might be no magazines (and someone would be getting an angry email). In all these cases, because you perform the action only upon receiving the magazine, you can think of this process as reactive (because you're *reacting* to receiving a magazine). A non-reactive version of this would be going to a newspaper stall at the airport. Here, you can also find magazines, but now you won't receive additional magazines, only the ones that you buy at the stall. In practice, this would mean that you receive updates only when you happen to be near a magazine stand rather than every time a new magazine becomes available.

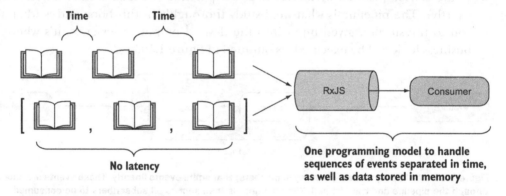

Figure 1.11 Not only does RxJS handle sequential events, but using the same programming model, it can just as easily work with asynchronous events (bound by time). This means that the same level of reasoning applied to linear programs can also be applied to non-linear programs with latency and wait times.

Rx allows you to take this magazine subscription metaphor and apply it to a wide range of use cases: loading files from disk or over a network, processing user input, or handling real-time services like RSS and Twitter feeds. Following the same examples as before, with RxJS you can consume a stream of time-based asynchronous sequences of events, just as you did with normal synchronous data:

```
Stream(loadMagazines('/subscriptions/magazines'))
  .filter(magazine => magazine.month === 'July')
  .subscribe(
    magazine => {
      console.log(magazine.title);
      //-> prints Dr. Dobbs "Composing Reactive Animations"
    }
);
```

Using the well-known Array.filter() operator, this time with magazine subscriptions, to retrieve only the July edition

These types of services produce data in real time at irregular intervals, and the data produced forms the foundation of an event stream. In the case of a service like Twitter, you can think of the Twitter API as a producer of tweets, of which some will be interesting and some not so much. In general, in most cases you're interested in creating logic that processes the content of the tweet rather than diving into the intricacies of network communication. As we mentioned earlier, this logic is made up of several components, which we'll look at in more detail.

1.4.5 Components of an Rx stream

The RxJS stream is made up of several basic components, each with specific tasks and lifetimes with respect to the overall stream. You saw some examples of these earlier, and now we'll introduce them more formally:

- Producers
- Consumers
- Data pipeline
- Time

PRODUCERS

Producers are the sources of your data. A stream must always have a producer of data, which will be the starting point for any logic that you'll perform in RxJS. In practice, a producer is created from something that generates events independently (anything from a single value, an array, mouse clicks, to a stream of bytes read from a file). The observer pattern defines producers as the *subject*; in RxJS, we call them *observables*, as in something that's *able to be observed*.

Observables are in charge of pushing notifications, so we refer to this behavior as fire-and-forget, which means that we'll never expect the producer to be involved in the *processing* of events, only the emission of them.

> **TC-39 OBSERVABLE SPEC**   The use of observables has proven to be so successful from the previous version of the library (RxJS 4) that a proposal has been made to include it in the next major release of JavaScript.[5] Fortunately, RxJS 5 follows this proposal closely to remain completely compatible.

CONSUMERS

To balance the producer half of the equation, you must also have a consumer to accept events from the producer and process them in some specific way. When the consumer begins listening to the producer for events to consume, you now have a stream, and it's at this point that the stream begins to push events; we'll refer to a consumer as an *observer*.

Streams travel only from the producer to the consumer, not the other way around. In other words, a user typing on the keyboard produces events that flow down to be consumed by some other process. This means that part of understanding of how to

---

[5] https://github.com/tc39/proposal-observable.

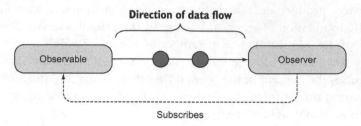

Figure 1.12   Events always move from observables to observers and never the other way around.

think in streams will mean understanding how to think about parts of an application as upstream or downstream to determine the direction in which the data will flow. With respect to RxJS, a stream will always flow from an upstream observable to a downstream observer, and both components are loosely coupled, which increases the modularity of your application, as shown in figure 1.12.

For instance, a keyboard event handler would be upstream because it would only produce events, not consume them, whereas code that should perform logic based on key presses would be downstream. At a fundamental level, a stream will only ever require the producer and the consumer. Once the latter is able to begin receiving events from the former, you have effectively created a stream. Now what can you do with this data? All of that happens within the data pipeline.

DATA PIPELINE

One advantage of RxJS is that you can manipulate or edit the data as it passes from the producer to the consumer. This is where the list of methods (known as observable operators) comes into play. Manipulating data en route means that you can adapt the output of the producer to match the expectations of the consumer. Doing so promotes a *separation of concerns*[6] between the two entities, and it's a big win for the modularity of your code. This design principle is typically extremely hard to accomplish in large-scale JavaScript applications, but RxJS facilitates this model of design.

TIME

The implicit factor behind all of this is time. For everything RxJS there's always an underlying concept of time, which you can use to manipulate streams. The time factor permeates all the components we've discussed so far. It's an important and abstract concept to grasp, so we'll look at it in detail in later chapters. For now, you need only understand that time need not always run at normal speed, and you can build streams that run slower or faster depending on your requirements. Luckily, this won't be an issue if you decide to use RxJS. Figure 1.13 provides a visualization of the parts of the RxJS stream.

---

[6]   *Separations of concerns* in this case refers to the use of functions with single responsibility.

```
Stream.timerInSeconds()  ◀━━━━━━━━━ ┌── Producer
       .interval()
       .map(x => x.value)                      ┐
Time   .filter(x => x % 2 === 0)               ├── Pipeline
       .take(10)                               ┘
       .subscribe(val=> console.log(val));  ◀━━━━━┌── Consumer
```

Figure 1.13 Sample code highlighting the different components of a stream

If you pay close attention to the structure of a stream, you'll notice that this closely resembles the pattern used in Promises. What started out as a nested callback "pyramid of doom"

```javascript
ajax('<host1>/items',
     items => {
        items.forEach(item => {
            ajax(`<host2>/items/${item.getId()}/info`,
            dataInfo => {
            ajax(`<host3>/files/${dataInfo.files}`,
            processFiles);
          });
        });
});
```

was drastically improved using Promises:

```javascript
ajax('<host1>/items')
    .then(items =>
       items.map(item => ajax(`<host2>/data/${item.getId()}/info`)
    )
    .then(promises => Promise.all(promises))
    .then(infos => infos.map(dataInfo =>
       ajax(`<host3>/data/files/${dataInfo.files}`))
    )
    .then(promises => Promise.all(promises))
    .then(processFiles);
```

And now, streams extend this behavior with powerful operators that break this down even further:

```javascript
Stream(ajax('<host1>/items')
  .streamMap(item =>
       Stream(ajax(`<host2>/data/${item.getId()}/info`)))     ◀┐  Streams can
  .streamMap(dataInfo =>                                        │  also compose
       Stream(ajax(`<host3>/data/files/${dataInfo.files}`)))  ◀┘  other streams.
  .subscribe(processFiles);
```

Remember that the Stream object here is merely an abstract artifact designed to show you how the paradigm works. In this book, you'll learn to use the actual objects that implement these abstract concepts to design your applications using a functional and reactive model. But RxJS doesn't obligate you to use only a single paradigm; it's often the combination of paradigms that creates the most flexible and maintainable designs.

1.5   *Reactive and other programming paradigms*

Every new paradigm that you'll encounter during your programming career will require you to modify your thinking to accommodate the primitives of the language. For example, object-oriented programming (OOP) puts *state* within objects, which are the central units of abstraction, and the intricacy of the paradigm comes from the interactions that arise when they interact with one another. In a similar fashion, FP places *behavior* at the center of all things, with functions as the main unit of work. Reactive programming, on the other hand, requires you to see data as a constantly *flowing stream of change* as opposed to monolithic data types or collections holding all of an application's state.

Now you're probably wondering, am I allowed to choose only one? Or can I combine them into the same code base? The beauty behind all this is that you can use all of them together. Many prominent figures in our industry have attested to this. In other words, RxJS doesn't force on you a certain style of development or design pattern to use—it is *unopinionated*. Thankfully, it also works orthogonally to most libraries. As you'll see later on, it's a simple matter in most cases to adapt an existing event stream such as a DOM event handler into an observable. The library provides many operators for such operations baked directly into it. It will even support unusual design patterns such as those you'll see when you use a library like React or Redux (which you'll see in the last chapter).

In practice, you can use OOP to model your domain and use a powerful combination of reactive and FP (a combination known as functional reactive programming) to drive your behavior and events. When it comes to managing events, you'll soon begin to see an important theme in code involving Rx. Unlike in OOP where state or data is *held* in variables or collections, state in RP is *transient*, which means that data never remains stored but actually flows through the streams that are being subscribed to, which makes event handling easy to reason about and test.

Another noticeable difference is the style used in both paradigms. On one hand, OOP is typically written imperatively. In other words, you instantiate objects that keep track of state while running through a sequence of statements revealing how those objects interact and transform to arrive at your desired solution.

On the other hand, RxJS code encourages you to write declaratively, which means your code expresses the *what* and not the *how* of what you're trying to accomplish. RxJS follows a simple and declarative design inspired by FP. No longer will you be required to create variables to track the progress of your callbacks or worry about inadvertently corrupting some closed-over outer state causing side effects to occur. Besides, with RxJS it becomes easy to manage multiple streams of data, filtering and transforming them at will. By creating operations that can be chained together, you can also fluently create pipelines of logic that sound very much like spoken sentences like this: "When I receive a magazine for the month of July, notify me."

In this chapter, you learned how RxJS elegantly combines both functional and reactive paradigms into a simple computing model that places observables (streams) at the forefront. Observables are pure and free of side effects, with a powerful arsenal of operators and transformations that allow you to elegantly compose your business logic with asynchronous operations. We chose to keep the code abstract for now as we work through some of the new concepts. But we'll quickly ramp up to a comprehensive theoretical and practical understanding of the library, so that you can begin to apply it immediately at work or on your personal projects. Now it's time to start really thinking in streams, and that's the topic of the next chapter.

1.6 Summary

- Asynchronous code can be very difficult to implement because existing programming patterns don't scale to complex behavior.
- Callbacks and Promises can be used to deal with asynchronous code, but they have many limitations when targeted against large streams generated from repeated button clicks or mouse movements.
- RxJS is a reactive solution that can more concisely and declaratively deal with large amounts of data separated over time.
- RxJS is a paradigm shift that requires seeing and understanding data in streams with propagation of change.
- Streams originate from a producer (observable), where data flows through a pipeline, arriving at a consumer (observer). This same programming model is used whether or not data is separated by time.

Reacting with RxJS

2

This chapter covers

- Looking at streams as the main unit of work
- Understanding functional programming's influence on RxJS
- Identifying different types of data sources and how to handle them
- Modeling data sources as RxJS observables
- Consuming observables with observers

When writing code in an object-oriented way, we're taught to decompose problems into components, interactions, and states. This breakdown occurs iteratively and on many levels, with each part further subdivided into more components, until at last we arrive at a set of cohesive classes that implement a well-defined set of interactions. Hence, in the object-oriented (OO) approach, classes are the main unit of work. Every time a component is created, it will have state associated with it, and the manipulation of that state in a structured fashion is what advances application logic. For example, consider a typical online banking website. Banking systems contain modules that encapsulate not only the business logic associated with withdrawing, depositing, and transferring money but also domain models that store and

28

manage other properties, such as account and user profiles. Manipulating this state (its behavior) causes the data to transform into the desired output. In other words, behavior is driven by the continuous mutation of a system's state. If such a system is designed using object-oriented programming, the units of work are the classes responsible for modeling accounts, users, money, and others.

RxJS programming works a bit differently. In reactive programming in general, the fundamental unit of work is the stream.

In this chapter, we ask you to think in terms of streams (think reactively) and design code that, instead of holding onto data, allows data to flow through and applies transformations along the way until it reaches your desired state. You'll learn how to handle different types of data sources, whether static or dynamic, as RxJS streams that use a consistent computational model based on the `Observable` data type. Unlike using other JavaScript libraries, however, using RxJS in your application means much more than implementing new APIs; it means that you must approach your problems not as the sum of the set of states manipulated by methods in classes but as a sequence of data that continuously travels from the producers to the consumers through a set of operators that implement your desired behavior.

This way of thinking places the notion of time at the forefront; this notion runs as the undercurrent through the components of an RxJS stream and causes data to be never stored but rather transiently flowing. Relating this to a real-world physical water stream, you can think of the data source as the top of the stream and the data consumer as the bottom of the stream. Hence, data is *always traveling downstream*, in a single direction, like water in a river, and along the way you can have control dams in charge of transforming the nature of this stream. Thinking this way will help you understand how data should move through an application.

This is not to say that this understanding will come easily—like any new skill, it must be built up over time and through iterative application of the concepts. As you saw in the pseudo streams example in chapter 1, the notion of data in motion versus data kept in variables is a difficult one for most people to wrap their head around. In this book, we'll provide you with the necessary tools to ease this learning curve. To begin building your toolkit, this chapter lays the groundwork to help you better understand streams. Many of the basic principles behind RP derive from functional programming, so let's start there.

2.1 Functional programming as the pillar of reactive programming

The abstractions that support RP are built on top of FP, so FP is the foundation for RP. Much of the hype around RP derives from the development communities and the industry realizing that FP offers a compelling way to design your code. This is why it's important for you to have at least a basic understanding of the FP principles. If you have a solid background in functional programming, you're free to skip this section, but we recommend you read along because it will help you better understand some of the design decisions behind RxJS.

Just like in chapter 1, we ask you to take another quick glance at the main website for the Reactive Extensions project (http://reactivex.io). In it, you'll find the following definition:

> *ReactiveX is a combination of the best ideas from the Observer pattern, the Iterator pattern, and functional programming.*

You learned about the main components of the observer pattern in chapter 1 (producer and consumer); now you'll learn the about the other parts that gave rise to the Rx project, which are functional programming and iterators. Here's a diagram (figure 2.1) that better illustrates the relationship between these paradigms.

Let's begin by exploring the basics of FP.

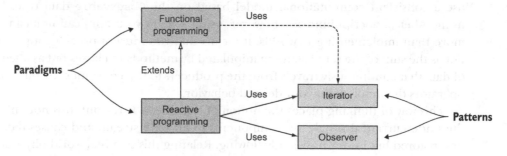

Figure 2.1 The RP paradigm builds and extends from FP. Also, it leverages commonly known design patterns such as iterator and observer.

2.1.1 *Functional programming*

Functional programming is a software paradigm that emphasizes the use of functions to create programs that are declarative, immutable, and side effect–free. Did you trip over the word *immutable*? We agree with you; the notion of a program that doesn't ever change state is a bit mind bending. After all, that's why we put data in variables and modify them to our heart's content. All of the object-oriented or procedural application code you've written so far relies on changing and passing variables back and forth to solve problems. So how can you accomplish the same goals without doing this? Take the example of a clock. When a clock goes from 1:00 p.m. to 2:00 p.m., it's undoubtedly changing, isn't it? But to frame this from a functional point of view, we argue that instead of a single clock instance mutating every second, it's best to return new clock instances every second. Theoretically, both would arrive at the same time, and both would give you a single state at the end.

RxJS borrows numerous principles from FP, particularly *function chaining, lazy evaluation,* and the notion of using an abstract data type to orchestrate data flows. These are some of the design decisions that drive the development of RxJS's stream programming via the `Observable` data type. Before we dive in, we'll explain the main parts of the FP definition we just gave and then show you a quick example involving arrays.

To reiterate, functional programs have the following characteristics:

- *Declarative*—Functional code has a peculiar style, which takes advantage of JavaScript's higher-order functions to apply specialized business logic. As you'll see later on, function chains (also known as *pipelines*) describe data transformation steps in an idiomatic manner. Most people see SQL syntax as a perfect example of declarative code.

- *Immutable*—An immutable program (and by this we mean any immutable function, module, or whole program) is one that never changes or modifies data after it's been created or after its variables have been declared. This can be a radical concept to grasp, especially when you're coming from an OO background. Functional programs treat data as immutable, constant values. A good example of a familiar module is the String type, because none of the operations change the string on which they operate; rather, they all return new strings. A good practice that you'll see us use throughout the book is to qualify all of our variables with const to create nicely block-scoped immutable variables that can't be reassigned. This doesn't solve all the problems of immutability, but it gives you a little extra support when your data and functions are shared globally.

- *Side effect–free*—Functions with side effects depend on data residing outside its own local scope. A function's scope is made up of its arguments and any local variables declared within. Interacting with anything outside this (like reading a file, writing to the console, rendering elements on an HTML page, and more) is considered a side effect and should be avoided or, at the very least, isolated. In this book, you'll learn how RxJS deals with these issues by pushing the effectful computations into the subscribers.

In general, mutations and side effects make functions unreliable and unpredictable. That is to say, if a function alters the contents of an object inadvertently, it will compromise other functions that expect this object to keep its original state. The OO solution to this is to encapsulate state and protect it from direct access from other components of the system. In contrast, FP deals with state by eliminating it, so that your functions can confidently rely on it to run.

For instance, figure 2.2 illustrates the dependency between the two functions doWork() and doMoreWork() through a shared state variable called data.

This coupling presents an issue because doMoreWork now relies on doWork to run first. Two issues may occur:

- The result of doMoreWork() depends entirely on the successful outcome of doWork() and on no other parts of the system changing this variable.

- Unit tests against this function can't be done in isolation as they should be, so your test results are susceptible to the order in which the test cases are run (in chapter 9, we'll explore testing in much more detail).

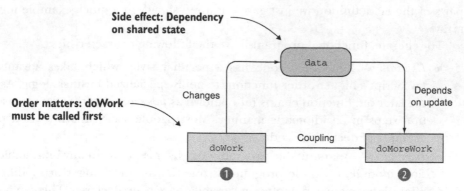

Figure 2.2   Function `doWork()` is temporarily coupled to `doMoreWork()` because of the dependency on shared state (side effect). Hence, `doWork()` must be called before `doMoreWork()` or the program will cease to work.

Shared variables, especially in the global scope, add to the cognitive load of reasoning about your code because these variables demand that you keep track of them as you trace through it. Another way you can think of global data is as a hidden parameter within all your functions. So the more global the state you have to maintain, the harder it is for you to maintain your code. The example in figure 2.2 is an obvious side effect, but they're not always this clear. Consider this trivial function that returns the lowest value in a numerical array:

```
const lowest = arr => arr.sort().shift();
```

Although this code may seem harmless to you, it packs a terrible side effect. Can you spot it? This function actually changes the contents of the input array, as shown in the following snippet. So if you used the first element of the array somewhere else, that's completely gone now:

```
let source = [3,1,9,8,3,7,4,6,5];
let result = lowest(source); //-> 1
console.log(source); //-> [3, 3, 4, 5, 6, 7, 8, 9]
```

The original array changed!

Later on, we'll talk about a functional library that provides a rich set of functions for working with arrays immutably, so that things like this don't inadvertently creep up on you.

Matters get worse if you have concurrent asynchronous processes where data structures are shared and used in different components. Because latency is unpredictable, you'd need to either nest your function calls or use some other robust synchronization mechanism to ensure they execute and mutate this state in the right order; otherwise, you'll experience random and hard-to-troubleshoot bugs.

Fortunately, JavaScript is single threaded, so you don't need to worry about shared state running through different threads. But as JavaScript developers, we deal quite often with concurrent code when either working with web workers or making simultaneous

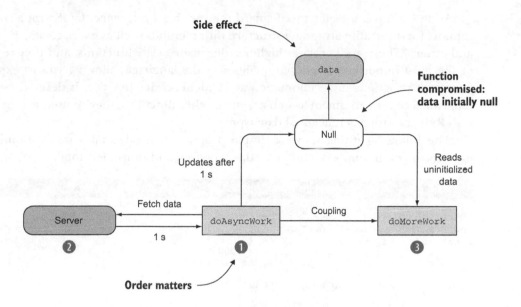

Figure 2.3 Function `doAsyncWork()` is an example of a remote call that fetches data from the server. Suppose this call has a latency around one second, depending on network conditions. Immediately after, the next function runs `doMoreWork()`, expecting that a piece of shared data has already been initialized. Because of this latency, the shared data has not been initialized, and the execution of `doMoreWork()` is compromised.

HTTP calls. Consider the trivial yet frequent use case illustrated in figure 2.3, which involves asynchronous code mixed with synchronous code. This presents a tremendous challenge because the latter assumes that the functions executing before it have completed successfully, which might not necessarily be the case if there's some latency.

In this scenario, `doAsyncWork()` fetches some data from the server, which never completes in a constant amount of time. So `doMoreWork()` fails to run properly because it reads data that hasn't yet been initialized. Callbacks and `Promises` help you solve this problem, so that you don't have to hardcode your own timeouts in order to anticipate latency. Dealing directly with time is a recipe for disaster because your code will be extremely brittle and hard to maintain and will cause you to come in to work during a weekend when your application is experiencing slightly more traffic than usual. Working with data immutably, using FP, and the help of an asynchronous library like RxJS can make these timing issues disappear—immutable variables are protected against time. In chapters 4 and 6, we'll cover timing and synchronization with observables, which offer a much superior solution to this problem.

Even though JavaScript isn't a pure functional language, with a bit of discipline and the help of the proper libraries you can use it completely functionally. As you learn to use RxJS, we ask that you also begin to embrace a functional coding style; it's something we believe strongly about and promote in all code samples in this book.

Aside from using `const` to safeguard the variable's reference, JavaScript also has support for a versatile array data structure with methods such as `map`, `reduce`, `filter`, and others. These are known as higher-order or first-class functions, and they're one of the most important functional qualities in the language, allowing you to express JavaScript programs in an idiomatic way. A higher-order function is defined as one that can accept as argument as well as return other functions; they're used extensively with RxJS, as with any functional data type.

The following listing shows a simple program that takes an array of numbers, extracts the even numbers, computes their squares, and sums their total.

Listing 2.1 Processing collections with `map`, `reduce`, and `filter`

```
const isEven = num => num % 2 === 0;
const square = num => num * num;
const add = (a, b) => a + b;

const arr = [1, 2, 3, 4, 5, 6, 7, 8, 9, 10];

arr.filter(isEven).map(square).reduce(add);   //-> 220
```

In this example, because these operations are side effect–free, this program will always produce the same value (220), given the same input array.

Where can I find this code?

All the code for this book can be found in the RxJS in Action GitHub repository at https://github.com/RxJSInAction. There, you'll find two subrepositories. Under rxjs-in-action, you'll find a simple application that contains the code for all individual chapter listings for chapters 1 through 9. All samples are presented as runnable snippets of RxJS code that you can interact with. Also, under the banking-in-action repository, you'll find our web application that showcases RxJS embedded into a React/Redux architecture. Some of the APIs that we interact with in the book don't allow cross-origin resource sharing (CORS). The simplest way to get around this is to disable it at the browser level by installing an extension or add-on.

If you imagine for a second having to write this program using a non-functional or imperative approach, you'll probably need to write a loop, a conditional statement, and a few variables to keep track of things. FP, on the other hand, raises the level of abstraction and encourages a style of declarative coding that clearly states the purpose of a program, describing *what* it does and not *how* it does it. Nowhere in this short program is the presence of a loop, `if/else`, or any imperative control flow mechanism.

One of the main themes in FP that you'll use as well in RP is *programming without loops*. In listing 2.1, you took advantage of `map`, `reduce`, and `filter` to hide manual looping constructs—allowing you to implement looping logic through functions' arguments. Moreover, these functions are also immutable, which means that new arrays are created at each step of the way, keeping the original intact.

Going back to our discussion, side effect–free functions are also known as *pure*, because they're predictable when you're working on collections of objects or streams. You should always strive for purity whenever possible because it makes your programs easy to test and reason about.

Want to learn more about functional programming?

JavaScript's `Array` object has a special place in functional programming because it behaves as an extremely powerful data type called a *functor*. In a simple sense, functors are containers that can wrap data and expose a mapping method that allows you to immutably apply transformations on this data, as shown by the `Array.map()` method. As you'll see later on, RxJS streams follow this same functor-like design.

Functional programming is a huge subject to cover. In this book, we'll cover only enough of FP to help you to understand and be proficient with RxJS and RP. If you'd like more information about FP and FP topics, you can read about them in detail in *Functional Programming in JavaScript* (Manning, 2016) by Luis Atencio.

The code shown in listing 2.1, which works well with arrays, also translates to streams. Along the lines of the pseudo `Stream` data type that we discussed in chapter 1, look at how similarly arrays and streams work when processing some number sequence:

```
Stream([1, 2, 3, 4, 5, 6, 7, 8, 9, 10])
  .filter(isEven)
  .map(square)
  .reduce(add)
  .subscribe(console.log);   //-> 220
```

You can clearly see how Rx was inspired by FP. All we had to do was wrap the array into a stream and then subscribe to it to listen for the computed values that derive from the sequence of steps declared in the stream's pipeline. This is the same as saying that streams are containers that you can use to lift data (events) into their context, so that you can apply sequences of operations on this data until reaching your desired outcome. Fortunately, you're already familiar with this concept from working with arrays for many years. You can lift a value into an array and map any functions to it. Suppose you declare some simple functions on strings like `toUpper`, `slice`, and `repeat`:

```
['rxjs'].map(toUpper).map(slice(0, 2)).map(repeat(2)); //-> 'RXRX'
```

The ancient Greek philosopher Heraclitus once said, "You can never step into the same river twice." He formulated this statement as part of his doctrine on *change* and *motion* being central components of the universe—everything is constantly in motion. This epic realization is what RxJS streams are all about: as data continuously flows and moves through the stream, orchestrated through this is the data type you're learning about called `Stream`. Despite being dynamic, `Stream`s are immutable data types. Once a `Stream` is declared to wrap an array, listen for mouse clicks, or respond to an HTTP call, you can't mutate it or add a new value to it afterward—you must do it at the time of declaration. Hence, you're *specifying the dynamic behavior of an object or value declaratively and immutably*. We'll revisit this topic a bit more in the next chapter.

Moreover, the business logic of this program is pure and takes advantage of side effect–free functions that are mapped onto the stream to transform the produced data into the desired outcome. The advantage of this is that all side effects are isolated and pushed onto the consumers (logging to the console, in this case). This separation of concerns is ideal and keeps your business logic clean and pure. Figure 2.4 shows the role that the producers and consumers play.

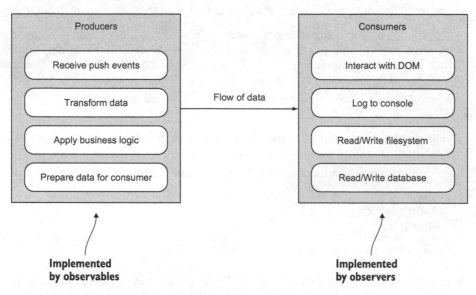

Figure 2.4 Events emitted by producers are pushed through a pipeline of side effect–free functions, which implement the business logic of your program. This data flows to all observers in charge of consuming and displaying it.

Another design principle of streams that's borrowed from FP is lazy evaluation. *Lazy evaluation* means that code is never called until actually needed. In other words, functions won't evaluate until their results are used as part of some other expression. In the following example, the idea is that a stream sits idle until a subscriber (a consumer) is attached to it; only then will it emit the values 1–10:

```
Stream([1, 2, 3, 4, 5, 6, 7, 8, 9, 10])
  .filter(isEven)
  .map(square)          Nothing runs here because
  .reduce(add);      ⟵ no subscriber is added.
```

When a subscriber begins listening, the stream will emit events downstream through the pipeline in a single, unidirectional flow from the producer to the consumer. This is beneficial if your functions have side effects because the pipeline runs in a single direction, helping to ensure an orderly execution of your function calls. This is another reason to avoid side effects at all costs, especially when you begin combining multiple streams, because things can revert into the tangled mess that you're trying to get rid of in the first place. Lazy evaluation is a mandatory requirement for streams because they emit data infinitely to handle mouse movements, key presses, and other asynchronous messages. Otherwise, storing the entire sequence of mouse movements in memory could make your programs crash.

> **Reactive Manifesto**
>
> One of the key principles of a reactive system is the ability to stay afloat under varying workloads—known as *elasticity*. Obviously, this has many architectural and infrastructural implications that extend beyond the scope of this book, but a corollary to this is that the paradigm you use shouldn't change whether you're dealing with one, one hundred, or thousands of events. RxJS offers a single computing model to handle finite as well as infinite streams.
>
> The Reactive Manifesto (http://www.reactivemanifesto.org) was published by a working group that aims at identifying patterns for building reactive systems. It has no direct relation to the Rx libraries, but philosophically there are many points in common.

For instance, without lazy evaluation, code that uses infinite streams like this will cause the application to run out of memory and halt:

```
//1
Stream.range(1, Number.POSITIVE_INFINITY)      ◁─┐ Reads infinitely many
   .take(100)                                      numbers in memory
   .subscribe(console.log);

//2
Stream.fromEvent('mousemove')                  ◁─┐ Listens to all mouse moves
    .map(e => [e.clientX, e.clientY])             the user is performing
    .subscribe(console.log);
```

In example 1, lazy evaluation makes the stream smart enough to understand that it will never need to actually run through all the positive numbers infinitely before taking the first 100. And even if the amount of numbers to store is big, streams won't persistently hold onto data; instead, any data emitted is immediately broadcast to all subscribers at the moment it gets generated. In example 2, imagine if you needed to store in memory the coordinates of all mouse movements on the screen; this could potentially take up a huge amount of memory. Instead of holding onto this data, RxJS lets it flow freely and uses the iterator pattern to traverse any type of data source irrespective of how it's created.

2.1.2   *The iterator pattern*

A key design principle behind RxJS streams is to give you a familiar traversal mechanism, just as you have with arrays. Iterators are used to traverse containers of data in a structure-agnostic way or independent of the underlying data structure used to harness these elements, whether it's an array, a tree, a map, or even a stream. In addition, this pattern is effective at *decoupling the business logic applied at each element from the iteration itself.* The goal is to provide a single protocol for accessing each element and moving on to the next, as shown in figure 2.5.

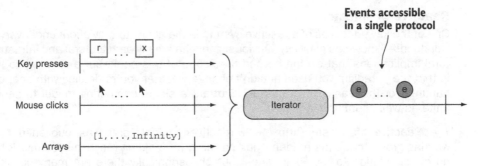

Figure 2.5   Iterators abstract the traversal mechanism, whether a `for` or a `while` loop, so that processing any type of data is done in the exact same way.

We'll explain this pattern briefly now, and later on you'll see how this applies to streams. The JavaScript ES6 (or ES2015) standard defines the iterator protocol, which allows you to define or customize the iteration behavior of any iterable object. The iterable objects you're most familiar with are arrays and strings. ES6 added `Map` and `Set`. With RxJS, we'll treat streams as iterable data types as well.

You can make any object iterable by manipulating its underlying iterator. We'll be using some ES6-specific syntax to show this. Consider an iterator object that traverses an array of numbers and buffers a set amount of contiguous elements. Here, the business logic performed is the buffering itself, which can be useful to group elements together to form numerical sets of any dimension, like the ones illustrated in figure 2.6.

Now let's see what the code would look like. The next listing shows the internal implementation of this custom iterator, which contains the buffer logic.

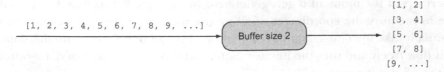

Figure 2.6   Using an iterator to display sets of numbers of size 2

Listing 2.2   Custom `BufferIterator` function

```
function BufferIterator(arr, bufferSize = 2) {        Assigns a default buffer size of 2
    this[Symbol.iterator] = function () {             Overrides the provided array's iterator
        let nextIndex = 0;                            mechanism. Symbol.iterator represents
                                                      the array's iterator function.
        return {
            next: () => {
                if(nextIndex >= arr.length) {
                    return {done: true};              Returns an object with a done =
                }                                     true property, which causes the
                else {                                iteration mechanism to stop
                    let buffer = new Array(bufferSize);
                    for(let i = 0; i < bufferSize; i++) {
                        buffer[i] = (arr[nextIndex++]);    Creates a temporary
                    }                                      buffer array to group
                    return {value: buffer, done: false};   contiguous elements
                }
            }
        }
    };
}
```

The next() function is part of the Iterator interface and marks the next element in the iteration.

Returns the buffered items and a status of done = false, which indicates to the iteration mechanism to continue

Any clients of this API need only interact with the next() function, as outlined in the class diagram in figure 2.7. The business logic is hidden from the caller, the for...of block, which is the main goal of the iterator pattern.

The next() function in listing 2.2 is used to customize the behavior of the iteration through for...of or any other looping mechanism. As you'll see later on, RxJS observers also implement a similar interface to signal to the stream to continue emitting elements.

DID ITERATORS THROW YOU FOR A LOOP?   The ES6 iterator/iterable protocols are powerful features of the language. RxJS development predates this protocol, so it doesn't use it at its core, but in many ways the pattern is still applied. We don't use iterators in this book; nevertheless, we recommend you learn about them. You can read more about this protocol here: https://developer.mozilla.org/en-US/docs/Web/JavaScript/Reference/Iteration_protocols#iterator.

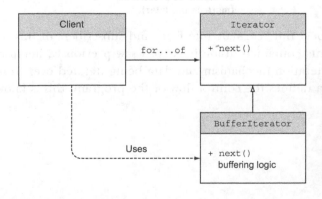

Figure 2.7   A class diagram (UML) highlighting the components of the iterator pattern. The `Iterator` interface defines the next() function, which is implemented by any concrete iterator (`BufferIterator`). Users of this API need only interact with the interface, which is general and applies to any custom traversal mechanism.

Iterators allow you to easily take advantage of the JavaScript runtime to take care of the iteration on your behalf. Following, we show some examples of this using our simple numerical domain. Buffering is built into RxJS, and it's really useful to gather up a sequence of events and make decisions about the nature of these events or apply additional logic. An example of this is when you need to invoke an expensive operation in response to a sequence of mouse events, like drag and drop. Instead of running expensive code at each mouse position, you buffer a specific number of them and emit a single response, taking all into account. Implementing this yourself would be tricky, because it would involve time management and keeping external state that tracks the frequency and speed with which the user moves the mouse; certainly, you'll want to delegate this to libraries that understand how to manage all this for you. We'll examine buffers in more detail in chapter 4. In RxJS, buffers aren't implemented as in listing 2.2, but it serves to show you an example of how you can buffer data using iterators, which is how you think about these sorts of operations. Here's our `BufferIterator` in action:

```
const arr = [1, 2, 3, 4, 5, 6];

for(let i of new BufferIterator(arr, 2)) {      ◁——— Buffers two elements at once
    console.log(i);
}
//-> [1, 2] [3, 4] [5, 6]
for(let i of new BufferIterator(arr, 3)) {  ◁—┐  Buffers three elements at once.
    console.log(i);                              Notice how the iteration
}                                                mechanism is completely separate
//-> [1, 2, 3] [4, 5, 6]                         from the buffering logic.
```

When you subscribe to a stream, you'll be traversing through many other data sources such as mouse clicks and key presses in the exact same way. Theoretically speaking, because our pseudo `Stream` type is an iterable object, you could traverse a set of key press events as well with a conventional loop:

```
const stream = Stream(R, x, J, S)[Symbol.iterator]();   ◁—┐  Creating a stream that
                                                             wraps key presses for
for(let keyEvent of stream) {  ◁—┐                           those four letters
    console.log(event.keyCode);
}                              Traversing a stream is semantically
//-> 82, 120, 74, 83           equivalent to subscribing to it
                               (more on this later).
```

Streams in RxJS also respect the `Iterator` interface, and subscribers of this stream will listen for all the events contained inside it. As you saw previously, iterators are great at decoupling the iteration mechanism and data being iterated over from the business logic. When data defines the control flow of the program, this is known as *data-driven code*.

2.2   *Stream's data-driven approach*

RxJS encourages a style of development known as data-driven programming. The data-driven approach is a way of writing code such that you can separate the behavior of an application from the data that's passing through it. This is a core design decision of RxJS and the main reason why you can use the same paradigm to process arrays, mouse clicks, or data from AJAX calls.

In the OO approach, you place more emphasis on the supporting structures than the data itself. This explains why pure OO languages like Java have many different implementations to store a sequential collection of elements, each tackling different use cases: `Array`, `ArrayList`, `LinkedList`, `DoublyLinkedList`, `ConcurrentLinkedList`, and others. To put it another way, imagine that you run a local florist that performs deliveries. Your business in this case is importing flowers, cutting them, packaging them, handling orders, and sending those orders out for delivery. These tasks are all part of your business logic; that is, they are the important bits that your customers care about and the parts that bring in revenue. Now imagine that in addition to those tasks, you're also tasked with designing the type of delivery van to use. Creating this structure is itself a full-time job and one that would likely distract from your primary business without meaningfully lending to it.

Data, as in the data that you care about and that which gives rise to search engines, websites, and video games, is the flower component of software design. Creating software should therefore be about how you manipulate data rather than how you create approximations of real-world objects (as you might in OO programming). Bringing data to the forefront and separating it from the behavior of the system is at the heart of data-driven/data-centric design. Similarly, loosely coupling functions from the objects that contain data is a design principle of FP and, by extension, RP.

To be driven by data is to be compelled to act by the presence of it and to let it fuel your logic. Without data to act on, behavior should do nothing. The idea of data giving life to behavior ties back to our earlier definition of what it means to be reactive— reacting to data instead of waiting for it. Streams are nothing more than a passive process that sits idle when nothing is pushed through them and no consumer is attached, as shown in figure 2.8.

This design pattern seems intuitive to most people because we think of data as requiring some sort of behavior in order to be meaningful. In a physics simulation, the mass of a ball is just a decimal number without context until the behavior of gravity is applied to it. Thus, if we are to imagine that both are intertwined by nature, it seems only natural that they should cohabitate logically within an object. In theory, this would seem to be a fairly obvious approach, and indeed the prevalence and popularity of OO programming stands testament to its power as a programming paradigm.

But it turns out that the greatest strength of OO design is also perhaps its greatest weakness. The intuition of representing components as objects with intrinsic behavior makes sense to a certain extent, but much like the real world, it can become difficult to reason about as the complexity of the application grows. For instance, if you hadn't

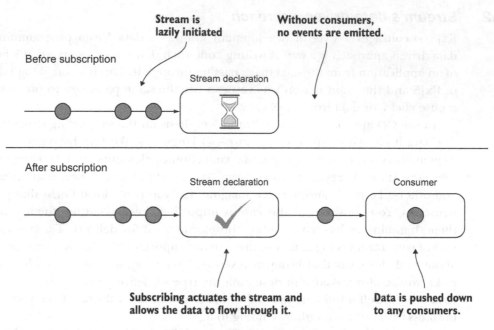

Figure 2.8   Initially, streams are lazy programs that wait for a subscriber to become available. Any events received at this point are discarded. Subscribing to the stream puts the wheels in motion, and event data flows through the pipeline and out for consumers to use.

used the `BufferIterator` type before, you would've had to implement the buffering logic with the application logic that uses this data. To keep things simple, you just logged the numbers to the screen, but in real life you'll use iterators for something more meaningful.

The data-centric approach seeks to remedy this issue by separating the concerns of data and behavior, through its producer/consumer model. Data would be lifted out of the behavior logic and instead would pass through it. Behavior could be loosely linked such that the data moved from one part of the application to another, independent of the underlying implementation. Earlier you saw how iterators help with this:

```
Stream([1, 2, 3, 4, 5, 6])
  .buffer(2)
  .subscribe(console.log)); //-> [1, 2] [3, 4] [5, 6]
```

Each step in the pipeline resides within its own scope that's externalized from the rest of the logic. In this case, you can see that just like iterators, the buffering step is done separately from the code acting on the data. By constructing it so, you've both declared the intent of each step and effectively decoupled the data from the underlying implementation, because each component reacts only to the step that preceded it.

Furthermore, producers come in all shapes and sizes. Event emitters are one of the most common ones; they're used to respond to events like mouse clicks or web requests. Also, there are timer-based sources like `setTimeout` and `setInterval` that will execute a task at a specified point in the future. There are subtler ones such as arrays and strings, which you might recognize as collections of data but not necessarily producers of data.

Traditionally, when dealing with each of these data sources, you've been conditioned to think of them as requiring a different approach. For instance, event emitters require named event handlers, `Promises` require the continuation-passing "thenable" function, `setTimeout` needs a callback, and arrays need a loop in order to iterate through them. What if we told you that all of these data sources can be consolidated and processed in the exact same way?

2.3   *Wrapping data sources with Rx.Observable*

All along, we've been using a pseudo data type called `Stream` as a substitute for the real `Rx.Observable` type available in RxJS 5. We did this to help you understand the paradigm and what it means to think in streams, rather than focus on the specifics of the library. In this section, we'll begin diving into the RxJS 5 APIs (for information about installing RxJS 5 on the client or on the server, please visit appendix A). Through the `Rx.Observable` type, you can subscribe to events produced from different types of data sources.

> **ES7 SPECIFICATION**   One of the key design decisions behind the development of RxJS 5 was to create an `Observable` type that follows the proposed observable specification slated for the next version of JavaScript ES7. You can find all the details of this API here: https://github.com/zenparsing/es-observable.

You can lift a heterogeneous set of inputs into the context of an observable object. Doing so allows you to unlock the power of RxJS to transform or manipulate them to reach your desired outcome. First, let's identify these different types of data.

2.3.1   *Identifying different sources of data*

We mentioned earlier that the advantage of separating data and behavior is that you can reason about a holistic model to account for any type of data. Hence, the first step to break the data free is to understand that all of these data sources are the same when viewed through a data-driven (or stream-driven?) lens. First, let's re-categorize the types of data we'll encounter. Rather than dealing with them as strict JavaScript types, let's look at some broader categories of data.

EMITTED DATA
Emitted data is data that will be created as a result of some sort of interaction with the system; this can be either from a user interaction such as a mouse click or a system event like a file read. As we alluded to in chapter 1, some of these will have at most one event; that is, you request data and then, at some point in the future, you receive a response. For this, `Promises` can be a good solution. Others, like a user's clicks and key presses, are part of a continuous process, and this requires you to treat them as event emitters that produce multiple discrete events at future times.

STATIC DATA

Static data is data that's already in existence and present in the system (in memory); for example, an array or a string. Artificial unit test data also falls into this category. Interacting with it is usually a matter of iterating through it. If you were wrapping a stream around an array, for instance, the stream would never actually store the array; it would extend it with a mechanism that flushes the elements within the array (based on iterators). Arrays are a common and heavily used static data source, but you could also think of associative arrays or maps as unordered static data. Most of the examples so far have dealt with static data such as strings, numbers, and arrays, which we used to illustrate some of the basic concepts. In later parts of the book, we'll focus on emitted data and generated data.

GENERATED DATA

Generated data is data that you create periodically or eventually, like a clock sounding a chime every quarter hour; it can also be something more procedural like generating the Fibonacci sequence using ES6 generators. In the latter case, because the sequence is infinite, it's not feasible to store it all in memory. Instead, each value should be generated on the fly and yielded to the client as needed. In this category, you can also place the traditional `setTimeout` and `setInterval` functions, which use a timer to trigger events in the future.

Just like the saying, "When you're a hammer, every problem looks like a nail," the `Rx.Observable` data type can be used to normalize and process each of these data sources using a single programming model—it's the hammer. With this approach, you gain the most code reuse and avoid creating specific ad hoc functions to deal with the idiosyncrasies of each event type.

2.3.2   *Creating RxJS observables*

In Rx, an observer subscribes to an observable. As you learned in chapter 1, this is analogous to the observer pattern with the subject acting as the observable; `Rx.Observable` represents the object that pushes notifications for observers to receive. The observers asynchronously react to any events emitted from the observable, which allows your application to remain responsive instead of blocking in the face of a deluge of events. This is ideal to implement asynchronous, responsive code both on the client and on the server.

`Rx.Observable` has different meanings to different people. To functional programming purists, it falls under a special category called a functor, an *endofunctor* to be exact. (We don't cover functors in this book because they're not essential to understanding Rx, but if you want learn more about them, you'll find them in the functional programming book mentioned earlier.) To most others, it's simply a data type that wraps a given data source, present in memory or eventually in the future, and allows you to chain operations onto it by invoking observable instance methods sequentially. Figure 2.9 shows a simple visualization of this concept.

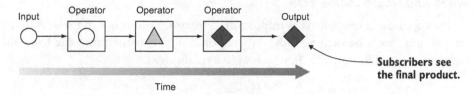

Figure 2.9   The sequential application of methods or operators that transform an input into the desired outcome, which is what subscribers see

Here's a quick look at how observables implement chaining extremely well:

```
Rx.Observable.from(<data-source>)        <──── Wraps a data source with a stream
   .operator1(...)            ◁─
   .operator2(...)                 Invokes a sequence of operations chained by
   .operator3(...)                 the dot operator. In chapter 3, we'll spend a lot
                                   more time with observable instance methods.
   .subscribe(<process-output>);   ◁─
                                   Processes the results
```

Whether you choose to accept one definition over the other, it's important to understand that an observable doesn't just represent a value *now* but also the *idea of a value occurring in the future*. In FP, this is the same definition given to pure functions, which are nothing more than to-be-computed values, and part of the reason why we refer to the "methods" invoked on an observable instance as *operators*.

Because observables in RxJS are immutable data types, this pattern works quite well and should not look that foreign to you. Consider a familiar data type, `String`. Look at this trivial example and notice its similarity to the previous pattern:

```
String('RxJS')
   .toUpperCase()
   .substring(0, 2)
   .concat(' ')
   .repeat(3)
   .trim()
   .concat('!') //->  "RX RX RX!"
```

Learning about a shiny new tool is always exciting, and there's a tendency among developers to try to use that tool in every conceivable situation where it might potentially apply. But as is often the case, no tool is meant for every situation, and it's just as important to understand where RxJS won't be used.

You can divide your computing tasks into four groups within two different dimensions. The first dimension is the number of pieces of data to process. The second is the manner in which the data must be processed, that is, synchronously or asynchronously. In enumerating these possibilities, we want to highlight where RxJS would be most beneficial to your applications.

2.3.3   *When and where to use RxJS*

Learning to use a new tool is as important as learning when not to use it. The types of data sources we'll be dealing with in this book can be classified into the four different categories listed in figure 2.10, which we'll explain next.

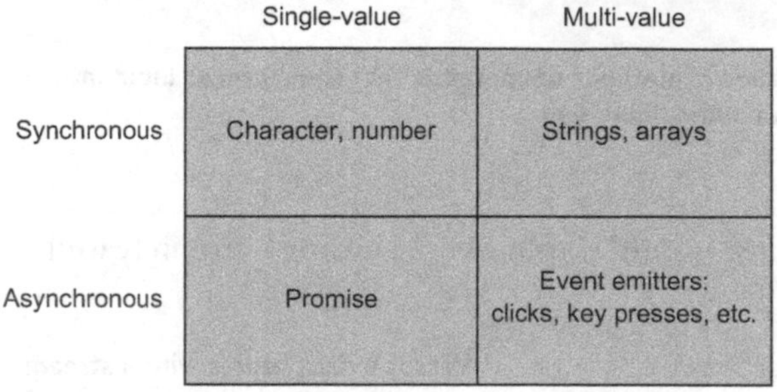

Figure 2.10   **Different types of data sources with examples in each quadrant**

SINGLE-VALUE, SYNCHRONOUS

The simplest case is that you have only a single piece of data. In programming, you know there are operations that return a single value for each invocation. This is the category of any function that returns a single object. You can use the `Rx.Observable .of()` function to wrap a single, synchronous value. As soon as the subscriber is attached, the value is emitted (we haven't yet explained the details behind `subscribe`, but we'll cover that in a bit):

```
Rx.Observable.of(42).subscribe(console.log); //-> 42
```

Although there are cases where you'll need to wrap single values, in most cases, if your goal is just to perform simple operations on them (concatenating another string, adding another number, and others), an observable wrapper may be overkill. The only time you'll wrap simple values with observables is when they combine with other streams.

MULTI-VALUE, SYNCHRONOUS

You can also group single items together to form collections of data, mainly for arrays. In order to apply the same operation that you used on the single item on all of the items, you would traditionally iterate over the collection and repeatedly apply the same operation to each item in the collection. With RxJS, it works in exactly the same way:

```
Rx.Observable.from([1, 2, 3]).subscribe(console.log);
// -> 1
       2
       3

Rx.Observable.from('RxJS').subscribe(console.log);
// -> "R"
       "x"
       "J"
       "S"
```

The RxJS `from()` operator is probably one of the most commonly used. And to make it a bit more idiomatic, RxJS has overloaded the `forEach` observable method as well, with the exact same semantics as `subscribe`:

```
const map = new Map();

map.set('key1', 'value1');
map.set('key2', 'value2');

Rx.Observable.from(map).forEach(console.log);
//-> ["key1", "value1"] ["key2", "value2"]
```

Both of these groups operate synchronously, which means each subsequent block of code must wait for the previous block to complete before executing. In the multi-value example, each item will be processed serially (one by one) until the collection is exhausted. This behavior is useful when dealing with items that have been preallocated, like arrays, sets, or maps, or if they can be generated, in place, on demand. Essentially, you can consider synchronous behavior to be actions on demand with results returning immediately (or at the very least before any further processing is done). When this is not the case, data is known as asynchronous.

SINGLE-VALUE, ASYNCHRONOUS

This brings us to the second dimension of computing tasks, where RxJS gives you the most benefits. This dimension addresses whether a task will execute synchronously or asynchronously. In the latter case, code is only guaranteed to run at some time in the future; thus, subsequent code blocks can't rely on any execution of a previous block having already taken place. Like with the first dimension, you also have a single-value case, where the result of a task will result in a single return value. This kind of operation is usually used to load some remote resource via an AJAX call or wait on the result of some non-local calculation wrapped in a `Promise`, without blocking the application. In either case, after the operation is initiated, it will expect a single return value or an error.

As we mentioned previously, in JavaScript this case is often handled using `Promises`. A `Promise` is similar to the single-value data case in that it resolves or errors only once. RxJS has methods to seamlessly integrate with `Promises`. Consider this simple example of a `Promise` resolving into a single, asynchronous value:

```
const fortyTwo = new Promise((resolve, reject) => {
    setTimeout(() => {
        resolve(42);
    }, 5000);
});

Rx.Observable.fromPromise(fortyTwo)
    .map(increment)
    .subscribe(console.log); //-> 43

console.log('Program terminated');
```

> **NOTE** The promised value is being computed asynchronously, but `Promises` differ from `Observables` in that they're executed *eagerly*, as soon as they're declared.

Running this program as is produces the following output:

```
'Program terminated'

43 //-> after 5 seconds elapse
```

And because `Promises` are single-value and immutable, they're never run again. So if you subscribe to one 10 seconds later, it will return the same value 10 times—this is a desirable trait of a `Promise` by design. In chapter 7, you'll learn that you can retry a `Promise Observable` and force it to be executed many times by nesting it within another `Observable`, which has support for retries. Using the version of `ajax(url)` that returns a `Promise`, you can write the following:

```
Rx.Observable.fromPromise(ajax('/data'))
   .subscribe(data => console.log(data.id));
```

Another frequently used alternative is to use jQuery's deferred objects, which also implement the `Promise` interface. In particular, you can use functions like `$.get(url)` or `$.getJSON(url)`:

```
Rx.Observable.fromPromise($.get('/data'))
   .subscribe(data => console.log(data.id));
```

MULTI-VALUE, ASYNCHRONOUS

For those keeping score, this brings us to our fourth and final group of computing tasks. The tasks in the fourth group are those that will produce multiple values over time, yet do so asynchronously. You create this category especially for the DOM events, which are all asynchronous and can occur infinitely many times. This means that you'll need a mix of semantics from both the iterator and the promise patterns. More specifically, you need a way to process infinitely many items in sequence and capture any errors that occur. These items could be data fetched from remote AJAX calls or data generated from dragging the mouse across the screen. For this you need to invert your control structures to operate asynchronously.

The typical solution to a problem of this nature would be to use an `EventEmitter`. It provides hooks or callbacks to which closures can be passed; in this way it's very much like the `Promise`. But an event emitter doesn't stop after a single event; instead, it can continue to invoke the registered callbacks for each event that arrives, creating a practically infinite stream of events. The emitter will fulfill both of your criteria for handling multi-value, asynchronous events. But it's not without its share of problems. Though simple to use, event emitters don't scale well for larger systems, because their simplicity leads to a lack of expressiveness. The semantics for unsubscribing and disposing of them can be cumbersome, and there's no native support for error handling. These deficits can make it difficult to compose and synchronize complex tasks where multiple events from different parts of the system can be in flight simultaneously.

Rather, you can use RxJS to wrap event emitters, with all their benefits and versatility. The following code attaches a callback to a `click` event on a `link` HTML element:

```
const link = document.querySelector('#google');   ◄─────────────
const clickStream = Rx.Observable.fromEvent(link, 'click')
  .map(event => event.currentTarget.getAttribute('href'))   ◄──
  .subscribe(console.log); //-> http://www.google.com
```

Queries the DOM for the link HTML element

Creates an observable around click events on this link

Extracts the link's href attribute

Note that in this example, the subscribe() method was used to process click events and perform the required business logic, in this case extracting the href attribute, as shown in figure 2.11. Later on, when we cover the Observable instance methods that form the pipeline, you'll see concrete examples of how to decouple the business logic from the printing of the result.

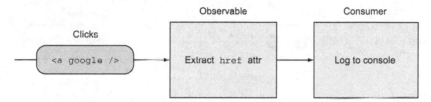

Figure 2.11 Observable that wraps `click` events and passes them down to the observer for processing

You can also use Observables to wrap any custom event emitters. Going back to our calculator emitter in Node.js, instead of listening for the add event,

```
addEmitter.on('add', (a, b) -> {
  console.log(a + b); //-> Prints 5
});
```

you can subscribe to it:

```
Rx.Observable.fromEvent(addEmitter, 'add', (a, b) => ({a: a, b: b}))
    .map(input -> input.a + input.b)
    .subscribe(console.log); //-> 5

addEmitter.emit('add', 2, 3);
```

In this section, we covered only a few of the ways for creating Observables with RxJS. Later on, we'll tackle more-complex problems as well as new Observable methods.

2.3.4   *To push or not to push*

Event emitters have been around as long as the JavaScript language. In that time, they haven't had any significant improvements to their interface in the latest releases of the language. This contrasts with Promises, iterators, and generators, which were part of the JavaScript ES6 specification and are already supported in many browsers at the time of writing. This is one of the reasons why RxJS is so important; it brings many improvements to JavaScript's event system.

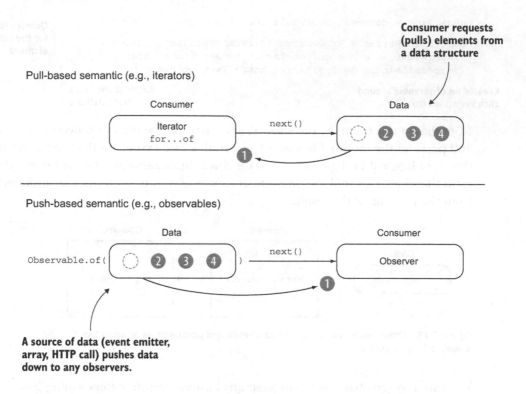

Figure 2.12   Notice the positions of the consumer and the direction of the data. In pull-based semantics, the consumer requests data (iterators work this way), whereas in pushed-based semantics, data is sent from the source to the consumer without it requesting it. Observables work this way.

Event emitters parse through a sequence of events asynchronously, so they come really close to being an iterator and, hence, a stream. The difference, however, lies in the way data is consumed by its clients—whether it is pulled or pushed. This is extremely important to understand, because most of the literature for RxJS defines observables as objects that represent *push-based* collections. Figure 2.12 highlights the main difference between the pull and push mechanisms, which we'll explain immediately.

Iterators use a pull-based semantic. This means that the consumer of the iterator is responsible for requesting the next item from the iterator. This data-on-demand model has two major benefits. First, it creates an abstraction over the data structure that's being used. Essentially, any data source that exposes some common method of iteration can be used interchangeably with another. The second benefit of data on demand is for sequences of data that result from some calculation. Such is the case with JavaScript generators.

For instance, for a Fibonacci number sequence, which is infinite, you need only calculate numbers as they're requested rather than wasting computing time generating parts of a sequence that the caller doesn't care about. This is immensely helpful if the data source is expensive or difficult to calculate. In the next listing, you use a generator to create a lazy Fibonacci calculator. Generators are nothing more than iterators behind the scenes, so each value will be produced only when the consumer calls (or pulls) the next() method.

Listing 2.3   Fibonacci function using generators

```
function* fibonacci() {
  let first = 1, second = 1;
  for(;;) {
    let sum = second + first;
    yield sum;
    first = second;
    second = sum;
  }
}

const iter = fibonacci();

console.log(iter.next()); //-> {value: 2, done: false}
console.log(iter.next()); //-> {value: 3, done: false}
console.log(iter.next()); //-> {value: 5, done: false}
```

A generator function is denoted by the * (star) notation.

Fibonacci sequence must be initialized with at least two values.

yield will return the result of each intermediate step in the loop.

Creates the generator

Want to learn more about generators?

Generators are a language feature added into JavaScript as part of the ES6 specification. From a syntax point of view, generators introduce the `function*` and `yield` keywords. A function with an asterisk declares that a function behaves as a generator, which means it can exit with a return value via `yield` and later reenter. Under the hood, generators don't actually execute immediately but return an `Iterator` object, which is accessed via its `next()` method. Through this `Iterator` object, a generator can pause and resume exactly where it left off, and any context (closure) is kept across reentrances. A generator is a rare but powerful construct for producing infinite data using a given formula or template. If you want to learn more about them, we recommend you read the documentation: https://developer.mozilla.org/en-US/docs/Web/JavaScript/Reference/Statements/function*.

A pull-based paradigm is useful in cases where you know that a value can be returned immediately from a computation. But in scenarios like listening for a mouse click, where the consumer has no way of knowing when the next piece of data will become available, this paradigm breaks down. For this reason, you require a corresponding type on the asynchronous side that is *push-based*—the opposite of the pull-based approach. In a push paradigm, the producer is responsible for creating the next item, whereas the consumer only listens for new events. As an example of this, consider your phone's email client. A pull-based mechanism that checks for new email every second can drain the resources of your mobile device quickly, whereas with push email, or any push notifications for that matter, your email client needs to react to any incoming messages only once.

RxJS observables use push-based notifications, which means they don't request data; rather, data is pushed onto them so that they can react to it. Push notifications bring the reactive paradigm to life. RxJS proposes observables as an improvement over event emitters because they're more versatile and extensible. The observable also serves as a better contemporary to the `Iterator` type, given that it possesses similar semantics but with a push-based mechanism.

You can see from our discussion so far how iterators and `Promises` can be potential data sources that can be wrapped as observables, even though we earlier classified them as distinct groups. This ability to adapt not just the types they are replacing but also types from other groups is immensely powerful—observables work equally well across synchronous and asynchronous boundaries. It not only makes interfacing with legacy code incredibly easy, but also it allows consumer code to be written independently of how the producer is implemented.

> **WATCH OUT!** This power comes with responsibility as well, for although you're *able* to convert anything your heart desires into `Observables`, it doesn't always mean that you *should*. In particular, processes that are strictly synchronous and iterative or will only ever deal with a single value do not need to be "Rx-ified" just for the sake of being cool. Even though `Observables` are cheap to create, there's a bit of overhead associated with applying simple operations on data. For instance, just transforming a string from lower- to uppercase does not require it to be wrapped with an observable; you should directly use the string methods. Don't be reactive just because you can.

In RxJS, you'll always have a pipeline that takes data from the source to the corresponding consumer. Data will always be created or materialized from a data source. Again, the type of data source isn't relevant to how your abstraction operates; when data reaches the end of its journey and must be consumed, it's immaterial where the data came from. We'll reiterate that the separation and abstraction of these two concepts, data production and data consumption, is important for three reasons:

- It enables you to hide differences of implementation behind a common interface, which lets you focus more on the business logic of your task. This has the benefit of not only optimizing development time but also reducing code complexity by removing extra noise from code.
- The separation of production and consumption builds a clear separation of concerns and makes the direction of data flow clear.
- It makes streams testable by allowing you to attach mock versions of the producer and wire the corresponding matching expectations in the observer.

Now that you understand how streams can be constructed, you're missing only the last place where observers come into play—stream consumption.

2.4   *Consuming data with observers*

Every piece of data that's emitted and processed through an observable needs a destination. In other words, what was the purpose of capturing and processing a certain
event? Observers are created within the context of a subscription, which means that
the result of calling `subscribe()` on an observable source is a `Subscription` object.
Because observables operate synchronously or asynchronously, the consumer of an
observable must in some way support the inversion of control that also happens with
callbacks. This is consistent with its push-based mechanism. That is, because you don't
know when a DOM element, for instance, will fire an event or when the result of an
AJAX call will return, observables must be able to call into or signal the observer structure that more data is available by using the observer's `next()` method, as illustrated
in figure 2.13. This mechanism is directly inspired in the iterator and observer patterns. An iterator doesn't know (or care) about the size of the data structure it's looping over or if it will ever end; it only knows whether there's more data to process.

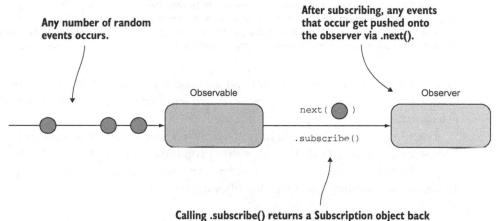

Figure 2.13   Observables calling into an observer's methods. Observers expose a simple iterator-like
API with a next() method. Upon subscription, an object of type `Subscription` is returned to the
calling code, which it can use for cancellation and disposal, as we'll discuss in a bit.

Through a concise iterator-like API, observables are able to signal to their subscribers
whether more events have occurred. This gives you the flexibility to control what data
observers receive.

2.4.1   *The Observer API*

An observer is registered with an observable in much the same way that you registered
callbacks on an event emitter. An observable becomes aware of an observer during the
subscription process, which you've seen a lot of so far. The subscription process is a
way for you to pass an observer reference into an observable, creating a managed,
one-way relationship.

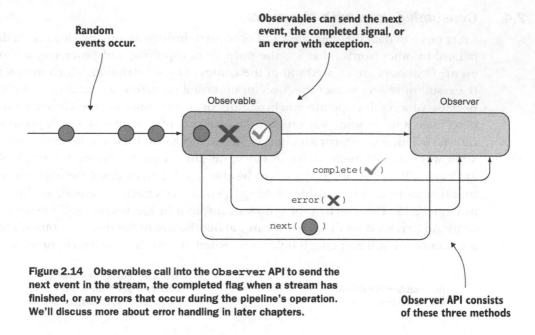

Figure 2.14   Observables call into the `Observer` API to send the next event in the stream, the completed flag when a stream has finished, or any errors that occur during the pipeline's operation. We'll discuss more about error handling in later chapters.

Figure 2.14 shows how observables call an observer's methods to signal more data, completion, and even errors. As you can see, aside from `next()`, two other methods are called on observers: `error()` and `complete()`.

Figure 2.14 shows that once the `subscribe` method is called, an observer is implicitly created with an API that exposes three (optional) methods: `next`, `complete`, and `error` (in RxJS 4 these were called `onNext`, `onCompleted`, and `onError`, respectively). In code, the resulting object has the following structure:

```
const observer = {
    next: function () {
        // process next value
    },
    error: function () {
        // alert user
    },
    complete: function () {

    }
}
```

Up until now, you've used a single function call only to process the results. This function maps to `next()`. Each method serves a specific purpose in the lifetime of the observer, as shown in table 2.1.

Alternatively, you can use this API directly by creating your own observable.

Table 2.1 Defining the `Observer` API

Name	Description
`next(val):void`	Receives the next value from an upstream observable. This is the equivalent of `update` in the observer pattern. When a single function is passed into `subscribe()` instead of an observer object, it maps to the observer's `next()`.
`complete():void`	Receives a completion notification from the upstream observable. Subsequent calls to `next()`, if any, are ignored.
`error(exception):void`	Receives an error notification from the upstream observable. This indicates that it encountered an exception and won't be emitting any more messages to the observer (subsequent calls to `next()` are ignored). Generally, error objects are passed in, but you could customize this to pass other types as well.

2.4.2 Creating bare observables

Most of the time, you'll use the RxJS factory operators like `from()` and `of()`, as you learned at the beginning of this chapter, to instantiate observables. In practice, these should cover all your needs. But it's important to understand how observables work under the nice RxJS abstraction and how they interact with the observer to emit events. We'll show you a barebones model of an observable that emits events asynchronously and exposes the mechanism to unsubscribe. At the core, an observable is a function that processes a set of inputs and returns a subscription to the caller to manage the disposal of the stream:

```
const observable = events => {
  const INTERVAL = 1 * 1000;
  let schedulerId;

  return {
    subscribe: observer => {
      schedulerId = setInterval(() => {
        if(events.length === 0) {
          observer.complete();
          clearInterval(schedulerId);
          schedulerId = undefined;
        }
        else {
          observer.next(events.shift());
        }
      }, INTERVAL);

      return {
        unsubscribe: () => {
          if(schedulerId) {
            clearInterval(schedulerId);
          }
        }
      }
    };
```

```
      }
    }
};
```

You can call this function by passing the observer object:

```
let sub = observable([1, 2, 3]).subscribe({
  next: console.log,
  complete: () => console.log('Done!')
});
//-> 1
     (...1 second)
   2
     (...1 second)
   3
     (...1 second)
   Done!
```

This is a simplistic model of RxJS, and there's much more that goes into it. But the main takeaway here is that an observable behaves like a function that begins chipping away at the data pushed into it as soon as a subscriber is available; the subscriber has the key to turn the stream off via sub.unsubscribe(). Now, let's move on to using RxJS.

Using RxJS, you can register an observer object through Rx.Observable.create(). Like the previous code, this function expects an observer object that you can use to signal the next emitted event by invoking its next() method. Most of the time, you'll provide the observer object literal directly into the subscription and use the static create() method when you want full control of how and when the data is emitted from the observable through the Observer API. For instance, you create observables artificially by calling into the observer's methods directly:

```
const source$ = Rx.Observable.create(observer => {
    observer.next('4111111111111111');
    observer.next('5105105105105100');
    observer.next('4342561111111118');
    observer.next('6500000000000002');
    observer.complete();
});

const subscription = source$.subscribe(console.log);
```

If an observable is finite, you can signal its completion by calling the observer's complete() method.

At this point, the observable stands idle and none of the data is emitted or passed into the observer.

With subscribe(), the observer logic is executed; in this case, it's printing to the console.

A marble diagram of this stream would look like figure 2.15.

This sample code is simple because it just emits a series of account numbers, but you could do much more. You could create your own observables with custom behavior that can be reused anywhere in your application.

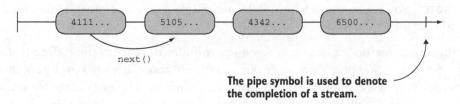

Figure 2.15 A marble diagram showing a synchronous set of events ended by a call to complete()

2.4.3 Observable modules

Directly calling the observer object allows you to define the data that's pushed to the subscriber. How this data is generated and where it comes are encapsulated into the observable's context—kind of like a module. For instance, suppose you wanted to create a simple progress indicator widget that can be used when a user is performing a long-running operation. This module will emit percentage values 0% to 100% at a certain speed, as shown in the following listing.

Listing 2.4 Custom progress indicator module using RxJS

```
const progressBar$ = Rx.Observable.create(observer => {
   const OFFSET = 3000;
   const SPEED =   50;

   let val = 0;
   function progress() {
     if(++val <= 100) {
       observer.next(val);
       setTimeout(progress, SPEED);
     }
     else {
       observer.complete();
     }
   };
   setTimeout(progress, OFFSET);
});

const label = document.querySelector('#progress-indicator');

progressBar$
  .subscribe(
    val   => label.textContent = (Number.isInteger(val) ? val + "%" : val),
    error => console.log(error.message),
    ()    => label.textContent = 'Complete!'
);
```

Annotations:
- Emits a new progress value every 50 milliseconds
- Starts the progress indicator counter after three seconds
- Calls the progress function recursively
- Sends the complete signal after reaching 100%

The business logic of how the values are generated and emitted belongs in the observable, whereas all the details of rendering, whether you want a simple number indicator or use some third-party progress bar widget, are for the caller to implement within the observer.

NOTE   You could also achieve this by using RxJS's time operators. More about this in the next chapter.

Using these methods gives you more opportunities to react to the different states of the program. Stepping back into our discussion about iterators and generators in chapter 2, observers operate similarly to these artifacts. The key difference is that the iterator uses a pull-based mechanism as opposed to an observable's push-based nature—an observable pushes values into an observer. For iterators and generators, the consuming code is controlling the pace of consumption. For instance, a `for` loop controls (or requests) what to pull from an iterator or a generator, not the other way around. This means that each time a new piece of data is needed (by a call to `next()` or `yield`), the consumer of the iterator will call the appropriate method to advance the state of the iterator. Figure 2.16 shows another example using the Fibonacci sequence.

The loop pulls the next element from the iterator by calling .next().

The loop pulls data from the generator function, requesting it to yield the next element.

```
for (let nums of new BufferIterator(arr, 2)) {
   console.log(nums);
}

for(let num of fibonacci()){
   console.log(num);
}
```

Figure 2.16   The pull mechanism of iterators

As a result, iterators must have a way to inform the consumer that there are no longer any items for consumption. Bank tellers are real-world iterators. Each time a customer comes up, that person must be handled before the next customer can be helped. When the teller becomes available, they yell "Next!" to "pull" the next customer in. If they were to call "Next!" and no one responded, they would know that the line was complete and it might be safe to take their lunch break.

Something to keep in mind, though, is that infinite event emitters, like the DOM, will never fire the `complete()` function (or `error()` for that matter) on any of its events. Therefore, it's entirely up to you to unsubscribe from them or roll your own autodispose mechanism. But for finite event sequences, when an observer is called with either of these methods, it knows that contractually it won't receive any more messages from its owning observable. This again is a tight parallel to an iterator, which by definition should stop returning values when the iteration generates an exception or completes.

Consider a simple `Promise` object that resolves to the value `42` after 5 seconds (shown in figure 2.17).

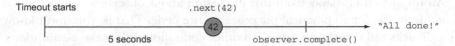

Figure 2.17   An observable (wrapped Promise) that emits a value after 5 seconds

We mentioned in chapter 1 that Promises can be used to model an immutable, single (future) value. You'll use the setTimeout() function to simulate this; now, instead of creating your own observable, you'll use the generic creational methods in RxJS, such as the following:

```
Rx.Observable.fromPromise():
const computeFutureValue = new Promise((resolve, reject) => {
  setTimeout(() => {
    resolve(42);                         ⟵┐ Resolves the Promise after
  }, 5000);                                │ 5 seconds have elapsed
});

Rx.Observable.fromPromise(computeFutureValue)
  .subscribe(
    val => {
      console.log(val);
    },
    err => {
      console.log(`Error occurred: ${err}`);
    },
    () => {
      console.log('All done!');
    });
```

Because Promises emit a single value, this stream will eventually send the completed status after 5 seconds have passed, printing "All done!" at the end. Now, suppose that instead of a resolved Promise, something goes wrong in computing this value and the Promise is rejected:

```
const computeFutureValue = new Promise((resolve, reject) => {
  setInterval(() => {
    reject(new Error('Unexpected Exception!'));
  }, 5000);
});
```

This will cause the observable to invoke the error() method on the observer and print the following message after 5 seconds:

```
"Error occurred: Unexpected Exception!"
```

This is quite remarkable because RxJS not only takes care of error handling for you (without messy, imperative try/catch statements) but also provides logic that ties in with Promise semantics of resolve/reject. We'll cover all there is to know about error handling in chapter 7.

An important takeaway from this discussion about observers is that the callbacks passed to it are, for all practical purposes, future code. That is, you don't know when the callbacks will actually be called, so other code shouldn't make assumptions about their execution. This relates to the larger point made earlier about the nature of the code within a stream. Because one of your goals is to move away from the messy business of keeping track of state changes, avoiding the introduction of side effects is one of the ways that you can keep your streams pure and prevent unwanted changes from adversely seeping into the application logic. This works well with RxJS because pure functions can run in any order and at any time (now or in the future) and will always yield the correct results.

With observers, we've finish introducing the three main parts of RxJS: producers (observables), the pipeline (business logic), and consumers (observers). This chapter is just the start of your journey of learning how to think reactively (and functionally). It will take much more time and many more examples to truly understand how you can think reactively, but you were able to get your feet wet on some advanced APIs. Much of what you've seen so far has been abstract in nature with very little coding, but this step is crucial for understanding how this approach differs from ones you've been taught in the past. In the next chapter, we'll look more closely at the operations that you can perform on streams as well as how you can cancel them if needed. By doing so, we're officially taking the training wheels off and introducing you to the core operations for building applications in RxJS.

2.5   Summary

- RxJS and, more generally, the concept of thinking in streams derive many of their foundational principles from functional programming.
- The declarative style of RxJS allows you to translate almost exactly from your problem statement into working code.
- Data sources can often operate quite differently, even within the observable contract.
- Mouse clicks, HTTP requests, or simple arrays are all the same under the eyes of observables.
- Push-based and pull-based semantics are represented through observables and iterators, respectively. Wrapping data sources is the first step in creating a pipeline/observable.
- Observables abstract the notion of production and consumption of events such that you can separate production, consumption, and processing into completely self-contained constructs.
- Observers expose an API with three methods: `next()`, `complete()`, and `error()`.

Core operators 3

This chapter covers

- Introducing disposal of streams
- Exploring common RxJS operators
- Building fluent method chains with `map`, `reduce`, and `filter`
- Additional aggregate operators

In the first two chapters, you learned that RxJS draws inspiration from functional programming and reactive programming. Both paradigms are oriented around data flows and the propagation of change through a chain of functions known as operators. Operators are pure functions that create a new observable based on the current one—the original is unchanged. In this chapter, you'll learn about some of the most widely used RxJS observable operators that you can use to create a pipeline that transforms a sequence of events into the output you desire.

A common theme in this chapter is creating observables using a declarative style of coding, which originates from FP. You can lift sequences of data of any size into an observable context, as well as data generated or emitted over time, with the goal of creating a unified programming model for any type of data source, static or dynamic. Before we dive into the operators used to apply transformations onto the data that flows through an observable sequence, it's important to understand that, unlike many AJAX libraries, observables can be cancelled.

61

3.1   *Evaluating and cancelling streams*

Imagine someone making a long-running AJAX call requesting considerable data from the server. But shortly after spawning this call, the user navigates away from the page by clicking some other button. What happens to the original AJAX request? Consider another example. You begin a client-side interval to poll for certain data to become available, but an exception occurs and the data never becomes available. Should these processes be allowed to run wild and take up system resources? We're guessing no.

A stream, as it exists in RxJS, is an object with a deterministic lifespan defined almost entirely by you, the programmer. JavaScript, unlike some other languages, has few distinct types, most of those types mirroring the simplicity of JSON. Additionally, there's little support within JavaScript for memory management because this has historically been left to browser manufacturers to worry about. Although both of these features make JavaScript a marvelously simple language to learn and use, they also somewhat obscure what's really happening under your application's plumbing.

In languages like C and C++, there exists an extremely fine-grained approach to control not only the specific data structure you use but also its exact lifetime in memory—you have complete control of allocating and deallocating objects in memory. On the other hand, in JavaScript, the lifetime of objects is controlled by the garbage collector, and rightfully so. The garbage collector is a process operated by the runtime engine that's running your application. It will periodically run and free up memory associated with any unused references. The garbage collector does so by keeping track of the references that are kept between various objects in the application—this is known as *ref counting*. When it detects that an object is no longer referenced, it becomes a candidate for disposal. A failure to find references that are no longer in use results in a memory leak. Memory leaks are generally an indicator of either sloppy design or reference tracking and can result in a runaway system footprint that results in either the user or the system killing your application, because it becomes unresponsive at that point.

> **CAUTION** This notion of automatic garbage collection gives us JavaScript developers a false impression that we need not care about memory management. This is a mistake when attempting to write our own event-handling code. RxJS frees us from this by implementing a mechanism to unsubscribe or effectively clean up attached listeners from any event emitters such as the DOM.

In older browser implementations, this used to be a big problem, particularly with Internet Explorer's event-handling system. Modern browsers are now much more efficient at this, and libraries such as RxJS are tuned to avoid many of these problems.

3.1.1   *Downside of eager allocation*

An important point to remember when dealing with RxJS is that the lifetime of a stream doesn't start with the creation of an observable. It begins when it's subscribed to. Hence, there's little overhead in creating and initializing one, because it begins in a dormant state and doesn't generate or emit events without an observer subscribed to it. It's analogous to the old adage "If an observable is created by your application, and no one subscribes to it, does it emit an event?"

In computing terms, an object that creates data only when needed is known as a *lazy data source*. This is in sharp contrast to JavaScript, which has strict eager evaluation. The terms *lazy* and *eager* refer to when an application requests memory from the system and how much it requests up front. Lazy allocation is always done when the space is actually needed (or on demand), whereas eager allocation is performed up front as soon as the object is scoped. In the eager scheme, there's an up-front cost to allocation and there exists the possibility that you'll overallocate because you don't know how much space will be used. Lazy allocation, on the other hand, waits until the space is needed and pays the penalty for allocation at runtime. This allows frameworks to be really smart and avoid overallocating space in certain situations. To illustrate the difference, we'll show you how a popular JavaScript array method, slice(), would work under eager and lazy evaluation. Consider a function called range(start, end), which generates an array of numbers from start to end. Generating an infinite number of elements and taking the first five would look like the scheme in figure 3.1.

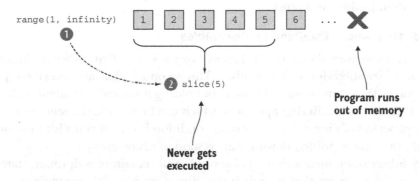

Figure 3.1 In an eager allocation scheme, the program halts before it can execute the slice(5) function because it runs out of memory.

Here it is in code:

```
range(1, Number.POSITIVE_INFINITY).slice(0, 5); //-> Browser halts
```

With JavaScript's eager evaluation, this code will never get past the range() function, because it needs to generate numbers infinitely (or until you run out of memory and crash). In other words, eager evaluation means executing each portion of an expression fully before moving on to the next. On the other hand, if JavaScript functions were lazy, then this code would only need to generate the first five elements, as shown in figure 3.2.

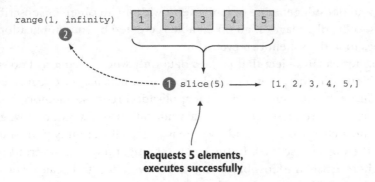

Figure 3.2 In a lazy allocation scheme, the runtime waits until the result of this expression is needed and only then runs it through the program, allocating only the resources it needs to request.

In this case, the entire evaluation of the expression waits until the result of the expression is needed. In RxJS, the strategy is precisely this: wait until a subscriber subscribes to the observable expression, and then begin to initialize any required data structures. You'll see later on that using lazy evaluation allows RxJS to perform internal data structure optimizations and reuse.

3.1.2 *Lazy allocation and subscribing to observables*

RxJS avoids premature allocation of data in two ways. The first, as we mentioned, is the use of a lazy subscription mechanism. The second is that an observable pushes data as soon as the event is emitted instead of holding it statically in memory. In chapter 4, we'll discuss the buffering operators, which can be used to transiently store data for either a period of time or until a certain condition is met, if you wish to do so. But by default, the data is emitted downstream as soon as it's received.

A lazy subscription means that an observable will remain in a dormant state until it's activated by an event that it finds interesting. Consider this example that again generates an infinite number of events separated by half a second:

```
const source$ = Rx.Observable.create(observer => {
  let i = 0;
  setInterval(() => {
    observer.next(i++);          This interval will keep on emitting
  }, 500);                       events every 500 milliseconds until
});                              something stops it.
```

The cost of allocating an observable instance is fixed, unlike an array, which is a dynamic object with potential unbounded growth. It must be this way; otherwise, it would be impossible to store each user's clicks, key presses, or mouse moves. To activate `source$`, an observer must first subscribe to it via `subscribe()`. A call to `subscribe` will take the observable out of its dormant state and inform it that it can begin producing values—in this case, starting the allocation for events 1, 2, 3, 4, 5, and so on every half-second. Because an observable is an abstraction over many different data sources, the effect will vary from source to source.

The second advantage to a lazy subscription is that the observable doesn't hold onto data by default. In the previous example, each event generated by the interval will be processed and then dropped. This is what we mean when we say that the observable is streaming in nature rather than pooled. This discard-by-default semantic means that you never have to worry about unbounded memory growth sneaking up on you, causing memory leaks. When writing native event-driven JavaScript code, especially in older browsers, memory leaks can occur if you neglect event management and disposal.

3.1.3 *Disposing of subscriptions: explicit cancellation*

Just as important as when memory is allocated is when it is deallocated or released back to the application. For example, rich JavaScript UIs bind event handlers to potentially thousands of elements. After the user has finished interacting with a certain part of the UI, there's no reason for those objects to exist and take up memory. As discussed earlier, the garbage collector is fairly smart about how it cleans up memory. Unfortunately, it's able to do so only if the references to those objects are found to be unused or if no reference cycles are formed, which tends to occur frequently in native event-handling code.

It's easy to initialize objects and then forget about them without removing references to them, which prevents the application from ever recovering that memory (this might not be a concern with small scripts but can easily become an issue with modern, client heavy applications). For example, you can see the problem better in this simple code where we listen for right-click events on a menu item, perhaps to show a custom context menu:

```
document.addEventListener('mouseup', e => {
  if (e.button === 2)
    showCustomContextMenu();
  e.stopPropagation();
});
```

Many developers may not even recognize the problem with this code. The problem arises from the fact that in order to unsubscribe from this event we need the reference to the function that was passed into the event handler (the inlined lambda expression). Because we're trying to use this idiom as much as possible, we end up creating a handler that we can't unsubscribe from—if we even remember to unsubscribe from it at all. To make matters worse, if we had nested event handlers or subscribed to other events from within this one, we'd create yet another level of complexity and potential for more memory to leak.

For older web applications (the Web 1.0 years), memory deallocation wasn't so much of a problem because navigation between pages forced a page reload, which cleared out JavaScript's runtime footprint. Today, as single-page applications grow in popularity (the Web 2.0+ era) and clients become more modern and richer, memory pressure becomes a real threat; objects can now conceivably exist for the duration of the entire application's lifespan loaded into the browser.

All this is not meant to sound alarmist. We expect that (just as they have since JavaScript's inception) garbage collectors will continue to improve, and many applications will run without issue. But proper memory management is still a good thing for all applications.

This is why we need sophisticated libraries like RxJS. In RxJS, the producer is the one responsible for unsubscribing. Managing a subscription is handled through an object of type `Subscription` (also known as a `Disposable` in RxJS 4) returned from a call to `subscribe()`, which implements the mechanism to dispose of the source stream. If we've finished with the observable and no longer wish to receive events from it, we can call `unsubscribe()` to tear it down; this is known as explicit cancellation. Here's a short example:

```
const mouseClicks = Rx.Observable.fromEvent(document, 'mouseup');
const subscription = mouseClicks.subscribe(someMouseClickObserver);

... moments later
subscription.unsubscribe();    ◁——————  Tears down the stream and frees up
                                         any allocated objects
```

This tearing-down process will stop further events from going to any registered observers and will immediately release all resources allocated by the observable. The subscription instance handles the entire unsubscription process, and it's able to do this because every observable also defines how it will be disposed. Additionally, as you'll see in later chapters, this behavior acts on the *entire* observable, meaning that *all* resources allocated by a given stream can be deallocated cleanly without additional boilerplate and without the risk of orphaning objects in memory.

Recall that in chapter 2 we introduced the `Rx.Observable.create()` method, which could be used to create arbitrary observables. The final step in creating it was to indicate how `subscribe` would dispose of it, and that's your responsibility to implement. Going back to our progress indicator code, add the unsubscription mechanism at the end, like this.

Listing 3.1   Disposing of an observable

```
const progressBar$ = Rx.Observable.create(observer => {
  const OFFSET = 3000;
  const SPEED =   50;

  let val = 0;
  let timeoutId = 0;
  function progress() {
    if(++val <= 100) {
      observer.next(val);
      timeoutId = setTimeout(progress, SPEED);
    }
```

```
    else {
      observer.complete();
    }
  };
  timeoutId = setTimeout(progress, OFFSET);

  return () => {          ◄─────────────
    clearTimeout(timeoutId);
  };
});
```

> **Function that executes when the unsubscribe method is called. Describes how to cancel that timeout upon disposal.**

CODE SAMPLES Remember that all the code for this chapter can be found in the RxJSinAction GitHub repository, https://github.com/RxJSInAction/rxjs-in-action.

The function added at the end of the observable body becomes the body of the unsubscribe() method of the returned Subscription object. In essence, each observable provides the keys to its own destruction during its creation. Every time a subscription occurs from an observer, it passes back a way to clean itself up (analogous to the finally clause after a try/catch). Because every observable provides this self-contained, self-destruct button, you can also compose its subscriptions such that you can always tear them down correctly no matter how complex the underlying observable is.

CUSTOM OBSERVABLES If you're creating a custom observable with create(), and it happens to emulate an infinite interval stream, you're responsible for supplying the proper unsubscribe behavior, or it will run indefinitely and cause memory to leak.

The examples we've shown so far for the most part involve setting timed intervals to generate events, which support cancellation through clearInterval(). But what happens to data sources that don't support cancellation? Let's jump into that next.

3.1.4 Cancellation mismatch between RxJS and other APIs

RxJS observables provide a straightforward mechanism for cancelling and disposing of event streams. But this simplicity can be deceiving when used in conjunction with other JavaScript APIs. For example, you might encounter problems when trying to cancel observables that wrap promises; look at the next listing.

Listing 3.2 Disposing of a promise

```
const promise = new Promise((resolve, reject) => {       ◄─┐
  setTimeout(() => {
    resolve(42);
  }, 10000);
});
promise.then(val => {
  console.log(`In then(): ${val}`);       ◄─┐
});
```

> **Creates a promise that resolves to 42 after 10**

> **Handles the resolved promise value**

```
const subscription$ = Rx.Observable.fromPromise(promise).subscribe(val => {
    console.log(`In subscribe(): ${val}`);                         Wraps an observable
});                                                                around the Promise API
subscription$.unsubscribe();          Attempts to dispose
                                       of the observable
```

As you can see from listing 3.2, you dispose of the observable thinking it would also take care of the underlying promise. The observable object itself was properly disposed of; surprisingly, although you attempt to explicitly cancel the event as well, after 10 seconds this program emits the following (apparently, JavaScript promises can't be broken after all):

```
"In then(): 42"
```

So, what happened? This process is explained in figure 3.3.

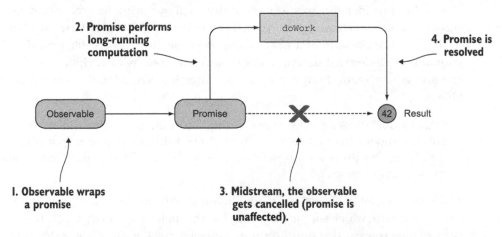

Figure 3.3   The cancellation of an observable doesn't affect the underlying promise.

What happens is that promises were not design to be cancelled. Once a `Promise` object begins executing (gets into a pending status), it tries to become fulfilled by either resolving or rejecting the underlying result, as the case may be.

RxJS makes it easy to integrate with external APIs, but you must be mindful that there's a mismatch of design philosophies between an API designed to emit a single value (promise) and one that supports infinite values (observable). This is one use case, but it could also happen if you integrate with other APIs that aren't RxJS aware. Most of the time, though, you don't have to worry about cancelling subscriptions yourself because many RxJS operators do this for you.

Now that we've covered creating and cancelling streams, in the next section we'll begin with the more popular operators that are essential to any RxJS program.

3.2   *Popular RxJS observable operators*

Though the subscription and disposal semantics of RxJS are useful in managing resources to avoid leaky event handlers, they're only part of the story. But keep in mind what thinking reactively is all about; instead of you controlling what goes on a stream by creating a custom observable and pushing events through `observer.next()`, it's preferable to relinquish that control and react when the time comes—you want to always be reactive! This means allowing RxJS factory operators (`of()`, `from()`, and others) to wrap an event source of interest and create the observable sequence with which to apply the business logic you desire. Hence, being reactive involves defining what a program will do when a value is pushed sometime in the future.

This is where RxJS shines, and it's because of its fully loaded arsenal of out-of-the-box operators, which you can use to create expressive streams of logical data flows. You can create flows to solve virtually any problem, including creating responsive web forms, drag and drop, and even games.

An operator is a small piece of declarative functionality that allows you to inject logic into an observable's pipeline. An operator is a pure, higher-order function as well, which means it never changes the observable object it's operating under (called the source), but rather it returns a new observable that continues the chain. FP best practices come into play at this point because the functions composing your business logic, the building blocks of your solution, should be done using pure functions as much as possible. These operators can be used to inspect, alter, create, or delay events after they leave the data source but before they reach the consumer; in other words, anything in your business logic pipeline is handled by the combination of one or more operators, which drive the execution of the pure functions of your program. And if that's not enough, RxJS operators are also lazily evaluated!

Recall that in chapter 2 (figure 2.10) we highlighted four fundamental types of computing tasks. We split them into two dimensions depending on whether they performed work synchronously or asynchronously and whether they acted on single values or collections. Manipulating a single value is a relatively trivial task (known as a *singleton stream*), given that you can inspect its properties and manipulate it directly. In most cases, though, you want streams to act across a range of values rather than just one and done. The computing model behind RxJS encourages you to work with function chains that process data, similar to a conveyor belt in an assembly line, as shown in figure 3.4.

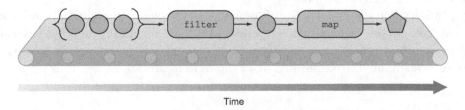

Time

Figure 3.4   An assembly line where operators represent individual stations and each has its own task to perform on each piece of data that passes by

Another important design principle of RxJS is to provide a computing model that's similar to what you're accustomed to. Inspired in the Array#extras APIs introduced in ES5, RxJS features its own version of core operators such as map, filter, and reduce. Because these are some of the more frequently used, let's start with them.

3.2.1 Introducing the core operators

Operators come in two varieties: as instance methods or as static methods of the observable type. Part of the RxJS 5 rework was the drastic simplification of the API surface, which consisted of a sheer reduction in the number of operators as well as a simplification of their usage. Hence, most of the operators in RxJS 5 can be invoked as static or as instance methods (when we say *instance*, we refer to invoking them using the dot (.) notation on an observable instance).

RxJS comes with many operators built in that handle many common tasks such as working with collections, extracting elements from the stream, manipulating and transforming the data, handling errors, and others. In this section, we'll focus on the three that you'll use about 80% of the time—map, filter, and reduce—as well as a variation of reduce called scan.

MAPPING OPERATIONS ON OBSERVABLES

By far the most common operator that you'll likely come across when dealing with RxJS is map(). RxJS isn't the only library to implement it, and all the libraries follow the same FP principles. In FP, map() belongs to a category of operations called *transformational* because it changes the nature of data running through the observable by applying a function; therefore, it's a single output value or a one-to-one transformation. In symbolic notation, you write it as map :: x -> f(x), where for a given value x you can associate an input of x with an output of f(x). Consider a quick example that applies a given percentage value onto a set of prices:

```
const addSixPercent = x => x + (x * .06);
Rx.Observable.of(10.0, 20.0, 30.0, 40.0)
  .map(addSixPercent)
  .subscribe(console.log); //-> 10.6, 21.2, 31.8, 42.4
```

<- **Applies this function onto each value of the source observable**

Mapping functions is a fundamental process when transforming data from one type to another. For example, say you had a list of user IDs for which you wanted to fetch GitHub information. Mapping a function like ajax() over the set of IDs yields an array of JSON account objects.

In RxJS, you want to map functions across all the elements emitted from an observable. To help you better visualize operators, we'll use the marble diagrams. Recall that arrows and symbolic characters represent the various operations that convert the input stream into the output stream, as shown in figure 3.5.

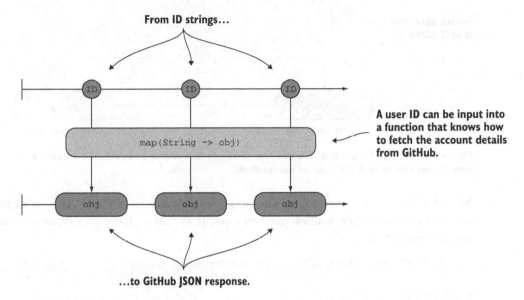

From ID strings...

map(String -> obj)

A user ID can be input into a function that knows how to fetch the account details from GitHub.

...to GitHub JSON response.

Figure 3.5 The `map` operator will produce a one-to-one transformation that will convert an input value into an output value by a given process. In this case, `map` takes a URL string and converts it into an array of users by means of the mapping function. In the diagram, operators are encoded inside a box that illustrates the function that's passed in.

We'll use these vertical transformations in figure 3.5 to depict operations that take one form of data and convert it to another. By design, this function in RxJS has the exact same signature as that of array:[1]

```
Array.prototype.map        :: a => b; for all a in Array<a>
Rx.Observable.prototype.map :: a => b; for all a in Observable<a>
```

Like with arrays, observable's map() is immutable, which means it won't change the original but instead will transform the value passed through it. Also, as you can see in figure 3.5, the output will always be the same size as the input because mapping is a one-to-one relationship that preserves structure. It's left up to you to decide exactly what the transform function is, depending on your business logic; map() simply guarantees that it will be called on every value passing through the stream as it's propagated downstream to the next operator in the chain.

We mentioned briefly before that all RxJS operators are pure. To show you what this means, we'll demonstrate the case of map(). Transforming a String into an ID looks like figure 3.6.

---

[1] https://developer.mozilla.org/en-US/docs/Web/JavaScript/Reference/Global_Objects/Array/map.

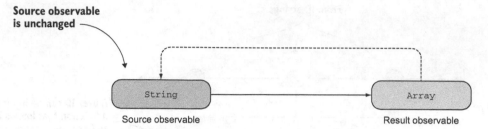

Figure 3.6   **Mapping a function from `String` to `Array` to a source `Observable` creates a new `Observable` with the result of the function.**

Now, let's look at the code for this. Suppose you need to convert a collection of strings into a corresponding comma-separated value (CSV) array. Here's a simple stream that will accomplish this.

Listing 3.3   Mapping functions over streams

```
Rx.Observable.from([
   'The quick brown fox',
   'jumps over the lazy dog'
   ])
 .map(str => str.split(' '))        ◄——  Maps a set of functions to
 .do(arr => console.log(arr.length))      extract the value from
 .subscribe(console.log);           ◄——  RxJS .do() is a utility operator that's useful
                                          for effective actions such as logging to the
                                          screen. This can be handy for debugging or
                                          tracing the values flowing through a stream.
```

For those familiar with design patterns, mapping functions is analogous to the adapter pattern (as shown in the famous "Gang of Four" book titled *Design Patterns: Elements of Reusable Object-Oriented Software*). In the adapter pattern, an object interacts with two otherwise incompatible interfaces and allows information to flow between them, adapting them to each other. In a similar fashion, you use map() to create a type compatibility between the producer and the consumer of data. The purpose of using it is to convert the raw input data into something the consumers can understand. In this way, the adaptation is done from the producer to the consumer.

But sometimes there can be too much data to process, and you may not be interested in all of it. For this, there's an operator to discard unwanted events.

FILTERING OUT UNWANTED EVENTS

Filtering is the process of removing unwanted items from a stream. The criteria to remove these elements is passed in as a selector function, also called the *predicate*. Here's a simple example of how this operator works. Say you need you need to place restrictions on input boxes for numerical quantities. It's probably a good idea to place a business rule over text boxes rejecting any non-numerical input. Whenever you're thinking about rejecting, removing, narrowing, or selecting data, you can do that easily using a filtering operator called `filter()` and inspecting the `keyCode` property of the keystroke, as shown in the following listing.

Listing 3.4   Filtering events from a stream

```
const isNumericalKeyCode = code => code >= 48 && code <= 57;
const input = document.querySelector('#input');
Rx.Observable.fromEvent(input, 'keyup')
  .pluck('keyCode')              ◄─────────────┐   Extracts this property from
  .filter(isNumericalKeyCode)    ◄─────────┐   │   the object passing through
  .subscribe(code => console.log(`User typed:   the observable
           ${String.fromCharCode(code)}`));
                                               Accepts only keys in
                                               the numerical range
```

Also, you can use it to ignore unwanted mouse clicks, touch events, and others. It could be that you're interested only in data that meets certain criteria, or you need only a certain subset of the data. In some cases, allowing too much data through can have an adverse effect on the performance of your application. Think about building an API for users to access their account history for the month; if on every request you simply dump their entire account history, you'd quickly find both your API and your clients overwhelmed. To make matters worse, your application won't scale to the size of data being processed. Filtering could be used to generate different views if the user wanted only debits, credits, or transactions after a certain month.

An easy way to think about filtering is to consider the job interview process (every developer's favorite activity). When recruiting people for a specific job, one of the first things to look for is the candidates' previous experience in order to determine if they have the right skill-set for the position. If the job requires programming, then you'd expect that the candidates should have some sort of programming background listed on their resume. If not, you could exclude them from your final interview list.

Suppose you modeled your applicant-screening process as an array; then, you could write your filtering operation using the array's `filter()`[2] method. Because observables implement the same filtering semantics, you're already familiar with using a predicate function (also called a *discriminant*) in `filter()` that returns `true` for candidates who will be selected to move on to the next round. Here's the dataset you'll use:

```
let candidates = [
    {name: 'Brendan Eich', experience : 'JavaScript Inventor'},
    {name: 'Emmet Brown', experience: 'Historian'},
    {name: 'George Lucas', experience: 'Sci-fi writer'},
    {name: 'Alberto Perez', experience: 'Zumba Instructor'},
    {name: 'Bjarne Stroustrup', experience: 'C++ Developer'}
];
```

Whether this data arrives because of an AJAX call or a DOM event, the observable treats it all the same way. So for now, you'll stick with a simple array. In this case, you

---

[2] https://developer.mozilla.org/en-US/docs/Web/JavaScript/Reference/Global_Objects/Array/filter.

can wrap the data with an observable and keep only the candidates who will be considered for this JavaScript job:

```
const hasJsExperience = bg => bg.toLowerCase().includes('javascript');

const candidates$ = Rx.Observable.from(candidates);
candidates$
  .filter(candidate => hasJsExperience(candidate.experience)) //#A
  .subscribe(console.log); //-> prints "Brendan Eich"
```

Figure 3.7 shows what's happening behind the scenes. Like `map()`, `filter()` works vertically removing values from the resulting stream.

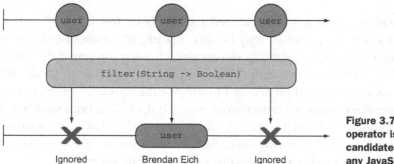

Figure 3.7 The `filter` operator is used to discard candidates who don't have any JavaScript experience.

Functions `map()` and `filter()` are similar in that they take a single function as their parameter. But whereas the function passed to `map` converted the input value into an output value, the `filter()` function is used merely as a criterion that decides whether to keep the event in the stream or not. As you know, JavaScript being loosely typed will accept any "truthy" value as a pass, while any "falsy" values will cause it to reject the event.

> **Truthy vs. falsy**
>
> In JavaScript, *truthy* is any value that can be coerced to a true Boolean value. This includes objects, arrays, non-zero numbers, non-empty strings, and of course the true Boolean value. Meanwhile, *falsy* would be represented by 0, ' ', null, undefined, or false. In practice, although JavaScript will accept all these types without question, it's often best for clarity's sake to return a Boolean value.

`map` and `filter` work well together in scenarios where you don't want to apply a mapping function to each element but apply it to only the subset you care about. But `filter` isn't the only function married to `map`; let's not forget about the powerful `map`/`reduce` combinations.

AGGREGATING RESULTS WITH REDUCE

Sometimes you aren't interested in acting on each item in a collection in isolation; sometimes you want to look at the collection in aggregate rather than piecemeal. For instance, suppose you want to take the average value of a collection of numbers or you want to turn a sequence into a mathematical series. This type of operation is called a *reduction* or an *aggregation*, with the result as a single value output instead of another collection. Once again, arrays come with a built-in reduce operator for this purpose,[3] and observables follow suit. reduce is a bit more involved than the other two; here's the function signature:

```
Rx.Observable.reduce(accumulatorFunction, [initialValue]);
```

The accumulator function is called on every element, and it's given the current running total and the new value as parameters. The initial value (optional) is used to begin the accumulation process; we're using 0 to begin the addition. Here's a simple example to illustrate how reduce() works. Suppose you want to compute the user's spending for the month by totaling all their transactions. For this example, these transaction objects have a property called amount.

Listing 3.5 Using `reduce()` to compute spending

```
const add = (x, y) => x + y;
Rx.Observable.from([
    {
        date: '2016-07-01',
        amount: -320.00,
    },
    {
        date: '2016-07-13',
        amount: 1000.00,
    },
    {
        date: '2016-07-22',
        amount: 45.0,
    },
])
.pluck('amount')         ⟵┐   Extracts the amount property
.reduce(add, 0)          ⟵─────── Reduces the set of amount
.subscribe(console.log);            values with an add function
```

It's important to notice that reduce() with observables works a bit differently than map() and filter(). With arrays, reduce() doesn't return another array; instead, it produces a single raw value, which is the result of the reduction. The observable's reduce(), on the other hand, continues the previous pattern of returning a new singleton observable. This distinction will become important in section 3.3 when we talk

---

[3] https://developer.mozilla.org/en-US/docs/Web/JavaScript/Reference/Global_Objects/Array/reduce.

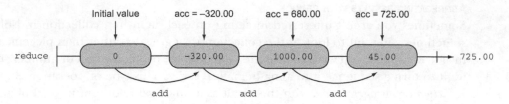

Figure 3.8   The `reduce` operator moving horizontally, accumulating every value through the stream using the `add` function

more about operator chaining. Figure 3.8 is a visual representation of the previous code. Reduction is an operation that moves horizontally through the stream.

Suppose you needed to traverse through the candidate stream and group all the candidates with a technical background (that is, with knowledge of C++ or JavaScript):

```
Rx.Observable.from(candidates)
  .filter(candidate => {                               Filters all candidates who have no
    const bg = candidate.experience.toLowerCase();     knowledge of a programming language
    return bg.includes('javascript') || bg.includes('c++');
  })
  .reduce((acc, obj) => {                   Adds a candidate name to the array
    acc.push(obj.name);
    return acc;
                                            Begins with an empty array
  }, [])                                    (called the seed)
  .subscribe(console.log); //-> ["Brendan Eich", "Bjarne Stroustrup"]
```

As you can see, `reduce` applies an accumulator function over the observable sequence initialized with the first seed value, which will be used to begin the aggregation process. Because `reduce()` returns a single value, there's a need for partial accumulation as well. We'll look at a variation of `reduce()` called `scan()`.

SCANNING AGGREGATE DATA

RxJS uses `scan()` to apply an accumulator function over an observable sequence (just like `reduce()`) but returns each intermediate result as the accumulation process is happening and not all at once. This is useful to obtain progress information about how data is being aggregated with each event.

Changing the previous code to use `scan()` as a direct swap-in replacement of `reduce()` reveals the intermediate steps of the accumulation:

```
Rx.Observable.from(candidates)
  .filter(candidate => {
    const bg = candidate.experience.toLowerCase();
    return bg.includes('javascript') || bg.includes('c++');
  })
  .scan((acc, obj) => {          Scan can be used as a direct replacement of reduce. In
    acc.push(obj.name);          RxJS 4, you would have had to change the seed
    return acc;                  parameter to be the first one. This was fixed in RxJS 5,
  }, [])                         with scan now having the same signature as reduce.
```

```
    .subscribe(console.log);
//-> ["Brendan Eich"]
    ["Brendan Eich", "Bjarne Stroustrup"]
```

> As soon as it finds the first event, it emits it and accumulates it. A second emission happens when the second event is found, returning the current state of the accumulation.

Aside from `scan()`, the symmetries between arrays and observables are no coincidence. This signature was chosen specifically because it's so simple and because it's one that many JavaScript developers are already familiar with. But here the similarities end. Remember that these methods by themselves don't cause any work to run on the stream (only a subscriber can); instead, when an operator is called on an observable, it's configuring the observable for future values. Recall our definition of a stream as a specification of a dynamic value. This is a key distinction between the operators that you'll see with arrays and those with observables, and you'll learn in later chapters that arrays represent work happening now, whereas observables represent work in the future.

3.3 Sequencing operator pipelines with aggregates

One principle of FP is the ability to construct lazy function chains. In this section, we'll show you how to mix and match the main observable operators you just learned about together with a few other functions known as *aggregates*. Aggregate functions let you do useful things like keeping track of a running total, taking only a subset of the total set of data, returning default values, and others. Some functional libraries you might have heard of or used before, such as Lodash.js and Underscore.js, have ample support for this. First, it's important to understand that observable sequences must be self-contained.

3.3.1 Self-contained pipelines and referential transparency

Function chains utilize JavaScript's power of higher-order functions to act as the single providers of the business logic. You saw examples of this before such as the `filter` function taking a predicate parameter. Also, observable pipelines should be self-contained, which essentially means they're side effect–free (keep in mind that if your business logic functions are pure, your entire program is pure and stable as well). A pure pipeline doesn't allow any references to leak out of the observable's context. Once an event is lifted into the context, it's contained and transformed through a sequence of operators. Earlier we showed that it's possible to group operations together to create more-expressive logic. In RxJS, we call this process *operator chaining* or *fluent programming*. The analogy of a self-contained pipeline works great as a visualization aid, as shown in figure 3.9.

Consider this example:

```
let sinceLast = new Date();

Rx.Observable.fromEvent(document, 'mouseup')
    .filter(e => {
```

```
         let timeElapsed = new Date() - sinceLast;      Careless side effects of
         sinceLast = new Date();                        reading and writing to
         return timeElapsed < 200;                      an external variable
}).subscribe(() => console.log('double clicked'));
```

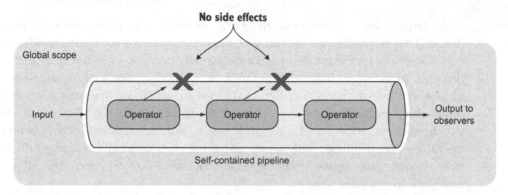

Figure 3.9 A self-contained pipeline is one where all of its operations are side effect–free and work strictly on the data coming from previous operators. Operators might be any of `map`, `filter`, `reduce`, and others you'll learn about in this book.

This code is an example of poorly designed scope management in which the state variable `sinceLast` is allowed to live outside the observable's context. The result is that the observable is no longer stateless, and the lifecycles of the state and the observable are now dependent on each other.

It's important to understand that when you create an observable, you're creating an ecosystem or a bounded context. That ecosystem is a closed loop that begins with a subscription and ends with a disposal. If you were to look at the observable through an FP lens, you'd see that the internals of that observable remain completely stateless and walled off somewhat from the rest of the application. The scope of the callbacks that are passed into the operators should remain small and local. Mixing code that has external side effects not only introduces difficult-to-track complexity but also removes one of the key advantages to using observables, which is their well-defined lifespan—creation and disposal should leave the system in the same state they found it in.

What is a bounded context?

A bounded context is a design principle originating from domain-driven design, which states that entities pertaining to a single domain model should be highly cohesive and expose only the necessary interface to interact with other contexts. You can extend this definition to the `Observable` type as a form of context that hides the nature of the data that's pushed through it, allowing you to transform it by a ubiquitous language made up from the limited set of operators being exposed and independently of what happens in the outside world.

At a glance, a single subscription to this observable will function correctly, assuming that no other code manipulates sinceLast. But if this observable is subscribed to a second time, the result is no longer the same. An observable must always produce the same results given the same events passing through it (that is, pressing the same key combination should always yield the same data to the observers), a quality known in FP as *referential transparency*.

Each invocation of subscribe() does more than start an event emitter. It spins off a brand-new pipeline that will be independent of any other pipelines that were created by subsequent calls to subscribe(). This behavior is intentional in order to minimize side effects and be referentially transparent; similarly, the result of an observable should be the result of the data passed through it, not the number of parallel observables that are also active. You'll see in the next chapter on dealing with time in RxJS that the sort of operation used in the previous code sample is unnecessary.

As mentioned earlier, the operator chain is core to the design of an RxJS operator: every operator must perform some work on the data passing through it and then wrap it into another observable instance that gets returned.[4] In this manner, the subscription gets internally passed around from one context to the next. To show how this works, you'll add your own operator using prototype extension (using ES6, you could also do it by extending from the Observable class); this operator is the logical inverse of filter(), called exclude(), and is shown in the next listing.

Listing 3.6 Custom exclude operator

```
function exclude(predicate) {
  return Rx.Observable.create(subscriber => {       Creates a new observable context
    let source = this;                              to return with the new result
    return source.subscribe(value => {
      try {                                         Because you're in a lambda function,
        if(!predicate(value)) {                     "this" points to the outer scope.
          subscriber.next(value);
        }                                           Passes the next value to the
      }                                             new operator in the chain
      catch(err) {
        subscriber.error(err);
      }
    },                                              Be sure to handle errors
    err => subscriber.error(err),                   appropriately and pass them along.
    () => subscriber.complete());
  });
}
Rx.Observable.prototype.exclude = exclude;          Adds the operator by extending
                                                    the Observable prototype
```

Catches errors from user-provided callbacks

As you can see from this snippet, every operator creates a brand-new observable, transforming the data in its own way and delegating it to the next subscriber in the chain. You can use it to exclude all even numbers as such:

[4] https://github.com/ReactiveX/rxjs/blob/master/doc/operator-creation.md#advanced.

```
Rx.Observable.from([1, 2, 3, 4, 5])
  .exclude(x => x % 2 === 0)
  .subscribe(console.log);
```

Furthermore, operation chaining in combination with an observable's lazy evaluation gives RxJS an important performance advantage over arrays, which we'll discuss next.

3.3.2 *Performance advantages of sequencing with RxJS*

Aside from the declarative style of development that encourages you to write side effect–free code, the primary advantage of using observable operators is that there is little or no performance penalty for chaining two methods like `map` and `filter`. Behind the scenes, RxJS produces little overhead because observables themselves are lightweight and inexpensive to create. On the other hand, operator calls on arrays create new instances along the way, which naturally incurs more memory allocations when the collection being processed is large. You can see this with a simple example that uses the full set of parameters for `map()` and `filter()` array functions:

```
const original = [1,2,3];
const result = original
    .filter((x, idx, arr) => {
      console.log(`filtering ${x}, same as original?
          ${original === arr}`);
      return x % 2 !== 0;
    })
    .map((x, idx, arr) => {
      console.log(`mapping, same as original?  ${original === arr}`);
      return x * x;
    });   result; //-> [1, 9]
```

map and filter expose extra parameters such as the current index and the source array. Typical implementations of these methods don't use these parameters, but it's good to know they're there.

Logging to the console within the pipeline is considered a side effect. We're bending the rule here a bit to illustrate this concept.

Running this code logs the following messages:

```
"filtering, same as original? true"
"filtering, same as original? true"
"filtering, same as original? true"
"mapping, same as original? false"
"mapping, same as original? false"
```

You can visualize the difference between both approaches in figure 3.10.

RxJS, by contrast, doesn't create intermediate data structures. As you can see in the previous example, `filter()` works on the same data structure as the original because it's first on the chain. This operation returns a brand-new array instance that becomes the new owning object on which you call `map`. This can be inefficient on very large collections because new data structures are created and used only once before being garbage collected. In RxJS, the underlying data structure is optimized to process each

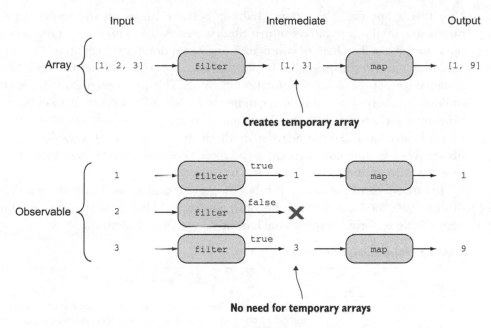

Figure 3.10 The array's `filter` and `map` operators generate intermediate, wasteful data structures. RxJS observables are optimized and process events entirely through all functions at once, avoiding intermediate storage altogether.

item through the pipeline from the producer to the consumer at once, avoiding the creation of extra data structures along the way. Let's convert the same code to use observables:

```
Rx.Observable.from(original)
    .filter(x => {
        console.log(`filtering ${x}`);
        return x % 2 !== 0;
    })
    .map(x => {
        console.log(`mapping ${x}`);
        return x * x;
    })
    .subscribe();
```

Running this code shows you that each element (or mouse click, key press, asynchronous data, and others) passes through the pipeline by itself without creating intermediary storage. The first value, 1, passes through filtering and then through mapping before 2 and 3 are looked at:

```
"filtering 1"
"mapping 1"
"filtering 2"
"filtering 3"
"mapping 3"
```

Now this is optimal. This fluent chaining pattern hinges on the return type of all observable methods to always return observables. As you know, in arrays, the `reduce` operator breaks the chain of commands because it doesn't return an array, so further chaining becomes impossible. In RxJS, every operator will return an observable instance so that it can support further chaining. This property means that a virtually unlimited variety of combinations can be assembled. Whereas observables are abstractions over various data sources, their operators are just abstractions of those abstractions. That is, just like the adapter methods used to create observables from other library types, an operator is simply an adapter to convert an existing observable into a new one with more-specific functionality.

Before we continue having fun building more chains, we'll introduce another set of aggregate methods that will become handy for building nice expressive business logic. Table 3.1 briefly explains each of these aggregate functions.

Table 3.1   More aggregate operators

Name	Description
`take(count)`	Filtering operator. Returns a specified amount (count) of contiguous elements from an observable sequence. Later, you'll see this is useful to extract a finite set of events from an otherwise infinite stream.
`first, last`	A refinement on the `take` function. Returns the first element in the observable stream or the last, respectively.
`min, max`	Filtering operators. Work on observables that emit numbers returning the minimum or maximum value of a finite stream, respectively.
`do`	Utility operator. Invokes an action for each element in the observable sequence to perform some type of side effect. This operator is for debugging and tracing purposes and can be plugged into any step in the pipeline.

Now, let's have fun with some examples that put some of these to work.

Listing 3.7   Using aggregate operators

```
Rx.Observable.from(candidates)
  .pluck('experience')
  .take(2)
  .do(val => console.log(`Visiting ${val}`))
  .subscribe(); // prints "Visiting JavaScript Guru"
                            "Visiting Historian"
```

Takes only the first two elements
(another filtering operator)

Performs the logging
routine and passes along
the observable sequence

> **Effectful computations**
>
> The do operator is known as an effectful computation, which means it will typically cause an effect such as I/O, a database insert, append to the DOM, or write to a file—all of these side effects, of course. The reason why do() still preserves the chain is rooted in an FP artifact called the *K combinator*. In simple terms, this is a function that executes any effect but ignores its outcome, just passing the value along in the stream to the next operator. In a way, it's a bridge that intercepts the stream that allows you to invoke any function. It's known in other libraries as the tap() operator.

Being able to use this repertoire of operators is certainly beneficial because it frees you from having to write them yourself, reducing the probably for bugs to occur (you can find a complete list of all the operators used in this book in appendix B—you're free to use it as a guide). Nevertheless, the functions passed into these operators are solely your responsibility, so please test them thoroughly. We'll revisit testing further in chapter 9.

In this chapter, we talked at length about several of the core operators that come bundled with RxJS. We purposely avoided specifically enumerating all the operators that are available for mapping, filtering, and other tasks. That job is better left to the reference material on GitHub or on the internet.[5] Instead, we wanted to demonstrate how operators are used in conjunction with observables to build chains of logic that let you write streams declaratively, so that they're both easy to understand and easy to extend. We chose what we think of as the set of core operators. We explored how you can build complex logic intuitively using fluent operators. These are operators that act primarily on a single observable and don't introduce any time-based operations. In the next chapter, we'll explore the time aspect of observables, which allows you to handle future data.

3.4   Summary

- Streams provide their own mechanisms for cancellation and disposal, which is an improvement over JavaScript's native event system.
- The Observable data type enables fluent function chaining that allows the sequential application of operators, using a model similar to that of arrays.
- Unlike JavaScript's native promises, observables have built-in capabilities for disposal and cancellation.
- Functions injected into the operators of an observable sequence contain the business logic of your application and should be side effect–free.
- Observables are self-contained with indefinitely chainable operators.

---

[5] http://xgrommx.github.io/rx-book/index.html.

- Operators act independent of each other and work only on the output of the operator that preceded them.
- The order and type of operators used determine the behavior and the performance characteristics of an observable.

It's about time you used RxJS

This chapter covers

- Understanding time in RxJS
- Using time as a new dimension of your programs
- Building observable streams with time
- Learning about RxJS operators like `debounce` and `throttle`
- Analyzing event data with buffering

Time is a tricky business. We spoke earlier about the challenges that exist when the code you write isn't synchronous; it may have unpredictable wait times from one instruction to the next. We defined observables as infinite sequences of events, and now we add the last part of the puzzle to this definition—*over time*. The ancient Greek Heraclitus implied that time is always in motion, and so are observables.

OBSERVABLES   are infinite sequences of events over time.

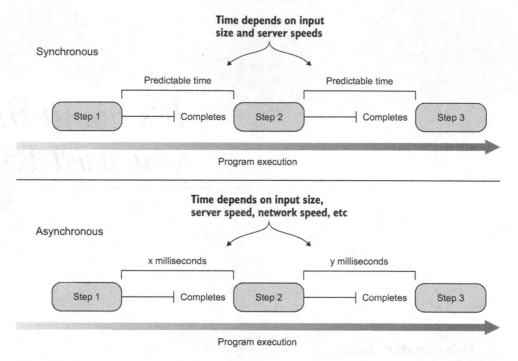

Figure 4.1 In synchronous code (top), operations are predictable and typically depend on the input size and speed of the environment. Asynchronous programs (bottom) depend on many other factors, including the speed of the network.

You can accurately measure the time a synchronous program takes by adding the execution time of its constituent functions, but this doesn't hold for asynchronous programs because instructions aren't linearly executed, as shown in figure 4.1.

Generally speaking, you should never try to inject wait times into your code in an attempt to time your operations. Asynchronous code is unpredictable, and many factors can alter the period of time an AJAX call takes to respond or a long-running computation to finish. So instead of dealing with time directly yourself and trying to guess when certain operations complete, you should *react* to them.

In previous chapters, we talked about how observables react to future events, but we skirted around the specifics of what the future is. We also mentioned the issue with latency in passing but never addressed it head-on. This chapter will first give you a brief introduction to time as viewed by RxJS and will then explore how to use operators to affect not only the output of a sequence of events but also when this output will occur and how that type of transformation can be useful. Having direct control over time, such as being able to schedule certain actions to occur or to generate data in set timed intervals, is essential to creating responsive user interfaces that interact with user actions. Keep in mind that modern users have high expectations that web UIs behave like native applications, so that any clicks, key presses, or any other types of action are immediately acknowledged.

4.1   *Why worry about time?*

Time is of the essence, and in computing it's essential. Many years ago, the world of user experience (UX) and design adopted the rule of the "Powers of Ten" to create guidelines about what is an acceptable amount of time a user can wait for an application to respond. The study can be summarized as such:

- At 0.1 seconds, the user feels as though their actions are causing a direct impact on the application. The interactions are real and pleasant.
- From 0.1 to 1 second, the user still feels in control of the application enough to stay focused on their activity. For web applications, pages or sections of a page should display within 1 second.
- From 1 to 10 seconds, the user gets impatient and notices that they're waiting for a slow computer to respond.
- After 10 seconds, the flow is completely broken and the user is likely to leave the site.

Time is the undercurrent that causes your data to flow within a stream. And you can see from this study that it's a crucial aspect of any successful application. JavaScript applications are notorious for being frequently exposed to time, and we don't mean using any date/time libraries. We're referring to the conflicting tasks of having to balance fetching data from remote locations, slow networks, user animations, scheduled events, and others—all making balance incredibly challenging.

Before we get into this topic, it's important to realize that time-based functions rely on external state directly or indirectly. What do we mean by this? From a pure functional programming perspective, functions that deal with time are inherently impure. Time is a dimension that's not necessarily local to a function—it's global to the entire application and forever changing.

> **IMPURE JAVASCRIPT FUNCTIONS**   Some frequently used JavaScript functions like `Date.now()` and `Math.random()` are impure because you can never guarantee a consistent return value.

Despite this incompatibility from a pure FP standpoint, RxJS is still the right tool for the job. When you chain operators, as you already know, most of these issues are addressed by virtue of sequenced, synchronous execution that threads through time and minimizes the impact of this side effect. In previous chapters, you saw how to build a pipeline out of array-like operators that use higher-order functions, such as `map()`, `filter()`, and `reduce()`. Time, being a dimension that doesn't exist with arrays, doesn't have a direct analogy to any array methods. But this doesn't mean you can't introduce time into operators and end up with the same fluent design.

RxJS comes bundled with many of the tools to inspect and manipulate time right out of the box (in chapter 9, you'll learn how to work with virtual time in unit tests, essentially by mocking time). Before we dive into these new operators, let's review JavaScript's own timing mechanisms and how they can easily interact with RxJS.

4.2   Understanding asynchronous timing with JavaScript

The runtime of an asynchronous application depends on factors outside its control such as network, filesystem, server speed, and others; all of these become bottlenecks to code that would otherwise execute instantly on a CPU. An asynchronous event has two main challenges:

- It's ambiguous in that it may or may not happen at any time in the future.
- It's conditional, meaning that it's dependent on the correct execution of a previous task, such as loading data from a file or database.

The reason RxJS is a game changer is that it allows you to treat asynchronous tasks as if their execution order were synchronous. In simpler terms, it's designed to serialize operations so that one piece of code executes only after another piece of code has completed. This is possible through the orchestration layer of observables so that you can handle time implicitly or explicitly.

4.2.1   Implicit timing

Consider the example of a relay race. In a relay race, the participants run as fast as they can around the track. Every time a runner finishes their set distance, they pass the baton to the next runner. The winner of the race is always the team who collectively crosses the finish line first. JavaScript functions that use callbacks work under this same philosophy. This is why all of the client-side AJAX APIs, as well as all of the streaming I/O APIs in Node.js, to name a few, declare callback parameters *batons*. Figure 4.2 shows that time factors into many types of JavaScript problems, whether it's fetching data from the server or a database or handling user input.

Both cases would involve the use of nested callbacks to pass the baton along the way and ensure their synchronicity. On the left, two nested HTTP calls depend on each other to fetch the required data from the server. On the right, a DOM event is intercepted, which causes some data to be fetched from the server. By treating both scenarios as streams, observables internally take care of passing the baton for you through the operator's internal subscription mechanism, which you learned about in chapter 3. Your job is to wait and react accordingly. Now let's look at another form of timing in JavaScript, explicit timing.

4.2.2   Explicit timing

Unlike implicit timing, explicit timing has the following desirable characteristics:

- *Concrete*—It will happen at a set time.
- *Explicit*—It will happen at a time you clearly define and control.
- *Unconditional*—It will always happen, unless an error occurs or the stream is cancelled.

Think of any time you've had to write an event that occurred a few seconds after the user performed some action, or maybe delayed an animation for a set amount of time.

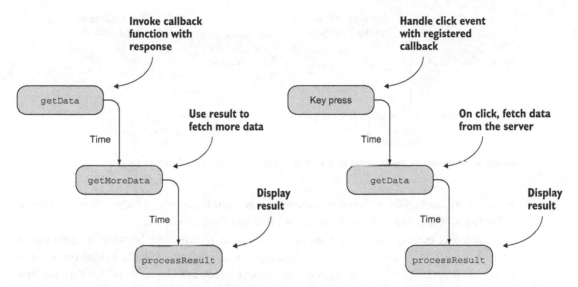

Figure 4.2 The dimension of time is implicit in I/O tasks such as fetching data from the server and handling user input. On the left, a sequence of AJAX calls fetches necessary data from the server before processing. On the right, you listen for a key press DOM event and a resultant fetch from the server. As each step completes, data (the baton) is passed from one step to the next.

These are examples of when you've explicitly declared that you wanted something to occur in the future as well as exactly when you wanted it to happen.

Use cases for these explicitly timed operations tend to revolve around two general categories: user-centric and resource-centric. In the former case, you're concerned with creating something that's perceivable to the human eye. An animation, a dialog, and a validation message are examples of user-centric timings. Although some animations are superfluous, they're also an important part of drawing the user's attention to where they should act next and creating a connection with the UI so that it's always responsive. By carefully timing how elements move and react to the user's interaction, you can subtly guide the user through what could otherwise be a difficult experience.

In the resource-centric case, you can use timing to reduce demands on a given resource. Network I/O operations, rapid user input, and CPU-intensive calculations are scenarios where reducing the number of method calls could significantly boost performance. In these cases, you could constrain either the number of calls or their impact by specifying a timeout. Another way of handling resources is through buffering or caching a certain subset of elements so that they can be accomplished at once. One example is when you need to apply many database operations and it's preferable to do a single bulk operation (at the end of this chapter we'll show how buffering helps you in this respect).

Explicit timing is similar to a train or airline schedule. Tasks such as moving passengers from point A to point B don't happen as soon as there's availability. Trains and planes depart at their scheduled time (for the most part, of course, but that's a separate

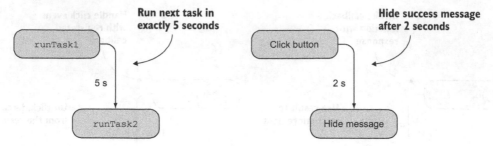

Figure 4.3   Explicitly timed tasks can execute with a delay or can overlap in time.

issue). You know that an airplane doesn't leave simply because you're on it (or you've subscribed to it). It will leave only on or after its departure time.

Explicitly timing events is a useful property in computing because it means that you can exercise some control over when a piece of code is run rather than rely on the implied timing of executing operations in sequence. The latter is unreliable for any sort of exact timing, because it's bound to the speed and availability of processors, memory, and network latency. In practical terms, this means that the behavior of an application would be very different on a desktop as opposed to a smartphone, so explicitly defined behavior is sometimes necessary. You can use explicit time to invoke timed tasks in sequence, such as hiding and showing messages to the user after a set number of seconds, displaying a notification dialog that guides the user to the next step, implementing a countdown clock indicating an action needs to be completed by a certain time, and others. Figure 4.3 shows a simple visualization of explicit time-dependent tasks.

Now that you understand both modalities, let's see what JavaScript has to offer. If you've used functions such as `setTimeout()` or `setInterval()`, then you've already been exposed to JavaScript's timing interfaces.

4.2.3   The JavaScript timing interfaces

There are two well-known interfaces for accomplishing explicit timing in JavaScript (there are actually several more, but they're not universal so we'll leave them out for now). Both methods use time relatively; that is, all declarations of future tasks will be done by a time offset relative to the current time ("now") within the application. For instance, if you show a countdown clock for an action that is to be completed within 3 seconds, this action would complete in 3 seconds relative to the execution of the timed operator in use (or now + 3 sec), as shown in figure 4.4.

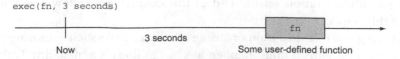

Figure 4.4   Explicitly timing some function after 3 seconds offset time

Generally, there are two types of explicit time in RxJS. *Relative time* is also called *offset time*, and it represents only a delta measurement from now. *Absolute time* always refers to a specific instance in time, which can be either in the past or in the future.

> **When is "now"?**
>
> "Now" in JavaScript is always the time provided by the system when a particular line of code executes. If you're declaring a time of `new Date()`, you'd expect the date to be the system time in milliseconds since 1970 at the moment the line is evaluated. For some of the examples involving dates and time, we'll be using a library called moment.js (installation instructions are available in appendix A). Moment.js provides a simple API for accessing and manipulating dates and time.

We'll go over JavaScript's most common timing operations that are part of the Window-Timers utilities and their equivalent operators in RxJS, starting with `setTimeout()`.

SETTIMEOUT

The `setTimeout()` function (a method of the global context object) sets up an explicit one-time task to execute at a specific point in the future (in milliseconds) relative to now. Invoking the function will tell the JavaScript runtime that some body of code should be executed milliseconds after `setTimeout()` is called, which is considered time zero milliseconds. This is the programmatic equivalent of setting an egg timer to notify you when your cake is done baking and is great if you don't want something to be executed synchronously with the rest of your program. For instance, you could schedule some CSS to slide the account details panel to the right after a short delay to make the interaction with the page richer:

```
setTimeout(() =>
  document.querySelector('#panel')
    .setAttribute('class', 'slide-right'), 1000);
```

The `setTimeout()` function is similar to the `Promise` in that its callback is invoked exactly once in the future. But it offers none of the same versatility that a `Promise` or RxJS does. For example, there's no mechanism for error handling or fluent composition. Clearly, you can do better!

With your new understanding of streams, you should also be able to recognize that this is again a simple observable, one that emits once to each subscriber. You can create an observable that wraps over `setTimeout()`, which applies some CSS action downstream into the observer to avoid conflating it with any business logic; see the following listing.

Listing 4.1   Working with observables and `setTimeout()`

```
const source$ = Rx.Observable.create(observer => {        ◁—— Wraps everything
    const timeoutId = setTimeout(() => {                       inside the observable
        observer.next();                                       factory method
        observer.complete();
    }, 1000);                                              ——— Sends the single next and
                                                               completed flags a second after
    return () => clearTimeout(timeoutId);                      the subscription occurs
});

source$.subscribe(() =>
        document.querySelector('#panel').style.backgroundColor = 'red');   ◁—
```

Defines
unsubscribe
behavior

Subscribes to the observable
to start the timer

Performs CSS
operations

CODE SAMPLES   Remember that all the code for this chapter can be found in
the RxJSinAction GitHub repository, https://github.com/RxJSInAction/rxjs-
in-action.

Listing 4.1 creates an observable that will fire once after a second and then complete,
without being tied to any business logic, and it provides the unsubscription mechanism of the timer by passing `clearTimeout(timeoutId)` back as the disposal logic. It
turns out, however, that this kind of boilerplate code is unnecessary because the RxJS
library already possess implementations for these base cases. The `setTimeout()`
method can be substituted with the `timer()` operator, which creates an observable
that will emit a single event after a given period of time. The next listing performs the
same action as before, using a one-second timer to emit an action that changes the lay-
out of an HTML element.

Listing 4.2   Creating a simple animation with an RxJS timer

```
Rx.Observable.timer(1000)   ◁—— Timer factory function in milliseconds
    .subscribe(()=>
        document.querySelector('#panel').style.backgroundColor = 'red');
```

Adds a custom CSS class to the selector
element after a set time has elapsed

We can illustrate this using a marble diagram, as shown in figure 4.5.

Notice that you no longer need to worry about unruly callbacks. Although the
result of listing 4.2 is the same as that of listing 4.1, taking advantage of RxJS operators
has, in our opinion, drastically improved the readability of this simple program. As an
additional plus, the timer is now emitting a generic event that can be used by several
consumers if you want it to go through subsequent subscriptions, rather than being
forced to cram several callbacks together.

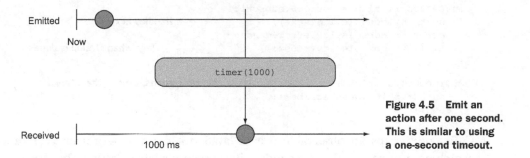

Figure 4.5 Emit an action after one second. This is similar to using a one-second timeout.

SETINTERVAL

The other commonly used method is setInterval(). Whereas setTimeout() bears similarities to a promise, setInterval() more closely resembles event emitters in that it can create multiple events over a span of time, specified in milliseconds. Now, instead of a single operation being performed, this function invokes the operation repeatedly by specifying how far apart in time those calls should be. Using this type of operation, you could easily create a simple counter that would tell the user how long they've been on the same page:

```
let tick = 0;              ◁——— External state keeping track of the ticker
setInterval(() => {
  document.querySelector('#ticker').innerHTML = `${tick}`;
  tick++;                                                          Updates the counter
}, 1000);        ◁——┐ Sets the time period for the interval       on the screen (clear
                     (in milliseconds) to 1 second                side effect)
```

Unfortunately, this sample code uses a global side effect to increment the counter. Instead, consider using a pure observable context to create a container around the effect and push out new counts as events into the observer. Listing 4.3 creates a simple observable in charge of spawning a two-second interval. At every interval, it increments a running counter and pushes the event to any downstream observers. In light of what you learned in chapter 3 and because JavaScript's time intervals can run infinitely, we included the cancellation of the event. The cancellation process also occurs explicitly after 8 seconds have elapsed.

Listing 4.3 Explicit time using JavaScript timing functions and RxJS

```
const source$ = Rx.Observable.create(observer => {
    let num = 0;
    const id = setInterval(() => {
      observer.next(`Next ${num++}`);          Every 2 seconds prints
    }, 2000);                            ◁——┘   the next number count

    return () => {                  ◁——┐ The returned object contains the
      clearInterval(id);                cancellation logic for this
    }                                   observable (the disposal handler).
});
```

```
const subscription = source$.subscribe(
    next  => console.log(next),                <——— Handles next
    error => console.log(error.message),
        () => console.log('Done!')             <——— Flags when stream is done
);

setTimeout(function () {              <——— After 8 seconds, cancels the interval
    subscription.unsubscribe();
}, 8000);
```

This code wraps an observable over a JavaScript explicit `setInterval()` function, which emits a count after 2 seconds. After 8 seconds have elapsed, the stream is cancelled and disposed of, generating a total of 8 / 2 = 4 events. Notice that because it was cancelled, the completed function of the observer is also omitted. Running this code yields the following:

```
"Next 0"
"Next 1"
"Next 2"
"Next 3"
"Done!"
```

As you saw in listing 4.3, `setInterval()` can be used within an observable. In its current form, however, it isn't particularly useful. For instance, there's no way to track the number of invocations, short of tracking it yourself with an external variable. An actual observable operator would be more useful because it can forward state downstream while remaining infinitely more extensible.

Fortunately, you don't have to implement this method either, because it already exists as the `interval()` operator, which gives you a simple compact, generic form. Essentially, you can subscribe to the interval and begin receiving periodic events, and in true RxJS form you gain automatic disposal semantics for free!

Both the interval and the timer emulate the existing behavior that you see from the traditional JavaScript interfaces, but they do so without the associated entanglement. Although `interval` emits the number of milliseconds in the interval, you don't have to use it. Most RxJS implementations use `interval` to monitor and react to an external resource. For instance, you can make periodic AJAX requests to an external API and detect when something has changed. This is useful for stock tickers, weather trackers, and other real-time applications. In the next section, we'll look at how to introduce time-based operators into a stream to implement a stock ticker component.

4.3   *Back to the future with RxJS*

The time-based operators in RxJS come in several different flavors. The factory functions that resemble generic versions of the `setInterval()` and `setTimeout()` methods have function signatures resembling these RxJS operators, respectively:

```
Rx.Observable.interval(periodInMillis)
Rx.Observable.timer(timeoutInMillis)
```

These static methods (`interval()` and `timer()`) work just like the other factory methods that you saw in previous chapters for creating observables, except that where most of those either wrapped other sources or emitted events immediately upon subscription, the time-based factory methods emit only after a provided amount of time has elapsed.

> **SCHEDULERS** There's another parameter called a *scheduler* that's passed into either `interval()` or `timer()`, as well as other operators. You can imagine that unit testing code with long timers is virtually impossible. You'll learn about schedulers when we cover unit testing in chapter 9.

We've illustrated these timing operators by themselves, but in real-world problems they're usually combined with observable streams that generate meaningful data. This combination is extremely powerful, because you can use the timers to synchronize the frequency with which you consume data from an observable.

We'll start implementing our stock ticker widget using only functional and reactive primitives. We'll come back to this example and add more features as you explore and get more comfortable with RxJS. At the moment, we'll use a made-up symbol, ABC, to keep things simple, and instead of fetching its stock price using a real web service, we'll emulate it using random numbers. In the next chapter, we'll tie everything together and fetch stock data using actual AJAX calls to a real service endpoint. Here's our simple function that fabricates random numbers:

```
const newRandomNumber = () => Math.floor(Math.random() * 100);
```
Maps the number into the range [0,100]

> **NOTE** This function is impure, but we're using it only as a random producer of events, not as part of our business logic.

At a high level, the process of fetching stock data works as shown in figure 4.6. Our program consists of generating a random value every 2 seconds, which we'll use to emulate continuous stock quote prices of our hypothetical ABC company.

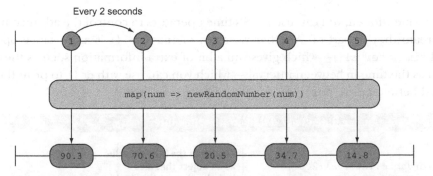

Figure 4.6 The process of fetching the stock data involves using a promise to make a remote HTTP call against a stock service. In this case, we'll use a random-number-generator function to emulate stock price changes, and we'll revisit this in chapter 5.

Stock prices are made up of a numerical portion and a currency string. You can model this with a simple `Money` value object:

```
const Money = function (currency, val) {
  return {
    value: function () {
      return val;
    },
    currency: function () {
      return currency;
    },
    toString: function () {
      return `${currency} ${val}`;
    }
  };
};
```

A *value object* is a design pattern used to represent simple immutable data structures whose equality is based not on the entity itself but on its values. In other words, two value objects are equal only if they have the same content or their corresponding properties contain the same values. These objects are ideal to transfer immutable state from one component to another.

The stock ticker widget is kicked off by a two-second interval, which will set the pace for how often notifications are pushed onto your observable stream. Subscribers receive each value and update the DOM, as shown in the following listing.

Listing 4.4 Simulating a simple stock ticker widget

```
Rx.Observable.interval(2000)         ◁——— Creates a two-second interval
  .skip(1)                           ◁——— Skips the first number emitted, zero
  .take(5)                                              ◁——┐ Because this is an
  .map(num => new Money('USD', newRandomNumber()))          │ infinite operator,
  .subscribe(price => {                                     │ simulates only five
      document.querySelector('#price').textContent = price; │ values
  });
```

As we've mentioned, you can use RxJS's time operators to control the advancement of the stream they're part of. Another variation of `interval()` is an instance operator called `timeInterval()`—which gives you a bit of extra information such as the count as well as the time in between intervals—which you can use with `do()` to print the time elapsed between price refreshes, as shown in the next listing.

Listing 4.5 Augmenting stock data with the time interval

```
Rx.Observable.interval(2000)        Augments the interval value
  .timeInterval()      ◁————————    as an object that also
  .skip(1)                          includes the precise number
  .take(5)                          of milliseconds between
  .do(int =>                        intervals
```

```
      console.log(`Checking every ${int.interval} milliseconds`))
   .map(int => new Money('USD', newRandomNumber()))
   .subscribe(price => {
      document.querySelector('#price').textContent = price;
   });
```

The interval property contains the number of milliseconds elapsed between one interval and the next.

The value property returns the number of intervals emitted by the observable.

This function reveals the fraction of delay present in the call needed to compute the random number; checking the log shows the following:

```
"Checking every 2000 milliseconds"
"Checking every 2002 milliseconds"
"Checking every 1999 milliseconds"
"Checking every 2001 milliseconds"
"Checking every 2000 milliseconds"
```

The two types of timing options we've discussed so far (explicit and implicit) aren't mutually exclusive. Using one doesn't preclude the use of the other. But using them together docs require an understanding of how time propagates to downstream operators. Unlike when you use only implicitly timed operations, where each operation will initiate directly after the previous one, explicit timing can introduce new issues with ordering.

This knowledge is especially important when introducing a new operator called `delay()`. It accepts a time in milliseconds and can be used to time shift the entire observable sequence. This means that if an event arrives at 1 second to `delay()`, it would be emitted to the subscribe method at 3 seconds if the delay was 2 seconds long. You can visualize this with the marble diagram in figure 4.7.

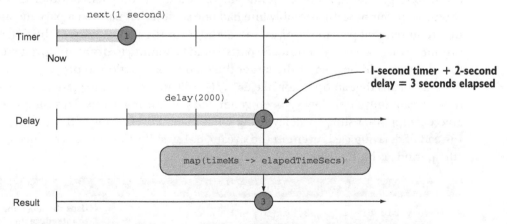

Figure 4.7 A marble diagram of how the `delay` operator affects the output observable

Here's a code sample to illustrate its use.

Listing 4.6 Showcase the `delay` operator

```
Rx.Observable.timer(1000          ⟵── Emits a value after 1 second
    .delay(2000)          ⟵─────────────────────────
    .timeInterval()
    .map(int => Math.floor(int.interval / 1000))
    .subscribe(seconds => console.log(`${seconds} seconds`));  ⟵──
```

Delays the entire sequence by a two-second offset

Computes the time elapsed using the interval value from timeInterval()

Converts and rounds the result to seconds

This code reflects what figure 4.7 shows: how the stream is affected by the `delay` operator to create a shifted observable sequence. Running this code will print "3 seconds" rather than the initial time. The effect of this process raises two important points about the nature of a delay:

- Each operator will affect only the propagation of an event, not its creation.
- Time operators act sequentially.

Let's discuss each of these points individually.

4.3.1 *Propagation*

The first effect applies to all operators but is especially critical with explicitly timed operations because it can have drastic effects on the performance of your application. Because operators have no knowledge about the specific observable to which they're attached, they're unable to affect the production of events (remember that you can think of each operator as a workstation on an assembly line). In order to maximize decoupling and throughput, each operator must work independently. This decoupling can lead to problems, however, if one station drastically outpaces another in terms of production. Suppose an assembly line had one station that painted a part and another that required that part to sit for at least an hour for the paint to dry. If the first station produced one part every minute, 60 parts would be waiting to dry at any given moment. The deficit would be greater the larger the ratio of production to propagation.

This means that an operator like `delay()` will affect the propagation of the events downstream only after they've been generated, not during. Consider a simple observable example that shows a delay firing all at once, for an array with multiple values. Instead of delaying each event in the stream, `delay` shifts the entire sequence by a specific period, as in this listing.

Listing 4.7 `delay` shifts the entire observable sequence

Uses the .do() operator to introduce an effectful computation; in this case, logs to the console the emitted data.

```
Rx.Observable.of([1, 2, 3, 4, 5])
    .do(x => console.log(`Emitted: ${x}`))          ⟵──
    .delay(200)
    .subscribe(x => console.log(`Received: ${x}`));
```

Delays propagation of the event by 200 ms

You might expect that each `Emitted` event would be followed immediately by a `Received`, followed by a delay of 200 ms before the next `Emitted/Received` pair. This is a common mistake for newcomers to RxJS. In reality, the result is this:

```
Output:
"Emitted: 1,2,3,4,5"

// 200 milliseconds later...

"Received: 1,2,3,4,5"
```

This result is much different than you might have expected, because the generation of the events is independent of the `delay` operator. This is exactly the same as the factory worker scenario where production and propagation are not matched. Figure 4.8 illustrates what's happening.

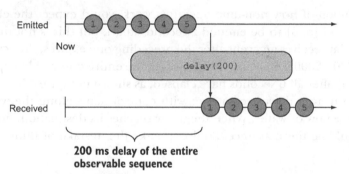

Figure 4.8   A 200 ms delay injected into the pipeline shifts the entire observable sequence instead of each event.

A corollary to this idea is that in order for a delay to work, it must buffer the events it receives before emitting them at the right time. The `delay()` operator has a fixed constant value called a *bounded upper limit* that's proportional to the number of events received and their frequency. You can calculate this with the following relation:

```
# of events received / time * (x time units)
```

For the most part, as long as an operator will eventually propagate, a buffer will always remain bounded, and it will not grow beyond a certain size (we'll come back to buffering in a bit). It's worth mentioning this behavior because it's often confusing for newcomers to RxJS who see `delay` and think that the production of the sequence can be delayed or somehow controlled downstream. Another important aspect of these time-based operators is that they act sequentially.

4.3.2   *Sequential time*

As you've already seen, when operators are chained together, they always operate in sequence, where operators earlier in the chain execute before operators later in the chain. This downstream flow is a core design of RxJS observables. You'd expect this to hold when dealing with time-based operators as well. That is to say, if you were to chain multiple delays, you'd expect that the actual delay downstream would be the sum of each of them. Although `delay()` is sequential, its execution as it appears in the stream declaration with respect to other non-time operators isn't, which can be confusing. The next listing shows how `delay()` stays true to its definition to shift the entire observable sequence, regardless of where it's placed in the sequence.

Listing 4.8   Sequential delay operators

```
Rx.Observable.from([1, 2])
    .delay(2000)
    .concat(Rx.Observable.from([3, 4]))    ◁─┐  Chaining multiple delay
    .delay(2000)                              │  operators together
    .concat(Rx.Observable.from([5, 6]))    ◁─┘
    .delay(2000)
    .subscribe(console.log);
```

Based on your intuition of how non-time operators work, you'd expect the element pairs [1, 2], [3, 4], and [5, 6] to be emitted 2 seconds apart, but this is not the case. Each subsequent delay receives an event after the preceding one expires, thus creating a delay of 2000 + 2000 + 2000 = 6000 ms with respect to the entire observable sequence, printing [1,2,3,4,5,6] after all 6 seconds have elapsed, as shown in figure 4.9.

You can relate this to a downstream river with control dams along the way that temporarily delay the flow of water. When the water reaches its destination, however, all of the water would be there at once. So don't make the mistake of thinking that

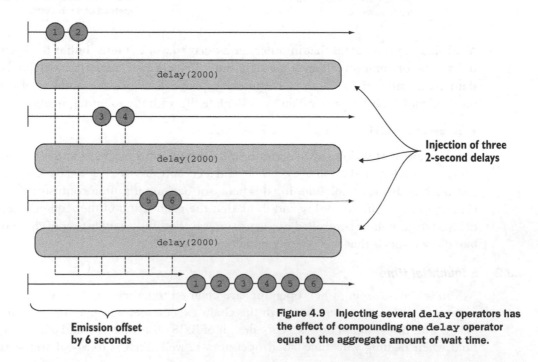

Figure 4.9   Injecting several `delay` operators has the effect of compounding one `delay` operator equal to the aggregate amount of wait time.

Emission offset by 6 seconds

Injection of three 2-second delays

embedding multiple delays into a stream will actually exert its effect at each stage in the pipeline.

Now that you've examined some RxJS time operators, let's put them in action and mix them up with other familiar operators. One of the main areas of concern when you build responsive UIs is dealing with user input. For instance, you'd expect that the application you're building would react accordingly whether the user was pressing a button once or rapidly many times. Consider the DOM events fired by a text box on each key press. Should the application handle every single change, or could you just process the result when the entire word is entered? Let's examine this next.

4.4   Handling user input

Both the `interval()` and `timer()` static methods are used to create observables and initiate an action after a timed offset. These, together with `delay()`, are probably the most familiar combinations when scheduling a future action that executes once, at a set interval, or after a set time. These operators are ideal for use with an explicit event for which you know the action to perform, and you want to schedule it to be run at some later time. But what happens when sequences of events are generated from a dynamic event emitter, like a user's mouse move or key presses, which can emit potentially many events in a short time? In this case, you're probably not interested in processing each of them but events in between.

In this section, we'll look at two of the most useful observable mechanisms: debounce and throttle. They perform similar functions, so first you'll learn to apply debouncing to implement a smart search program, starting with an imperative version before moving into a fully reactive version.

4.4.1   Debouncing

In signal and circuit design, it's common to debounce a signal so that a manual input signal doesn't appear like multiple signals. This is a common feature with switches and other types of manual user interactions. The same thing happens when software interacts with humans, for which RxJS offers an operator called `debounceTime()`, which emits an event from an observable sequence only after a particular time span (in milliseconds) has passed without it emitting any other item—essentially sending one and not many within a certain time frame. You can think of this operator as belonging to the filtering category of operators, using time as the predicate to decide which events to keep. In simple software terms, debouncing means "execute a function or some action only if a certain period has passed without it being called." In this case, it means that an event is emitted from an observable sequence if a set time span has passed without emitting another value, and it may be represented with the marble diagram in figure 4.10.

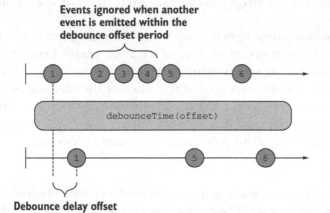

Figure 4.10   This generic debounce operation allows the emission of an item only after a certain time span has elapsed before another event is emitted.

Here's a simple example showcasing the debouncing operator, which emits the most recent click after a rapid succession of clicks:

```
Rx.Observable.fromEvent(document, 'click')
    .debounceTime(1000)
    .subscribe(c => {
      console.log(`Clicked at position
          ${c.clientX} and ${c.clientY}`)
    });
```

With this code, the user can generate a burst of click events, but only the last one will be emitted after a second of inactivity.

Observable factory vs. instance methods

Static methods and instance methods on some websites are referred to as observable methods and observable instance methods, respectively. The static methods are defined directly on the `Rx.Observable` object and are not part of the object's prototype. These are typically used for initiating the declaration of an observable instance, for example, `Rx.Observable.interval(500)`. The observable instance methods are included in the object's prototype and are used as members of the chained pipeline after you've initiated an observable declaration. We've referred to these simply as operators in previous chapters for brevity, for example, `Rx.Observable.prototype.delay()`, `Rx.Observable.prototype.debounceTime()`, and others.

Let's put this operator to the test. Consider the example shown in figure 4.11 of a smart search widget that allows you to easily look up articles from Wikipedia by giving you suggestions as you type.

Running this code generates the following output: if the user types r into the text box, it will suggest two possible results: "rxmarbles.com" and "reactivex.io." Additionally typing e into the box will filter the results further to just "reactivex.io." As the user

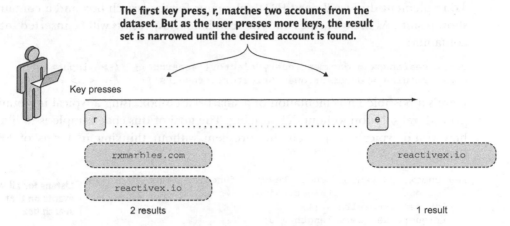

The first key press, r, matches two accounts from the dataset. But as the user presses more keys, the result set is narrowed until the desired account is found.

Key presses

r

e

rxmarbles.com

reactivex.io

reactivex.io

2 results

1 result

Figure 4.11 The user interacts with the search box. As the user types on the keyboard, the list of search results filters down. This is typical of modern search engines.

types their keywords, you recognize that making web requests after each letter typed is a bit wasteful, and you'd be better off if you allow the user to type first and wait for a specific amount of time before making the expensive round-trip request. This has the benefit of restricting the number of web requests made to the server while the user is still typing, which is better resource utilization overall. When interacting with a third-party service, such as the Wikipedia API, it's good to do this so that you don't hit your rate limit. Preferably, the program should back off until the user has stopped typing for a brief period (indicating that they're not sure what to type next) before looking for possible suggestions. This is both to prevent the additional network congestion of initiating requests that will never be seen and to avoid the annoying UX of having the type-ahead flicker as the user types.

Prior to RxJS, you'd need to implement this yourself, probably using `setTimeout()`. The timeout is reset every time the user types a new key. If the user doesn't type for a short duration, the timeout will expire and the function will execute. We'll need to cover a little more ground in order to start streaming from remote services, so in the meantime, we'll use a small dataset and return to this program in the next chapter:

```
let testData = [
    'github.com/Reactive-Extensions/RxJS',
    'github.com/ReactiveX/RxJS',
    'xgrommx.github.io/rx-book',
    'reactivex.io',
    'egghead.io/technologies/rx',
    'rxmarbles.com',
    'https://www.manning.com/books/rxjs-in-action'
];
```

To implement this, we'll need HTML elements for the search box and a container to show results. As the user types into the search box, any results will be inserted into this container:

```
const searchBox = document.querySelector('#search'); //-> <input>
const results = document.querySelector('#results');  //-> <ul>
```

Here's a possible implementation of a smart search box using a typical imperative or procedural solution without debouncing. The goal of this code sample is to illustrate how you'd typically approach this problem without thinking in terms of FP and streams:

```
searchBox.addEventListener('keyup', function (event) {        ⟵ Listens for all keyup
    let query = event.target.value;                             events on that
    let searchResults = [];                                     search box
    if(query && query.length > 0) {
      clearResults(results);
        for(let result of testData) {                         ⟵ Loops through all of
          if(result.startsWith(query)) {                        your test data URLs
            searchResults.push(result);                         and find matches
          }
        }
      }
    for(let result of searchResults) {                        ⟵ If no matches are found, clears the
        appendResults(result, results);                         list of search results; otherwise,
      }                                                         appends the items found
});

function clearResults(container) {                            ⟵ Function used to
  while(container.childElementCount > 0) {                      clear search results
    container.removeChild(container.firstChild);               container
  }
}

function appendResults(result, container) {                   ⟵ Function used to
    let li = document.createElement('li');                      append a result onto
    let text = document.createTextNode(result);                 the container
    li.appendChild(text);
    container.appendChild(li);
}
```

This code is simple. Building a smart search box involves binding the keyup event and using the value in the text box to look up possible search results. If there's a match, the results are appended to the DOM; otherwise, the DOM is cleared. For this, you created two functions, appendResults() and clearResults(), respectively. This flow is shown in figure 4.12.

This code has no debouncing logic, so essentially it will issue queries against the test array for every letter the user enters into the search box. By adding debouncing logic to this imperative code example, we end up with the following.

Listing 4.9 Manual debouncing logic for smart search widget

```
let timeoutId = null;                         ⟵── Registers the current timeout

searchBox.addEventListener('keyup', function (event) {

  clearTimeout(timeoutId);                    ⟵
                                                    As the user presses the key,
  timeoutId = setTimeout(function (query) {   ⟵    clears the current timeout
    console.log('querying...');                      to initiate a new one
    let searchResults = [];
    if(query && query.length > 0) {                 Starts a new timeout that
      clearResults(results);                        will fire after 1 second of
      for(let result of testData) {                 no interaction
        if(result.startsWith(query)) {
          searchResults.push(result);
        }
      }
    }
    for(let result of searchResults) {
      appendResults(result, results);
    }
  }, 1000, event.target.value);               ⟵── Debounces for 1 second
});
```

Whenever the user types a key, that key press event will trigger the event listener. Inside the event listener, you first clear any existing pending timeouts using `clear-Timeout()`. Then you reset the timer. The result of all this is that the task won't execute until the input has "cooled off" or there's a delay between inputs. In this case,

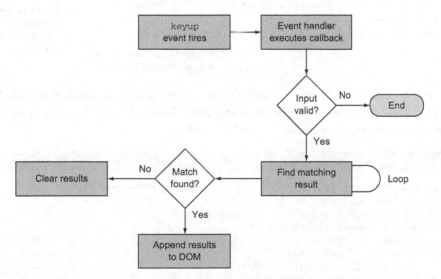

Figure 4.12 The stages of this simple program from the moment the event fires to finding a correct search result and writing the data on the page. Notice the use of a couple of conditional statements and loops. This is the mark of true imperative design.

the delay in inputs dovetails nicely with the perception of helping the user along if they hesitate when typing.

Although the number of lines of code added here is minimal, several things make this approach less than desirable. For one, you're forced to create an external `time-outId` variable that's accessible within the callback's closure and exists outside the scope of the event handler. This introduces more of the dreaded global state pollution, which is a clear sign of side effects. Further, there's no real separation of concerns. The operation itself isn't terribly indicative of what it's intended for, and the timeout value together with all the business logic get buried and entangled with the debouncing logic—adding additional logic is very invasive.

It would be nice if we could clean up this operation. Let's wear our functional hats and start by creating a method similar to `setTimeout()` that will encapsulate the debouncing mechanism, separate it from the rest of the business logic, and lift the method out of the closure. From that we could expect a function signature, as shown in the next listing.

Listing 4.10 Dedicated `debounce()` method using vanilla JavaScript

Stores timeoutId externally so it can be shared

Returns a function that wraps the original callback

Resets the timer

Captures the arguments object into an actual array

Proxies the arguments to the setTimeout() method

```
const copyToArray = arrayLike => Array.prototype.slice.call(arrayLike);

function debounce(fn, time) {
  let timeoutId;
  return function() {
    const args = [fn, time]
      .concat(copyToArray(arguments));
    clearTimeout(timeoutId);
    timeoutId = window.setTimeout.apply(window, args);
  }
}
```

This new `debounce()` can now wrap the request logic, allowing you to elegantly decouple event-handling logic from debouncing logic. Using this method, you can extend the imperative version of the search code, as follows.

Listing 4.11 Using custom `debounce()` method

Helper method to send HTTP

```
function sendRequest(query) {
  console.log('querying...');
  let searchResults = [];
  if(query && query.length > 0) {
    clearResults(results);
    for(result of testData) {
      if(result.startsWith(query)) {
        searchResults.push(result);
      }
    }
  }
}
```

```
    for(let result of searchResults) {
      appendResults(result, results);
    }
  }
}
let debouncedRequest = debounce(sendRequest, 1000);

searchBox.addEventListener('keyup', function (event) {
  debouncedRequest(event.target.value);
});
```

Wraps this helper method with debounce()

Invokes the debounced version of the function after handling user input

As you can see, just like in previous chapters, you're able to remove much of the ugly and bug-prone extrinsic state by compartmentalizing behavior into small functions. But doing this introduces another problem, which is that the result of the task completion is no longer readily available. You now need to push all of the event-handling logic into sendRequest() because there's no way to forward the result outside the closure. All this serves to show that implementing your own debounce logic can be quite daunting and imposes many limitations on your design.

Fortunately, with RxJS this becomes extremely simple, and the fact that you push all of the DOM interaction into the observer means your business logic is greatly simplified from the complex flow chart shown earlier to the abstract model shown in figure 4.13, where data always moves forward from producer to consumer in its typical unidirectional manner.

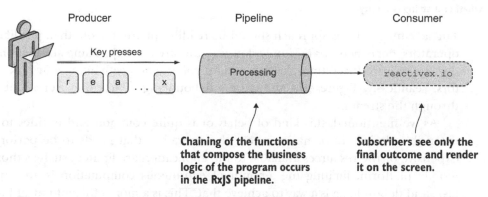

Figure 4.13 RxJS uses the pipeline to process data from the producers in a way that's consumable and acceptable to the consumers to display and do more work on. Reactive state machines are modeled using marble diagrams; more on this later in this section.

Thinking reactively, you can see a debounce operation as simply a filter embedded into the processing pipeline that uses time to remove certain events from the observer. Hence, you can use observables to explicitly inject time into your stream as a first-class entity. For this functional version of the program, you'll create a pure, more-streamlined version of sendRequest() and use debounceTime() to implement all of the debouncing logic for you. Here's the functional-reactive version.

Listing 4.12   A simple debounce-optimized search program

```
const notEmpty = input => !!input && input.trim().length > 0;

const sendRequest = function(arr, query) {                    ◄──── Refactors
  return arr.filter(item => {                                        sendRequest() to be
    return query.length > 0 && item.startsWith(query);              more functional and
  });                                                                returns the list of
}                                                                    matched search results

const search$ = Rx.Observable.fromEvent(searchBox, 'keyup')
    .debounceTime(1000)                           ◄──── Injects a debounce offset
    .pluck('target', 'value')                            of I second, after
 ┌► .filter(notEmpty)                                    capturing the user's
 │  .do(query => console.log(`Querying for ${query}...`))  input. This will allow the
 │  .map(query =>                             ◄────────── user to type any
 │    sendRequest(testData, query))                      characters in the time
 │  .subscribe(result => {                               span of a second, before
 │    if(result.length === 0) {                          requests are sent over.
 │      clearResults(results);
 │    }                                         Maps the search results into the
 │    else {                                    source observable. For now, you're
 │      appendResults(result, results);         creating a test dataset. In chapter
 │    }                                         5, you'll learn how to add AJAX calls
 │  });                                         into your streams.
 │
 └ Helper function to check
   whether a string is empty
```

The advantage of this approach should be readily apparent. Note that, just like other operators, `debounceTime()` simply slots into the stream. RxJS's time abstraction allows time to be introduced transparently and, in conjunction with all of your other operators, seamlessly. Figure 4.14 shows how debouncing affects the user input passed through the stream.

As we mentioned, this kind of behavior is quite common and testifies to RxJS's extensible design. In scenarios where the operation that needs to be performed is expensive or the resources available to the application are limited, such as those on a mobile platform, limiting the amount of extraneous computation is an important task, and debouncing is a way to achieve that. This is a more efficient way of handling user input, and the Wikipedia servers agree with us. Another way to achieve this is with the operator `throttle`, a sister to `debounce`.

4.4.2   *Throttling*

The `debounceTime()` operator has a close sister called `throttleTime()`. Throttling ignores values from an observable sequence that are followed by another value before a certain time. In simple terms, this means "execute a function at most once every period," as shown in the marble diagram in figure 4.15.

Let's say you're executing an expensive computation in response to a user scrolling or moving the mouse. It's probably best to wait for the user to finish scrolling instead of executing this function thousands of times. This can also work well with

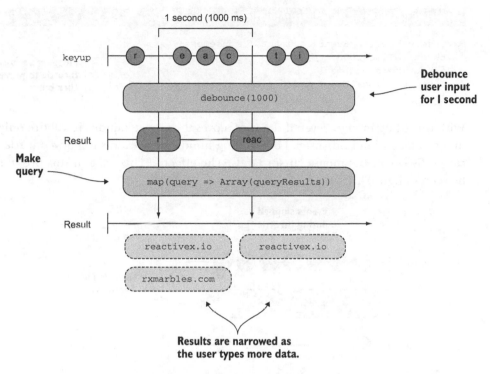

Figure 4.14 Debouncing the event stream allows the user to rapidly input a set of characters so that they can be processed all at once, instead of querying for data at every key press.

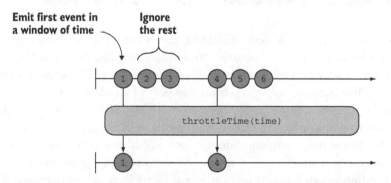

Figure 4.15 Throttling events so that at most one will be emitted in a specified period of time, in this case the first event in the time span window

banking sites for controlling important action buttons like withdrawing from an account or with popular shopping sites like Amazon to add extra logic around the "one-click buy" buttons. The next listing shows how to throttle mouse moves.

Listing 4.13   Controlling button action with `throttle`

```
Rx.Observable.fromEvent(document, 'mousemove')
  .throttleTime(2000)                                    ←———————  Plugging a two-second
  .subscribe(event => {                                            throttle to prevent
    console.log(`Mouse at: ${event.x} and ${event.y}`);            click bursts
  });
```

With throttling in place, even if the user moves the mouse rapidly, it will fire only once in a two-second period, instead of emitting hundreds of events in between. You really care only where the mouse cursor lands. The effect of `throttle` in this program can be seen in figure 4.16.

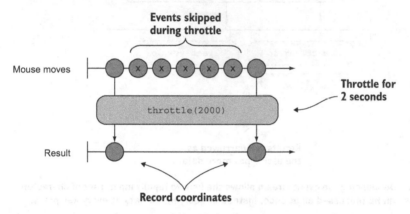

Figure 4.16   Throttling button clicks allows the application to ignore accidental repeated clicking, thereby preventing the withdraw action from executing multiple times.

Up until now, this chapter has been all about understanding the basics of time in RxJS. We explored several of the operators to demonstrate the power of RxJS to simplify the concepts of time and make coding with it much easier. We demonstrated that RxJS operators allow you to intuitively use time as part of an observable.

Time-based operators like `delay()` and others contain buffering or caching logic under the hood to temporarily defer emitting events without any loss of data; this is how RxJS is able to control or manipulate the time within the events of an observable sequence. This can be a powerful feature to use in your own applications as well, so RxJS exposes buffering operators for you to use directly in order to temporarily store data of a certain amount or for a certain period. This is analogous to building control dams along the way to harvest the streams, not only for a specific period but also of a certain size, so that you can make decisions and potentially transform the stream before it flows through. In the next section, we'll kick it up a notch. The plan is to use buffering as a means to temporarily cache data, together with timed operators to debounce or throttle user input.

4.5   *Buffering in RxJS*

We've mentioned many times that streams are stateless and don't store any data. In chapter 2, we showed how you can create a small repository of data within a custom iterator, called `BufferIterator`, which you used to format and change the nature of the elements being iterated over.

RxJS recognizes that it's useful to temporarily cache some events like mouse moves, clicks, and key presses, instead of processing a deluge of events all at once, and apply some business logic to them before broadcasting them out to subscribers. Depending on the nature of this cached data, you might allow the events to flow through as is or perhaps create a whole new event that subscribers see. The buffering operators provide underlying data structures that transiently store past data so that you can work with it in batches instead of as a whole, as shown in figure 4.17.

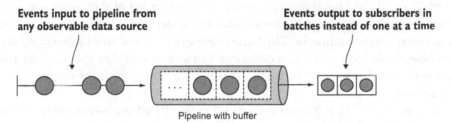

Events input to pipeline from any observable data source

Events output to subscribers in batches instead of one at a time

Pipeline with buffer

Figure 4.17   Buffers plugged into an RxJS pipeline. A buffer of size 3, as in this case, can store up to three events at a time and then emit them all at once as an array of observables.

One important thing to understand is what happens to the data emitted because of buffering. Instead of a single observable output, as you'd normally expect and as you've seen all along, subscribers receive an array of observables. Buffering is useful for tasks where the overhead of processing items is large, and therefore it's better to deal with multiple items at once. A good example of this is when reacting to a user moving the mouse or scrolling a web page. Because mouse movement emits hundreds of events at once, you might want to buffer a certain amount and then emit an observable in response to where the mouse or the page is.

Table 4.1 provides a list of the observable instance methods that we'll explore in this chapter.

Table 4.1   API documentation for buffer operators

Name	Description
`buffer(observable)`	Buffers the incoming observable values until the provided observable emits a value, at which point it emits the buffer on the returned observable and starts a new buffer internally, waiting for the next time an observable emits.

Table 4.1   API documentation for buffer operators *(continued)*

Name	Description
`bufferCount(number)`	Buffers a number of values from the source observable and then emits the buffer whole and clears it. At this point, a new buffer is internally initialized.
`bufferWhen(selector)`	Opens a buffer immediately and then closes the buffer when the observable returned by calling `selector` emits a value. At that time, it immediately opens a new buffer and repeats the process.
`bufferTime(time)`	Buffers events from the source for a specific period. After the time has passed, the data is emitted and a new buffer is initialized internally.

Generally speaking, this ability to capture a temporary set of data gives you a window of time that you can use to examine and make decisions about the nature or frequency of the data coming in. The buffer operators achieve this by grouping the data of an observable sequence into a collection (an array), and they also provide a second parameter called a selector function, which you can use to transform or format the data beforehand.

We'll start with the `buffer()` operator. `buffer()` gathers events emitted by source observables into a buffer until a passed-in observable, called the *closing* observable, emits an event. At this point, `buffer()` flushes out the buffered data and starts a new buffer internally. To show this, we'll use `timer(0, 50)`. A period argument of 50 causes the timer to emit subsequent values every 50 ms. We'll buffer the events with a closing timer observable of 500 ms; hence, you should expect 500 / 50 = 10 events to be emitted at once. Figure 4.18 is a marble diagram showing this process.

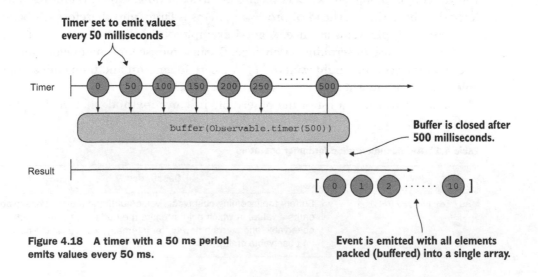

Figure 4.18   A timer with a 50 ms period emits values every 50 ms.

You can implement this with the following code:

```
Rx.Observable.timer(0, 50)
  .buffer(Rx.Observable.timer(500))          <───
  .subscribe(
    function (val) {
      console.log(`Data in buffer: [${val}]`);   <───
    });
//-> "Data in buffer: [0,1,2,3,4,5,6,7,8,9]"
```

buffer uses a closing observable, which is the criteria for when to stop buffering data, in this case after 500 ms of caching events.

buffer returns an array of observable sequences.

The fact that buffers emit an array of observables is analogous to the iterator example we discussed in chapter 2 because the client of the iterator (the `for...of` loop) would receive arrays of data as each element. In that example, creating a `BufferIterator(3)` would yield arrays of triplets at each iteration (or at each call to `next()`). The best way to illustrate this is by using the `bufferCount()` operator.

`bufferCount()` retains a certain amount of data at a time, which you define by passing a size. Once this number is reached, the data is emitted and a new buffer started. You'll use a buffer count to display a warning message for numerical inputs that involve large quantities (say, five digits or more). You'll listen for changes on the amount field so that you can display a warning next to it when the amount value is five digits long:

Listens for key events on the amount text box

```
const amountTextBox = document.querySelector('#amount');
const warningMessage = document.querySelector('#amount-warning');

Rx.Observable.fromEvent(amountTextBox, 'keyup')          <───
  .bufferCount(5)                                        <─── Buffers a total of five events at a time
  .map(events => events[0].target.value)
  .map(val => parseInt(val, 10))         <─── Ensures the amount entered is numeric
  .filter(val => !Number.isNaN(val))     <─── Filters out any empty numbers
  .subscribe(amount => {
    warningMessage.setAttribute('style', 'display: inline;');  <───
  });
```

Extracts the value of the input box. Because buffer returns an array of events, it's sufficient to use the first event's target DOM element that received the key input.

Displays a warning to alert the user they've entered a large quantity

As you can see, a buffer is in some ways similar to a delay. But nothing relates buffers and time more than the `bufferWhen()` and `bufferTime()` operators. We'll begin with `bufferWhen()`. This operator is useful for caching events until another observable emits a value. This operator differs slightly from `buffer()` in that it takes a selector function that creates an observable to signal when the buffer should emit. It doesn't just buffer at the pace of a subordinate observable; it calls this factory function to create the observable that dictates when it should emit, reset, and create a new buffer. For example, suppose you're implementing form fields that can keep track of previously entered values, so that you could revert to a value you had entered before changing it. First, let's look at the marble diagram for this entire interaction in figure 4.19.

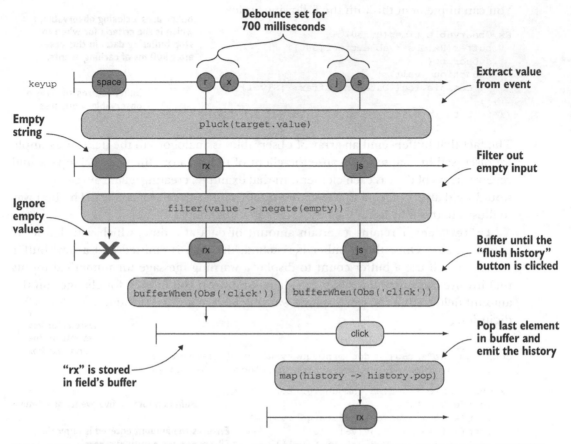

Figure 4.19   A stream listening for key presses, debounced in order to capture the event at a little over half a second. Any word entered is passed through a simple validation check. The data fills the buffer and is flushed only when requesting the history. This observable closes off the buffer and prints the history.

The goal of this program is that as values are entered into a form field, you keep them in a buffer so that you can always go back to any of them if you wish to do so. As you can see from listing 4.14, in this book we occasionally sprinkle a functional library called Ramda.js to replace utility functions like input validation, array manipulation, and others you'd otherwise have to write yourself (for details about installing Ramda, please visit appendix A). We also do it to show you how well RxJS interacts with functional libraries you may use (in chapter 10, "RxJS in the wild," expect to see a lot of this interaction).

Ramda loads its arsenal of functions under a single namespace, R. One special function you'll come to learn and love is R.compose() for functional composition. Used with RxJS, which is great at managing state, it's the perfect combination of functional and reactive programming. Here's the code to implement this business logic.

Listing 4.14   Creating form field history with `bufferWhen()`

```
const field = document.querySelector('.form-field');
const showHistoryButton = document.querySelector('#show-history');
const historyPanel = document.querySelector('#history');

const showHistory$ = Rx.Observable.fromEvent(showHistoryButton, 'click');

Rx.Observable.fromEvent(field, 'keyup')
  .debounceTime(200)
  .pluck('target', 'value')
  .filter(R.compose(R.not, R.isEmpty))          ⟵┐  Validates the input field by
  .bufferWhen(() => showHistory$)         ⟵      │  composing Ramda functions
  .do(history => history.pop())                  ┘  to check for non-empty
  .subscribe(history => {                         Signals that the stream should
    let contents = '';                            clear the buffer when the history
    if(history.length > 0) {    ⟵── Prints the history next to the button
      for(let item of history) {               button observable emits a value
        contents += '<li>' + item + '</li>';
      }
      historyPanel.innerHTML = contents;
    }
});
```

Pay attention to how the composition of `R.isEmpty()` and `R.not()` creates the behavior for "non-empty." Always remember that FP is powerful when you can create and combine functions with minimal logic that together solve complex tasks. We'll use Ramda again in the next code listing so that you can see how it benefits the readability of your code.

Finally, we'll take a look at `bufferTime()`. This operator holds onto data from an observable sequence for a specific period of time and then emits it as an observable array. You can think of this as equivalent to a `bufferWhen()` operator combined with an `Rx.Observable.timer()`. You'll see this in action in listing 4.15. You're going to run a buffer with a timer in the background to monitor a form with a text box and a button just like in the previous example. In this example, however, you'll use a rolling buffer to look for a specific key sequence, that is, a passcode. As with many of the operators, we suggest that you review the documentation for `bufferTime()` to understand all its possible uses.

Another twist added to this code in preparation for the next chapters is the use of the `combineLatest()` operator to combine the outputs from two independent streams. Take a look (make sure to click the Submit button *at least once* to see the result).

Listing 4.15   Buffering events for a specific period of time

```
const password = document.getElementById('password-field');
const submit = document.getElementById('submit');
const outputField = document.getElementById('output');
```

```
const password$ = Rx.Observable.fromEvent(password, 'keyup')
  .map(({keyCode}) => keyCode - 48)
  .filter(value => 0 <= value && value <= 9);

const submit$ = Rx.Observable.fromEvent(submit, 'click');

Rx.Observable.combineLatest(
  password$
  .bufferTime(7000)
  .filter(R.compose(R.not, R.isEmpty)),
  submit$
)
.take(10)
.subscribe(
  ([maybePassword]) => {
    if (maybePassword.join('') === '1337') {
      outputField.innerHTML = 'Correct Password!';
    } else {
      outputField.innerHTML = 'Wrong Password!';
    }
  },
  err => {},
  () => outputField.innerHTML = 'No more tries accepted!'
);
```

Determines the numeric key that was pressed

Submits the password

Combines the events emitted from both the text field and button simultaneously (you'll learn about this operator later in chapter 6)

Buffers input for 7 seconds and then flush it

Composes a series of Ramda functions to remove empty buffers from the output stream

ES6 destructuring, because you care only about the password field

Outputs when the stream has stopped accepting entries

Accepts only three password tries until locking the system

Determines if the password was correct

When combining buffers and time, you need to understand how your application gets used. Buffers use temporary data structures to cache events that occur in their window of operation. Ten seconds can be a very long time if you're caching hundreds of events per second, like mouse moves or scrolls. So exert caution by not overflowing the amount of memory you have, or your UI will become unresponsive. In the process of illustrating RxJS concepts, we introduced a new operator called combineLatest(), which is used to join multiple streams into one. At this point, you've seen the most frequently used operators that act on a single stream. In chapters 5 and 6, we'll begin to dive deeply into RxJS by taking on more real-world problems, and we'll explain more-advanced operators so that you can begin to work with multiple simultaneous streams.

4.6 Summary

- RxJS allows you greater control in manipulating and tracking the flow of time in an application.
- Operators can interact with time to change the output of an observable.
- Time can be implicit, or it can be explicitly declared when more fine-grained control is needed.

- Implicit time manifests in the latency waiting for asynchronous HTTP calls to respond. You have no control over how long these functions take.
- Explicit time is controlled by you and takes advantage of JavaScript's timers.
- Delaying shifts the observable sequence by a due time (in milliseconds).
- Debouncing emits an event from an observable sequence only after a particular time span (in milliseconds) has passed without it omitting any other item.
- Throttling enforces a maximum number of times a function can be called over time.
- Buffering operations use many of the same semantics as the timing operations.
- RxJS features size-based as well as time-based buffers.

Part 2

Observables in practice

Now that you understand the basics of RxJS observables and you're starting to become familiar with the syntactic style of the library, it's time to kick it up a notch and dive into some more-interesting use cases. In chapter 5, we'll examine nested observables, or streams within streams, and their ability to create more-powerful semantics for asynchronous control. Chapter 6 starts by dismantling the observable lifecycle and explaining how you can make use of different parts of the observable's life to manage state logic without exposing such state externally. Chapter 6 follows this with a discussion of how you can combine several observables and combine multiple events occurring at different times. In chapter 7, you'll learn about how observables manage exceptions neatly and allow you to program based on happy-path expectations, beginning with a functional programming introduction to the Try data type.

Applied reactive streams

This chapter covers

- Handling multiple observable sequences with one subscription
- Learning to make observable streams conformant
- Flattening nested observables structures
- Merging a collection of observables into a single output
- Preserving sequence order with concatenation
- Implementing real-world problems: search box, live stock ticker, and drag and drop

In the previous chapter, we firmly rooted the notion that an observable is a sequence of events over time. You can think about it as the orchestrator or channel through which events are pushed and transformed. So far, we've discussed how to process observable sequences in isolation for the most part, and you learned how you could apply familiar operators over all the elements within an observable in the same way that you could with an array, irrespective of when those elements were emitted. Toward the end of the chapter, we briefly gave you some exposure to an RxJS operator called combineLatest(), which is used to combine streams. The reason for these discussions is that other than trivial examples, most of your programming tasks will involve the use of these operators so that the events from one stream propagate and cause a reaction somewhere else. This is where RxJS and the entire reactive paradigm begin to shine and set themselves superior to other conventional asynchronous libraries.

Now you've entered into new, more sophisticated territory. This chapter is our point of inflection where we'll look at combinatorial operators similar to `combineLatest()` like `merge()`, `switch()`, `concat()`, and others to solve real-world, complex problems. Although there's still a lot to gain from using observables to handle a single event source, like a single button click, in all but the most trivial of applications, you'll quickly find that your logic will require more than a single stream to get the job done. You had a taste of this toward the end of chapter 4 when you implemented a slightly more complicated problem, which required you to combine and buffer the output of multiple streams.

Depending on the complexity of your application, your logic will likely involve the interplay between many observables, potentially containing different types of data. For instance, a user typing keys on the search bar kicks off an entirely different type of stream for fetching data from a server—to put it in Newton's terms, user actions may create reactions in different parts of the application. But combining different observables presents a challenge because you have to learn how to fuse them together. What if their interfaces are different? This happens quite often, especially when modeling complex state machines such as UIs or mashing up data from remote locations. Thus, in this chapter, we'll focus on an important principle in functional programming called *flattening a data type*, which stems from the need to project other observables carrying needed data into a single source. After learning this technique, you'll be prepared to tackle all sorts of complicated flows. Let's begin with the idea that all data sources, whether static or dynamic, can be treated in the exact same manner under the observable programming model, because everything is a stream.

5.1   *One for all, and all for one!*

The addition of time to the observable introduced a new dimension that let you delay, filter, and manipulate elements based on when they were dispatched. By playing with various types of operators and their corresponding selector functions, you were able to determine if, when, and how events made it downstream, so this gave your business logic full control of how data is transformed within the stream.

Up until now, we've been focusing on single streams. In this chapter, we expand our use of operators and introduce more-advanced ones that allow you to create complex flows and combine them into a single flow. This is essential for any non-trivial state machines where input taken from the user creates a ripple effect on other parts of the system in real time.

Multi-stream scenarios are common in the real world. Generally, you'll find that the more complex your system becomes, the more entangled your streams will be.

This linear relation shouldn't surprise you because complexity grows as you inject more business logic into your code. But this is far more maintainable than the exponential complexity growth of a system that deals with asynchronous flows relying only on nested callback functions or even solely on promises.

The combination operators you'll learn in this chapter are indispensable because if isolated streams were unable to interact with each other, it would be up to you to create the necessary boilerplate for those streams to work together. Ugh! You'd likely be no better off than before you started using RxJS!

> **REACTIVE MANIFESTO** According to the Reactive Manifesto, one of the central principles of reactive architectures is elasticity. An elastic system is one that stays responsive under a varying workload. RxJS nicely achieves this because multiple sources of data with varying input rates can be combined in different ways without you having to rewrite or refactor how your code works.

As an example of when multiple streams come into play, imagine that in addition to supporting mouse handling, you wanted to support touch interfaces. JavaScript already provides built-in support for touch events in most browsers, but adding touch support to an application means introducing a second set of events and logic. Without the right architecture, you'll most likely have to create a whole new set of event handlers for those as well. With your newly developed reactive mindset, you realize that those are all just different streams passing through the same channel. Whether you're using mouse or touch, most of the time those streams kick-start events that need to combine key presses with other HTTP calls, timed intervals, animations, and much more—complex UIs work this way.

Let's look at a quick example. Just as mouse events have mousedown, mouseup, and mousemove, touch events have touchstart, touchend, and touchmove, respectively. This means that, at a minimum, you'll need to create three new streams in order to emulate the same behaviors from mouse events as with touch events and have your code work on mobile browsers. Consider the scenario of two independent streams. The touchend event is probably equivalent to mouseup, which means that in most cases users will use it in the same way:

```
const mouseUp$ = Rx.Observable.fromEvent(document, 'mouseup');

const touchEnd$ = Rx.Observable.fromEvent(document, 'touchend');
```

Each of the streams represents the same action of completing some interaction with your application, whether it's through a mouse or the screen. You know from the previous chapters that you can subscribe to each of the handlers individually as such:

```
mouseUp$.subscribe(/* Handle mouse click */);

touchEnd$.subscribe(/* Handle touch click* /);
```

But this setup is less than ideal. For one, you now have two subscription blocks for what will most likely be identical code. Any code that must be shared between the two will

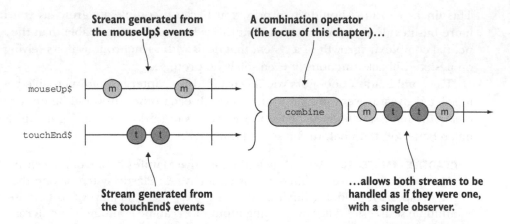

Figure 5.1   A simplified diagram of the desired behavior of ingesting two streams, `mouseUp$` and `touchEnd$`, through a combination operator, and creating a single output block for consumption. In this chapter, you'll learn about the most important combination operators in RxJS.

now require a shared external state. In addition, now two subscriptions must be tracked, which introduces one more area of potential memory leaks. It would be in many ways preferable if you could manage both subscriptions with a single block of code without having to worry about the synchronization of both streams, as shown in figure 5.1, especially in this case, because both observables will emit very similar events.

There are many different ways to join multiple streams into one and take advantage of using a single observer to handle them all. In this section, we'll look at the following strategies:

- *Interleave events by merging streams*—This strategy is useful for forwarding events from multiple streams and is ideal for handling different types of user interaction events like mouse or touch.
- *Preserve order of events by concatenating streams*—This one is used when the order of the events emitted by multiple streams needs to be preserved.
- *Switch to the latest stream data*—This is used when one type of event kicks off another, such as a button click initiating a remote HTTP call or beginning a timer.

5.1.1   Interleave events by merging streams

The simplest operator that combines multiple streams together is `merge()`. It's easy to understand; its purpose is to forward the events from several streams in order of arrival into one observable, like a funnel. Logically, you can think of `merge` as performing an OR of the two events, as shown in figure 5.2.

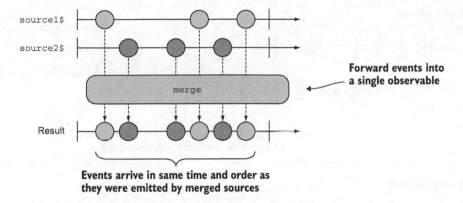

Forward events into a single observable

Events arrive in same time and order as they were emitted by merged sources

Figure 5.2   The `merge()` operator has no logic of its own, other than to combine events from multiple streams in the order in which they're emitted.

We can illustrate this with a simple example:

```
const source1$ = Rx.Observable.interval(1000)
    .map(x => `Source 1 ${x}`)
    .take(3);
const source2$ = Rx.Observable.interval(1000)
    .map(y => `Source 2 ${y}`)
    .take(3);

Rx.Observable.merge(source1$, source2$)
    .subscribe(console.log);
```

The resulting stream created from merge will emit values every second, alternating between sources 1 and 2. `merge()` has no logic of its own other than placing the events onto a single stream in the order in which they arrive.

In the example of mouse and touch streams, because the two types are virtually interchangeable, you can funnel both through this operator so that you can react to either one in the exact same way or with the same observer logic. Just like most of the operators you'll learn about soon, `merge()` can be found in the static method form:

```
Rx.Observable.merge(source1$, source2$, ...)
```

Or, it can be found in instance form:

```
source1$.merge(source$2).merge(...)
```

In the static form, it's a creational operator, as we showed in chapter 4. In other words, you're creating a new stream from the combination of two or more observables. Using it in instance form, we say that an observable is *projected* or *mapped* to the source observable. Both yield the same results, and because operators are pure, both create new observables.

Static operator

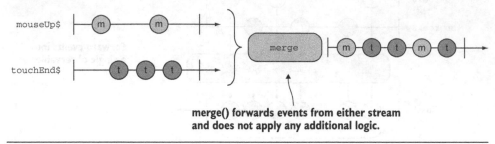

**merge() forwards events from either stream
and does not apply any additional logic.**

Instance operator

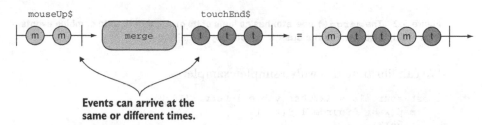

**Events can arrive at the
same or different times.**

Figure 5.3   Static and instance versions of the `merge` operator between two streams. The results
are the same. `merge()` is the simplest operator because it only forwards events from either
stream as they come.

`merge()` can accept either an array or a variable number of streams that are to have
their outputs merged into one. Thus, for the previous example, you can create a
merged stream easily by passing both sources into the `merge()` operator, as shown in
figure 5.3, for both static and instance forms.

Here's the code that combines both streams, in creational form:

```
Rx.Observable.merge(mouseUp$, touchEnd$)
    .subscribe(/* single observer to consume either event */);
```

Again, you can also write this code where a source observable merges onto another in
midstream in instance form:

```
mouseUp$.merge(touchEnd$)
    .subscribe(/*single observer to consume either event */);
```

**In this case, both mouseUp$ and touchEnd$
are still referred to as the source observables.**

The outcome of merging two observables is that they now appear as a single one from
the point of view of any instance methods used, all the way down to the observer, so all
their outputs are piped to a single output block. This is true for all of the combinatorial operators you'll learn about in this chapter. You now need only worry about a single subscription for the two streams.

Now, here's something to think about when merging streams is order. The `merge`
operator will interleave events from each stream in the order in which the events are

received; internally, RxJS does a good job of timestamping each event that gets pushed through the observable.

Each stream, though independent, contributes to the overall output of the sequence. In more statically typed languages, the compiler will also often constrain the types that can go into a merge. This forces the input streams to have a uniform and predicable type for the output. In JavaScript, because these constraints don't exist, it's much easier to merge types that may not even be compatible. But this flexibility can result in some unexpected errors downstream when you're looking to handle one type of event differently than the other. For this, one thing you could do is check your use cases to determine the type, as in the following listing. Again, going back to the touch and click streams, assume you need to print out the coordinates of both touch and click events.

Listing 5.1   Case matching event data resulting from merging mouse and touch streams

```
Rx.Observable.merge(mouseUp$, touchEnd$)   ⟵── Merges the outputs of the two streams
  .do(event => console.log(event.type))
  .map(event => {
      switch(event.type) {            ⟵─────────────────────  Detects the type of the
          case 'touchend':                                    event, builds a compatible
              return {left: event.changedTouches[0].clientX,  type, and constructs the
                      top: event.changedTouches[0].clientY};  object accordingly
          case 'mouseup':
              return {left: event.clientX,
                      top:  event.clientY};
      }
  }).subscribe(obj =>
      console.log(`Left: ${obj.left}, Top: ${obj.top}`));
```

CODE SAMPLES   Remember that all the code for this chapter can be found in the RxJSinAction GitHub repository, https://github.com/RxJSInAction/rxjs-in-action.

But this sort of behavior should raise some flags as a potential code smell. One of the main reasons to combine observables is that they possess some similarities that you'd like to leverage into simpler code. Introducing more boilerplate code into the mix, only to then switch on type, doesn't serve this purpose; it simply moves the complexity to a different location.

On another note, keep in mind that in FP you try to avoid imperative control statements like if/else whenever possible. Instead, each event should be at least contract compatible with any other, which means that the data emitted from all of them should at least follow the same protocols or structure in order to be consumed by the same observer code. Now, why you should avoid imperative control structures as much as possible has more to do with the notion of using RxJS in a functional style as well as to continue the fluent declaration of an observable chain.

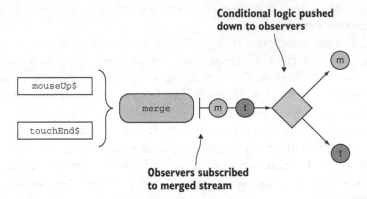

Figure 5.4   The logic that decides how to handle events from the merged streams is pushed down to the observer. The observer code at this point could use `if/else` or `switch` blocks based on type.

FUNCTIONAL VS. IMPERATIVE   Generally speaking, most of the cases using structures like `for/of` or `if/else` can be satisfied by using RxJS operators like `filter()`, `map()`, `reduce()`, `take()`, `first()`, `last()`, and others. In other words, most of the complex tasks for which you need to implement loops and branches are just instances of a certain combination of these operators. A familiar example of this is an array. Most uses of `for/of` and `if/else` statements can be supplanted by a combination of `map()` and `filter()`.

In cases where you absolutely need to apply specific logic, you can insert operators upstream of where the merge occurs in order to create compatible types ahead of time. Instead of forcing observers to use conditional logic to discern between different types of events (figure 5.4), you should make the stream data conformant before the merge (figure 5.5) to make your subscribers happier by avoiding any checks.

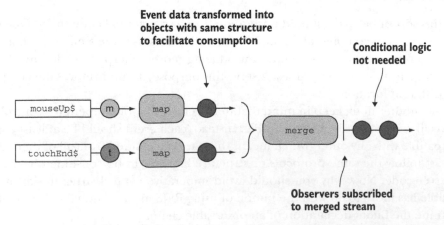

Figure 5.5   Applying an upstream transformation to both streams to normalize the data and facilitate the observer code

Listing 5.2 shows how you can do this with our mouse clicks and touch events example. As you can imagine, the touch interface doesn't exactly correspond to that of the mouse interface, so to make them work together, you need to normalize the events so that you can reuse the same functions to handle the merged stream. You do this in the next listing by creating conformant streams or streams that emit data with similar structure.

Listing 5.2 Normalizing upstream event data merges the streams

```
const conformantMouseUp$ = mouseUp$.map(event => ({        <─┐
  left: event.clientX,                                        │  Converts each type
  top: event.clientY                                          │  upstream before it's
}));                                                          │  merged into the final
                                                              │  stream
const conformantTouchEnd$ = touchEnd$.map(event => ({     <─┘
  left: event.changedTouches[0].clientX,
  top: event.changedTouches[0].clientY,        Merges the converted streams;
}));                                            the observer logic stays the same

Rx.Observable.merge(conformantMouseUp$, conformantTouchEnd$)   <─────────┘
  .subscribe(obj =>
    console.log(`Left: ${obj.left}, Top: ${obj.top}`));
```

It may seem more verbose to create separate streams, but as the complexity of the application grows, updating and managing a switch statement will become a tedious process. By requiring that the source observables be conformant with the expected output interface, you can more easily expand this and continue adding more logic as needed, in case you want to include streams generated from, say, the `pointerup` event of a pointer device, like a pen (https://w3c.github.io/pointerevents). The pointer event commands may have a completely different interface from either the mouse click or the touch events, but you can still use them to control your application by forcing the incoming stream to conform to the interface expected by the subscribe block.

One important point about `merge` that could be confusing to an RxJS beginner is that it will emit all the data that's immediately present in memory from any merged observables. The interleaving happens when events arrive asynchronously, like with `interval()` and mouse movements, but when the data is synchronously loaded, it will emit one entire stream before emitting the next. Consider this code:

```
const source1$ = Rx.Observable.of(1, 2, 3);
const source2$ = Rx.Observable.of('a', 'b', 'c');
Rx.Observable.merge(source1$, source2$).subscribe(console.log);
```

From what you just learned, you might think `merge()` alternates between numbers and letters, but it iterates through all numbers first and then all letters. This is because the data is synchronously available to emit. The same would happen whether you were passing scalar values one at a time, whole arrays, or generators.

Whether data is synchronous or asynchronous, if your goal is to preserve the order of events in the combined streams, then you need to use concatenation.

5.1.2   *Preserve order of events by concatenating streams*

The RxJS merge() operator uses a naïve strategy of outputting all the observable data in the order in which events are received from the source streams. But in other scenarios, you might be more interested in preserving the order of the entire observable sequences when you join them instead of interleaving them. That is, given two observables, you might want to receive all the events from source1$ and then all the events from source2$. This is useful in cases when you'd like to give priority to one type of event versus another. We refer to this type of operation as a *concatenation* of the two streams.

Just as you can concatenate two strings or two arrays, you can also concatenate two streams that will generate a brand-new observable made from the events of both constituent observables—similar to a set union operation. The signature is almost identical to that of the merge operator:

```
const source$ = Rx.Observable.concat(...streams)
```

The behavior of this new observable operator is shown in figure 5.6.

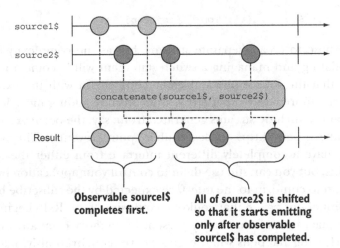

Observable source1$ completes first.

All of source2$ is shifted so that it starts emitting only after observable source1$ has completed.

Figure 5.6 A marble diagram of the concat() operator, which waits for the first observable to complete before subscribing to the next one. In concatenation, the data from both observables is appended rather than interleaved.

It's important to note that a merge differs from a concatenation on one key behavior: whereas the merge() operator will allow you to immediately subscribe to all of the source observables, concat() will subscribe to only one observable at a time. Although it continues to manage the subscriptions to each of the underlying streams, it will hold only a single subscription at a time and process that before the next one in order. You can see this behavior clearly with this simple example:

```
const source1$ = Rx.Observable.range(1, 3).delay(3000);
const source2$ = Rx.Observable.of('a', 'b', 'c');
const result = Rx.Observable.concat(source1$, source2$);
result.subscribe(console.log);
```

Second stream is set to three letters immediately

First stream is delayed by 3 seconds, which means it will start emitting after 3 seconds

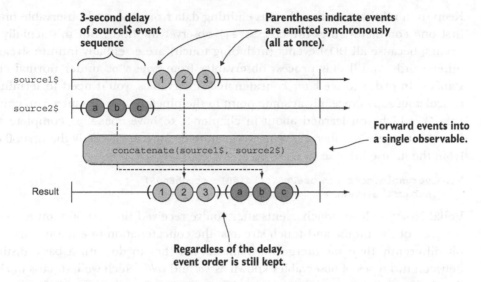

Figure 5.7 Marble diagram showing the interaction of sources with delay. Regardless of the delay offsetting the entire observable sequence, the order of the events in a stream is preserved using `concat`.

Intuitively, because the second stream is delayed by 3 seconds, you'd expect to see the letters a, b, and c emitted first. But because concat() keeps the order, it will complete the first stream before appending the next stream. So you'd see the numbers 1, 2, and 3 before the letters, as shown in figure 5.7.

Consequently, if you were to take the example of merging the touch events and the mouse events, for instance, changing from merge() to concat() would result in very different (possibly undesired) behavior, as figure 5.8 shows.

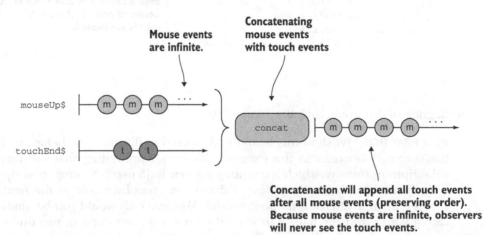

Figure 5.8 The concatenation of an infinite stream with any other stream will only ever emit an event from the first stream.

Keep in mind that `concat()` begins emitting data from a second observable once the first one completes (fires the `complete()` observer method). But this actually never occurs, because all DOM events (including touch) are essentially infinite streams. In other words, you'll only process observables from `mouseUp$` under normal circumstances. In order to see later concatenated observables, you'd need to terminate or cancel `mouseUp$` gracefully at some point in the pipeline. For instance, you could use `take()`, which you learned about in chapter 3, to have `mouseUp$` complete (made finite) after a set number of events were emitted. Say you take only the first 50 events from the mouse interface:

```
Rx.Observable.concat(mouseUp$.take(50), touchEnd$)
   .subscribe(event => console.log(event.type));
```

Voila! Now you'll see touch events after you've received the first 50 mouse events. In the case of the mouse and touch streams, the concatenation operation works a little bit differently than the merge mechanism. This has to do with a basic distinction between two types of observables known as *hot* and *cold*, which we'll discuss in chapter 8. In this case, when you do begin receiving touch events, they're only for events that occurred after the end of the mouse events and not from the beginning offset to the end. Essentially, this use of `concat()` is equivalent to a nested subscription of the following form:

```
mouseUp$
  .take(50)
  .subscribe(
    function next(event) {
      console.log(event.type);        ←——— Handles the first 50 mouse events
    },
    function error(e) {
      console.log(e);
    },                                      Starts the touch stream when mouse
                                            events finish. Any touch events that
    function complete() {                   occurred prior to the first 50 mouse
      touchEnd$.subscribe(          ←——┘    events are missed.
        event => console.log(event.type)
      );
    }
  );
```

A diagram of this would look like figure 5.9.

> **BEST PRACTICE**   We show this sample code merely to illustrate the behavior of the `concat()` operator in this example. We're not promoting that you nest subscriptions this way, which is tempting for new RxJS users. Nesting subscriptions breaks the downstream flow of data from one observable to the next, which is an antipattern in the RxJS model. Also, not only would you be duplicating your efforts by having to write the same observer code in two difference places, but you'd hamper RxJS's optimizations in the pipeline chain by impeding its ability to reuse internal data structures and lazy evaluation.

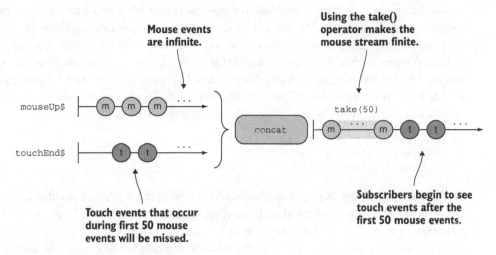

Figure 5.9 Because we've made the `mouseUp$` stream finite, subscribers will see data emitted from `touchEnd$` after the first 50 `mouseUp$` events.

As you can see, the type of strategy employed makes a huge difference in how a downstream observable will behave. It's therefore important to understand that when you combine streams, there's a difference between when a stream is created and when a subscriber subscribes to it. You can use `merge()` when you want to receive the latest event from any observable as it's emitted, whereas `concat()` is useful when you wish to preserve the absolute ordering between observables.

As we mentioned briefly, there will be cases when you'll need to cancel one of the observables and receive data from only another one. Let's look at another combinator, `switch()`.

5.1.3 Switch to the latest observable data

Both `merge` and `concat` propagate the input stream data forward into the pipeline. But suppose you wanted a different behavior, such as cancelling the first sequence when a new one begins emitting. Let's study this simple example:

```
Rx.Observable.fromEvent(document, 'click')    ⟵── Listens for any clicks on the page
   .map(click => Rx.Observable.range(1, 3))    ⟵┐ Maps another observable
   .switch()                           ⟵┐       │ to the source observable
   .subscribe(console.log);             │
                          Uses switch to begin emitting data
                          from the projected observable
```

Running this code logs the numbers 1, 2, 3 to the console after the mouse is clicked. In essence, when the click event occurs, this event is cancelled and replaced by another observable with numbers 1 through 3. In other words, subscribers never see the click event come in—a switch happened.

switch() occurs only as an instance operator, and it's one of the hardest ones to understand because it carries a bit of logic of its own. As you can see from the previous code, switch() takes another observable that has been mapped to the source observable and fuses it into the source observable. The caveat is that each time the source observable emits, switch() immediately unsubscribes from it and begins emitting events from the latest observable that was mapped. To showcase the difference, consider what the same code would look like using merge instead:

```
Rx.Observable.fromEvent(document, 'click')
  .merge(Rx.Observable.range(1, 3))
  .subscribe(console.log);
```

In this case, because the source observable (click events) is not cancelled, observers will receive click events mixed with numbers from 1 through 3. Hence, this sort of behavior can be useful when one stream (a button click, for instance) is used to initiate another stream. At this point, there's no interest in listening for the original stream's data (the button clicks). So switch() is also a suitable operator for our suggested search stream:

```
const search$ = Rx.Observable.fromEvent(inputText, 'keyup')
  .pluck('target', 'value')
  .debounceTime(1000)
  .do(query => console.log(`Querying for ${query}...`))
  .map(query =>
        sendRequest(testData, query)))
  .switch()          ⟵—  Switch operator causes the
  .subscribe(...);        observable stream to switch to
                          the projected observable
```

This is because as soon as the keyup event fires, there's no need to push that event onto the observers; instead, it's best to switch to the search results streams and push that data downstream to any subscribers, which is what gets displayed as search results. As you can see in the code, before calling switch(), you *mapped* (or *projected*) an observable to the source. This terminology is important, and you'll see us repeat it quite a bit in this chapter. At this point, switch() will cancel the previous subscription when the new one comes in. In this way, the downstream observable is always guaranteed to have the latest data by removing operations that have become stale or are no longer of interest. You can visualize this interaction in figure 5.10.

In using the latest value, you guarantee that no cycles will be wasted on data that will be overridden immediately when new data arrives, and you don't have to guard against that same data coming back out of order. Also, the observers don't need to worry about handling events from key presses because those are not of interest and have been suppressed by switch(). Because network requests can be processed and returned out of order, in certain scenarios you could see earlier requests arrive after later ones. If those requests were not excluded from the final stream, then you could see old data overwriting newer data, which is obviously not the desired behavior.

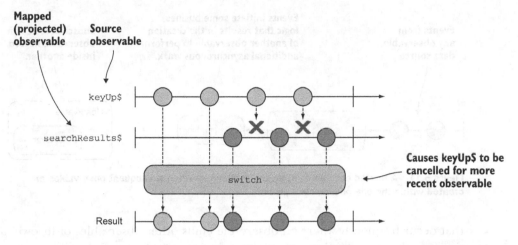

Figure 5.10 A marble diagram of the `switch()` operator, which allows only the most recently received observable to run

> **DISCLAIMER** If `switch()` is somewhat confusing at this point, there's a reason for this. Internally, this operator is addressing a fundamental need in functional programs, which is to flatten nested context types into a single one. In this case, the observable that's mapped to the source internally creates a nested observable object. You'll learn about this in the next section in the form of a single `switchMap()`, and then everything will be clear.

These three operators, `merge()`, `concat()`, and `switch()`, grouped observable data in a flat manner, each with a different strategy. In other words, you're receiving events from one source or another and processing them accordingly. All these operators have higher-order observable equivalents, which handle nested observables.

> **DEFINITION** The term *higher-order observable* originates from the notion of a higher-order function, which can receive other functions as parameters. In this case, we mean observables that receive other observables as arguments.

At this point in the book, you'll make the leap from a novice RxJS developer to a practitioner, and the techniques you're about to learn will drastically shape the way in which you approach reactive and functional programs. We began with the idea that all types of data are treated equally when wrapped with an observable; this includes the observable itself.

5.2 *Unwinding nested observables: the case of mergeMap*

The previous section detailed how streams can have their outputs combined simultaneously. In each case, the input consisted of several streams funneled into a single output stream. Depending on the strategy of combination, you can extract different behaviors from observables, as you saw in the previous section. But there are also cases

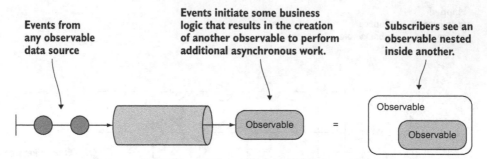

Events from any observable data source

Events initiate some business logic that results in the creation of another observable to perform additional asynchronous work.

Subscribers see an observable nested inside another.

Figure 5.11   A nested observable structure that occurs when subsequent observables are created within the one observable's pipeline.

that occur frequently where an observable emits other observables of its own, a situation we call *nesting the observable*, as shown in figure 5.11.

Nesting observables is useful when certain actions result in or initiate subsequent asynchronous operations whose results need to be brought back into the source observable. Recall that when you map a function to an observable, the result of this function (internally passed through to `subscriber.next()`) gets wrapped into another observable and propagated through. But what happens when the function you're trying to map also returns an observable? In other words, instead of mapping a function that returns some scalar value as you've been doing all along, the mapped function returns another observable—known as *projecting an observable onto another*, or an *observable of observables*. This is by no means a flaw in the design of RxJS; it's an expected and desired behavior.

This situation arises frequently in the world of FP because the protocol of `map()` is that it's a structure-preserving function (for example, `Array.map()` also returns a new array). This is the contractual obligation of the implementing data type, in this case the observable, so that it retains its functor-like behavior. Again, we don't cover functors in this book because they're a more advanced functional programming topic. Suffice it to say that RxJS has already implemented this for you because the `Rx.Observable` type, as you might have guessed, behaves very much like a functor.

Let's see how this can manifest itself in a real-world scenario. In chapter 4, we implemented a simple search box that streamed data from a small, static dataset. In that version, we used `map()` to transform a stream carrying a keyword entered by the user into an array of search results matching the term. Here are the relevant parts of it:

```
const search$ = Rx.Observable.fromEvent(inputText, 'keyup')
   ...
   .map(query => sendRequest(testData, query)))
   .subscribe(...)
```

But consider what would have happened if `sendRequest()` had returned an observable object, as it would have if it was actually invoking an AJAX call. As you know, all

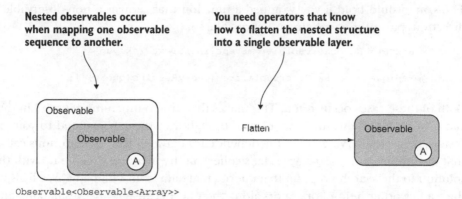

Observable<Observable<Array>>

Figure 5.12 Mapping an observable-returning function to a source observable yields a nested observable type. `switch` can be used to flatten this structure back to a single observable.

operators create new observable instances; as a result, mapping this function will produce values of this type:

```
Observable<Observable<Array>>
```

Now subscribers need to deal with `Observable<Array>` directly instead of the data that's contained within it. This is not the desired behavior.

The `search$` stream is now essentially a nested observable, as shown in figure 5.12. But observers shouldn't be reacting to a layer of wrapped observable values; this is unnecessary exposure or lack of proper encapsulation. They should always receive the underlying data that resulted from applying all of your business rules. So you need to somehow flatten or unwind these layers into a single one.

You can do this in two ways: either you can perform a nested subscribe, wherein you subscribe to the inner observable in the parent's subscription block (bad idea for the same reasons discussed earlier), or you can merge the streams such that `search$` actually appears as a simple stream of search results to any subscriber (better idea). To get there, you need to learn and master the `mergeMap()` operator (previously known as `flatMap()` in RxJS 4).

Unlike `merge()` and `concat()`, `mergeMap()` and others you'll learn about shortly have additional logic under the hood to compress the inner observable back into a single observable structure (you'll learn what this means in a bit):

```
const search$ = Rx.Observable.fromEvent(inputText, 'keyup')
  ...
  .mergeMap(query => sendRequest(testData, query)))    ◁── Merges the outputs and switches to the observable values emitted from the query results
  .subscribe(...)

search$; //-> Observable<Array>    ◁── Subscribers of this stream will deal only with values of type T.
```

The same would hold if you wrapped a function that returns a non-observable value directly as part of the mapping function, like so:

```
const search$ = Rx.Observable.fromEvent(inputText, 'keyup')
  ...
  .mergeMap(query => Rx.Observable.from(queryResults(query)));
```

Both of these cases occur often. This makes this stream much more useful in that you can now reason about the keystrokes as though they directly mapped to your search results, without worrying about the dependency between the asynchronous calls. Now that you understand `mergeMap()`, let's collect all the pieces and come up with the full solution to the search program that queries real data from Wikipedia. We'll also introduce a few other helpful operators along the way. Because it involves making an AJAX call, we'll use RxJS's version of `ajax()`, as well as `appendResults()`, `clearResults()`, and `notEmpty()` from the initial search code from chapter 4 (listing 4.12). The next listing combines most of the concepts you've learned up to now, including debouncing, into a single program.

Listing 5.3   Reactive search solution

```
const searchBox = document.querySelector('#search'); //-> <input>
const results = document.querySelector('#results');  //-> <ul>
const count = document.querySelector('#count');       //-> <label>

const URL = 'https://en.wikipedia.org/w/api.php
             ?action=query&format=json&list=search&utf8=1&srsearch=';
const search$ = Rx.Observable.fromEvent(searchBox, 'keyup')
  .pluck('target','value')
  .debounceTime(500)
  .filter(notEmpty)
  .do(term => console.log(`Searching with term ${term}`))
  .map(query => URL + query)
  .mergeMap(query =>
     Rx.Observable.ajax(query)
        .pluck('response', 'query', 'search')
        .defaultIfEmpty([]))
  .mergeMap(R.map(R.prop('title')))
  .subscribe(arr => {
    count.innerHTML = `${arr.length} results`;
    clearResults(results);
    appendResults(arr, results);
  });
```

Wikipedia's API URL [points to the `const URL` line]

Mapping an observable-returning function and flattening it (or merging it) into the source observable [points to the `.mergeMap(query =>` line]

If the result of the AJAX call happens to be an empty object, converts it to an empty array by default [points to the `.defaultIfEmpty([]))` line]

Extracts all title properties of the resulting response array [points to the `.mergeMap(R.map(R.prop('title')))` line]

Warning: Working with CORS

Throughout the book, we'll make use of several external APIs; if you plan to copy and paste these samples directly into your browser, make sure that you have CORS protection disabled or a plugin for your browser active. If you don't want to worry about these issues, please use the code in the sample repository (https://github.com/RxJSInAction/rxjs-in-action), which uses a simple proxy method to bypass CORS issues.

Figure 5.13   Reactive
search program querying for
"reactive programming"

Figure 5.13 shows how running this program looks with a little CSS.

You just implemented your first sample program, and despite the added complexity, you still hold true to all the principles of immutability and side effect–free coding. You'll continue to tackle problems of different types as you get comfortable with the RxJS operators. This will prepare you for chapter 10, which will show you a complete end-to-end application that integrates RxJS into React and Redux, to create a fully reactive solution.

Where does the notion of flattening data come from?

The notion of flattening data comes from the world of arrays when you need to reduce the levels of a multidimensional array. Here's an example:

```
[[0, 1], [2, 3], [4, 5]].flatten(); //-> [0, 1, 2, 3, 4, 5]
```

JavaScript doesn't actually have an array-flatten method, but you can easily use reduce with subsequent array concatenation to achieve the same effect:

```
[[0, 1], [2, 3], [4, 5]].reduce(function(a, b) {
  return a.concat(b);
}, []); //-> [0, 1, 2, 3, 4, 5]
```

As you can see, flattening is achieved by repeated concatenation at each nested level of the multidimensional array. For this reason, flatten() also goes by the name concatAll().

Instead of rolling your own, use a functional library like Ramda.js to achieve this:

```
R.flatten([[0, 1], [2, 3], [4, 5]]); //-> [0, 1, 2, 3, 4, 5]
```

If you come from an OO background, you might not be accustomed to flattening data structures as a core operation. This is because observables manage and control the data that flows through them—this idea is known as *containerizing data.* There are various benefits to doing this, some of which you've already been exposed to, such as enforcing immutability and side effect–free code, data-handling abstractions to support many event types seamlessly, and using higher-order functions to declaratively chain operators fluently. You want to have all these benefits regardless of how complex or deep your observable graph is.

Working with nested observables is analogous to inserting an array into another array and expecting `map()` and `filter()` to work with just the data inside them. Now, instead of you having to deal with the nested structure explicitly, you allow operators to take care of this for you so that you can reason about your code better. Graphically, the notion of flattening observables means extracting the value from a nested observable and consolidating the nested structure so that the user sees only one level. This process is shown in figure 5.14.

We'll show an example that uses simple arrays so that you can see more clearly the difference between flattening an array and leaving it as is. Consider some simple code that fills in numbers in an array:

```
const source = [1, 2, 3];

source.map(value =>
    Array(value).fill(value));
//-> [[1],[2,2],[3,3,3]]

source.map(value => Array(value).fill(value)).concatAll();
//-> [1,2,2,3,3,3]
```

Mapping a function that returns an array onto an array results in a multidimensional array.

After a call to concatAll (or flatten), the resulting array is single dimensional and much easier to work with.

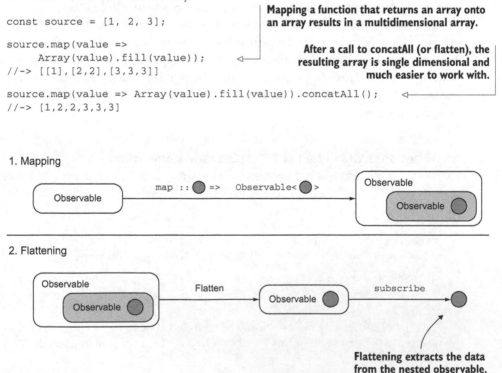

1. Mapping

2. Flattening

Flattening extracts the data from the nested observable.

Figure 5.14 The process of mapping a function onto an observable, resulting in a nested observable, and then flattening to extract its value. You do this so that subscribers deal with only the processed data. Here, `flatten` can be any one of the RxJS operators, such as `switch()` or `merge()`.

Wrapping your head around the idea of observables propagating other observables may take some time, but we guarantee it will come to you naturally by the end of the book. This software pattern is at the root of the FP paradigm and implemented data types known as monads. In simple terms, a monad exposes an interface with three simple requirements that observables satisfy: a unit function to lift values into the monadic context (`of()`, `from()`, and the like), a mapping function (`map()`), and a map-with-flatten function (`flatMap()` or `mergeMap()`).

> **More information about monads**
>
> We don't cover monads in this book, but we encourage you to learn more about them because they're a central pillar of FP. If you're interested in learning more, please read chapter 5 of *Functional Programming in JavaScript* (Manning, 2016) by Luis Atencio.

In the real world, nested streams occur so frequently that for most of the combinatorial operators there exists a set of joint operators so that you don't have to use two every time you need to use switching, merging, and concatenating. We introduced `mergeMap()` in this section, and now we're going to use it to tackle more-complex problems.

5.3 *Mastering asynchronous streams*

Recall that for our initial implementation of our stock ticker widget in chapter 4 we used a simple random-number generator to model the variability of our hypothetical company ABC and its stock price in the market. In this chapter, we'll integrate with a real stock service, such as Yahoo Finance, to fetch data for a given symbol. The task at hand is to use the Yahoo Finance API to query for a company's real stock price in real time so that the user sees updates pushed to the application reflecting changes in the stock's value. This simple-to-use API responds with CSV. To start off, let's use one symbol, Facebook (FB). This time, instead of using RxJS's `ajax()`, we'll show you how to plug in promise-based AJAX calls. The process is roughly outlined in figure 5.15.

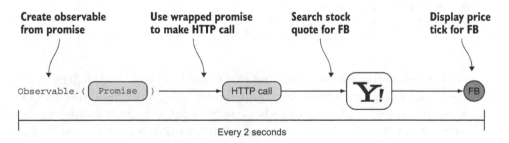

Figure 5.15 Using a promise call to the Yahoo web service for Facebook's stock data

You'll approach this stream by tackling its individual components. The first one you'll need is a stream that uses a promise to query stock data via AJAX, as shown in the following listing.

Listing 5.4   The request quote stream

```
const csv = str => str.split(/,\s*/);                          ◄———  Helper function that
                                                                      creates an array
const webservice = 'http://download.finance.yahoo.com                 from a CSV string
/d/quotes.csv?s=$symbol&f=sa&e=.csv';                          ◄———
                                                                      Yahoo Finance REST API
const requestQuote$ = symbol =>                                       link and requesting output
    Rx.Observable.fromPromise(                                        format to be CSV
        ajax(webservice.replace(/\$symbol/, symbol)))          ◄———
    .map(response => response.replace(/"/g, ''))                      Uses the promise
    .map(csv);                                                        based ajax() to
                                                                      query the service
```

Cleans up
and parses
the CSV
output

The CSV response string emitted by the Yahoo API needs to be cleaned up and parsed into a string. Here, you create a function that returns an observable capable of fetching data from a remote service and publishing the result. You'll combine this with a two-second interval to poll and provide the real-time feed:

```
const twoSecond$ = Rx.Observable.interval(2000);
```

Now, you have two isolated streams that need to be combined, or mapped one to the other. You can use `mergeMap()` to accomplish this. You can create a function that takes any stock symbol and creates a stream that requests stock quote data every 2 seconds. You'll call this resulting observable function `fetchDataInterval$`, as shown here.

Listing 5.5   Mapping one stream into another

```
const fetchDataInterval$ = symbol => twoSecond$
    .mergeMap(() => requestQuote$(symbol));
```

All that's left to do now is call this function with any stock symbol, in this case FB:

```
fetchDataInterval$('FB')
  .subscribe(([symbol, price])=>
     console.log(`${symbol}, ${price}`)
  );
```

Notice how declarative, succinct, and easy to read this code is. At a glance, it describes the process of taking a two-second poll and mapping a function to fetch stock data—as simple as that. This works well for a single item, but when scaling out to multiple items, it's common to lift the collection of stock symbols to search for into an observable context and then map other operations to it. The next listing shows how to use `mergeMap()` again to fetch quotes for companies: Facebook (FB), Citrix Systems (CTXS), and Apple Inc. (AAPL).

Listing 5.6 Updating multiple stock symbols

```
const symbols$ = Rx.Observable.of('FB', 'CTXS', 'AAPL');

const ticks$ = symbols$.mergeMap(fetchDataInterval$);

ticks$.subscribe(
  ([symbol, price]) => {
    let id = 'row-' + symbol.toLowerCase();
    let row = document.querySelector(`#${id}`);
    if(!row) {
        addRow(id, symbol, price);
    }
    else {
        updateRow(row, symbol, price);
    }
  },
  error => console.log(error.message));
```

For brevity, we won't show the body of these functions that simply manipulate HTML to add or update rows. You can visit the code repository to get all the details.

Essentially, the semantic meaning of `mergeMap()` is to transform the nature of the stream (map) by merging a projected observable. This operator is incredibly useful because now you can use it to orchestrate a complex business process containing multiple observable levels. The program flow looks like figure 5.16.

This program is simple and high level, but it accomplishes a lot:

1 You start by lifting the stock symbols involved in your component into a stream so that you can begin to fetch their quote data. This technique of lifting or wrapping a scalar value into an observable is beneficial because you can initiate

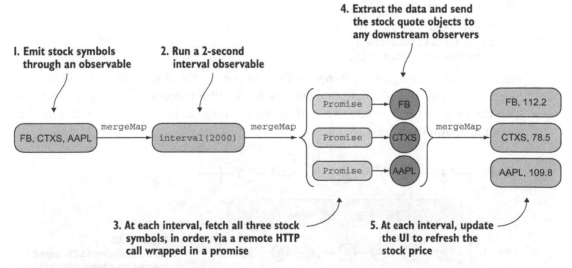

Figure 5.16 Steps to implement the stock ticker widget with multiple symbols and a refresh interval of 2 seconds. Every step involves the use of nested observables that are merged or concatenated accordingly as the information gets transformed into different types of streams. At the end, subscribers will see only the scalar values representing the stock symbols and their respective prices.

asynchronous processes involving these values. Also, you unlock the power of RxJS when involving blocks of code related to these values.

2 You map an interval (every 2 seconds) to this observable, so that you cycle through the stock symbols every minute. This gives it the appearance of real time.

3 At each interval, you execute AJAX calls for each stock symbol against the Yahoo web service.

4 Finally, you map functions that strip out unnecessary company data and leave just the stock symbol and price, before emitting it to subscribers.

The result is that the subscribers see the data pairs shown in figure 5.17 emitted every 2 seconds.

There's room for improvement here, because in cases when there's not a whole lot of fluctuation in a company's stock price, you don't want to bother updating the DOM unnecessarily. One optimization you can do is to allow the stream to flow down to the observer only when a change is detected, by means of a filtering operator called `distinctUntil-Changed()`. First, we'll show you how this operator works, and then we'll include it in our code. Here's an example of using it with a simple input:

Stocks

Symbol	Total
FB	128.40 USD
CTXS	85.27 USD
AAPL	113.02 USD

Figure 5.17   A Stocks table that updates with real stock symbols every 2 seconds

```
Rx.Observable.of('a', 'b', 'c', 'a', 'a', 'b', 'b')
  .distinctUntilChanged()
  .subscribe(console.log);
```

`distinctUntilChanged()` belongs in the category of filtering operators and emits a sequence of distinct, contiguous elements. So the fifth element, a, is skipped because it's the same as the previous one, and the same for the last, b. You can see this mechanism in action in figure 5.18.

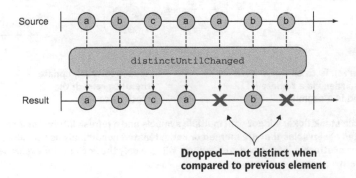

Dropped—not distinct when compared to previous element

Figure 5.18
`distinctUntilChanged()` returns an observable that emits all items emitted by the source observable that are distinct when compared to the previous item.

This is perfect for the task at hand. Adding this feature to your stream involves using it with a key selector function, a function that instructs the operator what to use as the property to compare:

```
const fetchDataInterval$ = symbol => twoSecond$
    .mergeMap(() => requestQuote$(symbol))
    .distinctUntilChanged(([symbol, price]) => price);  <──┐
```

Performs a distinct comparison based on price, so that the DOM will get updated only when the price changes

Now, you'll update the DOM strictly on a price change, which is much more optimal than doing it naïvely every 2 seconds.

You were able to combine observable flows and solve this problem without creating a single external variable, conditional, or `for` loop. Because this task involves the combination of multiple streams—iterating through the symbols, a timed interval, and remote HTTP requests with promises—you had to unwind nested streams using a combination of a couple of nested `mergeMap()` operators to convert the intricate business logic into a more flattened and linear sequence of data that observers subscribe to and easily consume. As we mentioned previously, it's much more efficient and fluent to do it this way, rather than to subscribe to each nested stream at each step. Using RxJS operators to handle this, as well as all the business logic, is always preferred over sending raw nested observables to any downstream observers.

As you can see from this example, RxJS's combinatorial operators like `mergeMap()` are about more than simply reducing the number of subscribe blocks you have to write and the number of subscriptions to keep. They also serve as an important way to craft more-intricate flows to support complex business logic. By leveraging nested streams, you can think of each block within a nest as a mini application (that can be partitioned out into its own stream, as you learned previously). This is a clear sign of modularity in your code and something that functional programs exhibit extremely well. By breaking down problems into individual, independent blocks, you can create code that's more modular and composable. Now that we've covered merging complex observable flows, let's look at a more complex example.

Aside from `mergeMap()`, other operators work in a similar manner but with a slightly different flavor driven by the behavior of the composed function, whether it be `switch()`, `merge()`, or `concat()`, depending on what you're trying to accomplish. Table 5.1 describes the three joint operators we'll use in this book.

Table 5.1 A breakdown of the three most used RxJS joint operators

Split operator	Joint operator	Description
`map()...merge()`	`mergeMap()`	Projects an observable-returning function to each item value in the source observable and flattens the output observable. You might know this operator by `flatMap()`, as used in previous versions of RxJS.

Table 5.1   A breakdown of the three most used RxJS joint operators *(continued)*

Split operator	Joint operator	Description
map()...concatAll()	concatMap()	Similar to mergeMap() with the merging happening serially; in other words, each observable waits for the previous one to complete. Why not map()...concat()? We'll explain this disparity shortly.
map()...switch()	switchMap()	Similar to mergeMap() as well but emitting only values from the recently projected observable. In other words, it switches to the projected observable emitting its most recent values, cancelling any previous inner observables. You might know this operator by flatMapLatest(), as used in previous versions of RxJS. We'll come back to this operator in chapter 6.

Now that you've mastered handling nested observables, let's move on to other types of higher-order observable combinations, continuing with concatMap().

5.4   *Drag and drop with concatMap*

We've looked at two ways of composing streams such that they produce a single output stream. In each case, the resulting stream appears identical to an observer. Both

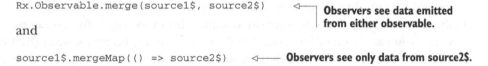

```
Rx.Observable.merge(source1$, source2$)
```
Observers see data emitted from either observable.

and

```
source1$.mergeMap(() => source2$)
```
Observers see only data from source2$.

result in observables that return a type compatible with either source. As we mentioned before, this is entirely up to you because JavaScript won't enforce that observables wrap values of the same type, as statically typed languages will.

But the behavior of these two approaches is slightly different. In the former case, you create a set of simultaneous streams; this means that both streams are subscribed to at the same time and the resulting observable can output from either observable—both are active simultaneously.

Sequential streams, on the other hand, are streams in which the output of one stream generates a new one. In the second case, the observer won't receive any events from the first stream; an observer will only see the results of the observable projected by mergeMap(). By combining sequential and simultaneous streams, you can make fairly complex logic relatively easily.

One canonical example of a sequential stream is drag and drop, present in most modern web content management systems and customizable dashboards. Implementing this behavior in vanilla JavaScript is fairly difficult to get right because it involves keeping track of fast-changing states with multiple targets and interaction rules. Using streams, you can implement this in a somewhat streamlined manner.

To implement drag and drop, you need to first identify the three types of mouse events that are necessary for basic drag and drop. First, you need to know when the mouse button is clicked, because this indicates that the drag has started, and then the mouse-button-up event to determine when it has stopped, because this indicates a drop. In order to track the drag, you need to capture the mouse-move event as well. You'll need only those three events (mouseup, mousemove, and mousedown); each, of course, modeled as a stream.

A drag starts when the user clicks and stops only when the mouse button is released or until the mouseup event fires. As the mouse is moved with the button down, the object is being dragged; it also moves in a fluent manner, so you'll anticipate performing a side effect by manipulating the DOM element. When the button is released, you drop that object into the coordinates of the location of the mouse on the screen—thus terminating the mousemove event. As before, the gist is to combine these streams, representing the three mouse events emitting data.

First, you'll create streams from the different types of events you're interested in, as shown in the following listing.

Listing 5.7 Streams needed to implement drag and drop with a mouse

A reference to the panel or target you want to drag (My Stocks widget)

Observable for mousedown events on the target

```
const panel = document.querySelector('#dragTarget');

const mouseDown$ = Rx.Observable.fromEvent(panel, 'mousedown');
const mouseUp$ = Rx.Observable.fromEvent(document, 'mouseup');
const mouseMove$ = Rx.Observable.fromEvent(document, 'mousemove');
```

Observable for mouseup events over the entire page

Observable for mousemove events over the entire page

After you've established the streams that will be used to control the drag, you can build logic around it. In the next step, you need to implement the logic, first to handle detecting a click on a drag target that will initiate the drag event. Then, you need to have the element follow the mouse around the screen until it's released and dropped somewhere. You've learned in this chapter how you can use the RxJS joint operators to combine and flatten multiple nested streams so that subscribers see a simple representation of the data flowing through the stream. So you need an order-preserving operator (the mouse is pressed, then dragged, and finally released), just like concat(), but you also need to be able to flatten the observable that's pushed through it. Care to take a guess? Yes, this is the job of concatMap(). This operator works just like mergeMap() but performs the additional logic of retaining the order of the observable sequences, instead of interleaving the events.

The logic for handling the drag is made up of a sequence of streams that emit mouse events together, as shown in the next listing.

Listing 5.8 Drag-and-drop stream logic

```
const drag$ = mouseDown$.concatMap(() => mouseMove$.takeUntil(mouseUp$));

drag$.subscribe(event => {
  panel.style.left = event.clientX + 'px';
  panel.style.top = event.clientY + 'px';
});
```

Sorry, were you expecting more? This is all that's required to drag the stock widget around the page. If you think about it—likely, you've implemented drag and drop before—you're probably aware that using plain JavaScript would take much more code, using many more variables to store some transient state. This code is not only shorter, but it also has a higher level of abstraction, because all side effects were pushed elegantly onto the observer.

Here, we've introduced another variation of the `take()` operator called `take-Until()`. The name is straightforward; this operator also belongs to the filtering category and allows the source observable to emit values until the provided notifier observable emits a value. The notion of notifier observables occurs frequently in RxJS, to be used as signals to either start or stop some kind of interaction; in this case, to take any `mousemove` concatenated with the `mousedown` events until a `mouseup` event is fired. This is the gist behind dragging.

Here's a simple use of `takeUntil()` so that you can fully appreciate how it works. This example starts a simple one-second interval, which will print values to the console until the user clicks a button. This could be useful to implement a site inactivity feature, for instance:

```
const interval$ = Rx.Observable.interval(1000);
const clicks$ = Rx.Observable.fromEvent(document, 'click');

interval$.takeUntil(clicks$)           ◁──┐  As soon as a click event is emitted,
    .subscribe(                              the interval stream is cancelled.
        x   => console.log(x),
        err => console.log(`Error: ${err}`),
        ()  => console.log('OK, user is back!'));
```

The other benefit of RxJS's unified computing model is that if you were implementing drag through a touch interface, it would just be a matter of changing the event names in the stream declaration to `touchmove`, `touchstart`, and `touchend`, respectively. The business logic stays the same, and the code would work exactly the same!

There's a small caveat here. From our earlier discussions, you might be led to believe that calling `map()...concat()` would work in a fashion similar to the split operator `concatMap()`. You might intuitively think that this code would work exactly the same way as listing 5.7:

```
const drag$ = mouseDown$.map(() =>
    mouseMove$.takeUntil(mouseUp$))        Using the instance operator
    .concat();                          ◁─┘ concat() in place of concatMap()
```

Unfortunately, it doesn't, because there's no mechanism here to flatten the observable type running through the stream. Recall that the `concat()` instance method takes a number of observables and concatenates them in order. It's not designed to work with an observable of observable type—a higher-order observable. For this, you need to use a variation of `concat()` that works with nested observables and also flattens them, called `concatAll()` (just as you implemented with arrays before). So the RxJS nomenclature here is a little inconsistent, because `concatMap()` is really `map()...concatAll()`.

Now this code works just like listing 5.7:

```
const drag$ = mouseDown$
  .map(() => mouseMove$.takeUntil(mouseUp$))
  .concatAll();
```

Figure 5.19 is a visual of how `concatAll()` works.

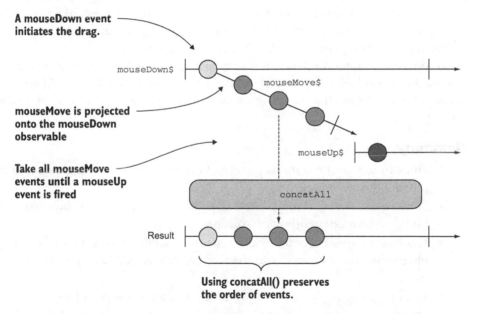

Figure 5.19 Workings of `concatAll()` combining three mouse events. This operator not only preserves order but can also flatten a sequence of nested observables. Also, the use of `takeUntil()` causes `mouseMove$` to cancel as soon as `mouseUp$` emits a value.

In the code repository, you'll find a more complete version of this example, which we simplified for the sake of highlighting the important elements. In reality, you can add any number of bells and whistles to this functionality, and for our sample application, we added some helper code for dealing with CSS. For instance, if you wanted to prevent users from accidentally dragging a widget by allowing them to confirm the drag, you could just filter the mouseup stream to include this confirmation:

```
const drag$ = mouseDown$.
  concatMap(() =>
    mouseMove$.takeUntil(
      mouseUp$.filter(() => confirm('Drop widget here?')))));
```

It's as simple as that. The examples that we've discussed in this chapter are only a small portion of the total number of use cases we could support. As we mentioned at the outset, almost all non-trivial applications will use flattened streams, so understanding them is a huge step toward understanding RxJS.

In this chapter, we entered more complex territory by combining the outputs of multiple streams. This was key for us to begin implementing more real-world tasks instead of just showcasing the different operators. Initially, we looked at static streams that merely had their outputs piped together to appear as a single stream. But as a more complex case, we examined how to nest observables within each other and then flatten the result to deliver the appropriate data to observers. We discussed how making more-complex applications, especially those that deal with UIs and other state machines, will almost always necessitate the use of nested or merged streams. Finally, we explored a couple of practical examples of flattening and merging that helped you understand the design principle behind projecting observables.

In the next chapter, we'll continue expanding on this topic by examining how you can further coordinate observables and have them work together. We'll also explore other interesting ways that observables combine, using an operator called `combine-Latest()`.

5.5   *Summary*

- You can merge the outputs of several observables into a single stream to simplify subscription logic.
- You can use different merge strategies that contain different behavior for combining streams, depending on your needs.
- You can interleave streams with `merge()`, cancel and switch to a new projected observable with `switch()`, or preserve entire observable sequences in order by using `concat()`.
- You can use split operators to combine and flatten a series of nested observable streams.
- You can combine and project observables into a source observable using the higher-order operators such as `mergeMap()` and `concatMap()`.
- You implemented an auto-suggest search box.
- You implemented a live stock ticker with deeply nested streams.
- You implemented drag and drop using stream concatenation.

6

Coordinating
business processes

This chapter covers

- Synchronizing the emission of several observables
- Using observables as signaling devices
- Building complex interactions from multiple inputs
- Spawning streams simultaneously
- Streamlining database storage operations using observables

The previous chapter examined how converting multiple observables into a single one can simplify their consumption and reduce the management overhead. This mechanism is important because it allows you to reuse a single subscription to handle data that's being transformed or created by the composition of multiple tasks, such as AJAX requests, business logic transformations, timers, and others. The various strategies for how these different types of merging operations (merge(), concat(), or switch()) occurred, as in whether we cared about the order of the events or cancelled others, was determined by the operator itself—each had a different flavor. We also showed examples like search and drag and drop that use the output of one observable to signal the start or completion of another.

In this chapter, we'll continue with this theme and expand where we left off in chapter 5. You'll learn that you don't always have to care about the result of an observable if you simply want to leverage the semantics of when one emits to cause some other process to begin. Furthermore, we'll explore scenarios where events from multiple streams can be aggregated and combined so that the resulting observable is emitting the sum of two observables: in other words, two streams cooperating with each other, working together toward a common goal. To illustrate this, in this chapter, we'll tackle problems that involve authentication, data persistence, and stream parallelization. The interplay of using observables as a signaling device and the more interesting uses we can achieve through joining observables forms the foundation of the more complex logic you're likely to see in the wild. In order for you to understand how observables can collaborate, you must first understand how to tap into their lifecycle.

6.1   *Hooking into the observable lifecycle*

The representational power of a single observable is limited. Although you can create a stream to represent just about any data type, a single stream can contain logic for only a single set of inputs and outputs, like the results of a series of keystrokes or an individual web request. Even using the combinational operators from the previous chapters like mergeMap(), there's still only a single task to which a observable can be assigned without introducing side effects. Remember that in the last chapter you were able to combine mouse and touch events to support drag and drop. Trying to also support, say, free-form drawing using the same stream would be very difficult because it would no longer be clear which use case an observer should be expecting. It's important to realize that, by design, a single stream can carry out only a single task; therefore, performing multiple actions whether serially or in parallel depends on how you combine streams.

By now, you've learned how to transform and filter data in flight, even coming from different sources. Separating tasks into loosely coupled streams is advantageous because you can compartmentalize their respective logic without bleeding state into other areas of the application—we call this *upstream compartmentalization* or *conformance*. You saw examples of this in the mouse and touch code when you needed to make two streams conformant to a single observer block. You could, alternatively, combine the stream data as is and group all your business logic into the observer, or *downstream compartmentalization*. We highly recommend the former over the latter.

But there are times when those operations are insufficient because you need several streams to interact while also maintaining the same semantically easy-to-understand flow of code that you've come to expect from RxJS. So instead of creating separate streams and building the scaffolding to connect them yourself, you learned in the previous chapter how to combine and map observables to other observables. You did this for real-world tasks such as smart search, a stock widget, and others. In this chapter, you'll continue building on those techniques and continue the theme of observables working in unison to achieve a certain goal.

6.1.1 Web hooks and the observer pattern

RxJS's `Observable` type is comparable to an `EventEmitter` data type, which we briefly mentioned in chapter 1, in that both belong to a general class of objects known as *event hooks*. Event hooks are just a way of targeting certain points in an object's lifecycle with the objective of triggering further actions. When an action associated with a hook is triggered, you say that the hook has *fired*. Event hooks can operate within or beyond the confines of a single application. For instance, GitHub, the most popular version control repository for hosting code, provides access to a whole slew of external hooks that allow multiple services to coordinate with events such as the creation of pull requests, new commits, or branches. Each time an action is performed, the associated event hooks will fire and any listeners will receive those events, as shown in figure 6.1.

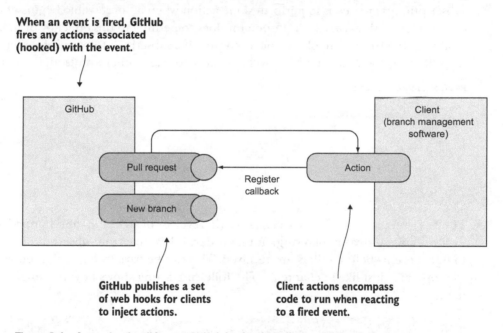

When an event is fired, GitHub fires any actions associated (hooked) with the event.

GitHub

Pull request

New branch

Register callback

Action

Client (branch management software)

GitHub publishes a set of web hooks for clients to inject actions.

Client actions encompass code to run when reacting to a fired event.

Figure 6.1 A couple of well-known GitHub hooks that clients can plug logic into

In general, event hooks provide two main benefits:

- They allow the developer of the application to retain control over what constitutes a hook, thereby maintaining final say over where and when events will be fired.
- They allow third parties to execute arbitrary code without having to worry about detecting internal system implementation.

It's not hard to realize that event hooks are just another manifestation of the observer pattern omnipresent in RxJS. Similarly, every observable also has a set of events, or hooks, in its lifecycle that can be plugged into, all of which should be familiar to you by now:

- Observable start (subscription)
- Observable stop (completion or error)
- Observable next (normal event)

6.1.2 Hooked on observables

Let's discuss each one a bit further and offer some operators that work during these stages. The first item, the observable start (or the onSubscribe hook), may not be as obvious as the other two, which you've seen in some form several times up to this point, but it's also perhaps the easiest to understand. The goal of listening to when a subscription is created is to perform some action when an observable begins emitting events. Hence, the startWith() operator does something to this effect by prepending a value to the front of an observable each time it's subscribed to by an observer. So in the following code, the number 0 will appear before any other events on the console:

```
Rx.Observable.range(1, 5)
  .startWith(0)
  .subscribe(console.log);
//-> 0
     1
     2
     3
     4
     5
```

The startWith() operator is a concat() (in reverse) of all of the values provided to it with the source stream following, in that order. It leverages the subscription behavior to inject events before others are received. This can be trivially implemented as a custom operator just like in chapter 3. The following listing shows how you might implement it.

Listing 6.1 Hooking into the start of a stream

```
function startWith(value) {
  return Rx.Observable.create(subscriber => {      ⟵ Uses the factory method
    let source = this;                                to create the stream
    try {
      subscriber.next(value);      ⟵ Always emits the value
    }                                 before anything else
    catch(err) {
      subscriber.error(err);
    }
    return source.subscribe(subscriber);      ⟵ Emits the rest of the stream
  });
};

Rx.Observable.prototype.startWith = startWith;
```

CODE SAMPLES   Remember that all the code for this chapter can be found in the RxJSinAction GitHub repository: https://github.com/RxJSInAction/rxjs-in-action.

This operator makes sure that every time the stream is subscribed to, it produces that value first. Now, normally you wouldn't reinvent your own startWith() because RxJS already implements the necessary hooks for you; all you have to do is inject any function you want. But this serves to show how extensible observables are.

On the opposite side of the spectrum, you can also think of the completion event as its own kind of event. It occurs when invoking the observer's complete() method when some observable finishes and before the subscription is disposed of. As you've seen all along, this hook is used to perform all of your side effect logic, operations outside the scope of the observable (such as logging to the console, printing data to the screen, writing to a database), and others.

RXJS FINALLY   RxJS's error-handling mechanism also introduces the finally() operator. Semantically similar to the traditional finally block in JavaScript, this operator is the last step in the observable lifecycle, regardless of whether any errors occurred. The function passed to the finally operator will be executed when the observable is shutting down for any reason, so even if the observable terminates with an exception, the block will still be run. This gives you the opportunity to recover from errors and clean up any necessary resources. We'll cover error handling and all of the wonderful things you can do to recover from errors in chapter 7.

In addition, you can combine logic that's tied to the start and end of an observable. You can do this with a new operator, called using(). Figure 6.2 demonstrates how this operator works.

This operator (using()) takes two parameters: a function that creates a disposable resource (like an object) and a function that creates an observable. The created object is called a *disposable* because it provides the mechanism to clean itself up—an unsubscribe() method. Both of these functions are known as *factory functions* in RxJS parlance. The resource is tied to the lifecycle of the observable created by this function, so that when the latter is disposed of, so is the resource. When an observer subscribes to the observable returned from using(), the first factory function is invoked to create an instance of the resource. The resource is then passed to the second factory function as a parameter, and that second factory function returns the actual observable that will be subscribed to. Disposing of the resource is as simple as disposing of the stream through normal means. When the subscription goes through the disposal process, it will also attempt to dispose of the resource that was created by the resource factory. The completion of the observable will also attempt to dispose of the resource, whichever comes first. Essentially, what you're doing is linking the lifespan of an object using an observable.

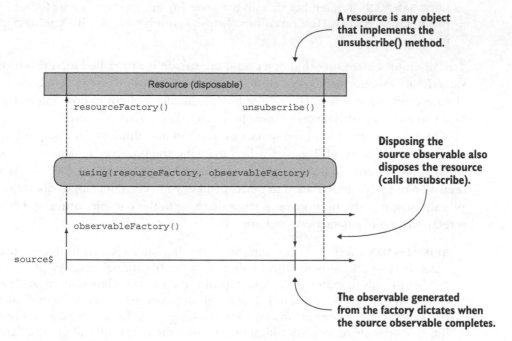

Figure 6.2   The using() operator controls the lifespan of a resource object (created via a resourceFactory()) through the lifespan of an observable (created via an observableFactory()).

Here's an example that will help you understand how it works. Consider an arbitrary disposable resource object, called DisposableResource:

```
class DisposableResource {
  constructor(value) {
    this.value = value;
    this.disposed = false;
  }

  getValue() {
    if (this.disposed) {
      throw new Error('Object is disposed');
    }
    return this.value;
  }

  unsubscribe() {                          ◁─── A disposable resource
    if (!this.disposed) {                        must provide an
      this.disposed = true;                      implementation for the
      this.value = null;                         unsubscribe() behavior.
    }
    console.log('Disposed');
  }
}
```

You can tie the behavior of this object and its state with the lifespan of any observable with using(), as follows:

```
const source$ = Rx.Observable.using(          ◁——  using() receives two
  ()=> new DisposableResource(42),                  parameters: a resource
  resource => Rx.Observable.interval(1000)          object and an observable.
);

const subscription = source$.subscribe(
    next => console.log(`Next: ${next}`),
    err  => console.log(`Error: ${err}`),
    ()   => console.log('Completed')
);                                             Seconds later, you unsubscribe from
                                               the source, which will unsubscribe
//...                                          from the observable managing the
subscription.unsubscribe();          ◁——       resource as well as the resource itself.
```

Running this code will begin emitting one value every second. Seconds later (after subscription but before emission), you unsubscribe from the source. This cleans up the resource observable as well as the DisposableResource instance by calling its unsubscribe method.

The idea behind it is that you often have resources that are completely subject to the lifespan of the observable. In order to hook into this stage, the only requirement is that the object you plug in must be disposable-like, which is to say that it must declare an unsubscribe() method in order to be cleaned up properly if needed. As an example, suppose you want to manage the login session of the user through an observable. When the user logs in, you can create a session token that can be stored in the cookies that keep track of the authenticated user session. But when the user logs out or closes the window, the session needs to be deleted. The closing of the browser signals an event that you can listen for, so you can use observables for this.

First, you need to create an object that will manage the lifecycle of the session token, similar to the previous code sample. Upon construction, it will set the session to expire in 24 hours, as shown here.

Listing 6.2 SessionDisposable object implementing the dispose functionality

```
class SessionDisposable {
  constructor(sessionToken) {
    this.token = sessionToken;
    this.disposed = false;
    let expiration = moment().add(1, 'days').toDate();   ◁——
    document.cookie = `session_token=${sessionToken};
        expires=${expiration.toUTCString()}`;            ◁——
    console.log('Session created: ' + this.token);
  }
                                                   Adds the
  getToken() {                                     cookie
    return this.token;
  }

  unsubscribe() {              ◁—— Clears the cookie
```

Creates a cookie with an expiration date 24 hours from now, using the popular moment.js library to manipulate dates easily (installation instructions found in appendix A)

```
        if (!this.disposed) {
            this.disposed = true;
            this.token = null;
            document.cookie = 'session_token=; expires=Thu, 01 Jan 1970
                00:00:00 GMT';
            console.log('Ended session! This object has been disposed.');
        }
    }
}
```

The most important aspect to note from this class is the declaration of the unsubscribe()
method, so that objects of this type conform to the disposable specification.

> **DISPOSE OR UNSUBSCRIBE**   The terms *dispose* and *unsubscribe* are interchange-
> able. The notion of disposing was used predominantly in RxJS 4, so the termi-
> nology became part of the RxJS jargon. RxJS 5 changes this to *unsubscribe*, yet
> it's still easier to say *disposable* than *unsubscribable*.

If you have a Java or C# background, this is analogous to saying that your class implements the Disposable interface. The logic here is simple; it only resets the value of
the token and sets the time back to the epoch (01/01/1970) so that the browser
deletes it before closing. Now, let's tie the SessionDisposable object to a stream. For
this example, you'll be using the using() operator to construct an observable sequence
that depends on an object whose lifetime is tied to the resulting observable sequence's
lifetime; in other words, you'll make one stream dependent on another one. This
using() operator takes a factory function that creates the SessionDisposable object
and a second method that makes that object available to the stream.

Here's how you can use using() to manage a session token available for the duration of a countdown.

Listing 6.3   Managing a temporary session token with using()

```
function generateSessionToken() {                    ◁──── Simple function to
    return 'xyxyxyxy'.replace(/[xy]/g, c => {              generate a random
        return Math.floor(Math.random() * 10);            session token
    });
}

const $countDownSession = Rx.Observable.using(         Attaches the session
    () => new SessionDisposable(generateSessionToken()),  ◁── to the lifespan of this
    () => Rx.Observable.interval(1000)                    observable
        .startWith(10)
        .scan(val => val - 1)          When this subscription completes,
        .take(10)                      the subordinate session disposable
);                                     token will be disposed of and the
                                       cookie deleted.
$countDownSession.subscribe(console.log);   ◁──┘
```

With this code, your user's login state is now tied into the lifetime of the session, such
that when the user closes the window or logs out (thereby unsubscribing from the

subscription), they're also logged out of the application. This kind of pattern is used a lot in e-commerce sites where you need to perform some action within a certain time span. This kind of coordination takes advantage of the hooks to create side effects around the observable, but you can do much more by incorporating more streams into the mix.

> **ABOUT THE RX.OBSERVABLE.USING() OPERATOR** The using operator actually comes from C#, where a using(resource){ ... } block is a synchronous construct that manages the lifetime of a resource by invoking the garbage collector and cleaning up the resource once the inner block (between the curly braces) exits.

Using a disposable object allowed you to tap into RxJS's unsubscription mechanism. It turns out that you can handle many different use cases when observables coordinate with others through signals.

Another form of coordination occurs when multiple streams join together to produce a result. You learned in the previous chapters about combination operators such as merge(), switch(), and concat(), and we briefly introduced combineLatest(). In the areas of signaling and coordination, combineLatest() can have many practical effects. Let's spend more time exploring how important this operator is when it comes to parallel streams.

6.2 Joining parallel streams with combineLatest and forkJoin

Building asynchronous flows is a difficult endeavor, because each possible permutation of data arrival times—which you can never guarantee—must be accounted for. Using the browser's multiple connections, you can retrieve some of the data in parallel. But when data is causally linked, it needs to be fetched serially. In this section, we'll show you how to use RxJS to coordinate between observable streams that can originate from independent and dependent actions. That is to say, a stream's data can come from events causally linked to other data sources (dependent), like a button click that kicks off an AJAX request, or it can be run in parallel with other streams (independent), like simultaneously invoking two AJAX requests. There are ways to do this with plain-vanilla JavaScript using our long-lost friends, callbacks and Promises. Consider writing an event handler for a button that, when clicked, queries two remote data sources for data using an ajax() function with a callback:

```
button.addEventListener('click', () => {
   let result1, result2 = {};
   ajax('/source1', data => {
     result1 = data;
   });

   ajax('/source2', data => {
     result2 = data;
   });
```

```
    setTimeout(() => {
      processResults(result1, result2);
    }, arbitraryWaitTimeMs);
});
```

**Would need to be long enough
so that both AJAX calls have
enough time to finish**

Of course, the chances of this working are slim to none because you can never predict how long both AJAX calls will take. Other options include writing custom waiting routines based on setInterval() and semaphores, yet they're convoluted and invasive to the business logic. This code would allow both AJAX requests to happen in parallel, but waiting and combining the results later is difficult without proper wait semantics. Inserting sleep functions into a single-threaded JavaScript code is frowned on, because browsers may deem your scripts unresponsive. In order for this to work, you have to either sacrifice parallelism and nest your AJAX calls or create a variable visible at a higher scope. Neither of these solutions is terribly wieldy:

```
button.addEventListener('click', () => {
  ajax('/source1', result1 => {
    ajax('/source2', result2 => {
      processResults(result1, result2);
    });
  });
});
```

Or:

```
button.addEventListener('click', () => {
  let firstResult;
  ajax('/source1', result => {
    if (firstResult) processResults(result, firstResult);
    else firstResult = result;
  });
  ajax('/source2', result => {
    if (firstResult) processResults(firstResult, result);
    else firstResult = result;
  });
});
```

And just in case you're thinking about this, we'll mention that using observables this way goes against the RxJS philosophy—it's an antipattern. What we mean to say is that you could think of nesting subscribe() blocks like this:

```
click$.subscribe(() => {
  source1$.subscribe(result1 => {
    source2$.subscribe(result2 => {
      processResults(result1, result2);
    });
  });
});
```

But just like the previous snippet, this would lead you to the very familiar callback hell you're trying to stay away from in the first place. In addition, this solution would apply

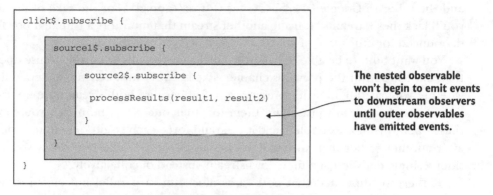

```
click$.subscribe {

   source1$.subscribe {

      source2$.subscribe {

      processResults(result1, result2)

      }

   }

}
```

The nested observable won't begin to emit events to downstream observers until outer observables have emitted events.

Figure 6.3   The issue with nested subscription blocks

only if the inner observables were eagerly loaded, which is not the case. Consequently, the inner subscriptions would begin executing only after the outer subscription had produced its first value. This makes your code blocks dependent and tightly coupled to each other, not parallel, as shown in figure 6.3.

In the previous chapter, you learned that you can project observables using operators such as mergeMap() and switchMap(), but these won't work either, for two reasons:

- Nesting observables implies causality: that a source observable dictates how the other executes.
- You need to preserve the data from all the observables at the same time without cancelling any of them.

Note that nesting callbacks does eliminate the need for an arbitrary wait time. But in either case, you won't be able to perform tasks in parallel, which is what you're trying to do here. Given how frequently this occurs in JavaScript, other libraries address this problem, such as Async.js (https://github.com/caolan/async), which you can use to write code of the following form:

```
button.addEventListener('click', () => {
    async.parallel([              ⟵── Runs all functions in parallel
       ajax('/source1'),
       ajax('/source2')
    ],
    (err, ([result1, result2])) => {    ⟵── The final callback in async.parallel()
       processResults(result1, result1);      receives an array with the outcome
    });                                        of both AJAX calls.
});
```

Luckily, you don't need to include another library, because RxJS is the right tool for the job. In this section, we'll explore an operator called combineLatest() that applies parallel semantics similar to Async.js but in line with the RxJS operator philosophy. To frame this problem more concretely, consider two streams that access two popular APIs to shorten a URL. One makes an AJAX request to Bitly (https://app.bitly.com), and the other to Google URL Shortener (https://goo.gl). For the sake of discussion, you'll kick these streams off using another stream that monitors a URL text box field—debounced for efficiency, of course.

You want both to be able to run in parallel, and you might be able to use operators that you learned in the previous chapter, like `merge()` and `concat()`, depending on whether you care about order preservation. But because both streams are not causally linked (as in you can't just chain them together one after the next), you can't use these operators. For example, `concat()` would force each result to emit in order, one after another rather than in parallel, whereas `merge()` would only allow you to consider a single emission at a time downstream, instead of collectively.

Rather, we stipulated that both tasks must run in parallel but emit results only when all of them have emitted, which may be at any point in the future. You tried using callbacks; let's see if `Promises` fair better.

6.2.1 *Limitations of using Promises*

Certainly, you need a new pattern or set of operators to accomplish your goal, such that you can execute all the statements in parallel while also being able to gather them collectively when they've all completed. Promise libraries that follow the Promise/A+ protocol include a collection operation called `Promise.all()`, which creates a new `Promise` that awaits the completion of all the `Promises` or rejects with the error of the first one to reject. Let's use this method here, but instead of using callbacks, you'll use a version of `ajax()` that returns `Promises` that wrap the HTTP request:

```
button.addEventListener('click', () => {
    Promise.all(ajax('/source1'), ajax('/source2'))    ◁─┐  Executes all Promises and
        .then(([result1, result2]) => {          ◁─       waits for all to complete
            processResults(result1, result2);
        });
});
```

> **Executes all Promises and waits for all to complete**
>
> **Processes the joined value, an array, returned from the call to .all(), which is destructured and passed into a method that knows how to render account details**

Already, you see that the use of `Promises` helps your code not only in indentation and readability but also in parallel, effectively, because you're using a mechanism that knows to emit the value only when all have arrived. But the more these types have to be mixed and matched, the more difficult this becomes, because each variation will require a more intricate solution. In the previous code, you mix two fundamentally different paradigms: event-driven listeners with the more functional `Promises`. Nevertheless, it does achieve parallelism and moves the needle in the right direction.

You already know the desired traits of the new operator you need. It should provide the fluent API design of `Promises` plus the parallelism semantics of Async.js. This operator should take multiple sources, like the static `merge()` operator, but at the same time, it should be able to combine and emit the collective result from all inputs as an event of its own. Let's take a look at `combineLatest()`.

6.2.2   Combining parallel streams

Whereas operators such as `merge()`, `concat()`, and `switch()` combine a series of observables (or an array of them) to output a single observable, `combineLatest()` gives you a way to emit and capture events from multiple sources at the same time. This operator creates an observable whose values are calculated from the latest values of each of its input observables. `combineLatest()` is ideal for situations where you need to spawn to long-running processes in parallel and then use the combined result. For example, suppose you want to use third-party services to shorten URLs. Because both streams act independently, you can use both services in parallel and then present the user with both outputs. This is the task we'll tackle in this section.

Before we begin developing the solution to this problem, we'll briefly introduce you to `combineLatest()` with a simple example. The data emitted is similar to how buffering worked in chapter 3. In other words, the output is an array that combines the latest data from all of the input observables—the same semantics as `Promise .all()` or `async.parallel()`. Here's a quick example to showcase how this operator works. You'll combine the output of two streams: one emits letters every second, and the other emits numbers every second.

> **Listing 6.4   Synchronizing streams with `combineLatest()`**

```
const letter$ =
    Rx.Observable.interval(1000)          <-- Emits A, B, C, ... every second
    .map(num => String.fromCharCode(65 + num))
    .map(letter => `Source 1 -> ${letter}`);

const number$ = Rx.Observable.interval(1000)     <-- Emits 0, 1, 2, 3, ...
    .map(num => `Source 2 -> ${num}`);               every second

Rx.Observable.combineLatest(letter$, number$)
    .take(5)
    .subscribe(console.log);
```

Running this code prints the following:

```
["Source 1 -> A", "Source 2 -> 0"]
["Source 1 -> B", "Source 2 -> 0"]     <--  Source 1 emits "B" with the
["Source 1 -> B", "Source 2 -> 1"]     <--  latest value in source 2, "0."
["Source 1 -> C", "Source 2 -> 1"]          Source 2 emits "1" with the
["Source 1 -> C", "Source 2 -> 2"]          latest value in source 1, "B."
```

Here, you have two independent streams that emit every second: one, letters starting with *A*, and the other, numbers starting at zero. Each emission will cause a collective emission of the latest value present in the stream. So after the first emission, A -> 0, each result alternates emitting the latest from the other stream. In other words, when Source 1 emits B, it sends the result with the latest value in Source 2 at that time, 0. Then, when Source 2 emits the next value, 1, it sends the result with the latest value in the stream at that time, 0. In summary, an emission from any stream in the combination causes all of them to publish their latest value, all sent to the observer via an array.

In this simple case, both data sources are asynchronous intervals. With synchronous data sources, you have to be careful because RxJS will immediately run through the events of the first source stream and combine its latest value with the latest value of the combined stream instead of pairing each number with a letter.

```
const letter$ = Rx.Observable.from(['a', 'b', 'c']);
const number$ = Rx.Observable.from([1, 2, 3]);
Rx.Observable.combineLatest(letter$, number$).subscribe(console.log);
```

Running this code will output a very different result:

```
["c", 1]
["c", 2]
["c", 3]
```

Now that you understand how this operator works, let's jump into your task. Again, you want to spawn parallel AJAX calls to shorten some URL. The user is expected to type a valid URL into a text box; when the user removes focus from it, it will kick off these independent streams. So you're mixing one causally linked stream with two parallel streams, which should suggest the use or `mergeMap()` (or `switchMap()`) and `combineLatest()`, respectively.

> **CAUSALITY** Generally, causal streams (one depends on the other) are combined using `mergeMap()` or `switchMap()`, whereas independent streams are combined using `combineLatest()` and others you'll learn about shortly.

Reasoning about this problem this way—thinking in streams—we came up with the following program for a URL shortener stream that uses both Bitly and Google.

Listing 6.5 Combining multiple URL shortener streams

```
const urlField = document.querySelector('#url');

const url$ = Rx.Observable.fromEvent(urlField, 'blur')
  .pluck('target', 'value')
  .filter(isUrl)                              ◁── Checks using a regex
  .switchMap(input =>                            that the input provided
    Rx.Observable.combineLatest(bitly$(input), goog$(input)))   matches a valid URL
  .subscribe(([bitly, goog]) => {                (omitted for brevity)
    console.log(`From Bitly: ${bitly}`);
    console.log(`From Google: ${goog}`)
  });
```

Combines the latest events of both services

Projects an observable that will emit results when both subordinate streams emit

To run this program, type any URL into the input field; we'll use these providers to shorten this URL. So, for https://www.manning.com/books/rxjs-in-action, the output is

```
From Bitly: http://bit.ly/2dkHUau
From Google: https://goo.gl/plTbDG
```

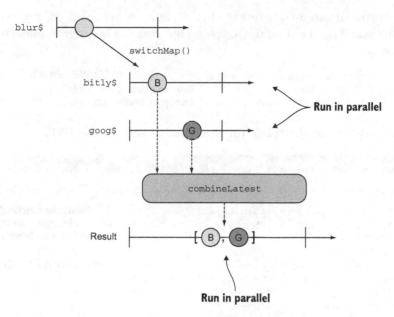

Figure 6.4 The workings of `combineLatest()`. This operator outputs an array containing the latest values from all of its input observables.

These all resolve to the original link (so feel free to share it on your favorite social media!). Of course, you don't understand exactly how `bitly$` and `goog$` work, but the abstraction provided by RxJS means you can still reason about this code as is, from its declarative nature. Figure 6.4 is a simple graph to show you what's happening.

Fortunately, `combineLatest()` allows you to provide a selector function that makes the stream more conformant, so that you can avoid the direct array access, which can be tedious and error prone when you need only one of the results. This selector function receives as arguments the data emitted from each subordinate observable. So, by using a selector function that measures the length, you can compute the shorter of the URLs:

```
const url$ = Rx.Observable.fromEvent(urlField, 'blur')
   .pluck('target', 'value')
   .filter(isUrl)
   .switchMap(input =>
        Rx.Observable.combineLatest(bitly$(input), goog$(input),
           (b, g) => b.length > g.length ? b : g))
   .subscribe(shortUrl => {
      console.log(`The shorter URL is: ${shortUrl}`);
   });
```

> Using a selector function to pick the data from the stream that emits the shorted URL

For the sake of completing this example, let's finish implementing each individual stream, because they pack another interesting technique used to deal with third-party APIs that work with callbacks. You'll implement both services as functions that accept a URL and return a stream used to shorten it. You'll start with bitly$. When you open a Bitly account, you'll need to find the following information in order to make remote web API requests:

```
const API = 'https://api-ssl.bitly.com';          ◄── Bitly's Web API URL
const LOGIN = '<YOUR LOGIN>';                      You can obtain these fields
const KEY = '<YOUR GENERATED KEY>';                from your profile settings.
```

The next listing shows the observable function used to shorten this URL.

Listing 6.6   Bitly URL shortener stream

```
const ajaxAsObservable = Rx.Observable.bindCallback(ajax);          ◄──

const bitly$ = url => Rx.Observable.of(url)                Binds the function's
   .filter(R.compose(R.not, R.isEmpty))                    callback internally to the
   .map(encodeURIComponent)                                observer's next function
   .map(encodedUrl =>
   `${API}/v3/shorten?longUrl=${encodedUrl}&login=${LOGIN}&apiKey=${KEY}`)
   .switchMap(url => ajaxAsObservable(url).map(R.head))
   .filter(obj => obj.status_code === 200 && obj.status_txt === 'OK')
   .pluck('data', 'url');          ◄──
```

Builds the API path

Invokes an AJAX call against Bitly with the longUrl to shorten

Extracts the URL property

For starters, we need to explain the first line in listing 6.6, which you haven't encountered before. It's a fact that many JavaScript APIs, particularly Node.js, still use callback functions heavily. Just as RxJS works well with Promises, it's important to be able to adapt callback-based APIs to RxJS. The way to do this is by internally binding the callback as the observer's next() method and publishing that value as an observable to continue the chain, as shown in figure 6.5.

This way, when the bound ajax() function is invoked with the URL argument, it will execute and the result intended for the callback will be proxied into a new observable. Because you're returning an observable, you use switchMap() to project it and

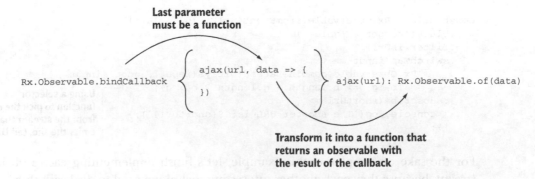

Figure 6.5 bindCallback transforms any function f(x, callback) into a function g, such that calling g(x) outputs an observable with the result of the callback.

replace the source stream. This is the only new part; everything else should be straightforward.

Furthermore, working with Google's URL shortener is similar, except that for reasons of security and authentication, it's best to use their JavaScript client APIs instead of making a raw request (details about installing this library can be found in appendix A). Just like Bitly, Google's service expects you to have a Google account, have this particular API enabled, and have generated a security OAuth2 token. This client API library gapi gives you access to many of Google's web APIs, and it works partially with callbacks and Promises. So integrating it into RxJS involves wrapping those promisified method calls to configure the library and pushing it downstream as you set up to make the shorten call; see the following listing.

Listing 6.7   Google URL shortener stream

Uses your OAuth2 token generated through the Google APIs console

Binds the callback into the load method so that you can integrate it into the observable

```
const GKEY = '<YOUR-GENERATED-OAUTH-KEY>';

const gAPILoadAsObservable = Rx.Observable.bindCallback(gapi.load);

const goog$ = url => Rx.Observable.of(url)
    .filter(R.compose(R.not, R.isEmpty))
    .map(encodeURIComponent)
    .switchMap(() =>
      gAPILoadAsObservable('client'))          ⟵── Loads the client library
    .do(() => gapi.client.setApiKey(GKEY))     ⟵── Passes the generated token
    .switchMap(() =>
        Rx.Observable.fromPromise(gapi.client.load('urlshortener', 'v1')))
    .switchMap(() =>
        Rx.Observable.fromPromise(gapi.client.urlshortener.url.insert(
        {'longUrl': example_url}))
    )
    .filter(obj => obj.status === 200)
    .pluck('result', 'id');
```

Loads the URL shortener API

Shortens the URL and inserts it into your personal list of URLs

---

As you can see, you can compartmentalize both services as individual observables, only to embed them into an orchestrating observable using combineLatest() to run those services in parallel in reaction to the URL field changing. Here's that code once more:

```
const url$ = Rx.Observable.fromEvent(urlField, 'blur')
    .pluck('target', 'value')
    .filter(isUrl)
    .switchMap(input =>
        Rx.Observable.combineLatest(bitly$(input), goog$(input)))
    .subscribe(([bitly, goog]) => {
      console.log(`From Bitly: ${bitly}`);
      console.log(`From Google: ${goog}`)
    });
```

This code reveals that spawning and joining streams gets first-class citizen treatment in RxJS. To nail this point home, let's look at an operator called forkJoin().

6.2.3   *More coordination with forkJoin*

RxJS provides an operator called `forkJoin()`, in many ways similar to `combine-Latest()`, in charge of running multiple observable sequences in parallel and collecting their last element. In contrast to `combineLatest()`, `forkJoin()` will emit only the last value of each forked stream. This is important, so we'll come back to it to make this really clear. At the time of writing, most modern browsers allow you to make up to 10 requests for data simultaneously, and `forkJoin()` takes advantage of this to maximize throughput. For the stock ticker widget, this operator is a plus because you can look up multiple stock symbols simultaneously and then add them all up to reflect the grand total of the user's entire stock portfolio. Take a look at this example in figure 6.6. Here's an outline of the steps:

1 Create a function that uses an observable to fetch the stock data for a company's symbol with price.
2 Iterate through the user's preferred stock symbols: FB (Facebook), AAPL (Apple), and CTXS (Citrix).
3 Use `forkJoin()` to spawn these simultaneous processes and join the result.
4 Add the final result.

To implement our widget, the first thing you'll do is reuse the function that fetches a stock symbol's price `requestQuote$()` from our stock ticker widget in chapter 5:

```
const requestQuote$ = symbol =>
    Rx.Observable.fromPromise(
      ajax(webservice.replace(/\$symbol/, symbol)))
    .map(response => response.replace(/"/g, ''))
    .map(csv);
```

There are so many things you can do, and it all depends on your needs. In this case, you're optimizing for parallelism. One of the things you did in chapter 5 was make the stream conformant in that it returns only the price property of the fetched company symbol as a numerical float.

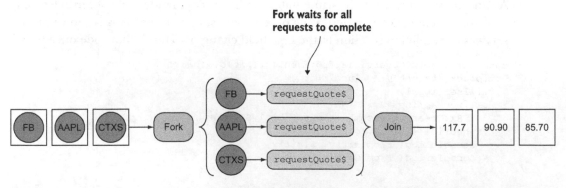

Figure 6.6   The fork operation spawns several requests, waits for them to complete, and emits when all streams have completed. The result is an array mapping to the output of each stream.

Remember from previous chapters that the user has chosen to fetch stock information for three companies:

```
const symbols = ['FB', 'AAPL', 'CTXS'];
```

To compute the total price, you need to query for each of these symbols in parallel and add up the joined result. For this, you'll use `forkJoin()`. You could pass each request observable one by one:

```
Rx.Observable.forkJoin(
    requestQuote$('FB'),
    requestQuote$('AAPL'),
    requestQuote$('CTXS')
);
```

This is clean and declarative. Preferably, use your FP skills to map this function over the symbols array, as shown here.

Listing 6.8   Using `forkJoin` to fetch multiple stock symbols simultaneously

```
Rx.Observable.forkJoin(symbols.map(requestQuote$))
  .map(data => data.map(arr => parseInt(arr[1])))     <── Reads the price amount only
  .subscribe(allPrices => {
     console.log('Total Portfolio Value: ' +
         new USDMoney(allPrices.reduce(add).toLocaleString()));
  });
```

Just like `combineLatest()`, `forkJoin()` will return an array with all stock prices all at once. The subscriber receives the array and reduces it with a simple `const add = (x, y) => x + y;` function to produce the result, which at the time of this run is

```
"Total Portfolio Value: USD 293.25"   <──| Total value subject to change
                                          | depending on market conditions
```

As you can see, this flow is declarative, immutable, and uses functional expressions to obtain the final answer. A simple look at the browser's console, shown in figure 6.7, reveals that all simultaneous processes began at the same time:

`forkJoin()` and `combineLatest()` are similar, yet each imparts its own flavor. Aside from the former being strictly a static factory method and the latter used interchangeably as a factory and instance operator, they differ in the criteria with which they emit their values. `forkJoin()` emits only the latest values from each of the input

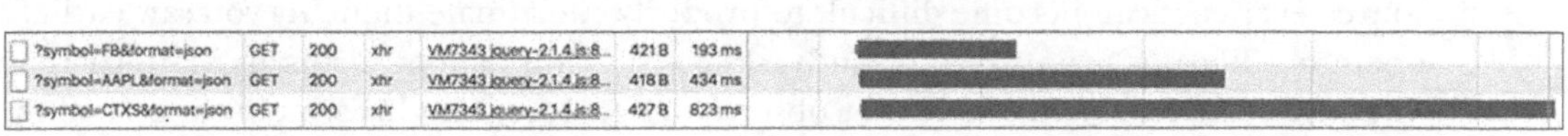

☐ ?symbol=FB&format=json	GET	200	xhr	VM7343 jquery-2.1.4.js:8...	421 B	193 ms	
☐ ?symbol=AAPL&format=json	GET	200	xhr	VM7343 jquery-2.1.4.js:8...	418 B	434 ms	
☐ ?symbol=CTXS&format=json	GET	200	xhr	VM7343 jquery-2.1.4.js:8...	427 B	823 ms	

Figure 6.7   The browser's view of network traffic shows the remote HTTP requests all start at the same time. The `forkJoin()` operator spawns these requests and waits for all to emit before emitting its result.

observables. So if a sequence emits five values, it will sit there and wait for the last one (certainly expect some level of in-memory caching occurring here):

```
Rx.Observable.forkJoin(
  Rx.Observable.of(42),
  Rx.Observable.interval(1000).take(5))
.subscribe(console.log);   //-> [42,4]
```

> It will hold on to 42 for about 5 seconds and then emit the last value seen from all streams.

On the other hand, `combineLatest()` is closer to a merge in the sense that it will emit values for the latest values when any of its input observables emits, namely:

```
Rx.Observable.combineLatest(
  Rx.Observable.of(42),
  Rx.Observable.interval(1000).take(5))
.subscribe(console.log);

//-> [42, 0]
    [42, 1]
    [42, 2]
    [42, 3]
    [42, 4]
```

As you saw in these examples, asynchronous data may arrive at any time, which makes coordination difficult to implement without a tool like RxJS. This is particularly important when synchronizing data operations into a database, for instance. Let's see how RxJS fares with these kinds of problems.

Pitfalls of combinatorial operators

For many operators that combine streams, even those like `combineLatest()`, which emits on any change, each observable is expected to emit at least once before the combining operator emits. So, don't try to do this,

```
Observable.combineLatest(
  Observable.empty(),
  Observable.range(1, 3)
)
```

and expect to get any values.

6.3   *Building a reactive database*

When data sources are expected to arrive at different times or are tied to different source events, it can become difficult to properly coordinate them. As you saw earlier, operators like `combineLatest()` and `forkJoin()` implement a joining pattern that one way or another waits for input observables to complete before emitting a value. This is incredibly powerful and the sort of behavior you'll find in sophisticated concurrency frameworks. You can also find plenty of uses cases of this pattern in backend systems, especially when dealing with data persistence.

The use case you'll tackle here is a simple banking transaction system that keeps track of all transactions as a user withdraws money from their account. Thinking reactively here, you should recognize instances of join patterns because reacting to some action triggers another to occur. In this case, you'll need to join together or sequence a set of database calls to reflect a withdraw action and a transaction record being created. Around this problem domain, you'll implement a few tasks such as loading all of a user's transactions from the database.

A common problem with sophisticated client-side applications is loading all the data from the backend into the browser, an environment restricted to a limited amount of memory. Some architectures load the data as needed; this is called *progressive loading*. But this doesn't work well if an application has high demands for performance or needs to work without an internet connection. Most modern applications are expected to work this way. Another approach is to bypass the browser's memory and load the data into persistent storage. Let's go over the technology you'll be using.

IndexedDB is a great and relatively underutilized web standard for client-side databases. It takes what was traditionally a server-side process of storing data efficiently in some structured manner and allows those same types of operations for the web. Unfortunately, the standard has a less-than-straightforward interface. So for this example, you'll use an abstracted library modeled after the more popular CouchDB library, called PouchDB, which is more readable and handles browser differences (please visit appendix A for installation instructions).

The benefit of using PouchDB, like most modern asynchronous JavaScript APIs you interacted with earlier, is that it uses `Promises` to model all of its asynchronous operations, which means you can use `Rx.Observable.fromPromise()` to adapt all the API calls if you want to use observables, which is exactly what you'll do because you're smarter about preferring observables to regular `Promises`. For instance, the output of `PouchDB.put()`, a `Promise` method, can be converted to an observable, as in figure 6.8.

You can use RxJS to move this static, persistent data into flows of asynchronous operations that compose or cascade the outcome of one into the next seamlessly. Hence, RxJS becomes your query language, treating data as constantly moving and changing infinitely. Keep in mind that PouchDB is a schemaless document store, so this means you don't need to define and create schema before writing data to its tables. You'll start with a simple example that loads a set of banking transactions into the document store. Constructing an instance of the database is as simple as this:

```
const txDb = new PouchDB('transactions');
```

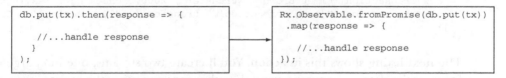

```
db.put(tx).then(response => {

  //...handle response
  }
);
```

```
Rx.Observable.fromPromise(db.put(tx))
  .map(response => {

    //...handle response
});
```

Figure 6.8 Adapting the callback-based API into an observable

This database stores transaction documents in JSON form. A transaction has the following structure.

```
class Transaction {
  constructor(name, type, amount, from, to = null) {
    this.name = name;
    this.type = type;
    this.from = from;
    this.to   = to;
    this.amount = amount;
  }

}
```

Next, you'll populate your database with a few transaction records that represent a user transferring money from one account to another.

6.3.1   *Populating a database reactively*

The code to create and store several transactions involves looping through `Transaction` objects (whether they come from a locally stored array or from a remote HTTP call), date-stamping each transaction with an RxJS timestamp, and posting it to the database, as shown in figure 6.9.

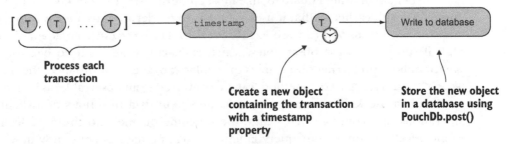

Figure 6.9   Steps to populate data into local storage using streams

You'll start by artificially populating the database with this dataset:

```
function getTransactionsArray() {
  return [
    new Transaction('Brendan Eich', 'withdraw', 500, 'checking'),
    new Transaction('George Lucas', 'deposit',  800, 'savings'),
    new Transaction('Emmet Brown', 'transfer', 2000, 'checking', 'savings'),
    new Transaction('Bjarne Stroustrup', 'transfer', 1000, 'savings', 'CD'),
  ];
}
```

The next listing shows this in action. You'll create two streams, one in charge of performing the database operation and the other for processing the input.

Listing 6.10   Populating the database

Attaches a timestamp to each emitted item that
indicates when it was emitted. The resulting object
has two properties, obj.value, which points to the
emitted object (transaction), and obj.timestamp,
which contains the time the event was emitted.

Uses ES6 Object.assign() to create a copy of the
transaction object with the additional date
property. This preserves immutability. You could
also use the ES6 spread operator (partially
supported in some JavaScript environments).

```
const writeTx$ = tx => Rx.Observable.of(tx)
  .timestamp()
  .map(obj => Object.assign({}, obj.value, {
              date: obj.timestamp
            })
  )
  .do(tx => console.log(`Processing transaction for: ${tx.name}`))
  .mergeMap(datedTx => Rx.Observable.fromPromise(txDb.post(datedTx)));

Rx.Observable.from(getTransactionsArray())
  .concatMap(writeTx$)
  .subscribe(
    rec => console.log(`New record created: ${rec.id}`),
    err => console.log('Error: ' + err),
    () => console.log('Database populated!')
  );
```

Reads the
transaction objects
from a local array

Posts the object into the database by wrapping the
PouchDB.post() operation with an observable. This
assigns the stored document a unique _id.

Joins the stream to
process and creates
the new transaction
document

Before we get into the details of this code, it's important to note that you were able to
process and manipulate a set of objects and store them in a database, all in an
immutable manner; this is compelling and reduces the probability of bugs. Listing
6.10 involves multiple steps and new concepts:

1 You know you'll need to modify the transaction objects to include the date
   when the transaction was processed. This is typical of any banking application
   because most transactions are sorted based on date. Because functional programs are immutable, instead of mapping a function to the transactions array
   and modifying the object's internal structure directly, you can use JavaScript's
   ES6 Object.assign() to immutably create or set a new property into the object,
   leaving the original intact—you want your code to be as stateless as possible.

2 Next, you retrieve the transaction data into an array. Given RxJS's unifying
   model of computation, you could easily retrieve data from a local array, or you
   could just as easily fetch it with a remote HTTP call, such as this:

   ```
   Rx.Observable.fromPromise(ajax('/transactions'))
     .timestamp()
     ...
   ```

3 You use the Object.assign() function to add a date to the transaction object
   iterated over by passing the generated RxJS timestamp() operator. This operator

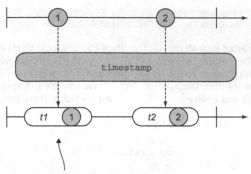

The timestamp operator creates a temporary object with a timestamp property and a value property that points to the original object.

Figure 6.10   RxJS timestamp operator

creates an object with a timestamp and a value property, containing the original object's data, as shown in figure 6.10.

4 You create each transaction object using the `post()` method of the `PouchDB` object. This object also sets a randomly generated key in the database table. Although this method call inevitably creates a side effect in your application (writing to a database), it's one that's managed by RxJS and isolated to its own function—the rest of the code remains pure. As we said earlier, because PouchDB exposes a thenable API, you can wrap observables over it, creating your reactive database.

5 Finally, because the call to `post()` returns a `Promise`, which you convert to an observable, you use `mergeMap()` to flatten the projected observable.

6 Running this code prints the following:

```
"Processing transaction for: Brendan Eich"
"New record created: 4F7404AF-10D2-8438-AEAB-CC21CDC23810"
"Processing transaction for: George Lucas"
"New record created: A9ACE7FE-85DB-484E-AA74-B47A7F4D32B1"
"Processing transaction for: Emmet Brown"
"New record created: DD469ACA-BC5C-A5C6-8E4A-0FB544C62231"
"Processing transaction for: Bjarne Stroustrup"
"New record created: B5C8B8C7-127B-11C7-A90E-64D79C8315E2"
"Database populated!"
```

Another benefit of wrapping observables over the database API is that all side effects are pushed downstream to observers instead of each `Promise.then()` call. It's nice to keep your business logic pure as much as possible and side effects isolated.

Depending on the size of the transaction objects, when storing thousands of them in an array, you could end up with very large memory footprints. Of course, you'd like to avoid keeping all of that data directly in memory, which is why you leverage the browser's database to store this data within it but persisted out of memory. To make this example simple, you use a small array. Most likely you'll also want to keep transactions created locally as well as data coming in remotely. Can you guess which operator you need? Correct! You can use RxJS's merge() to plug in all of the data from multiple sources:

```
Rx.Observable.merge(                              ◄──────────────    Merging the output from
    getTransactionsArray(),                                          local and remote streams
    Rx.Observable.fromPromise(ajax('/transactions')))
  .concatMap(writeTx$)
  .subscribe(
    rec => console.log(`New record created: ${rec.id}`),
    err => console.log('Error: ' + err),
    ()  => console.log('Database populated!')
  );
```

The rest of the code continues to work exactly the same way. Brilliant! The asynchronicity of code is seamless in reactive programming!

And in the event that the remote HTTP call response is not an array, remember that you can make the observable conformant, just as we discussed earlier, and push some logic upstream like this. It's typical of remote calls to return an object with a status and a payload. So if you're response object is something like

```
{
    status: 'OK',
    payload: [{name: 'Brendan Eich', ...}]
}
```

you can make it conformant as you inject it into the stream:

```
Rx.Observable.merge(
    getTransactionsArray(),
    Rx.Observable.fromPromise(ajax('/transactions'))
      .mergeMap(response => Rx.Observable.from(response.payload))  ◄──────┐
  )                                                                       │
  .concatMap(writeTx$)              Converts the JSON response object into an array
  ...                                 that gets combined with the other transaction
                                       records and pushed through the stream │
```

Moreover, databases are full of optimizations to improve read and write speed. You can further help these optimizations by performing bulk operations whenever possible.

6.3.2 *Writing bulk data*

The previous code samples create single bank transaction records at a time. You can optimize this process with bulk operations. Bulk operations write an entire set of records with a single post request. Naturally, the PouchDB operation bulkDocs() takes an array. Earlier, we talked about how much memory was used to build this set, and this is completely in your control using RxJS buffers.

The buffer() operator that you saw back in chapter 4 would come in handy here when you're processing not just a handful of transactions but hundreds of them. Let's optimize listing 6.10 with the following listing.

Listing 6.11   Optimizing write operations using bulk writes

```
Rx.Observable.from(getTransactionsArray())
  .bufferCount(20)                    ←———— Buffers 20 transactions at a time
  .timestamp()                        ←———— Timestamps the entire set of items at once
  .map(obj => {
     return obj.value.map(tx => {     ←———┐ Loops within each set and assigns
       return Object.assign({}, tx, {       │ a date to each transaction object
          date: obj.timestamp
       })
     })
  })
  .do(txs => console.log(`Processing ${txs.length} transactions`))
  .mergeMap(datedTxs =>
       Rx.Observable.fromPromise(txDb.bulkDocs(datedTxs)))  ←——┐ Performs bulk
  .subscribe(                                                   │ operation upon
    rec => console.log('New records created'),                 │ passing the
    err => console.log('Error: ' + err),                       │ entire buffer
    ()  => console.log('Database populated!')
  );
```

To support this optimization, you had to make a few adjustments. After collecting 20 objects with `bufferCount(20)`, the data passing through the stream is now an array instead of a single record, as shown in figure 6.11.

Alternatively, you could have also buffered for a certain period of time with `buffer(Rx.Observable.interval(500))`; this decision depends on the amount of data your application will process. In this case, each record will be kept in a buffer for 500 milliseconds, at which point it will be released and all the records can be written in bulk to the database.

But there's a problem with just using a count- or time-based buffer. If the user attempts to navigate away from the page while the data is being cached, you could potentially lose anything waiting in the buffer, up to 20 transactions in this case, which

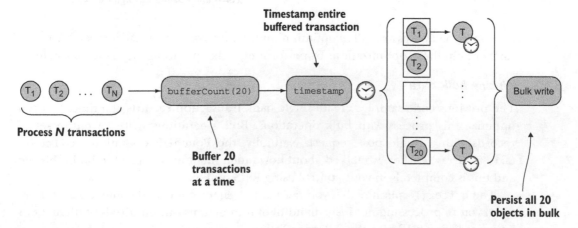

Figure 6.11   Flow followed to add items in bulk (in this case, 20 at a time)

will never get saved. To fix this, let's introduce another observable to trigger a buffer write. Buffers also support signaling, so that the emission can occur in response to the execution of some browser hook, such as the closing of the window. To implement this you can use the `bufferWhen()` operator with an observable that's smart enough to support both use cases: to cache the results for a specific period of time or emit before the browser closes:

```
Rx.Observable.from(getTransactionsArray())          Buffers events from the source observable
  .bufferWhen(() =>                                  until the provided observable emits
    Rx.Observable.race(
      Rx.Observable.interval(500),
      Rx.Observable.fromEvent(window, 'beforeunload'))
  )
  ...
```

Creates an observable that mirrors the first observable to emit a value of the ones provided to it. In this case, it will emit after half a second or when the window closes, whichever comes first.

Hooking into the browser closing event. Because the contents within the buffer storage are emitted as a single array object and processed synchronously, there's no danger of the browser shutting down before the buffer gets processed.

`bufferWhen()`, instead of taking an observable to trigger the start of each new buffer, accepts a closing selector method that's re-invoked every time the buffer is closed, and the resulting observable is used to determine when the next buffer should close. Using this, you can create a signal observable that has a host of possible constraint states. Now that you know how to get data into the database, let's join with a query that can count the total number of records.

6.3.3 Joining related database operations

All of the local store operations, whether you're using IndexedDB directly or PouchDB, happen asynchronously, but with RxJS you can treat your operations almost as if they were synchronous because of the abstraction that it poses over the latency involved in database calls. To illustrate this, you'll chain together an operation to insert a record, followed by an operation that retrieves the total count.

PouchDB is a map/reduce database, so in order to query the data, you must first define how the projection or the mapping function works. This object is called a *design document*, which you need to include as part of the query. For your purposes, you'll keep it simple and count the number of transactions performed. So your design document—you'll call it count—looks like this:

```
const count = {
  map: function (doc) {
    emit(doc.name);          Counts the number of users
  },
  reduce: '_count'           Uses the reduce PouchDB aggregate operator _count
};
```

The next listing shows how you can join two queries with a single stream declaration.

Listing 6.12   Two queries in a single stream declaration

```
Rx.Observable.from(getTransactionsArray())
  .switchMap(writeTx$)                          <─── Posts a single transaction
  .mergeMap(() => Rx.Observable.fromPromise(
    txDb.query(count, {reduce: true})))         <─┐  Runs a reduction query
  .subscribe(                                      │  to count the total
    recs  => console.log('Total: ' + recs.rows[0].value),  │  number of documents
    error => console.log('Error: ' + error),       │  in the table
    ()    => console.log('Query completed!')
  );
```

Prints the total value ▷

PouchDB also has some reduction operations of its own, and you understand what a reduction is because you're an experienced functional programmer by now. Aside from count, you can perform other reductions such as sum and stats. Let's go over another example that combines all of what you've learned thus far. It performs a withdraw from the account database and creates a new transaction document, as shown in figure 6.12.

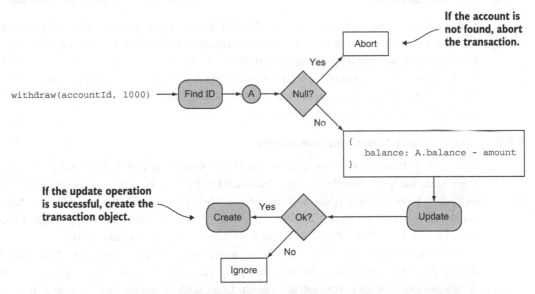

Figure 6.12   The backend workflow that takes place when a withdraw operation occurs. First, you find the account by ID, and if it results in a valid object, you subtract the withdraw amount and update the account.

First, you'll need to seed a set of user accounts with the following structure (again, you'll keep your domain simple).

Listing 6.13   The Account class

```
class Account {
  constructor(id, name, type, balance) {
    this._id = id;                    <─── The _id field is used to tell PouchDB's put()
    this.name = name;                      method to use your provided ID instead of
                                           generating a new one. You can use
                                           PouchDB's get() method to query by this ID.
```

```
        this.type = type;
        this.balance = balance;
    }
    get id() {
        return this._id;
    }
}
```

Similarly, you'll create a few different types of accounts for your user Emmet Brown—

```
const accounts = [
    new Account('1', 'Emmet Brown', 'savings', 1000),
    new Account('2', 'Emmet Brown', 'checking', 2000),
    new Account('3', 'Emmet Brown', 'CD', 20000),
];
```

—to populate a new document store:

```
const accountsDb = new PouchDB('accounts');
```

Because you're already familiar with creating databases and populating them from the earlier example, you'll jump right into the withdraw() function, which returns an observable responsible for creating the flow to query and update multiple databases, as shown in the next listing.

Listing 6.14 withdraw function

```
function withdraw$({name, accountId, type, amount}) {                  ◁─────────
    return Rx.Observable.fromPromise(accountsDb.get(accountId))
        .do(doc => console.log(                                        Unpacks the
            doc.balance < amount ?                                     input into the
                'WARN: This operation will cause an overdraft!' :      parameters
                'Sufficient funds'                                     needed for the
        ))                                                             transaction
        .mergeMap(doc =>
            Rx.Observable.fromPromise(        ◁──── Updates the user balance
                accountsDb.put({
                    _id: doc._id,
                    _rev: doc._rev,
                    balance: doc.balance - amount
                }))
        )
        .filter(response => response.ok)      ◁──┐ Continues only if the DB
        .do(() =>                                 │ update was successful
            console.log('Withdraw succeeded. Creating transaction document'))
        .concatMap(() => writeTx$(
            new Transaction(name, 'withdraw', amount, type)));   ◁──┐ Creates the
}                                                                    │ transaction record
                                                                     │ and return it
```

Retrieves the existing account info

You can run this code by passing it an operation object literal:

```
withdraw$({
    name: 'Emmet Brown',
```

```
    accountId: '3',
    type: 'checking',
    amount: 1000
})
.subscribe(
    tx    => console.log(`Transaction number: ${tx.id}`),
    error => console.log('Error: ' + error),
    ()    => console.log('Operation completed!!')
);
```

This will generate the following output:

```
"Sufficient funds"
"Withdraw succeeded. Creating transaction document"
"Processing transaction for: Emmet Brown"
"Transaction number: DB6FF825-C703-0F1A-B860-DA6B1138F723"
"Operation completed!!"
```

As you can see, because the API of PouchDB uses `Promises`, it's easy to integrate your database code with your business logic, all wrapped and coordinated via the observable operators. Although database calls are a form of side effect, it's one you're willing to take in practice and rely on the unidirectional flow of streams to streamline the use of this shared state. But wrapping API calls is not the only thing you can do with PouchDB. In addition, you can build support for a reactive database.

6.3.4   *Reactive databases*

PouchDB is an event emitter, which means it exposes a set of events or hooks for you to use to plug logic into certain phases of its lifecycle. Just as GitHub exposes hooks to tap into when branches are created, you can add event listeners that fire when databases are created and destroyed.

This is important in browser storage where the lifespan of a database is temporary because it can be destroyed and re-created at any time. So before you begin adding any documents, it will be good to do so in the context of a database-created hook.

Using the `Rx.Observable.fromEvent()` operator, you can transform any event emitter into an observable sequence. Hooking into the database-creation event looks like the following:

```
Rx.Observable.fromEvent(txDb, 'created')
  .subscribe(
    () => console.log('Database to accept data!')
  );
```

Adding this check in your streams is easy. All you need to do is key off of that hook to perform all your logic. This is somewhat similar to waiting for the document to be ready before executing any of your JavaScript code. The withdraw operation would look like this:

```
Rx.Observable.fromEvent(txDb, 'created')        ⟵── Reacts to the 'created' event
  .switchMap(() =>
```

```
withdraw$({
 name: 'Charlie Brown',
 accountId: '1',
 type: 'checking',
 amount: 1000
})
    )
    ...
```

In this chapter, you saw how you can bring together multiple distinct subsystems and build coherent state machines from them. Each example brought out a small piece of functionality that could be independently attached to and handled. The combinatorial operators allow you to join each stream while maintaining the same separation of concerns that you achieved with single streams. Notice that, so far, none of the code you've written has accounted for errors or exceptions. What if there's an error inserting a record into a database? What if there's an exception happening when you call some third-party function? In the next chapter, we'll take these same concepts and show you how to make your applications more fault tolerant against the unexpected.

6.4 Summary

- You joined parallel URL shortening services with `combineLatest()` and spawned multiple observable sequences with `forkJoin()`.
- You used buffering to improve the performance database queries.
- You used observables to control the lifespans of non-observables like user sessions.
- You saw how reactive databases allow you to orchestrate business flows involving permanent storage.

Error handling with RxJS

7

This chapter covers

- The issues with imperative error–handling schemes
- Using functional data types to abstract exception handling
- Using observable operators to handle exceptions
- Different strategies for retrying observable sequences

Until now, we've explored only happy-path examples involving RxJS for tackling many different use cases. We suspect that at some point you've probably asked yourself, "What would happen if a remote HTTP call failed while fetching data for my stock quote widget?" Observers see the outcome of combining and transforming sequences of streams that you use to map your business logic to. But if an exception occurs midstream, what will the observer see at that point? These are some valid and important questions, but it was important that you first understand and learn to think reactively with ideal scenarios. Now, we're going to sprinkle a dose of the real world onto your code. The brutal reality is that software will likely fail at some point during its execution.

Many issues can arise in software where data inadvertently becomes null or undefined, exceptions are thrown, network connectivity is lost, and so on. Your code needs to account for the potential occurrence of these issues, which unavoidably creates complexity. In other words, you can't escape errors, but you can learn how to deal with them. One strategy that developers often use is to scatter error-handling code around every function call. We do this to make our code more robust and fault tolerant, but it has the detrimental effect of making it even more complex and harder to read.

In this chapter, you'll learn that the key to elegant error handling in RxJS is done in part by the effective use of observables and by following proper FP principles, as you've seen all along. Given a properly constructed observable stream, the next step is to learn about the different RxJS observable operators that you can plug in to respond to any adversity. Before we get started, it's important for you to understand that you need to put aside the imperative error-handling techniques you're accustomed to, like try/catch, in favor of a functional approach as implemented in RxJS.

7.1 Common error-handling techniques

JavaScript errors can occur in many situations, especially when an application fails to communicate with a server when invoking an AJAX call. Also, third-party libraries that you load into your project can have functions that throw exceptions to signal special error conditions. Hence, you always need to be prepared for the worst and design with failure in mind, instead of letting it become an afterthought and a source of regret.

In the imperative world, exceptions are typically handled with the common try/catch idiom, which occurs frequently with synchronous code. Conversely, in the asynchronous world—remote HTTP calls and event emitters—you're required to interface with functions that delegate failures to callback functions. And recently with JavaScript ES6, many libraries have switched to using Promises to wrap their asynchronous computations. Let's examine each of these cases individually.

7.1.1 Error handling with try/catch

JavaScript's default exception-handling mechanism is geared toward throwing and catching exceptions through the popular try/catch block, which is also pervasive in most modern programming languages. Here's a sample:

```
try {
    someDangerousFunction();
}
catch (error) {
    // statements to handle any exceptions
    console.log(error.message);
}
```

As you know, the purpose of this structure is to surround a piece of code that you deem to be unsafe. Upon throwing an exception, the JavaScript runtime abruptly halts the program's execution and creates a stack trace of all the function calls leading up to the problematic instruction. Specific details about the error, such as the message, line number, and filename, are populated into an object of type Error and passed into the catch block.

RXJS 5 EXCEPTIONS   RxJS 5 has a number of improvements over its previous version. One of them involves the simplification of the internal mechanisms of RxJS, resulting in a stack trace that's much easier to parse.

The `catch` block becomes a safe haven so that you can potentially recover your program. But with your knowledge about observables, you can see how this imperative style of dealing with exceptions is structurally very different from what you've done so far. So, adding `try/catch` to your RxJS code to provide error-handling logic to a stream would look like the following:

```
try {
   const data$ = Rx.Observable.fromPromise(ajax('/data'))
      .subscribe(console.log);
}
catch(error) {
   console.log(`Error processing stream: ${error.message}`);
}
```

Now, imagine having to merge multiple streams, each with its own type of failure, and you can see how this pattern couldn't possibly be effective if you need to wrap each stream with its own `try/catch`. With asynchronous functions, the common JavaScript pattern is to provide the error callback alongside the success callback.

7.1.2   *Delegating errors to callbacks*

As is common with asynchronous functions in many JavaScript libraries, there's typically a function that responds to the success case and one that handles errors. This is necessary because asynchronous functions are unpredictable in terms of if and when they return, and if errors occur. Until now, we purposely avoided talking about error cases when using an asynchronous function like `ajax()`. You've been using this function all along, as a kind of black box that always ran correctly. You could use it in two different ways: with callbacks or with `Promises`. Let's peek under the hood of this function using callbacks.

> **Listing 7.1   Function `ajax()` with success and error callbacks**

```
const ajax = function (url, success, error) {
   let req = new XMLHttpRequest();        ◁─┐ Initializes an XmlHttpRequest
   req.responseType = 'json';               │ object used to fetch data remotely
   req.open('GET', url);
   req.onload = function() {
      if(req.status == 200) {
         let data = JSON.parse(req.responseText);
         success(data);                   ◁─┐ On success, parses the data as JSON
      }                                      │ and invokes the success() callback
      else {
         req.onerror();
      }
   }
   req.onerror = function () {
```

```
      if(error) {
         error(new Error('IO Error'));      ◁─┐  On error, converts the error
      }                                        │  message into an exception object
   };
   req.send();
};
```

CODE SAMPLES   Remember that the code for this chapter can be found in the RxJSinAction GitHub repository, https://github.com/RxJSInAction/rxjs-in-action.

Using this function, code that would require multiple nested sequences of HTTP calls, such as when mashing up different sources of data, would look like the next listing.

Listing 7.2   Imperative error handling with asynchronous code

```
ajax('/data',
  data => {
    for (let item of data) {
      ajax(`/data/${item.getId()}/info`,
        dataInfo => {
          ajax(`/data/images/${dataInfo.img}`,   ─┐  Handles the innermost
            showImage,                             │  HTTP call
            error => {                       ◁─────┘
              console.log(`Error image: ${error.message}`);
            });
        },
        error => {                           ─┐  Handles second-level
          console.log(`Error each data item: ${error.message}`);  │  HTTP call
        });                              ◁────┘
    }
  },                                     ─┐  Handles the outermost
  error => {                              │  HTTP call
    console.log(`Error fetching data: ${error.message}`);  ◁─┘
  }
});
```

Looking at this code from just a structural point of view, you can picture it as nested code blocks, such as the ones shown in figure 7.1.

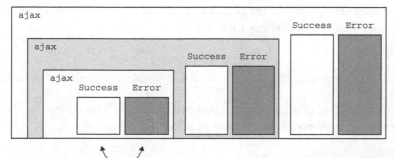

Each ajax provides callbacks for Success and Error.

Figure 7.1   Imperative asynchronous error handling tends to nest when processing a series of asynchronous calls.

Indeed, although our code is more fault tolerant, all we've done here is exacerbate the problem of having to parse this nested "pyramid of doom," which we spoke about in chapter 1. Because of this type of situation, the JavaScript ES6 specification introduced Promises, which elegantly streamline the invocation of a sequence of asynchronous functions.

7.1.3 *Errors and Promises*

The Promise.then() function acts as the mapping function (similar to Rx.Observable .map()) used to project (or map) another Promise to a source Promise. This is the reason why we decided to "promisify" ajax(), and it's what we've been using for most of the examples as a form much superior to its callback counterpart. Here's the code for that.

Listing 7.3 Promisified ajax()

```
const ajax = function (url) {
    return new Promise(function(resolve, reject) {      // Creates and returns
        let req = new XMLHttpRequest();                  // the HTTP call wrapped
        req.responseType = 'json';                       // in a Promise
        req.open('GET', url);
        req.onload = function() {
            if(req.status == 200) {
                let data = JSON.parse(req.responseText);
                resolve(data);                           // Promise is resolved if data
            }                                            // is fetched successfully
            else {
                reject(new Error(req.statusText));       // Promise is rejected in
            }                                            // case failure occurs
        };                                               // while performing the
        req.onerror = function () {                      // remote request
            reject(new Error('IO Error'));
        };
        req.send();
    });
};
```

Much as you can with observables, you can chain multiple asynchronous calls by mapping new Promises to a source Promise. Then, you can use the Promise.catch() operator to implement an error-handling strategy that answers to any of the rejected Promises or ones that throw exceptions, as such:

```
ajax('/data')
  .then(...)
  .catch(error => console.log(`Error fetching data: ${error.message}`))
```

Because catch() itself returns a Promise, you can implement specific errors by inserting multiple asynchronous calls to catch() in series, like this:

```
ajax('/data')
  .then(item => ajax(`/data/${item.getId()}/info`))
  .catch(error => console.log(`Error fetching data: ${error.message}`))
```

```
.then(dataInfo => ajax(`/data/images/${dataInfo.img}`))
.catch(error => console.log(`Error each data item: ${error.message}`))

.then(showImg);
.catch(error => console.log(`Error image: ${error.message}`))
```

Arguably, in comparison to figure 7.1, the statement in figure 7.2 resembles a much easier structure to parse.

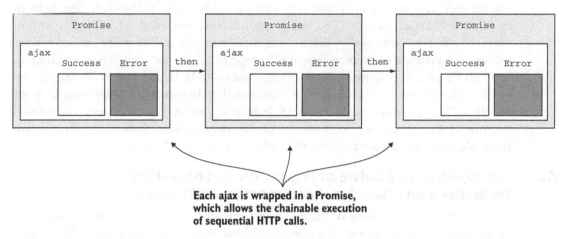

Each ajax is wrapped in a Promise, which allows the chainable execution of sequential HTTP calls.

Figure 7.2 `Promises` allow you to chain subsequent asynchronous calls, each with its own success and error (`catch`) callbacks.

If the first `ajax()` fails, the first `catch()` operator runs before jumping into the next `Promise` in the chain. Each `catch` can be thought of as a recovery block for the previous `Promise`; the `Promise` allows you to resume processing in some known state.

> **CONTINUOUS CATCH**   The previous code example introduces a small bug that we ignored to prevent cluttering up the code. Because catches are also part of the continuation, the handler method can return either a value or another `Promise`; if no value is returned, then an undefined value will be passed to the next continuation block.

Just like with a synchronous `try/catch`, you can either continue by recovering from the error, in this case by returning a non-error value, or you can rethrow the error. In the `catch` block, that's done by either returning a `Promise.reject()` or throwing within the callback method. But because you're basically just transferring control from one `Promise` to the next, it's more typical to just implement a single, global `catch()` operator (this is essentially equivalent to placing an overarching `try/catch` block over your entire function body). In this case, when any `Promise` fails, the `catch()` operator is run and the entire body of code is exited:

```
ajax('/data')
    .then(item => ajax(`/data/${item.getId()}/info`))
    .then(dataInfo => ajax(`/data/images/${dataInfo.img}`))
```

```
.then(showImg)
.catch(error => console.log(error.message));
```

Certainly, `Promises` get you closer to where you want to be. Unfortunately, all these approaches limit your ability to make your code responsive and reactive; in other words, you can't easily return a default value in case a request failed or perhaps retry a rejected `Promise`. You can get around passing default values down the chain by introducing side effects in your code. And you can implement retries with the help of third-party libraries, such as Q.js (https://github.com/kriskowal/q). But more importantly, recall from our earlier discussions that `Promises` model single asynchronous values, not a deluge of them, which are the type of problems you solve when combining functional and reactive programming—and to make matters worse, `Promises` can swallow exceptions if no error handler is provided. (This is true only for older browser versions. Newer browsers and NodeJS bubble up errors thrown from unhandled promises.) Let's examine in more detail the reasons why these imperative error-handling mechanisms are incompatible with a reactive application.

7.2   *Incompatibilities between imperative error-handling techniques and functional and reactive code bases*

The structured mechanism of throwing and catching exceptions in imperative JavaScript code has many drawbacks when used in a functional or reactive style. In general, functions that throw exceptions

- Can't be composed or chained like other functional artifacts.
- Violate the principle of pure functions that advocates a single, predictable value because throwing exceptions constitutes another exit path from your function calls.
- Cause side effects to occur because an unanticipated unwinding of the stack impacts the entire system beyond just the function call or the stream declaration.
- Violate the principle of non-locality because the code used to recover from the error is distanced from the originating function call. When an error is thrown, a function leaves the local stack and environment, for instance:

```
try {
    let record = findRecordById('123');

    ... potentially many lines of code in between
}
catch (e) {
    console.log('ERROR: Record not found!');

    // Handle error here
}
```

- Put a great deal of responsibility on the caller to declare matching `catch` blocks to manage specific exceptions instead of just worrying about a function's single return value.
- Are hard to use asynchronously. The `try/catch` idiom is effective when enclosing synchronous code, where errors are syntactically bounded by the enclosing

`try` blocks. This code is predictable and not affected by time and latency. Asynchronous functions, on the other hand, are unpredictable and typically provide an error callback mechanism to give control of the program back to the user.

- Are hard to use when multiple error conditions create nested levels of exception-handling blocks:

```
let record = null;
try {
    record = findRecordByName('RecordA');
}
catch (e) {
    console.log('ERROR: Cannot locate record by name');

    try {
        record = findRecordById('123');
    }
    catch (e) {
        console.log('ERROR: Record is nowhere to be found!');
    }
}
```

After reading all these statements, you're probably asking yourself, "Is throwing exceptions completely off the table?" We certainly don't believe so. In practice, they can never be off the table because there are many factors outside your control that you may need to account for, like system or environmental errors or calls to third-party code.

We're not recommending you don't use exceptions at all, because they do serve a purpose—just use them for truly exceptional conditions. When you need to use exceptions or deal with errors, the functional approach is to allow functional data types to abstract them away from your main business logic; this prevents you from creating side effects or code that becomes hard to maintain.

7.3 Understanding the functional error-handling approach

The functional approach to error handling is quite simple. As we mentioned before, we won't get too deep into any functional topics in this book, so we'll provide a simplistic view of this approach that will serve to help you better understand the design of RxJS's error-handling mechanism. The goal here is to reify, or make a first-class citizen, the idea of a wrapper around a function or body of code that has the potential of throwing an exception. If you think about it, that's what you've been doing all along when you use a `try`/`catch` block. The function `findRecordById()` can throw an exception in the event that a database record is not found, as illustrated in figure 7.3.

```
try {
    let record = findRecordById('123');

    //... processing account
}
catch(e) {
    console.log(`Exception caught: ${e.message}`);
}
```

The curly braces imposed by the try block create an invisible container around the function call.

Figure 7.3 A `try`/`catch` block creates an invisible section that protects any section of code.

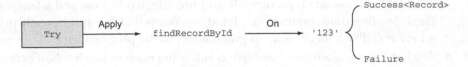

Figure 7.4   Use a data type called `Try` to make errors first-class citizens of your application. This can be used to wrap any value and then safely apply or map functions to it. If a function invocation is successful (no exceptions produced), a data type called `Success` is returned; otherwise, an object of `Failure` is returned.

The `try` block creates an invisible enclosure around the function call so that you can implement all your error-handling logic inside the `catch` block. In the functional world, you'll reify this container with a data type called `Try`.

> **NOTE**   The `Try` data type is a common pattern in FP that we introduce here merely as a theoretical construct. This will help you later, when we discuss how observables implement this pattern.

Figure 7.4 shows how this data type would work.

You can use this type to apply or map a function to a certain value. This is equivalent to invoking the function with that parameter. With this extra plumbing, `Try` allows you to provide the necessary abstraction to return an object of type `Success` if a record object is found; otherwise, an object of type `Failure`, signaling that something unexpected occurred. Notice that this requires the input to be a function so that it can properly capture a thrown exception:

```
Try.of(() => findRecordById('123')); //-> Success(Record)
Try.of(() => findRecordById('456')); //-> Failure
Try.of(() => findRecordById('xxxxx'))
   .getOrElse(new Record(...));   //-> Default value
```

Now, just like any functional data type, suppose `Try` also had a `map()` operator, which you can use to perform any action on the resolved object, if one is found:

```
Try.of(() => findRecordById('123')).map(processRecord);
```

Using `Try` as the return type of your functions is quite handy, because not only do you protect the value it returns from a possible null access, but also you let your users know that this particular function might produce an invalid result—it's self-documenting. This is why other languages such as Scala, Java, and Haskell one way or another provide native APIs for this data type.

For the purpose of our discussion, we show some of the pieces of `Try` in the next listing, as well as its derived types `Success` and `Failure`.

Listing 7.4   Internals of the `Try` functional data type

```
class Try {
  constructor(val) {                    ◄─── Creates a new instance of this data type
    this._val = val;
  }
  static of(fn) {                       ◄─
    try {                                    If Try yields a successful
      return new Success(fn());              computation, wraps the result in
    } catch (error) {                        a Success; otherwise, wraps the
      return new Failure(error);             result in a Failure
    }
  }
  map(fn) {                             ◄─
    return Try.of(() => fn(this._val));      Map applies a function to a value with internal
  }                                          try/catch logic and returns an instance of Try
}                                            to continue chaining more operations (this is
                                             analogous to Rx.Observable.map()).

class Success extends Try {           ◄─
                                           Success represents a successful
  getOrElse(anotherVal) {                  computation, with a method to
    return this._val;                      get the value.
  }

  getOrElseThrow() {
    return this._val;
  }
}

class Failure extends Try {           ◄─
                                           Failure represents a function that
  map(fn) {                                resulted in an exception being
    return this;                           thrown. Any subsequent mapping
  }                                        operations are skipped.

  getOrElse(anotherVal) {
    return anotherVal;
  }

  getOrElseThrow() {
    if(this._val !== null) {
      throw this._val;
    }
  }
}
```

SYNTAX   Listing 7.4 uses the class syntax in ES6 to model the `Try` data type. We use classes only because they're syntactically shorter than using functions and object prototypes. As you probably know by now, classes are nothing more than syntactic sugar over JavaScript's existing prototype-based inheritance. Whether you decide to implement this using function or class syntax is entirely up to you.

Listing 7.4 shows just a few of the key details of this functional data type. `Try` models two scenarios:

- If an instance of `Try<Record>` represents a successful computation, it's an instance of `Success<Record>` internally that's used to continue the chain.
- If, on the other hand, it represents a computation in which an error has occurred, it's an instance of `Failure<Error>`, wrapping an `Error` object or an exception.

What you accomplish with this is a simple data type that allows you to pipeline, or chain operations on objects, catching exceptions along the way, without impacting your business logic and hiding the imperative `try/catch` structure. Here's how you can use it. Suppose you execute a function `processRecord()` that works on a record fetched from a database. If the record is not found, `processRecord()` will throw an exception:

```
let record = Try.of(() => findRecordById('123')
   .map(processRecord)
   .getOrElse(new Record('123', 'RecordA'));
```

This code works by lifting a value into the `Try` context and then mapping a function to it. `map()` is where the `try/catch` logic lives, consolidated in one place. Arguably, this code is much more readable and pure compared to the following:

```
let record;
try {
   record = findRecordById('123');
   processRecord(record);
}
catch (e) {
   record = new Record('123', 'RecordA');
}
```

In the functional case, if the process operation were to fail, nothing in this logic would actually change because the error would be propagated internally via `Failure` instances, finally resulting in the `getOrElse()` function that creates and returns a default record object. This simple design pattern is really powerful, because it abstracts error handling completely from your business logic so that your functions worry only about writing code to solve your task at hand, while remaining side effect–free. You can see the workings of this in the diagram in figure 7.5.

Does this discussion about propagation of change and the mapping of functions ring a bell? That's right! The `Observable` data type works exactly the same way, and now you'll see how it implements its own exception-handling operators.

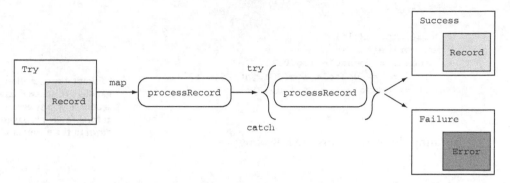

Figure 7.5 Mapping a function to a `Try` returns the result wrapped in a `Success` type or an exception wrapped in a `Failure`.

7.4 The RxJS way of dealing with failure

Just as observables abstract data flow and processing, they also abstract errors and exception handling. RxJS's `Observable` type provides several strategies for you to manage the errors that could arise midstream. In this section, you'll learn about these strategies:

- Propagating errors to observers
- Catching errors and reacting accordingly
- Retrying a failed operation for a fixed number of times
- Reacting to failed retries

7.4.1 Errors propagated downstream to observers

In chapter 2, we mentioned that at the end of the observable stream is a subscriber waiting to pounce on the next event to occur. This subscriber implements the `Observer` interface, consisting of three methods: `next()`, `error()`, and `complete()`.

In general, *errors don't escape the observable pipeline.* They are contained and guarded to prevent side effects from happening—much like `Try`, as shown in figure 7.6.

Errors that occur at the beginning of the stream or in the middle are propagated down to any observers, finally resulting in a call to `error()`. Here's a quick example to illustrate this concept.

Listing 7.5 Calling the `error` method on observers when an exception is thrown

```
const computeHalf = x => Math.floor(x / 2);
Rx.Observable.of(2,4,5,8,10)
    .map(num => {
      if(num % 2 !== 0) {
        throw new Error(`Unexpected odd number: ${num}`);
      }
```
The business logic spits out an exception somewhere midstream.

```
    return num;
  })
  .map(computeHalf)
  .subscribe(
    (next) => console.log(val),
    (error) => console.log(`Caught: ${err}`),
    () => console.log('All done!');

  );
```

⊲─┐ **Without any exception handlers (discussed later in section 7.4), any errors are automatically propagated down to the observers.**

Running this code prints the following:

```
1
2
"Caught: Error: Unexpected odd number: 5"
```

You can consider this approach similar in structure to an overarching `try/catch` block. The important aspect to note from this example is how the `Observable` data type acts like a `Try` by disallowing the exception to leak from the stream's context. Because there's no way to recover, the first exception that fires will result in the entire stream being cancelled. Think of parsing data from a network call; you'd obviously want to skip parsing the object if the network call was unsuccessful. The error is pushed down to any subscribers so that they can perform any side effects, such as showing an alert pop-up or a modal dialog. Most of the time, though, you'll want to catch and recover from the error that occurred. To make understanding the different recovery strategies easier, we'll continue using this simple numerical example from listing 7.5 as our theme.

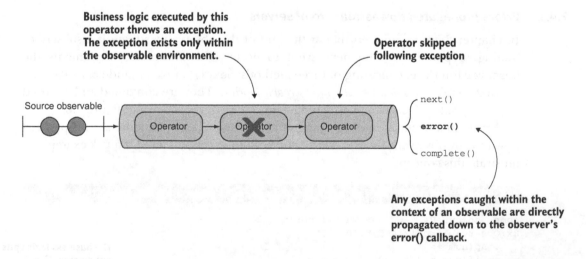

Figure 7.6   Errors that occur within an operator are not allowed to escape the context of the observable. Rather, errors can be handled within the pipeline (as you'll see later in section 7.4); otherwise, the observer's `error()` function is called.

7.4.2 Catching and reacting to errors

Most of the time, you'll want to catch and recover from any errors so that your application is always responsive and resilient—one of the main requirements of being reactive is always being responsive.

> **REACTIVE MANIFESTO** One of the main principles of reactive systems is the notion of resiliency, which states that systems should stay responsive in the face of failure. Reacting to errors using RxJS operators is one way to work toward this goal.

The basic error-handling mechanism that RxJS provides is the `catch()` operator, used to intercept any error in the `Observable` and give you the option to handle by returning a new `Observable` or, again, by propagating it down to observers in case there's a recoverability path, as shown in figure 7.7.

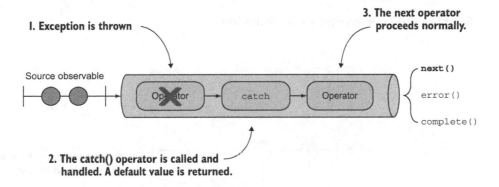

Figure 7.7 Exception caught in an operator upstream by using the `catch()` operator

Just like with regular `try/catch` usage, you want to place the `catch()` operator close to the segment of code that might fail. `catch()` allows you to insert a default value in place of the event that caused the error; any subsequent operators in the chain will never know that an exception occurred. Imagine if you experienced a login error to the server or had a problem accessing your local DB. The `catch` could be used to capture that error and inject a default or in-memory value into the stream without the downstream being any the wiser!

You can use marble diagrams to show error handling in a stream as well, just like with any other operator. Figure 7.8 shows an example of a stream that rejects odd numbers and returns evens instead.

Here's the code for figure 7.8.

Listing 7.6   Recovering from an exception using catch()

```
Rx.Observable.of(2,4,5,8,10)
  .map(num => {
    if(num % 2 !== 0) {
      throw new Error(`Unexpected odd number: ${num}`);
    }
    return num;
  })
  .catch(err => Rx.Observable.of(6))      ⟵  Catches or intercepts the error and
  .map(n => n / 2)                             returns an observable in its place
  .subscribe(
    (next) => console.log(val),              In this case, because the
    (error) => console.log(`Caught: ${err}`),  ⟵ exception is caught and
    () => console.log('All done!');           handled, the error method
  );                                          on the observer is never
                                              executed.
```

Running this code now prints the following:

```
1
2
3
"All done!"
```

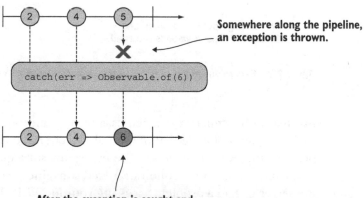

Somewhere along the pipeline, an exception is thrown.

After the exception is caught and handled, the observable sequence completes with a default value.

Figure 7.8   Error handling using marble diagrams

As you can see, the stream continues to be cancelled when the exception occurs, but now you're at least able to recover. Some errors, however, might be intermittent and shouldn't halt the stream. For instance, a server is unavailable for a short period of time because of a planned outage. In cases like this, you may want to retry your failed operations.

7.4.3 *Retrying failed streams for a fixed number of times*

The catch() operator is passed a function that takes an error argument (shown in listing 7.6) as well as the source observable that was caught, which you can return to tell the source observable to retry from the beginning. Let's take a look:

```
Rx.Observable.of(2,4,5,8,10)
  .map(num => {
    if(num % 2 !== 0) {
      throw new Error(`Unexpected odd number: ${num}`);
    }
    return num;                          Returning the original observable, which
  })                                     will begin to emit the entire observable
  .catch((err, source) => source)   ◄───┘ sequence, starting with the first value, 2
  ...
```

This operation can be dangerous when the exception is unavoidable or not transient because you've now entered an infinite loop; there's no condition in the business logic that will change for the error to disappear. Figure 7.9 shows what's occurring.

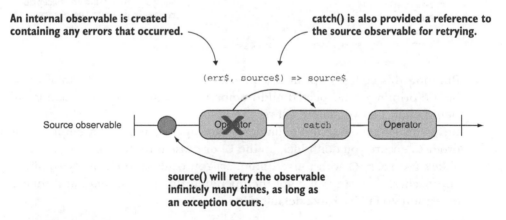

Figure 7.9 The catch() operator is provided an Observable sequence populated with any errors that occurred as well as the source observable, which you can use to retry the sequence from the beginning.

Another place looping can occur is when using Promises. A Promise can emit two types of errors: either an unexpected exception is thrown during the body of the computation, or the Promise becomes unfulfilled and gets rejected. Because Promises are not retriable artifacts, dereferencing the value of a Promise will always return its fulfilled value or error, as the case may be. The following code creates a big problem:

```
const requestQuote$ = symbol =>
    Rx.Observable.fromPromise(
      ajax(webservice.replace(/\$symbol/, symbol)))
```

```
.catch((err$, promise$) => promise$)
.map(response => response.replace(/"/g, ''))
.map(csv);
```

Using the selector function to reiterate the execution of this Promise stream. Bad idea!

Just like in figure 7.9, if the server you're trying to access is offline, the exception thrown would also create an infinite loop and exhaust the main thread, because you would be retrying the same exception (failed `Promise`) over and over again. You'll see how to solve this problem in a bit.

RxJS provides more-intuitive ways of retrying via the `retry()` operator, which combines this notion of catching and reexecuting the source observable into one function. Here's a simple example:

```
Rx.Observable.of(2,4,5,8,10)
  .map(num => {
    if(num % 2 !== 0) {
      throw new Error(`Unexpected odd number: ${num}`);
    }
    return num;
  })
  .retry(3)
  .subscribe(
    num => console.log(num),
    err => console.log(err.message)
  );
```

Repeats this sequence three more times (a total of four) if there's an error before giving up and letting the exception propagate down to the observer

Running this code will print a sequence of numbers 2 and 4 a total of four times before printing "Unexpected odd number: 5." So unless you're dealing with a transient failure that you know will resolve itself somehow, avoid catching and returning the same sequence or the equivalent retry operation with an empty argument. In order to ensure you don't lock up the UI or cause infinite loops to occur, you should always use `retry()` with a fixed number. You could also elegantly combine the two approaches. You can reattempt the operation three more times and then catch the exception, to fall back to a default value:

```
Rx.Observable.of(2,4,5,8,10)
  .map(num => {
    if(num % 2 !== 0) {
      throw new Error(`Unexpected odd number: ${num}`);
    }
    return num;
  })
  .retry(3)
  .catch(err$ => Rx.Observable.of(6))
  .subscribe(
    num => console.log(num),
    err => console.log(err.message));
```

Instead of propagating the error down, you can use this placeholder value.

Again the effect of this is that the sequence would be tried a total of four times before the `catch` block executes, emitting the default value 6 and then completing the sequence. Notice that using a default value with `catch` doesn't simply replace the value in the sequence and allow it to continue. After an exception occurs, the Observable is terminated at that point.

Now that we've talked about catch/retry, you're probably thinking it would be appropriate to embed retry into your stock ticker code, so that if the server were to fail due to a restart or a small outage, you could at least retry to fetch stock information:

```
const requestQuote$ = symbol =>
    Rx.Observable.fromPromise(
      ajax(webservice.replace(/\$symbol/, symbol)))
    .retry(3)
    .map(response => response.replace(/"/g, ''))
    .map(csv);
```

But there's a small caveat here. Recall from our previous discussions that Promises have no retry capability (you don't get second chances with Promises). Unlike Promises, streams are retriable artifacts, so you can easily get around this limitation by wrapping the Promise observable into another stream that is retriable—again creating a higher-order observable. Effectively, what you want to do is apply the retry function to an outer observable that wraps the inner Promise. You can use mergeMap() to flatten it back into a single stream, so placing the retry at fetchDataInterval$ solves this problem:

```
const fetchDataInterval$ = symbol => twoSecond$
    .mergeMap(() => requestQuote$(symbol)         ◀──
        .distinctUntilChanged((previous, next) => {
            ...
        }))
    .retry(3);
```

> requestQuote$ invokes the Promise. This source observable is an outer observable that you can use to make the Promise observable retry three more times.

This code will cause the Promise internally to reinstantiate and retry three more times if it encounters an exception or a rejection, which is really nice. Keep in mind that it will become a single observable layer once mergeMap() projects requestQuote$(symbol) onto the source. The fact that streams can reemit or replay events upon multiple subscriptions is important, but there's a bit more you need to understand that's happening behind the scenes. We'll come back to this solution in the next chapter in the context of hot observables. Another way of implementing retries effectively is to add a backoff strategy, which introduces some wait time in between retry actions.

7.4.4 *Reacting to failed retries*

Using retries with backoff is an effective way to retry more times without overloading the server. Examples of a backoff strategy are constant, linear, exponential, and random (also known as jitter). The exponential and linear types are more commonly used, but in any case, the goal is to use progressively longer waits between retries for consecutive periods of time. RxJS allows you to accomplish this using the retryWhen() operator. retryWhen() takes a notifier observable argument (an internal Observable object that contains any errors that occurred during the execution of the stream, just like with catch()) and repeats the source observable that errors at the pace of when this notifier emits values. For instance, you can say "retry after 3 seconds," as shown in figure 7.10.

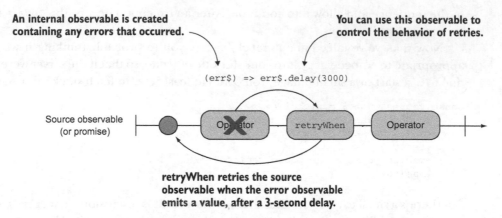

**An internal observable is created
containing any errors that occurred.**

**You can use this observable to
control the behavior of retries.**

`(err$) => err$.delay(3000)`

Source observable
(or promise)

Operator

retryWhen

Operator

**retryWhen retries the source
observable when the error observable
emits a value, after a 3-second delay.**

Figure 7.10   Implementing retries with a constant wait of 3 seconds between retries

In other words, if the provided error observable emits a value, the retry action is executed. So you can use this observable to control when and how retries should take place; it's common to use timer observables to accomplish this. Let's go back to our numbers example to see this clearly:

```
Rx.Observable.of(2,4,5,8,10)
    .map(num => {
       if(num % 2 !== 0) {
          throw new Error(`Unexpected odd number: ${num}`);
       }
       return num;
    })
    .retryWhen(errors$ => errors$.delay(3000))     ⟵  Using the delay operator to
    ...                                                plug in a three-second delay
                                                       between when each error
                                                       value is emitted
```

This will retry the observable sequence from the start and every 3 seconds thereafter and repeat the numbers indefinitely or until the operation that threw the exception becomes successful:

```
1
2
// 3 seconds wait...
1
2
// 3 seconds wait...
...
// and so on
```

You can also use `retryWhen()` to implement a fixed number of retries by keeping track of the number of times the source observable has been retried. Remember, you can use `scan()` to emit values at every accumulated interval:

```
const maxRetries = 3;

Rx.Observable.of(2,4,5,8,10)
    .map(num => {
```

```
    if(num % 2 !== 0) {
        throw new Error(`Unexpected odd number: ${num}`);
    }
    return num;
})
.retryWhen(errors$ =>
    errors$.scan((errorCount, err) => {
        if(errorCount >= maxRetries) {
            throw err;
        }
        return errorCount + 1;
    }, 0)
)
...
```

Running this code prints the same result as previously, with the difference that instead of running indefinitely, it will retry up to the maxRetries limit and then error, calling the error() method on the observers. A more effective retry strategy used in cases where remote requests are being made is a linear backoff, which alleviates the overall load on the server. This technique is readily implemented in most major modern websites; the first retry action occurs immediately, and subsequent actions occur after a certain lag time, which increases linearly, as shown in figure 7.11.

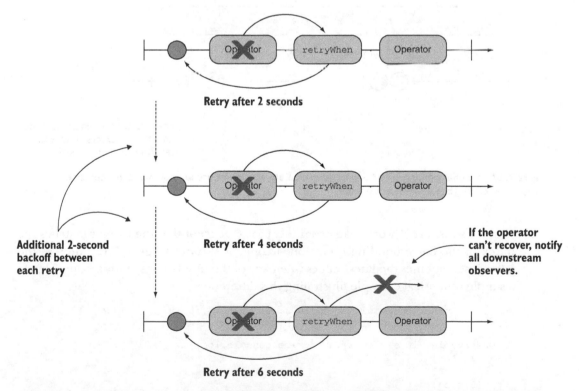

Figure 7.11 After each retry, the time between retries grows linearly. It starts with a two-second wait, and then invokes the next retry call after 4 seconds, and then after 6 seconds, and so on.

Before we get into the code that implements this, we'll introduce a new operator called `zip()`. This operator merges the specified observable sequence into one by using a selector function (a function that you provide to instruct `zip()` how to format the events emitted) whenever all of the observable sequences have emitted values at a corresponding index. This operator is frequently used in FP to merge two corresponding arrays; for instance, `zip()` is implemented in Ramda.js:

```
const records = R.zip(
   ['RecordA', 'RecordB', 'RecordC'],
   ['123', '456', '789']
);
//=> [['RecordA', '123'],
      ['RecordB', '456'],
      ['RecordC', '789']
     ]
```

zip combines both arrays into a multidimensional array, associating each value at the corresponding key.

This works with streams just as well, as shown in the marble diagram in figure 7.12.

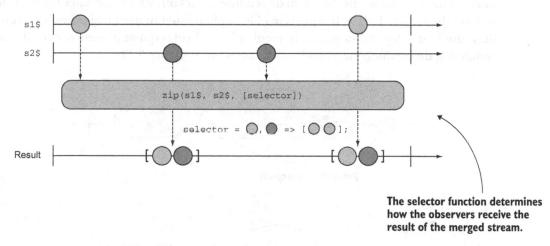

The selector function determines how the observers receive the result of the merged stream.

Figure 7.12   Internal workings of `zip` with streams. Both stream events are combined at each index irrespective of the time either event occurs.

In some ways, `zip()` works like `combineLatest()`, except that the former matches the index of the corresponding events one-to-one, as shown in figure 7.12, whereas the latter just combines the latest values when any of the observables emits a value. Here's a simple numerical example illustrating this difference:

```
const s1$ = Rx.Observable.of(1, 2, 3, 4, 5, 6, 7, 8, 9);
const s2$ = Rx.Observable.of('a', 'b', 'c', 'd', 'e');

Rx.Observable.zip(s1$, s2$).subscribe(console.log);
//-> [1, "a"]
      [2, "b"]
      [3, "c"]
      [4, "d"]
      [5, "e"]
```

```
    Rx.Observable.combineLatest(s1$, s2$).subscribe(console.log);
//-> [9, "a"]
    [9, "b"]
    [9, "c"]
    [9, "d"]
    [9, "e"]
```

As you can see, `zip()` sticks to the array definition, merges both events, and matches the corresponding indexes between the streams. In this case, `s1$` continues to emit more values, but because `s2$` doesn't, `zip()` ignores them—both have to emit events. On the other hand, `combineLatest()` just merges the latest event of `s1$` with whatever is the latest value emitted by `s2$`.

Now that you know how to use `zip()`, you'll implement a linear backoff that retries the first time after 1 second, the next time after 2 seconds, and so on, as shown in the following listing.

Listing 7.7 Implementing a linear backoff retry for our stock ticker stream

```
const maxRetries = 3;
Rx.Observable.of(2,4,5,8,10)
    .map(num => {
      if(num % 2 !== 0) {
        throw new Error(`Unexpected odd number: ${num}`);
      }
      return num;
    })
    .retryWhen(errors$ =>
      Rx.Observable.range(0, maxRetries)         ◄——— Returns an observable that
        .zip(errors$, val => val)                      will emit a maxRetries
        .mergeMap(i =>                    ◄———          number of events. So, if
          Rx.Observable.timer(i * 1000)                maxRetries is 3, it will emit
            .do(() => console.log(`Retrying after ${i} second(s)...`)))   events 3 - 0 = 3 times.
    )
    .subscribe(console.log);
```

zip is used to combine one-to-one values from the source observable (range) with the error observable. You pass a selector function, known in FP as the identity function, that returns the value of the first argument passed to it.

Merges map with a timer observable based on the number of attempts. This is what allows you to emulate the backoff mechanism.

With this retry strategy, the stream will attempt to run for a fixed number of times (given by `maxRetries`), with a linearly incrementing time of 1 second between retries, before finally giving up. Because you're not throwing the exception, the stream halts execution on every retry, generating the following output:

```
2
4
Retrying after 0 second(s)...
2
4
Retrying after 1 second(s)...
```

```
2
4
Retrying after 2 second(s)...
2
4
```

Although the following listing is pretty advanced, you can also bundle throwing the exception if your goal is to signal the unrecoverable condition on your last retry action, as shown in the next listing. You can do this by implementing some conditional logic within the projected observable returned from `mergeMap()`. In this case, if you've reached the last retry, you'll project an observable with an exception; otherwise, you'll project the timer, just as before.

Listing 7.8   Fixed count, linear backoff, and throwing exception if error persists

```
const maxRetries = 3;

Rx.Observable.of(2,4,5,8,10)
  .map(num => {
    if(num % 2 !== 0) {
      throw new Error(`Unexpected odd number: ${num}`);
    }
    return num;
  })
  .retryWhen(errors$ =>
    Rx.Observable.range(0, maxRetries + 1)
      .zip(errors$, (i, err) => ({'i': i, 'err': err}))
      .mergeMap( ({i, err}) => {
        if(i === maxRetries) {
          return Rx.Observable.throw(err);
        }
        return Rx.Observable.timer(i * 1000)
          .do(() =>
               console.log(`Retrying after ${i} second(s)...`));
      })
  )
  .subscribe(
    console.log,
    error => console.log(error.message)
  );
```

Uses a selector function that combines events from both zipped streams into a single object ← (annotation pointing to the `.zip` line)

Destructures the parameter to extract the attempt count and the last error object that occurred → (annotation pointing to the `.mergeMap` line)

← (annotation pointing to the `return Rx.Observable.throw(err);` line)

Because this code is inside a mergeMap() operator, it expects you to return an observable object. You can use the throw() operator to create an observable that safely wraps an exception object (throwing the error would also work, but this approach is more elegant).

Running this code prints the following:

```
2
4
Retrying after 0 second(s)...
2
4
Retrying after 1 second(s)...
```

```
2
4
Retrying after 2 second(s)...
2
4
Unexpected odd number: 5
```

Using `if/else` here is not the most functional way of writing code, but it's acceptable in practice given that the scope is internal to the pipeline. But if you're looking for a purer approach that uses more lambda expressions and keeps the FP spirit high, RxJS provides `Rx.Observable.if(condition, then$, else$)`, which evaluates a given condition function and either returns the `then$` observable or the `else$`, respectively. You'll use this to refactor just that segment of code:

Uses the if() operator (also called the functional combinator) to select between two streams, depending on the evaluation of the condition function

If the condition returns true, project this observable; otherwise, project the observable created in the else block.

```
...
.retryWhen(errors$ =>
    Rx.Observable.range(1, maxRetries)
      .zip(errors$, (i, err) => ({'i': i, 'err': err}))
      .mergeMap(({i, err}) =>
        Rx.Observable.if(() => i <= maxRetries - 1,
          Rx.Observable.timer(i * 1000)
            .do(() => console.log(`Retrying after ${i} second(s)...`)),
          Rx.Observable.throw(err))
    )
  )
...
```

Otherwise, use throw() to propagate an exception downstream to subscribers.

BEST PRACTICE The `zip()` operator can be very useful in cases when you need to spread out a stream synchronously over time, just as you did in the previous code samples. It's not recommended when coordinating asynchronous streams that emit at different times—`combineLatest()` is the operator of choice in these cases. The reason for this is that `zip()` pairs the events one-to-one, so it's effective when the asynchronous streams it's operating over emit values with similar time intervals, which you can't control all of the time. So if you're pairing a mouse-move observable that emits rapidly, for example, with an AJAX call that emits every few seconds, you can easily cause its internal, unbounded buffer to overflow and your application to crash.

Finally, in order to be at feature parity with the imperative world of `try/catch/finally`, RxJS provides the `finally()` operator. Just like the `do()` operator, this operator mirrors the source observable and invokes a specified void function after the source observable terminates by invoking the observer's `complete()` or `error()` methods. So the expectation is that `finally()` could perform some kind of side effect, if need be, such as cleanup actions. This is perfect for our stock ticker widget, which shows a counter of the last time the stock quotes were updated. In this case, you can add another subscription to the `twoSecond$` observable for updating the last updated date:

```
const lastUpdated = document.querySelector('#last-updated');

const updateSubscription = twoSecond$.subscribe(() => {
  lastUpdated.innerHTML = new Date().toLocaleTimeString();
});
```

Remember that you can have a list of subscribers for the same event, so separating the logic for updating different portions of the site keeps the code under the observer nice and simple. If you had, say, three components that needed to change as a result of a stream emitting events, you could attach three observers and update the different portions of the site accordingly. So you have two subscribers: the one we just showed you and another used to fetch the stock data, to which you'll add error-handling code. If the web service call made in the `fetchDataInterval$` observable were to fail (returning a 500 HTTP response code, for example), the `catch()` operator would react and return a default value for that stock quote section, as shown in the next listing.

Listing 7.9   Stock ticker with error handling

```
const requestQuote$ = symbol =>                                    Adds catch() to handle
    Rx.Observable.fromPromise(                                       the exception
      ajax(webservice.replace(/\$symbol/, symbol)))              potentially thrown
    .map(response => response.replace(/"/g, ''))                 from requestQuote$
    .map(csv)
    .catch(() =>
        Rx.Observable.of([new Error('Check again later...'), 0]))
    .finally(() => {
      updateSubscription.unsubscribe();        ◁──    In the event an error occurs, cancels
    });                                                the twoSecond$ interval observable
                                                       through its subscription object.
```

The other code you added was the `finally()` operator, which fires when a stream completes or when it errors. Because you're running a two-second interval, you don't expect a completion, but in the event of an error, you should also clean up the interval and cancel the subscription, so that the updated time shown reflects the last quoted update received before the error occurred. You can see this process in the graph in figure 7.13.

And now you need to make a small adjustment to the `tick$` observable, so that it knows how to handle an error. You can use our `Try` functional data type to handle this, and if a failure does occur, delegate the exception to the error callback of the observer. Here's that code once more with the new addition:

```
ticks$
  .map(([symbol, price]) => [Try.of(symbol).getOrElseThrow(), price])
  .subscribe(
    ([symbol, price]) => {

        let id = 'row-' + symbol.toLowerCase();
        let row = document.querySelector(`#${id}`);
        if(!row) {
            addRow(id, symbol, price);
        }
        else {
            updateRow(row, symbol, price);
        }
    },
    error => console.log(error.message));
```

Before the data is handed down to the subscriber, Try can inspect it and decide if the data flowing in is an exception that needs to be thrown.

If this service were to fail (or your internet disconnect), you'd see "Check again later…" printed in the console.

As you can see, RxJS provides a comprehensive set of error-handling operations that allows you to easily retry an entire observable sequence when an error is detected in the pipeline. But we made a huge assumption about the nature of the observable sequences. That is, the observables that we created and retried in this chapter belong to a category known as *cold* observables. Cold observables are passive (dormant) and emit values only when subscribed to: an array of numbers, a Promise, intervals, and the like. In other words, retrying a cold observable basically resubscribes to it and requests that it emit its values again. In the next chapter, you'll learn to create and handle the different types of observables: cold and hot.

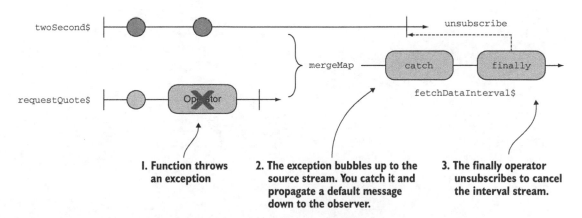

1. **Function throws an exception**

2. **The exception bubbles up to the source stream. You catch it and propagate a default message down to the observer.**

3. **The finally operator unsubscribes to cancel the interval stream.**

Figure 7.13 Using finally to clean up and cancel any outstanding streams

7.5   *Summary*

- Imperative error handling has many drawbacks that make it incompatible with FP.
- Value containers, like `Try`, provide a fluent, expressive mechanism for transforming values immutably.
- The `Try` wrapper is a functional data type used to consolidate and abstract exception handling so that you can sequentially map functions to values.
- RxJS implements many useful and powerful operators that allow you to catch and retry failed operations in a way that doesn't break the flow of the stream and the declarative nature of an RxJS stream declaration.
- RxJS provides operators such as `catch()`, `retry()`, `retryWhen()`, and `finally()` that you can combine to create sophisticated error-handling schemes.

Part 3

Mastering RxJS

Now that you have a firm grasp of the basics of RxJS, it's time to start working with some advanced techniques. We'll cover sharing your streams between observers, as well as a detailed discussion of eager versus lazy types and how observables are able to handle both scenarios gracefully. We'll also go back to some concepts about time that we only teased you with in the first part of the book; we'll show you how to use them to build powerful declarative tests that can run with user-defined concepts of time.

In chapter 8, we'll talk about the difference between hot and cold streams, how to identify the two types, and how to move between them easily using RxJS operators. Chapter 9 covers reactive testing and provides an introduction to the scheduling abstraction, which is a powerful concept that allows you to run tests faster than real time. Finally, in chapter 10 we'll wrap up by bringing together everything you've learned to create a basic banking application using React, Redux, and RxJS. This combo will help give you an idea of the potential for integration afforded by RxJS, as well as the strategies and benefits of maintaining a single-directional flow of events through an application.

Heating up observables

8

This chapter covers

- The difference between hot and cold observables
- Working with WebSockets and event emitters via RxJS
- Sharing streams with multiple subscribers
- Understanding how hot and cold pertains to how the producer is created
- Sending events as unicast or multicast to one or multiple subscribers

As you know, an observable function is a lazy computation, which means the entire sequence of operators that encompass the observable declaration won't begin executing until an observer subscribes to it. But have you ever thought about what happens to all the events that occur before subscription happens? For instance, what does a mouse move observable do with all the mouse events or a WebSocket that has received a set of messages? Do these potentially very important occurrences get lost in the ether? The reality is that these active data sources won't wait for subscribers to listen to begin emitting events, and it's vital for you to know how to deal with this situation. Earlier, we briefly called out this idea that observables come in two different flavors: hot and cold. This isn't a simple topic to grasp; it's probably one of the most complex in the RxJS world, which is why we dedicate an entire chapter to it.

In this chapter, we'll take a closer look at hot and cold observables, how they differ, the benefits of each, and how you can take advantage of this in your own code. Up until now, we've had only a single subscriber to a stream, and we even looked at combining multiple streams funneled through one observer in chapter 6. Now, we take the opposite approach as we look into sharing a single observable sequence with multiple observers. For instance, we can take a simple numerical stream and share its values with multiple subscribers or take a single WebSocket message and broadcast it to multiple subscribers. This is very different from the single-stream subscriber cases we've dealt with. We'll begin by demonstrating the differences between hot and cold observables.

8.1   Introducing hot and cold observables

Think about when you turn on your TV set and switch to the channel of your favorite show. If you catch the show 10 minutes after it began, will it start from the beginning? Restarting the show would mean that cable companies broadcast independent streams to every subscriber—which would be great. Instead, the same content is broadcast to all subscribers at a set time. So unless you have a recording device, which you can associate with a buffer operator, you can't replay content that aired in the past.

A TV's live stream is equivalent to a hot observable. RxJS divides observable sources into either of two categories: hot or cold. These categories determine the behavioral characteristics, not just of subscription semantics, but also of the entire lifetime of the stream. An observable's temperature also affects whether the stream and the producer are managed together or separately, which can greatly affect resource utilization (we'll get to this shortly). We classify an observable as either hot or cold based on the nature of the data source that it's listening to. Let's begin with cold observables.

8.1.1   Cold observables

In simple terms, a *cold observable* is one that doesn't begin emitting all of its values until an observer subscribes to it. Cold observables are typically used to wrap bounded data types such as numbers, ranges of numbers, strings, arrays, and HTTP requests, as well as unbounded types like generator functions. These resources are known as *passive* in the sense that their declaration is independent of their execution. This also means that these observables are truly lazy in their creation and execution.

Now, this isn't news to you, because that's what we've defined an observable to be all along, so what's the catch? Being cold means that each new subscription is creating a new independent stream with a new starting point for that stream. This means that subscribers will independently receive the exact same set of events always, from the beginning. Here's another way to conceptualize it: when creating a cold observable, you're actually creating a plan or recipe to be executed later—repeatedly, top to bottom. The recipe itself is just a set of instructions (operators) that tell the JavaScript runtime engine how to combine and cook the ingredients (data); cold observables begin emitting events only when you choose to start cooking.

PURE OBSERVABLES   Observables are pure when they abide by the FP principles of a pure function, which is immutable, side effect–free, and repeatable. We've talked about the first two principles at length in this book, and now we tag on this third quality. In order to support the desirable functional property of referential transparency, functions must be repeatable and predictable, which means that invoking a function with the same arguments always yields the same result. The same holds for cold observables when viewed simply as functions that produce (return) a set of values.

From a pure FP perspective, you can think of cold observables as behaving very much like functions. A function can be thought of as a lazy or to-be-computed value that's returned when you invoke it, only when needed (languages with lazy evaluation, like Haskell, work this way). Similarly, observable objects won't run until subscribed to, and you can use the provided observers to process their return values. You can visualize this resemblance in figure 8.1.

Furthermore, the declaration of a cold observable frequently begins with static operators such as of() or from(), and timing observables interval() and timer() also behave coldly. Here's a quick example:

```
const arr$ = Rx.Observable.from([1,2,3,4,5,6,7,8,9]);

const sub1 = arr$.subscribe(console.log);

// ... moments later ... //
const sub2 = arr$.subscribe(console.log);
```

Every subscriber gets their own independent copy of the same data no matter when the subscription happens.

sub2 could have subscribed moments later, yet it still receives the entire array of elements.

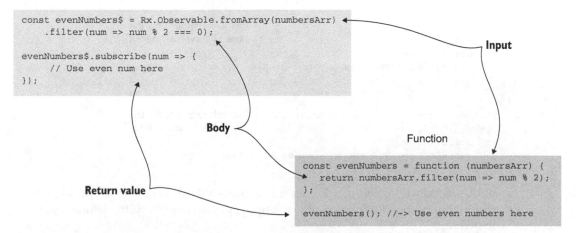

```
const evenNumbers$ = Rx.Observable.fromArray(numbersArr)
    .filter(num => num % 2 === 0);

evenNumbers$.subscribe(num => {
    // Use even num here
});
```

Cold observable

Input

Body

Function

Return value

```
const evenNumbers = function (numbersArr) {
    return numbersArr.filter(num => num % 2);
};

evenNumbers(); //-> Use even numbers here
```

Figure 8.1   A cold observable can be thought of as a function that takes input—data that is to be processed—and, based on this, returns an output to the caller.

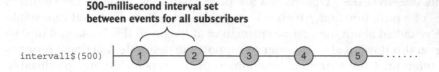

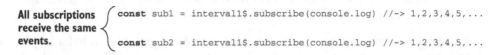

Figure 8.2   A cold observable is like an object factory, which can be used to create a family of subscriptions that will receive their own independent copy of all the events pushed through them.

With cold observables, all subscribers, no matter at what point the subscription occurred, will observe the same events. Another example is the `interval()` operator. Each time a new subscription occurs, a brand-new interval instance is created, like in figure 8.2.

  `interval` acts like a factory for timers, where each timer operates on its own schedule and each subscription can, therefore, be independently created and cancelled as needed. Cold observables can be likened to a factory function that produces stream instances according to a template (its pipeline) for each subscriber to consume fully. The following listing demonstrates that you can use the same observable with two subscribers that listen for even and odd numbers only, respectively.

Listing 8.1   Interval factory

```
const interval$ = Rx.Observable.interval(500);

const isEven = x => x % 2 === 0;

interval$
  .filter(isEven)                              Two subscriptions for the
  .take(5)                                     same observable, interval$
  .subscribe(x => {              ◄─┐
      console.log(`Even number found: ${x}`);
  });
interval$
  .filter(R.compose(R.not, isEven))            Two subscriptions for the
  .take(5)                                     same observable, interval$
  .subscribe(x => {              ◄─┐
      console.log(`Odd number found: ${x}`);
  });
```

CODE SAMPLES   Remember that all the code for this chapter can be found in the RxJSinAction GitHub repository, https://github.com/RxJSInAction/rxjs-in-action.

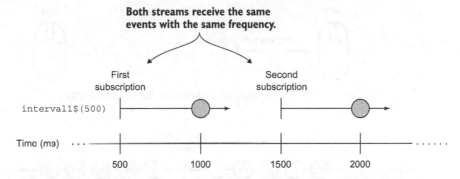

Figure 8.3 Resubscribing to an interval observable yields two independent sequences, with the same events happening with the same frequency; hence, this is a cold observable.

In the example in listing 8.1, the streams are independently created from one another. Each time a new subscriber subscribes, the logic in the pipeline is reexecuted from scratch. So these streams all receive the same numbers and don't affect each other's progress—they're isolated, as shown in figure 8.3.

> **DEFINITION**   A cold observable is one that, when subscribed to, emits the entire sequence of events to any active subscribers.

Now, we're ready to heat things up and look closely at the other side of the coin: hot observables.

8.1.2 *Hot observables*

Streams don't always start when you want them to, nor can you reasonably expect that you'd always want every event from every observable. It may be the case that by delaying subscription, you deliberately avoid certain events like an implicit version of `skip()`.

Hot observables are those that produce events regardless of the presence of subscribers—they are active. In the real world, hot observables are used to model events like clicks, mouse movement, touch, or any other events exposed via event emitters. This means that, unlike the cold counterpart where each subscription triggers a new stream, subscribers to hot observables tend to receive only the events that are emitted after the subscription is created, as shown in figure 8.4.

A hot observable continues to remain lazy in the sense that without a subscriber, the events are simply emitted and ignored. Only when an observer subscribes to the stream does the pipeline of operators begin to do its job and the data flow downstream.

This type of stream is often more intuitive to many developers because it closely mirrors behaviors they're already familiar with in `Promises` and event emitters.

> **PROMISES AND HTTP CALLS**   Although a conventional HTTP request is cold, it isn't when a `Promise` is used to resolve it. As you'll learn in a bit, a `Promise` of any type represents a hot observable because it's not reexecuted after it's been fulfilled.

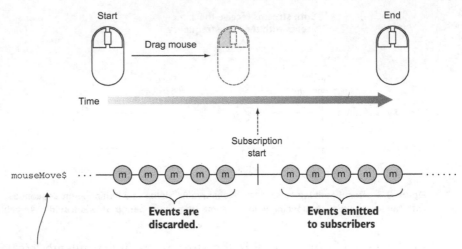

As the mouse moves, it generates an unpredictable number of events.

Figure 8.4 A mouse move handler generates unbounded events that can be captured as soon as the HTML document loads, but these events will be ignored until the stream has been created and the observer subscribed to it.

Because of the unpredictable and unrepeatable nature of the data that hot observables emit, you can reason that they're not completely pure, from a theoretical perspective. After all, reacting to an external stimulus, like a button click, can be considered a form of side effect dependent on the behavior of some other resource, like the DOM, or simply time. Nevertheless, from the point of view of the application and your code, all observables can be considered pure.

Unlike cold observables that create independent copies of the data source to emit to every subscriber, a hot observable shares the same subscription to all observers that listen to it, as shown in figure 8.5. Therefore, you can conclude that a hot observable is one that, when subscribed to, emits the ongoing sequence of events from the point of subscription and not from the beginning.

Whether an observable is hot or cold is partly related to the type of source that it's wrapping. For instance, in the case of any mouse event handler, short of creating some new mechanism for handling mouse events, an observable is merely abstracting the existing `addEventListener()` call for a given emitter. As a result, the behavior of mouse event observables is contingent on the behavior of the system's handling of mouse events. You can further categorize this source as natively hot, because the source is determining the behavior. You can also make sources hot, programmatically, using operators as well, and we'll discuss this further in the sections to come.

On the other hand, observables that either wrap a static data source (array) or use generated data (via a generator function) are typically cold, which means they don't begin producing values without a subscriber listening to them. This is intuitive because, like iteration, stepping through a data source requires a consumer or a client.

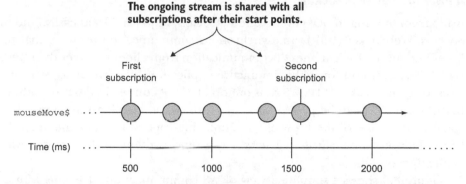

Figure 8.5　Hot observables share the same stream of events to all subscribers. Each subscriber will start receiving events currently flowing through the stream after subscription.

A key selling point for using RxJS is that it allows you to build logic independently of the type of data source you need to interact with—we called this a *unifying computing model*. A source can emit zero to thousands of events unpredictably fired at different times. Nevertheless, the abstraction provided by the observable type means that you don't have to worry about these peculiarities when building the logic inside the stream or within the context of the observable. This interface abstracts the underlying implementation out of sight and out of mind—for the most part.

> **DEFINITION**　Hot observables are those that produce events regardless of the presence of subscribers.

In general, it's better to use cold observables wherever possible because they're inherently stateless. This means that each subscription is independent of every other subscription, so there's less shared state to worry about, from an internal RxJS perspective, because you know a new stream is starting on every subscription.

8.2　A new type of data source: WebSockets

In chapter 4, we mentioned that time ubiquitously exists in observables—in hot observables, to be exact. This disparity between when a data source begins emitting events and when a subscriber starts listening can lead to issues. Think about that TV show that you switched to midprogram. In such contexts, unless you've watched the show before tuning in, you'll miss some context or plot that was presented at the beginning. In the same vein, you can imagine a simple messaging system using a protocol like WebSockets—or any other event emitter, for that matter. In these cases, missing any messages can be critical to the proper functioning of your application. So if a subscription to a hot observable occurs after a critical message packet arrives, then those instructions might be lost. We haven't talked about using WebSockets with RxJS, so let's begin by briefly examining what they are and how RxJS can help you handle these asynchronous message flows.

8.2.1   *A brief look at WebSocket*

Aside from binding to DOM events and AJAX calls, RxJS can just as easily bind to Web-Sockets. WebSocket (WS) is an asynchronous communication protocol that provides faster and more efficient lines of communication from client to server than traditional HTTP. This is useful for highly interactive applications like live chats, streaming services, or games. Like HTTP, WS runs on top of a TCP connection, but the advantage is that information can be passed back and forth while keeping the connection open (taking advantage of the browser's multiplexing capabilities and the keep-alive feature). The other benefit is that servers can send content to the browser without it explicitly requesting it.

Figure 8.6 shows a simplified view of WS communication. It begins with a handshake, which bridges the world of HTTP to WS. At this time, details about the connection and security are discussed to pave the way for secure, efficient communication between the parties involved.

The steps taken between the client and the server, illustrated in figure 8.6, are these:

1 Establish a socket connection between parties for the initial handshake.
2 Switch or upgrade the communication protocol from regular HTTP to a socket-based protocol.
3 Send messages in both directions (known as *full duplex*).
4 Issue a disconnect, via either the server or the client.

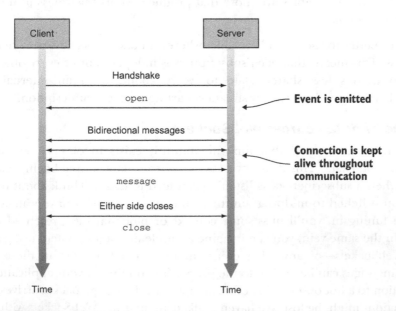

Figure 8.6   WebSocket communication diagram showing communication that begins with a handshake where client and server negotiate the terms of the connection. Afterward, communication flows freely until one of the parties closes.

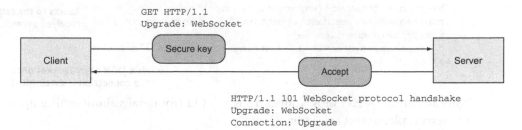

Figure 8.7 The handshake negotiation process begins with the client's GET request containing a secure key and instructions for the server to attempt to upgrade to a message-based WebSocket connection. If the server understands WebSocket, it will respond with a unique hash confirming the protocol upgrade.

The crucial point of this process is the initial handshake that negotiates the upgrade process. The upgrade needs to happen because WebSocket uses the same ports 80 and 443 for HTTP and HTTPS, respectively (443 is used by the WebSockets Secure protocol). Routing requests through the same ports is advantageous because firewalls are typically configured to allow this information to flow freely. At a very high level, this process happens with an initial secure request by the client and a proper response by the WebSocket-supporting server, shown in figure 8.7.

From the point of view of asynchronous event messaging, you can think of Web-Socket as an event emitter for client-server communication. We haven't really talked about server-side RxJS, but little changes there. You can easily use RxJS to support both sides of the coin, starting with the server.

8.2.2 A simple WebSocket server in Node.js

In the spirit of a JavaScript book, we'll write our server using Node.js. But you can use any other platform of your liking such as Python, PHP, Java, or any other platform with a socket API. Our server side will be a simple TCP application listening on port 1337 (chosen arbitrarily) using the Node.js WebSocket API. WebSocket negotiates with the HTTP server to be the vehicle to send and receive messages. Once the server receives a request, it will respond with the message "Hello Socket," as follows.

Listing 8.2 Simple RxJS Node.js server

```
const Rx = require('rxjs/Rx');                          ◁── Imports the RxJS core APIs
const WebSocketServer = require('websocket').server;    ◁── Imports the WebSocket
const http = require('http');                                server library

// ws port                                              Imports the
const server = http.createServer();    ◁──              HTTP library
server.listen(1337);

// create the server                    Instantiates an HTTP server to
wsServer = new WebSocketServer({        begin listening on port 1337
    httpServer: server
});
```

```
Rx.Observable.fromEvent(wsServer, 'request')      ◁───┐ Reacts to the request
   .map(request => request.accept(null, request.origin))    received event
   .subscribe(connection => {
      connection.sendUTF(JSON.stringify({ msg:'Hello Socket' }));   ◁───┐
   });
```

Reacts to the request received event

Sends a JSON object packet once a connection is established

You can run the server with Node.js using the CLI (for details about setting up RxJS on the server, please visit appendix A):

```
> node server.js
```

Now that your server is up and listening, you can build the client again using RxJS—one library to rule them all!

8.2.3 WebSocket client

Modern browsers come equipped with the WebSocket APIs, which allow for an interactive communication with a server. Using these APIs, you can send messages to a server and receive event-driven responses (server push) without you having to explicitly poll for data, which is what you would do with regular HTTP requests. The next listing shows a simple WebSocket connection using RxJS.

Listing 8.3   WebSocket client with RxJS

Connects to port 1337 using the WebSocket (ws) protocol

Listens for the 'message' events used to transmit messages between client and server

```
const websocket = new WebSocket('ws://localhost:1337');

Rx.Observable.fromEvent(websocket, 'message')      ◁───
   .map(msg => JSON.parse(msg.data))      ◁───┐ Parses the serialized
   .pluck('msg')                                string into a JSON object
   .subscribe(console.log);
```

Reads the message

Parses the serialized string into a JSON object

WebSockets are a form of loosely decoupled communication between two entities, in this case a browser and a server, that act as event emitters. This goes back to the idea of using a familiar computing model for everything. In essence, with RxJS, the details of setting up event listeners for WebSocket communication are completely abstracted and removed from your code.

> **REACTIVE MANIFESTO**   A good design principle of reactive systems is that they communicate using asynchronous message passing, in order to establish a boundary between loosely coupled components.[1] This not only allows components to evolve independently but also delegates failures as messages. This means non-local components can react to errors appropriately.

Just like any event emitter, using RxJS with WebSocket creates a hot observable, which means it won't reenact all the messages emitted upon subscription but merely begin

---

[1] http://www.reactivemanifesto.org/.

pushing any that occur thereafter. This can be tricky because subscribing to a hot observable a little too late can result in a loss of data. Consider this slight variation of listing 8.3:

```
Rx.Observable.timer(3000)                    ◄──────────────────────────
  .mergeMap(() => Rx.Observable.fromEvent(websocket, 'message'))
  .map(msg => JSON.parse(msg.data))
  .pluck('msg')                              Wraps the socket object after
  .subscribe(console.log);                   a three-second delay
```

In this stream, you tie WebSocket subscription to a wait time (3 seconds). You arbitrarily set this wait time in order to simulate a delay such as one caused by page initialization—essentially, you create a time dependency. Recall the WebSocket handshake diagram; as soon as the socket fires the open event, this hot observable can begin emitting events. Thus, if the socket opening occurs before the page has completed its initialization step, the observable will potentially miss any events emitted in the intervening period.

As an added complication, time dependencies aren't necessarily deterministic. In this scenario, you added a simple three-second timeout, but your page load or initialization logic could be much more complex. It could be affected by any number of variables, such as whether the application was loaded from a cache, how many resources the user's system has available for processing requests, how much network latency is present, or even how much animation is on the page, because they all can change when the page initialization occurs or when the WebSocket connects and begins sending events.

Certainly a dependency on time can be significant in an observable's behavior, to the point of breaking the nice functional quality that cold observables possess. Ideally, every subscriber to a cold observable should see the same sequence of events replayed, but this isn't always the case, because there's a big difference between resubscribing and replaying when side effects are at play.

8.3 *The impact of side effects on a resubscribe or a replay*

As you saw from the previous use case, hot observables, for the most part, follow a strict you-snooze-you-lose policy, which means you can't replay the contents of a hot observable by resubscribing to it, as you can with cold observables (there are ways of doing it, but this isn't the default behavior). Now, this doesn't mean that all cold observables behave this way, especially when you introduce side effects into your code. Before we discuss this further, you need to understand the difference between resubscribing and replaying in RxJS:

- A *replay* is about reemitting the same sequence of events to each subscriber—in effect, replaying the entire sequence. You must use caution when attempting to replay sequences because they potentially require using lots of memory (often with unbounded buffers) to store the contents of a stream that is to be reemitted at a later time. For obvious reasons, we recommend against doing this with streams like mouse clicks or any other infinite event emitter.

- A good example of replay semantics is a `Promise`. Replaying the observable created from a `Promise` by means of a retry or simply attaching new subscribers doesn't cause the fulfilled `Promise` to invoke again but simply to return the value or the error, as the case may be.
- A *resubscribe* re-creates the same pipeline and reexecutes the code that produces events. Although the results emitted by the producer will be implementation dependent, if your observable pipeline remains pure, then you can guarantee that all subscribers will receive the same events for the same input produced.

8.3.1 *Replay vs. resubscribe*

The difference is subtle but important. In essence, it's about whether the pipeline (your business logic) gets reexecuted or not when another subscriber starts listening. Most of the canned observable factory methods—`create()`, `interval()`, `range()`, `from(Array|scalar|generator*)`, and others—are cold by default. The diagram in figure 8.8 illustrates the differences between these mechanisms. A replay emits the same output to all subscribers without invoking the operator sequence.

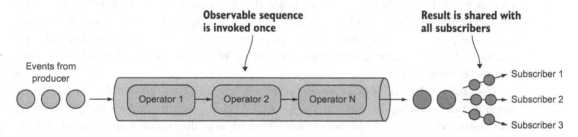

Figure 8.8 When replaying, the output emitted by an observable sequence is shared or broadcast to all subscribers.

In contrast, a cold resubscribe (figure 8.9) invokes the sequence of operators that lead to the result for every subscriber.

We'll show a simple example showcasing both scenarios and the impact a side effect can have. For this, you'll build custom observables whose behavior depends on the time of day (a side effect). In this case, you'll emit events until the time reaches 10:00 p.m., at which point they'll fire the complete signal.

8.3.2 *Replaying the logic of a stream*

To showcase how a replay works, consider a body of time-sensitive code wrapped in a `Promise` that will emit a value of "Success!" before 10:00 p.m. or throw an exception if executed after. The first observer that subscribes before 10:00 p.m. will cause the

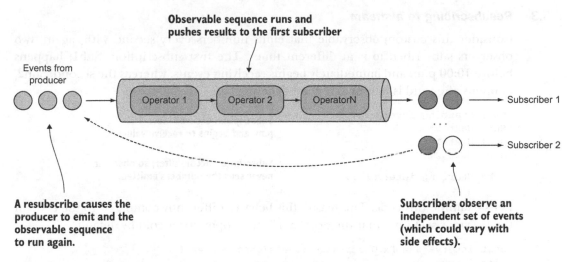

Figure 8.9 A resubscribe causes the producer and the observable sequence to execute. If the operator sequence has side effects, then new subscribers could see different results.

`Promise` to execute and resolve. Any observers that subscribe later will receive the same value without invoking the body of the `Promise`. The business logic is ignored:

```
const p = new Promise((resolve, reject) => {
  setTimeout(() =>{                                    ⟵ Uses moment.js to check if
    let isAtAfter10pm = moment().hour() >= 20;             the current time is 10:00 p.m.
    if(isAtAfter10pm) {
      reject(new Error('Too late!'));
    }
    else {
      resolve('Success!');
    }
  }, 5000);
});

const promise$ = Rx.Observable.fromPromise(p);           First subscriber
                                                         executes the Promise
promise$.subscribe(val => console.log(`Sub1 ${val}`));   ⟵

// ... after 10 pm ...//
promise$.subscribe(val => console.log(`Sub2 ${val}`));   ⟵
```

> Second subscriber will emit the same value, regardless
> of the time it subscribed, because it won't run the code
> within the body of the Promise

Regardless of the time of the subscription, any observers that subscribe to this stream receive the same value, whether it's a success or failure. This cold observable behaved predictably, but this is only because of the way `Promise`s work. Querying the result of a fulfilled `Promise` always outputs the same value. So the body of the `Promise`, in this case, doesn't actually run when the second subscribe occurs—this is a replay, and the `fromPromise()` static operator is hot. Now let's look at the case of a resubscribe.

8.3.3   *Resubscribing to a stream*

Consider this custom observable that emits numbers every second with, again, two observers subscribed to it at different times. The first subscription, Sub1, happens before 10:00 p.m. and immediately begins receiving events, whereas the second, Sub2, happens after and is terminated immediately:

```
"Sub1 Starting interval..."          ◁─┐  Subscription occurs before 10
"Sub1 Next 0"                          │  p.m. and begins to receive values
"Sub1 Next 1"
"Sub1 Next 2"
                                          Subscription occurs after, so observer
"Sub2 Starting interval..."          ◁─┘  never sees the numbers emitted.
```

Let's examine this code. The reason this behaves differently compared to the code in the previous section is that the `create()` factory operator is cold by default:

```
const interval$ = Rx.Observable.create(observer => {
  let i = 0;

  observer.next('Starting interval...');
  let intervalId = setInterval(() => {                    Uses moment.js to check if the
                                                          current time is 10:00 p.m.
    let isAtAfter10pm = moment().hour() >= 20;   ◁─┘

    if(isAtAfter10pm) {
      clearInterval(intervalId);            ◁──── Stops emitting events
      observer.complete();
    }

    observer.next(`Next ${i++}`);
  }, 1000);                                                    Subscriber sub1
});                                                            begins listening.

  // ... before 10 pm ... //
const sub1 = interval$.subscribe(val => console.log(`Sub1 ${val}`));   ◁─┘

// ... after 10 pm ... //
const sub2 = interval$.subscribe(val => console.log(`Sub2 ${val}`));
```

After 10 p.m., sub2 subscribes but ends immediately.

Resubscribing to this stream (with sub2) would create a new, independent stream, but it won't just blindly propagate the same values again. Instead it re-invokes the logic so that different subscribers would receive (or not) events based on when they subscribed. If the time reaches 10:00 p.m. before subscriber sub2 has a chance to listen, it won't receive any events at all. So the fact that the observable begins emitting events when subscribed to indicates that it's a cold observable. But because you have a side effect in your code, preventing it from replaying the sequence, the results that subscribers see might be significantly different.

> **SIDE EFFECT ALERT**   As we mentioned, the direct use of time in your code is clearly a sign of a side effect because, intuitively, it's global to your application and ever changing. This is why hot observables are the less-pure form when compared to cold observables, which should reemit (or replay) all the items to any subscribers.

In the same vein, consider an operator you saw in the last chapter, `retry()`, which performs a resubscribe on an observable when an error occurs. Let's revisit using it as part of your stock ticker stream. Using `retry()` directly on the `Promise` seemed like a good idea:

```
const requestQuote$ = symbol =>
    Rx.Observable.fromPromise(
      ajax(webservice.replace(/\$symbol/, symbol)))
    .retry(3)
    .map(response => response.replace(/"/g, ''))
    .map(csv);
```

You might expect to retry a web request if it fails, resulting in up to four requests sent to the server before an error is finally served. But we mentioned a small caveat in that you may have then been surprised to see that the network debugger showed only a single request being executed. Why? Let's look at this in the context of hot and cold observables.

This goes back to our examination of how sources affect the behavior of observables. A `Promise` is an eager data type (read *hot observable*), which means that upon creation it can only ever resolve or reject and will do so even without listeners. `Promises` are not retriable. So once it's in one of those two states, it stays there, and every new handler will receive either the resolved value or the error that caused the rejection. Because `Promises` don't have retry, any attempt to retry through `fromPromise()` is futile because it just replays whatever the final state of the `Promise` is, by design. Recall that to get around this limitation, you wrapped the creation of the `Promise` in another observable, which *is* retriable, so that the operation contained inside it (the `Promise`) could be retried. That's why you moved it to its outer observable:

```
const fetchDataInterval$ = symbol => twoSecond$
    .mergeMap(() => requestQuote$(symbol))  ◁──┐  The inner observable that's projected
    .retry(3)                                   │  onto the two-second stream
    .catch(err => Rx.Observable.throw(
       new Error('Stock data not available. Try again later!')));
```

This is the observable that retries the failed stream three more times; if not successful, it catches and propagates the error downstream.

Remember that this worked because you actually created a new `Promise` within the `mergeMap()` operator and the retry is resubscribing to the projected observable and not to the one created directly in `fromPromise()`. The resubscription rebuilds the pipeline and reexecutes it for the single value that you passed into it. So now you have a complete and deep understanding of why this technique works. You changed the temperature of this observable, so that it essentially behaves cold.

To summarize, resubscribing to a cold observable creates independent event channels for each subscriber, which means each observer creates its own copy of the producer. In most situations, this is desirable. For instance, if you use observables to process a set of objects originating from a generator function, you'll definitely want to work on copies of this producer (created via the cold `from()` static operator) instead of sharing it. On the other hand, replaying can be effective and save you precious computing cycles when your intent is to broadcast or share the output of an observable sequence to multiple observers.

In practice, when the producer resource is expensive to create, such as a remote HTTP call or a WebSocket, then sharing it is a smart thing to do. Let's examine how to heat up observables to accomplish this.

8.4   *Changing the temperature of an observable*

The resubscription mechanism of cold observables is easy to reason about because each stream carries its own copy of the producer, spawning a new pipeline back up to the source. This happens in RxJS by default when wrapping synchronous data sources like scalars and arrays but also through custom observables containing asynchronous data sources such as remote event emitters, AJAX calls, or WebSockets that are created within the observable context. In all these cases, you deal with cold observables. From a functional point of view, this is the purest solution because no data is being shared and the observable acts like a template (or a recipe, as we mentioned previously) for creating data, as shown in figure 8.10.

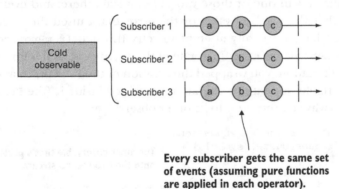

Every subscriber gets the same set of events (assuming pure functions are applied in each operator).

Figure 8.10   New subscribers to cold observables fork the event sequence and obtain their own copy.

But when resources are scarce, doing this can pose significant problems. In practice, it's beneficial to spawn one HTTP request, have a single event emitter instance, or create one WebSocket connection that many observers can share, instead of one for each. In section 8.3, we showed that wrapping an external socket (created outside the observable context) represents a hot observable. The WebSocket object in this case is the producer of data, and it's important to understand that the scope in which it's created is the ultimate thermometer, so to speak, to measure whether an observable is considered hot or cold.

8.4.1 Producers as thermometers

Ben Lesh, who is the project lead for RxJS 5, wrote an interesting piece on Medium.com[2] that explains hot and cold observables from the perspective of the producer (that is, WebSockets, eager HTTP requests via `Promises`, and event emitters). He articulates it eloquently as follows:

> *COLD is when your observable creates the producer.*
>
> *HOT is when your observable closes over the producer.*

In this article, he treats producers as a generic object of type `Producer`, which represents any object capable of emitting data asynchronously—without necessarily being iterated over. Let's examine the terminology he uses. A cold observable "creates the producer," meaning that it's created within the scope of the observable context, for instance:

```
const cold$ = new Rx.Observable(observer => {
    const producer = new Producer();        <──────┐  The lifecycle of the producer
                                                    │  entity (a generic object) is bound
    // ...Observer listens to producer,            │  to that of the observable's
    //    producer pushes events to the observer...┘

    producer.addEventListener('some-event', e => observer.next(e));

    return () => producer.dispose();
});
```

When this stream object is garbage collected, the underlying producer object gets collected with it. Likewise, when the stream is disposed of, it will invoke the mechanism to discard the producer as well. The other implication is that anything that subscribes to `cold$` will obtain its own copy of the producer object, as we've mentioned before. This one-to-one communication between a producer and a consumer (observer) is referred to as *unicast*.

> **UNICAST** In the world of computer networking, a unicast transmission involves the sending of messages to a single network destination identified by a unique source address.

On the other hand, hot observables "close over the producer object" that's created or activated outside the observable context. In this case, the lifecycle of the event emitter source is independent of that of the observable. The term *closes over* derives from the idea that the producer object is accessible through the closure formed around the observable declaration.

```
const producer = new Producer();        <──────┐  Producer object is in scope
                                               │  through the closure formed
const hot$ = new Rx.Observable(observer => {   │  around the observable
    // ...Observer listens to producer,        │  declaration
    //    and pushes events onto it...         │
    producer.addEventListener('some-event', e => observer.next(e));  <──┘
```

---

[2] https://medium.com/@benlesh/hot-vs-cold-observables-f8094ed53339#.966re47vq.

```
    // producer gets disposed of outside of Observable context
});
```

From our FP discussion, you can see that this is not pure because the observable object (or function) is accessing external data directly, which is a side effect. In practice, though, the benefit of doing this is that the producer is now shared by all subscribers to hot$ and emits data to all of them—a model known as *multicast*.

> **MULTICAST**   In computer networking, *multicast* refers to a one-to-many form of communication where information is addressed to multiple destinations from a single source.

Figure 8.11 explains the difference between the two modes of message passing.

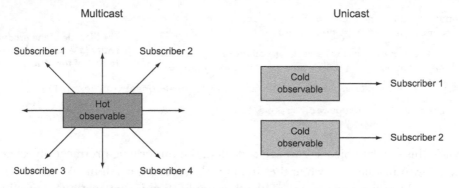

Figure 8.11   Multicast transmits messages from one source to many destinations; unicast sends dedicated messages to one destination address.

To sum up, the multicast mode is the process behind hot observables, whereas unicast messaging occurs with cold observables. Depending on your needs, you can use RxJS to make hot observables cold for isolated, dedicated connections or vice versa for shared access to resources. Let's look at examples of each scenario.

8.4.2   *Making a hot observable cold*

So far, our de facto mechanism for fetching remote data has always involved using Promises. Without you realizing it, you've already had to convert observable types; you did this in chapter 5 so that you could use Promises to fetch fresh stock data. Now we can discuss that technique more in depth and frame the problem this way: if Promises are hot because the value they emit is shared among all subscribers and are not repeatable or retriable, how can you use them to fetch new stock quotes? Wouldn't the stock price be the same all the time? Again, this has everything to do with where the observable was instantiated. If you execute the Promise request globally (eagerly), as in this simple code, the same value (or error) is essentially broadcast to all subscribers:

```
const futureVal = new Promise((resolve, reject) => {

    const value = computeValue();

    resolve(value);
});

const promise$ = Rx.Observable.fromPromise(futureVal);

promise$.subscribe(console.log);          ⟵—— Begins invoking the Promise

promise$.subscribe(console.log);   ⟵
```
After the first invocation of the Promise resolves, all subsequent subscriptions will resolve to the same value.

To make this observable cold, you move the instantiation of the `Promise` within the observable context through `ajax()`. Here's a snippet of that code once more:

```
const requestQuote$ = symbol =>
    Rx.Observable.fromPromise(ajax(...))    ⟵
...
```
ajax() instantiates a new Promise within the observable context.

```
const fetchDataInterval$ = symbol => twoSecond$
    .mergeMap(() => requestQuote$(symbol)
    ...
```

In essence, this is analogous to what you just learned, which is to move the source or the producer of events into the observable context:

```
const coldPromise$ = new Rx.Observable(observer => {
    const futureVal = new Promise((resolve, reject) => {     ⟵
```
Shoves the instantiation of the Promise into the observable

```
        const value = computeValue();

        resolve(value);
    });

    futureVal.then(result => {
        observer.next(result);      ⟵
        observer.complete();      ⟵
    });
});
```
Emits the value from the Promise

Because you're expecting only a single value, completes the stream

```
coldPromise$.subscribe(console.log);

coldPromise$.subscribe(console.log);
```
Both subscribers will invoke the internal Promise object.

You can apply this same principle to WebSockets. In section 8.3.3, you used an observable to wrap a global, shared WebSocket object. Here it is once more:

```
const websocket = new WebSocket('ws://localhost:1337');    ⟵
```
Globally shared object

```
const sub = Rx.Observable.fromEvent(websocket, 'message')
    .map(msg => JSON.parse(msg.data))
    .pluck('msg')
    .subscribe(console.log);

websocket.onclose = () => sub.unsubscribe();    ⟵
```
Socket's lifecycle is managed outside the observable sequence

If you instead wanted to have dedicated connections to each subscriber, you could enclose the activation of the producer within the observable context. This way, every subscriber of the stream would create its own socket connection:

```
const ws$ = new Rx.Observable(observer => {
  const socket = new WebSocket('ws://localhost:1337');      Not global but
  socket.addEventListener('message', e => observer.next(e));  instantiated
  return () => socket.close();                                 with every
});                                                            observer

const sub1 = ws$.map(msg => JSON.parse(msg.data))
  .subscribe(msg => console.log(`Sub1 ${msg}`));

const sub2 = ws$.map(msg => JSON.parse(msg.data))         Gets its own dedicated
  .subscribe(msg => console.log(`Sub2 ${msg}`));           socket connection
```

This also applies to the RxJS static factory operators such as `create()`, `from()`, `interval()`, `range()`, and others. As mentioned previously, because they're cold by default, you may want to make them hot with the intention of sharing their content and avoiding not only duplicating your efforts but also duplicating resources. Let's look at doing that next.

8.4.3   *Making a cold observable hot*

In this section, you'll apply the reverse logic. To make a cold observables hot, you need to focus on how they emit data and how subscribers access this data. Circling back to your stock ticker widget, this means that you must move the source of events (stock ticks) away from the observable pipeline. You would want to do something like this if you had stock data being pushed into different parts of the application and you wanted them all in sync with the same event timer. In this case, simply subscribing with multiple observers won't do the trick.

```
const sub1 = ticks$.subscribe(
  quoteDetails => updatePanel1(quoteDetails.symbol, quoteDetails.price)
);

const sub2 = ticks$.subscribe(
  quoteDetails => updatePanel2(quoteDetails.symbol, quoteDetails.price)
);
```

sub1 and sub2 will use their own two-second intervals, which could get out of sync, and also fetch their own copies of stock data. You could optimize this so that the HTTP response can be parsed once and consumed by multiple observers.

The other problem with this approach is resource usage. With two subscribers, if you were to open the developer console, you'd notice that for each refresh action (2 seconds apart) there would be not one but two separate requests being sent to the server with each observer. This means that every subscriber would have its own independent interval stream, which would incur the expense of establishing the same remote connection multiple times to fetch data against the Yahoo API, as shown in figure 8.12.

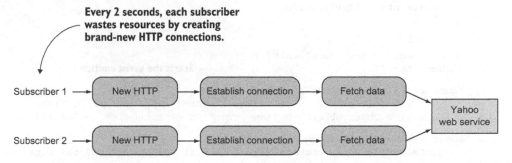

Figure 8.12   With two cold subscriptions, each one is responsible for initiating and allocating resources to make AJAX calls against the same service.

Why create new HTTP connections when you could just share this data downstream to multiple subscribers? Again, the answer lies in how the source of the stream is activated—as a globally accessible resource or within the observable context—we can't stress that enough. You can expose your service that fetches stock data as a resource that multiple subscribers can observe. But how can you make AJAX calls hot? There are many ways of doing this, but one idea involves using event emitters with an internal polling mechanism, so that, in conjunction with the hot Rx.Observable.from-Event() observable, you can pump stock data to all subscribers. This works just like a WebSocket, broadcasting stock ticks independently of when a subscriber exists. Take a look at an example of this in the next listing.

Listing 8.4   Stock ticker as event emitter

```
class StockTicker extends EventEmitter {        ◄──┐ Event emitter to
  constructor(symbol) {                               │ encapsulate a StockTicker
    super();
    this.symbol = symbol;
    this.intId = 0;
  }

  tick(symbol, price) {               ◄────── This represents the 'tick' event.
    this.emit('tick', symbol, price);
  }

  start() {                                    │ Every two seconds, polls the
    this.intId = setInterval(() => {      ◄──┘ stock service for new price data
    const webservice =
      `http://finance.yahoo.com/d/quotes.csv?s=${this.symbol}&f=sa&e=.csv`;

      ajax(webservice).then(csv).then(
        ([symbol, price]) => {
          this.tick(symbol.replace(/\"/g, ''), price);
      });
    }, 2000);
  }
  stop() {
```

```
          clearInterval(this.intId);
    }
}

const ticker = new StockTicker('FB');
ticker.start();                         <──── Starts the event emitter
const tick$ = Rx.Observable.fromEvent(ticker, 'tick',
        (symbol, price) => ({'symbol': symbol, 'price': price}))
    .catch(Rx.Observable.throw(new Error('Stock ticker exception'))));
const sub1 = ticks$.subscribe( //#E
    quoteDetails => updatePanel1(quoteDetails.symbol, quoteDetails.price)
);
const sub2 = ticks$.subscribe( //#E
    quoteDetails => updatePanel2(quoteDetails.symbol, quoteDetails.price)
);
```

**sub1 and sub2 will share the data
from the same source of events.**

As you can see from this code, whether you subscribe to the source or not, it will continue to fetch and send out price ticks. The big difference here is that you've decoupled the subscription from the activation of the event source, essentially now a hot observable. Because of this decoupling, the observable is also removed from the lifecycle of the event source (that is, `start()` and `stop()`), just like with WebSockets earlier. Thus, when all subscribers unsubscribe, the event emitter will continue to send data—it's just that no one is there to listen. This is expected, and most of the hot observables you'll find in the wild (DOM elements, a database, or the filesystem) won't emit a complete signal, because their lifecycle extends that of the observable.

You shouldn't expect that to make cold observables hot you need to have them depend on global producers all the time. You want the best of both worlds and certainly the nice functional qualities of cold observables. There are many benefits to encapsulating the event source and having it managed through the observable's lifecycle (this also ensures fewer possibilities of memory leaks because all resources are collected and disposed of when they're completely unsubscribed from). On the other hand, you also don't want to duplicate your efforts and instead share the events from a single source to multiple subscribers.

8.4.4   *Creating hot-by-operator streams*

So far, you've seen that the process of converting a cold stream to hot is to place the activation of the producer resource within the context of an observable. But this isn't the only way. Fortunately, RxJS provides a convenient operator called `share()`that does just that. It's so named because it shares a single subscription to a stream among multiple subscribers (kind of like the old days of DIRECTV, where a single satellite feed could operate multiple TVs in the same house). This means that you can place this operator right after a set of operations whose results should be common, and the subscribers to each of them will all get the same stream instance (without replaying the

pipeline). Just as important, this operator takes care of the management of the underlying stream's state such that upon the first subscriber subscribing, the underlying
stream is also subscribed to, and when all the subscribers stop listening (either
through error or cancellation), the underlying subscription is disposed of as well. Brilliant! When a new subscriber comes in, the source is reconnected and the process is
restarted. Here's a quick example that shows the same result shared without replaying
the entire sequence:

```
const source$ = Rx.Observable.interval(1000)
  .take(10)
  .do(num => {
      console.log(`Running some code with ${num}`);
  });
```

```
const shared$ = source$.share();          ⟵—— Converts the cold observable to hot
```

```
shared$.subscribe(createObserver('SourceA'));
shared$.subscribe(createObserver('SourceB'));

function createObserver(tag) {
    return {
        next: x => {
            console.log(`Next: ${tag} ${x}`);
        },
        error: err => {
            console.log(`Error: ${err}`);
        },
        complete: () => {
            console.log('Completed');
        }
    };
}
```

When the number of observers subscribed to a published observable goes from 0 to 1, you connect to the underlying observable sequence.

When the second subscriber is added, no additional subscriptions are added to the underlying observable sequence. As a result, the operations that result in side effects are not repeated per subscriber.

Helper method to create a simple observer for standard out

Once the observable in front of share() is subscribed to, it's for all intents and purposes hot; this is known as *hot-by-operator*, and it's the best way to heat up a cold observable. Running this code illustrates that a single subscription is shared to the
underlying sequence:

```
"Running some code with 0"
"Next: SubA 0"
"Next: SubB 0"
"Running some code with 1"
"Next: SubA 1"
"Next: SubB 1"

... and so on...

"Completed"
"Completed"
```

Pitfall: sharing with a synchronous event source

The `share()` operator is useful in many cases where subscribers subscribe at different times but are somewhat tolerant of data loss. Because it can be used following any observable, it's sometimes confusing to newcomers who might be tempted to do the following:

```
const source$ = Rx.Observable.from([1,2,3,4])
  .filter(isEven)
  .map(x => x * x)
  .share();
source$.subscribe(x => console.log(`Stream 1 ${x}`));
source$.subscribe(x => console.log(`Stream 2 ${x}`));
```

This code is often seen as an easy, efficient win for those new to reactive programming. If the pipeline executes for each subscription, then it makes sense that by adding the `share` operator you can force it to execute only once, and both observers can use the results. As the console will tell you, however, this does not appear to occur. Instead, only Stream 1 seems to get executed. The reason for this is twofold. The first is scheduling, which we'll gloss over for now because it's covered in a later chapter. In basic terms, subscribing to a synchronous source like an array will execute and complete before the second subscribe statement is even reached. The second reason is that `share()` has introduced state into your application. With it, the first subscription always results in the observable beginning to emit, and so long as at least one subscriber continues to listen, it will continue to emit until the source completes. If you're not careful, this kind of behavior can become a subtle bug.

When dealing with observables that run immediately, like those in the example, this can result in only a single subscriber receiving the events.

Let's apply this to your original stock ticker stream so that you can avoid making unnecessary HTTP calls with each subscriber that subscribes to the stream; instead, you make only one call that broadcasts to any subscribers. Making your stock ticker stream hot is as simple as adding `share()` at the end of it:

```
const ticks$ = symbol$.mergeMap(fetchDataInterval$).share();
const sub1 = ticks$.subscribe(
    quoteDetails => updatePanel1(quoteDetails.symbol, quoteDetails.price)
);

const sub1 = ticks$.subscribe(
    quoteDetails => updatePanel2(quoteDetails.symbol, quoteDetails.price)
);
```

Just like with the global event emitter example, all subscribers will receive the same tick data. We'll show a more complete version of this code in a bit.

And now you've officially completed the stock ticker code. Here's the full rendition with all the parts added from the operators you learned about in chapters 5 through 8. Let's recap:

- *Chapter 5*—You learned how to use higher-order observables and flattening operators such as `mergeMap()`.
- *Chapter 6*—You learned to coordinate multiple observables with `combineLatest()`.
- *Chapter 7*—You added fault tolerance to your streams with retry and error handling.
- *Chapter 8*—You learned how to convert a cold observable into a hot observable that shares its event data with many subscribers. To demonstrate this, you'll have two subscribers updating different parts of the site.

You'll put all of this together in listing 8.5 and enhance your stock widget with the ability to track the price and day's change for all stocks (we omit the CSS and HTML code, which you can find in the GitHub repository). With these changes, your UI is updated to look like figure 8.13.

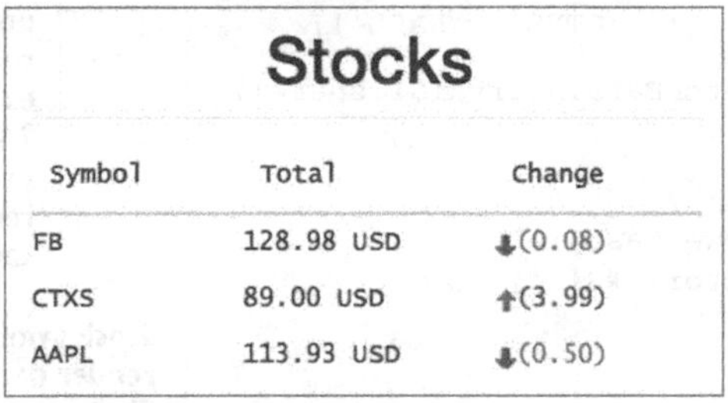

Stocks

Symbol	Total	Change
FB	128.98 USD	↓(0.08)
CTXS	89.00 USD	↑(3.99)
AAPL	113.93 USD	↓(0.50)

Figure 8.13 Screenshot of the live HTML stock ticker component as it ticks every 2 seconds and includes additional logic to compute the stock's price change from the opening price (prices are subject to market conditions)

You'll make several changes to the code you started with in listing 5.6, because you'll combine the stock ticker stream with another stream against the same service to read the stock's opening price. Subtracting the current price from the previous price gives you the next change. These will be two independent subscriptions parting from the commonly shared `tick$` stream, which is now hot. The following listing shows the complete code and uses many of the techniques you've learned about so far.

Listing 8.5 Complete stock ticker widget with change tracking

The Yahoo Finance web service to use with additional options used to query for the pertinent data

Applies options to the request URI. s = symbol; a = asking price; o = open.

Helper function to split a string into a comma-separated set of values (CSV)

Function used to create a stream that invokes a Promise that fetches data from the web service and parses the result into CSV

```
const csv = str => str.split(/,\s*/);
const cleanStr = str => str.replace(/\"|\s*/g, '');

const webservice = 'http://download.finance.yahoo.com/d/quotes.csv
    ?s=$symbol&f=$options&e=.csv';

const requestQuote$ = (symbol, opts = 'sa') =>
    Rx.Observable.fromPromise(
        ajax(webservice.replace(/\$symbol/, symbol)
            .replace(/\$options/, opts)))
```

```
                    .retry(3)
                    .catch(err => Rx.Observable.throw(
                        new Error('Stock data not available. Try again later!')))
                    .map(cleanStr)
                    .map(data => data.indexOf(',') > 0 ? csv(data) : data);
```

Converts output to CSV → (points to `.map(cleanStr)`)

Cleans string of any white spaces and unnecessary characters → (points to `.map(data => ...`)

```
    const twoSecond$ = Rx.Observable.interval(2000);

    const fetchDataInterval$ = symbol => twoSecond$
        .mergeMap(() => requestQuote$(symbol)
            .distinctUntilChanged((previous, next) => {
                let prevPrice = parseFloat(previous[1]).toFixed(2);
                let nextPrice = parseFloat(next[1]).toFixed(2);
                return prevPrice === nextPrice;
            }));
```

The two-second observable used to drive the execution of the real-time poll → (points to `const twoSecond$`)

Propagates stock price values only when they've changed. This avoids unnecessary code from executing every 2 seconds when price values remain the same. → (points to `.distinctUntilChanged`)

```
    const symbol$ = Rx.Observable.of('FB', 'CTXS', 'AAPL');

    const ticks$ = symbol$.mergeMap(fetchDataInterval$).share();

    ticks$.subscribe(
        ([symbol, price]) => {
            let id = 'row-' + symbol.toLowerCase();
            let row = document.querySelector(`#${id}`);
            if(!row) {
                addRow(id, symbol, price);
            }
            else {
                updateRow(row, symbol, price);
            }
        },
        error => console.log(error.message));
```

Shares the stock data with all subscribers → (points to `const ticks$`)

First subscription. Creates all necessary rows and updates the price amount in USD. → (points to `ticks$.subscribe(`)

Stock symbols to render data for. These can be any symbols; keep in mind that to see live changes, you must run the program during market hours. → (points to `const symbol$`)

```
    ticks$
        .mergeMap(([symbol, price]) =>
          Rx.Observable.of([symbol, price])
            .combineLatest(requestQuote$(symbol, 'o')))
        .map(R.flatten)
        .map(([symbol, current, open]) => [symbol, (current - open).toFixed(2)])
        .do(console.log)
        .subscribe(([symbol, change]) => {
            let id = 'row-' + symbol.toLowerCase();
            let row = document.querySelector(`#${id}`);
            if(row) {
                updatePriceChange(row, change);
            }
        },
        error => console.log(`Fetch error occurred: ${error}`)
        );
```

Second subscription. A conformant stream that combines the price of the stock at the open, so that it can compute the change amount for the day. It appends the next change price in the stock.

Uses Ramda to flatten the internal array of data passing through, making it easier to parse, for example, [[symbol, price], open] -> [symbol, price, open]

```
const updatePriceChange = (rowElem, change) => {
    let [,, changeElem] = rowElem.childNodes;
    let priceClass = "green-text", priceIcon="up-green";
    if(parseFloat(change) < 0) {
        priceClass = "red-text"; priceIcon="down-red";
    }
    changeElem.innerHTML =
      `<span class="${priceClass}">
          <span class="${priceIcon}">
              (${parseFloat(Math.abs(change)).toFixed(2)})
          </span>
      </span>`;
};
```

The `share()` method is a useful and powerful shortcut to implement these complex examples with relatively few lines of code. But to understand what's really happening under the hood, you need to dive a little deeper and explore the domain of an observable variety called `ConnectableObservable`.

8.5   *Connecting one observable to many observers*

We mentioned previously that in RxJS and the networking world, a single point-to-point transmission is known as unicast, and the one-to-many transmission is known as multicast. As you saw from the previous example, `share()` is a multicast operator, but there are other flavors or specializations of it, all derived from a single generic function known as `multicast()`. In practice, typically you'll never actually use `multicast()` directly, but rather one of its specializations.

> **RXJS 5 IMPROVEMENT** It's important to recall that the RxJS 5 team has done a great job at cutting the API surface pertaining to the set of operators used to share and publish values by about 75%.

A thorough explanation of all the specializations for multicasting (also known as the *multicasting operators* in RxJS parlance) can require a whole book of its own. We won't be using them much in this book, and you won't need them in your initial exploration of RxJS. When the time arises, `share()` is all you need (no pun intended). Nevertheless, it's important to be aware that RxJS gives you a lot more control over the amount and types of data to emit when you need it. So we'll spend some time talking about the most common ones:

- Publish
- Publish with replay
- Publish last

8.5.1   *Publish*

The first specialization is the operator `publish()`. This is the vanilla multicast specialization. The idea is to create an observable (like `share()`) that allows a single subscription to be distributed to several subscribers. The difference between these operators is one of simplicity versus control. Whereas `share()` automatically managed the subscription and unsubscription of the source stream based solely on the number of subscribers, `publish()` is slightly more low-level. Here it is, using the same `source$` stream as before:

```
const source$ = Rx.Observable.interval(1000)
  .take(10)                          <──── Makes your stream finite
  .do(num => {
      console.log(`Running some code with ${num}`);
  });

const published$ = source$.publish();

published$.subscribe(createObserver('SubA'));

published$.subscribe(createObserver('SubB'));
```

Now, when you run this code, there's no output, as if the stream is sitting idle. The issue you encounter is that `publish()` returns a derivation of observables known as a `ConnectableObservable`. This new type requires a more explicit initiation step than `share()`. Whereas the latter connects on the first subscription, the former requires another call to build the underlying subscription. You can start the source observable by calling `connect()` on the resulting `ConnectableObservable`:

```
published$.connect();          <──── Can be invoked at any point after the call to publish()
```

> **CAUTION**   We made our stream finite in this code sample for an important reason. `connect()` is a low-level operator, which means you're bypassing all of the nice subscription management logic available in the core RxJS creational operators. In other words, it's not a managed subscription. `connect()` can be a powerful tool, but it's up to you to ensure that the stream is unsubscribed from at some point; otherwise, you'll cause memory leaks.

As soon as you call the `connect()` method, your observable will act just like the one in the previous example. You can visualize this process with figure 8.14.

If you were to examine `ConnectableObservable`, you'd see an interface roughly shaped like this:

```
interface ConnectableObservable<T> extends Observable<T> {
  connect() : Subscription
  refCount(): Observable<T>
}
```

> **NOTE**   Observables that share subscriptions are generally called hot, whereas those that don't are called cold. But there are also observables that start emitting events only after the first subscription (a quality seen only in cold observables) and thereafter share their data to all subscribers (a hot quality). We sometimes refer to these observables as *warm*.

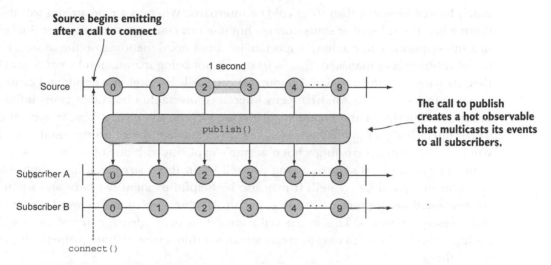

Figure 8.14 Publish creates a hot observable whereby all subscribers begin receiving the events as soon as the call to connect is made. Otherwise, the source stream behaves like a cold observable, sitting idle until `connect()` is called. The `share()` operator would yield the same results except that the call to `connect()` would be done internally by the library.

These are two important concepts to understand:

- The `connect()` method returns a `Subscription` instance that represents the shared underlying subscription. Unsubscribing from it will result in both subscribers no longer receiving any events. You saw how to use `connect` in the previous example.

- The `refCount()` method is named after the garbage collection concept known as *ref counting*, or *reference counting*. The point is that it returns an observable sequence that stays connected to the source as long as there's a least one active subscription. Does this sound familiar? It should because the `share()` operator we discussed a moment ago is little more than an alias for `publish().refCount()`.

Now you understand why `share()` is just a shortcut for what's happening under the hood. RxJS creates warm observables that multicast their values to all connected subscribers managed through the connectable observable, which keeps a count of all active subscribers. When all subscribers have unsubscribed, it will unsubscribe from the source observable.

The use of internal ref counting is crucial to the efficiency of RxJS. As we mentioned earlier, an important difference between hot and cold observables is when their lives start and when they can be considered to have ended. Hot observables can produce events in the absence of observers, whereas cold observables don't become active until they have a subscription. A result of this is that hot streams will often have much longer lifespans than their cold counterparts. Whereas a cold stream will shut down when the subscriber shuts down, a hot one can continue running after the end of a subscription. This can have important implications, depending on the source. If a hot observable is unmanaged, that is, its state is not being maintained by refCount(), then its state (and the associated resources) can easily be forgotten about and cause a memory leak—which is what happens when a connectable observable emits infinite events. A majority of the included operators, such as Rx.Observable.fromEvent() which intrinsically wrap hot sources, take care to manage their own disposed state. If you ever find yourself creating a hot observable explicitly with one of the multicast() family of operators, it's worth asking yourself when those streams will be destroyed and how many will be created. It may also be helpful to identify where and when a stream would be disposed of and to explicitly unsubscribe from it to avoid taking up unnecessary resources. This is especially important in single-page applications with multiple views, where it's easy to create streams within a view without properly disposing of them.

Publish is just one flavor of hot observable; several others can be useful, depending on the desired behavior on subsequent subscription. Suppose you wanted to have a moving window of past values to be emitted to all observables. Earlier, we talked about the differences between replaying the results of a sequence and resubscribing to execute the entire sequence again. You can mix that concept with publish.

8.5.2 *Publish with replay*

You could use another specialization of multicast called publishReplay() to emit the last 1, 10, 100, or all of the most recent values to all subscribers (obviously, this is another case of a warm observable). This operator uses several parameters to determine the characteristics of a buffer to maintain. And as with any of the buffering operators you learned about in chapter 4, we caution you again that the use of buffers can be dangerous when replaying entire sequences and the buffer grows indefinitely. You can see this clearly if you inspect the signature of this operator:

```
publishReplay(bufferSize = Number.POSITIVE_INFINITY,
              windowTime = Number.POSITIVE_INFINITY)
```

This operator is analogous to the RxJS 4 shareReplay() operator, which had the same issue. So using publishReplay() with empty arguments can be dangerous. Here's an example of this operator. Unlike the publish example, to showcase the use of this operator, you have to simulate a subscriber coming at a later time:

```
const source$ = Rx.Observable.interval(1000)   ◁── Begins a counter that pushes integers every second, starting at zero
  .take(10)
  .do(num => {
      console.log(`Running some code with ${num}`);   ◁── Creates a side effect to show that it's running
  });
```

```
const published$ = source$.publishReplay(2);

published$.subscribe(createObserver('SubA'));

setTimeout(() => {
  published$.subscribe(createObserver('SubB'));
}, 5000)

published$.connect();
```

Creates an observable that can store two past events and reemit them to any new subscribers

Subscribing 5 seconds later, subscriber B should begin receiving events starting with the number 4, but because of the replay it will first receive 2 and 3.

Subscriber A connects subscribers immediately, and begins receiving events from count 0.

Running this code would print the following output. What you'll notice here is that as soon as the second subscriber comes, it will first make sure to emit the last events in the stream (current and previous); afterward, both streams will replay the same events:

```
"Running some code with 0"
"Next: SubA 0"
"Running some code with 1"
"Next: SubA 1"
"Running some code with 2"
"Next: SubA 2"
"Running some code with 3"
"Next: SubA 3"
"Next: SubB 2"
"Next: SubB 3"
"Running some code with 4"
"Next: SubA 4"
"Next: SubB 4"
"Running some code with 5"
"Next: SubA 5"
"Next: SubB 5"
...
"Next: SubA 9"
"Next: SubB 9"
"Completed"
"Completed"
```

SubB will begin receiving the last two events (previous and current).

Both subscribers receive the same data.

Figure 8.15 is a diagram of what's happening in the code sample.

Alternatively, when you want only the last value to be emitted, `publishLast()` will do the trick.

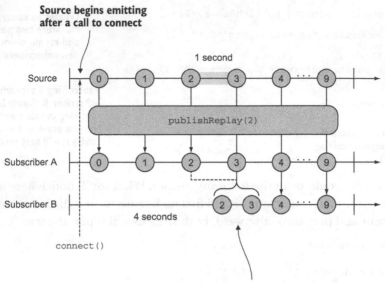

When Subscriber B subscribes, it receives the current element 3 and the previous element 2 (replay 2 events). This is not done at once with an array but with two calls to the observer's next().

Figure 8.15 `publishReplay` with a buffer count of 2 will emit the last two elements in the buffer (current and previous) at the moment the subscriber subscribes to the stream. Afterward, both streams receive the latest value emitted.

8.5.3   *Publish last*

`publishLast()` is simple to understand. It returns a connectable observable sequence that shares a single subscription containing only the last notification. This operator is analogous to `last()` (except non-blocking) in that it multicasts the last observable value from a sequence to all subscribers. Follow our simple example once more:

```
const published$ = source$.publishLast();

published$.subscribe(createObserver('SubA'));

published$.subscribe(createObserver('SubB'));

published$.connect();
```

Running this code prints out the following:

```
"Running some code with 0"
"Running some code with 1"
...
"Running some code with 9"
"Next: SubA 9"
"Next: SubB 9"
"Completed"
"Completed"
```

There are many overloaded specializations of `multicast()` in RxJS. You can find them all here: https://github.com/ReactiveX/rxjs/blob/master/src/operator/publish.ts. If you inspect these operators, you'll find that they delegate most of their work to entities called subjects.

> **Further reading**
>
> Theoretically, subjects can be used to supplant virtually all of your observable needs, and the possibilities are endless. Because this is an advanced topic, in this book we prefer sticking to the managed observables created via RxJS factory methods. But if you would like to read on further, we recommend you begin with the RxJS manual: http://reactivex.io/rxjs/manual/overview.html#subject.

RxJS provides hot and cold observables because the designers recognized that different types of sources must often be addressed, with different needs. There is no one-size-fits-all solution to every problem, but `share()` will get you a long way ahead. But to that end, there's also a steeper learning curve to mount in order to fully understand the library, especially the topic of multicasting operators. We hope this chapter has demystified some of the strangeness around these different observable types. But when all else fails, here's a good analogy to keep in mind (taken from the Reactive Extensions GitHub project[3]):

- A cold observable is like watching a movie.
- A hot observable is like watching live theater.
- A hot observable replayed is like watching a play on video.

These lessons will be useful when we move into the next chapter and discuss how to test your Rx pipelines.

8.6 Summary

- A cold observable is passive in that it waits until a subscriber is listening to execute an individual pipeline for each subscriber. Cold observables manage the lifecycle of the event producer.
- Hot observables are active and can begin emitting events regardless of whether subscribers are listening. Hot observables close over the producer of events, so their lifecycles are independent of the source.
- Event emitters such as WebSockets and DOM elements are examples of hot observables.
- Events from hot observables will be lost if no one is listening, whereas cold observables will always rebuild their pipeline upon every subscription.

---

[3] https://github.com/Reactive-Extensions/RxJS/blob/master/doc/gettingstarted/creating.md.

- share() makes observers use the same underlying source stream and disconnects when all the subscribers stop listening. This operator can be used to make a cold observable hot—or at least warm.
- Using operators such as publish(), publishReplay(), and publishLast() creates multicast observables.

Toward testable, reactive programs

This chapter covers

- Understanding functional programming's inherent testability
- Testing asynchronous code with Mocha.js
- Exploring the tools for testing observables
- Understanding the need for using virtual time instead of physical time
- Introducing RxJS schedulers
- Refactoring streams to enhance testability

If you've been in the software industry for any appreciable amount of time, you've likely encountered some form of testing. In production software, there's no escaping the need for tests (or there shouldn't be), whether they target newly written code or a system-wide refactoring. Changes to complex applications can easily produce unforeseen consequences in different paths of execution; it's particularly problematic when multiple developers work with code that they're not intimately familiar with. For instance, when a user types a negative number in the withdraw field or presses this number rapidly many times, your banking application should handle it gracefully. As you know, in JavaScript, a misspelled variable or a forgotten return statement means that certain execution paths may produce undefined values. These sorts of errors may be obvious or subtle, and no developer—no matter how experienced—is safe from them.

Tests not only help catch programmatic errors and find places where code is brittle, but they also ensure that there's a unified understanding of the requirements. In other words, tests also document the expected behavior of your code.

There are multiple types of testing methods, probably more than we can keep track of, but in this chapter, we'll focus strictly on unit tests. Unit tests are used to create expectations or assertions about the functionality of a single unit of work—a function.

We'll begin this chapter by demonstrating that pure functions are inherently much easier to test than stateful functions, because they have clear inputs and predictable outputs—known as *boundary conditions*. Likewise, observables are functional data types that can be tested in the same manner as pure functions by translating these pure function boundaries to the world of producers and observers. But this isn't always easy. In JavaScript, with so many asynchronous processes to coordinate, testing can be difficult to wrap your head around. You'll learn to use RxJS's observable-based testing to make asynchronous testing easier. With the help of a JavaScript testing framework, Mocha.js, as well as an RxJS instrumentation tool known as a *virtual scheduler*, you can learn to test streams that compose any sort of asynchronous code easily. Toward the end of this chapter, you'll learn about RxJS schedulers. Although they can be powerful, using schedulers in JavaScript applications, especially client-side, is not all that common and intended only for edge cases where the schedulers that accompany the RxJS operators aren't sufficient.

In the end, one of the main advantages of writing your programs functionally is that you've organized the code in such a way that favors testability. Let's start here.

9.1   *Testing is inherently built into functional programs*

Think back to when you last wrote a set of unit tests for some complex functionality. Do you remember running into any challenges? If this application was written using OOP, most likely you experienced at least one of the following:

- Methods rely on external state that must be properly set up and destroyed for each test.
- Methods are tightly coupled to other modules of the system, making it impossible to test each one independently.
- Your application design lacks a proper dependency injection strategy, so you're unable to properly mock calls to all third-party dependencies.
- Methods are long and complex, so they contain many internal logic paths (lots of if/else blocks), which requires you to write multiple tests against the same method just to cover all the flows.

- The order in which tests are run can impact the results that output from the functions under test, so changing the order or possibly commenting out a unit can cause others to fail.

This is by no means an exhaustive list, just some of the more common pain points that we've all experienced while unit testing. Now we don't mean to say that functional tests won't ever have these problems, but what you'll begin to see is that by using pure functions, you can significantly diminish their occurrence.

Pure functions tend to be small in scope, have at most three clearly defined parameters (rarely more), and have a predictable, consistent output—like a black box with simple boundary conditions, as shown in figure 9.1. Moreover, a pure function is deterministic, which means its result is directly determined from the arguments that are passed to it, so half of the testing battle is just coming up with comprehensive sets of inputs. These can be any primitive type like a number or a string, or complex types such as objects and mocks (object impersonators), also shown in figure 9.1.

The other half of the battle is asserting that the return value matches solely the logic behind the function under test, which isn't influenced by what's happening externally. In this book, we'll use Mocha.js as our unit test framework (you can find setup information in appendix A). Let's look at a quick example of its basic usage. Aside from loading the necessary scripts on the page, there's a minor setup step for you to specify the API style you'll use for your assertions and expectations, known as the UI of the test. You'll use the BDD UI, which is the default. If you're using it in the browser, you can use this:

```
mocha.setup({ ui: 'bdd', checkLeaks: true});
```

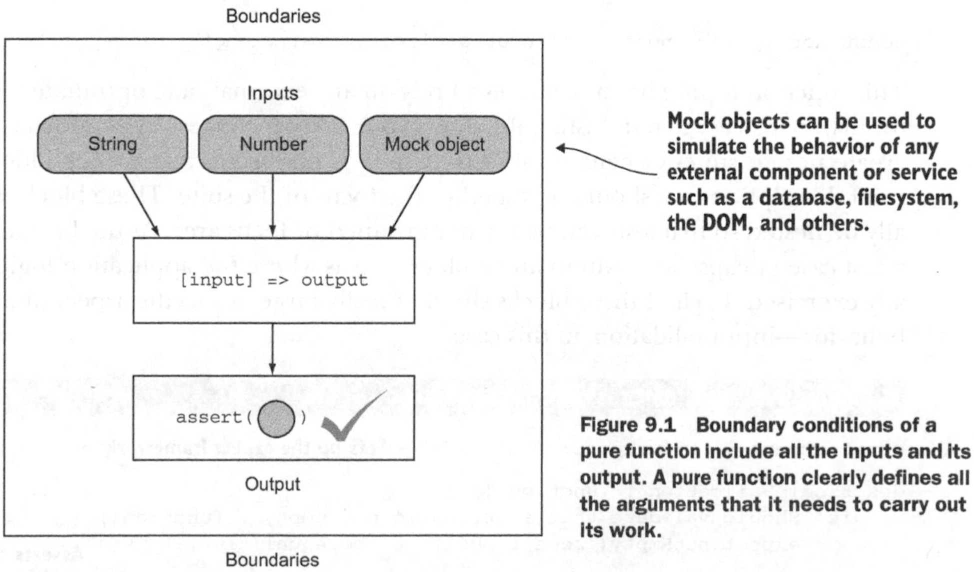

Boundaries

Inputs

String   Number   Mock object

[input] => output

assert(◯) ✓

Output

Boundaries

Mock objects can be used to simulate the behavior of any external component or service such as a database, filesystem, the DOM, and others.

Figure 9.1 Boundary conditions of a pure function include all the inputs and its output. A pure function clearly defines all the arguments that it needs to carry out its work.

On the server, you can run your scripts as

```
mocha --check-leaks --ui tests.js
```

The second parameter is very interesting (as a functional programmer, you'll particularly appreciate this). Mocha also has the ability to detect if global variables "leak" during a single test. A leaked variable is global to the entire test suite with a lifespan that exceeds the test that created it. You may want to leak variables in order to share them with another test, but more often than not, that could cause a programmatic error. For instance, can you spot the leak in this function?

```
function average(arr) {
    let len = arr.length;
        total = arr.reduce((a, b) => a + b);    ◁┐  Accidentally used ";" instead of
    return Math.floor(total / len);                 "," for multivariable assignment.
}                                                    As a result, the "total" variable is
average([80, 90, 100]) //-> 90                       declared globally.
```

As you know by now, a leaked variable is a side effect that can compromise both the order and the results of your unit tests. Each `it()` block in your tests should be an isolated set of expectations, which is to say that the order and outcome of other tests within the suite should not affect the outcome of any one test. Each test case must start and end with a clean environment, sometimes referred to as a *sandbox*.

All the same principles of pure functions apply as best practices for test development, particularly the property of idempotency that states you should be able to run the tests as many times as needed and always obtain the same results.

Now, let's look at the first function you want to test. Earlier in developing your search widget, you used a function to validate the user's input typed in the search field. Here's that function again to refresh your mind:

```
const notEmpty = input => !!input && input.trim().length > 0;
```

This function is pure because it doesn't rely on any external state or mutate any of the inputs, so it's easy to test. Listing 9.1 shows your first Mocha test. With Mocha, you can create nested suites of behavioral tests. A suite is marked as a `describe` block with a brief description that should tie together the focus of the suite. These blocks can usually be nested so that tests can be further grouped by focus area. At the bottom level is a test case encapsulated within an `it` block; this is where the application logic is actually exercised. Each of these blocks should ideally target a specific aspect of a specific behavior—input validation, in this case.

Listing 9.1   First unit test of a pure function `notEmpty`

```
const expect = chai.expect;                ◁——— Sets up the expect framework

describe('Validation', function () {
    it('Should validate that a string is not empty', function() {
        expect(notEmpty('some input')).to.be.equal(true);    ◁┐  Asserts the
                                                                 positive use case
```

```
        expect(notEmpty(' ')).to.be.equal(false);        ⟵  Asserts the
        expect(notEmpty(null)).to.be.equal(false);            negative
        expect(notEmpty(undefined)).to.be.equal(false);       use cases
    });
});
```

Finally, to run this unit test you invoke

```
mocha.run();    or        mocha --check-leaks --ui validation.js
```

And everything works as expected:

✓ Should validate that a string is not empty

CODE SAMPLES Remember that all the code for this chapter can be found in the RxJSinAction GitHub repository, https://github.com/RxJSInAction/rxjs-in-action.

As you can see, testing this pure function was easy, and setup was minimal. Now that you know what a simple Mocha test looks like, let's play with the leak-detection feature for a bit. Running a test for our fishy average function

```
describe('Average numbers', function () {
  it('Leak the variable total', function () {
     expect(average([80, 90, 100])).to.be.equal(90);
   });
});
```

causes the result

```
Error: global leak detected: total
```

identifying exactly which variable caused a side effect. Inadvertently changing total, a globally declared variable, because of a subtle code bug could have caused any other tests that depended on it to fail. So as a general rule of thumb, try not to read from or mutate any global state.

Mocha with Chai

Mocha.js is a full-fledged JavaScript testing framework built for both the browser and Node.js. It runs all of your unit tests serially and creates detailed reports. One of the nice features of Mocha is that it allows you to easily plug in any assertion library you want, whether you're familiar with the xUnit assertion APIs like assert.js or other varieties such as expect.js (used previously) and should.js, to name a few. In this book, because we have synchronous as well as asynchronous test requirements, we'll use a flexible API or a domain-specific language (DSL) called Chai.js, which includes support for all the testing APIs mentioned previously. Should.js will be instrumental when running tests involving Promises.

(continued)

Mocha also has great reporting capabilities. It prints out the results as human-readable sentences—allowing you to tell exactly which behaviors are failing in the application—and lets you isolate debugging efforts to a specific region.

One of the main reasons for using Mocha is its ample support for asynchronous testing and promises. Hence, it's the framework with which core RxJS code is tested. More details about installing Mocha can be found in appendix A. To explore the RxJS test suites, you can visit http://reactivex.io/rxjs/test.html.

Undeniably, the world would be a better place if all your code was this easy to unit test (certainly people would be less afraid of it). But asynchronous functions throw a monkey wrench into the whole process, and JavaScript applications are notorious for dealing with lots of asynchronous behavior. So let's talk about how you can use Mocha to test these types of programs.

9.2   Testing asynchronous code and promises

Asynchronous code creates a big wrinkle in your ability to write unit tests. Although it's true that Mocha is designed to run your individual test cases serially (one by one), how can you instruct it to wait for the completion of some long-running computation instead of sweeping through your entire test suite synchronously? In this section, we'll examine two testing scenarios: invoking AJAX requests directly and working with Promises.

9.2.1   Testing AJAX requests

The smart search widget we developed in chapter 5 made AJAX requests against the Wikipedia API to suggest potential search results using the RxJS DOM operator called Rx.Observable.ajax(). As you can imagine, under the hood, this operator uses the common XmlHttpRequest object to communicate with the server. Before you work your way up to testing entire observables, let's focus on testing plain asynchronous calls for now. Consider this simple alternative:

```
const ajax = (url, success, error) => {
  let req = new XMLHttpRequest();
  req.responseType = 'json';
  req.open('GET', url);
  req.onload = function() {
    if(req.status == 200) {
      let data = JSON.parse(req.responseText);
      success(data);
    }
    else {
      req.onerror();
    }
  }
  req.onerror = function () {
```

```
    if(error) {
      error(new Error('IO Error'));
    }
  };
  req.send();
};
```

You'll use Mocha to set up a unit test for this just like before:

```
describe('Asynchronous Test', function () {
  it('Should fetch Wikipedia pages for search term +
      `"reactive programming"', function() {             Sets up initial
                                                          conditions
    const searchTerm = 'reactive+programming';        ◄─┘
    const url = `https://en.wikipedia.org/w/api.php?action=query +
                `&format=json&list=search&utf8=1&srsearch=${searchTerm}`;

    let result = undefined;

    ajax(url, response => {                   Makes the request and assigns the
      result = response;                  ◄─┘ response to the result variable
    });
                                              Asserts the result
    expect(result).to.not.be.undefined;   ◄─┘ variable has a value
  });
});
```

> **WATCH OUT: CORS** Remember, if you're running any of these examples in the browser, make sure you disable CORS so that you can access the tested endpoints. Otherwise, just use the example directory located at https://github.com/RxJSInAction/rxjs-in-action, which handles these issues for you.

At a glance, this test seems pretty simple. Set up the initial conditions, make the asynchronous request, capture its response, and assert it. Nothing to it, yet running it prints this:

```
AssertionError: expected undefined not to be undefined
```

What happened? To be and not to be? The issue here is that your unit test is not async-aware. In other words, it thinks it can run synchronously and execute every single statement top to bottom, disregarding the latency present in the HTTP request.

Luckily, Mocha provides excellent support for testing functions that execute asynchronously. It's pretty straightforward: provide a function (usually) called done() into the callback passed to it(), and Mocha will understand that it needs to wait for this function to be called. Instead of running these tests in parallel and printing randomly ordered test reports, it's advantageous that Mocha runs your tests serially and properly waits for one test to finish before proceeding to the next (if you were thinking for a second that the use of a done function looks familiar, it's because you've gotten used to the complete() function of observers by now). Let's write a test suite that checks for the success and error cases of ajax().

Listing 9.2   Using Mocha/Chai to test an asynchronous function

```
const assert = chai.assert;          ◁──── Loads the assert style of assertions

describe('Ajax test', function () {
  it('Should fetch Wikipedia pages for search term +
    `"reactive programming"',
    function (done) {                                   ◁──
    const searchTerm = 'reactive+programming';
    const url = `https://en.wikipedia.org/w/api.php?action=query& +
               `format=json&list=search&utf8=1&srsearch=${searchTerm}`;

    const success = results => {          ◁──
      expect(results)
             .to.have.property('query')
             .with.property('search')
             .with.length(10);
      done();
    };

    const error = (err) => {
      done(err);                          ◁──
    };

    ajax(url, success, error);
  });

  it('Should fail for invalid URL', function (done) {   ◁──

    const url = 'invalid-url';

    const success = data => {                           ◁──
      done(new Error('Should not have been successful!'));
    };

    const error = (err) => {                            ◁──
      expect(err).to.have.property('message').to.equal('IO Error');
      done();
    };

    ajax(url, success, error);
  });
});
```

Passing the done function instructs Mocha to halt, waiting for the async ajax() function to return.

Sets up the success function and the assertion

In the successful case, you don't expect the call to fail.

Within the same test, includes the error case

In the error case, you don't expect the call to be successful.

Asserts that the failure occurred and that you received the correct error message

The suite in listing 9.2 contains two test cases: one to test the Wikipedia response object returned from invoking a successful AJAX query with matched results, and the other asserting the error condition when no search results match.

As you can imagine, the ability to test asynchronous functions is a necessity for applications involving RxJS. But recall that with promises you have several options when working with these longer-running tasks. You could use the AJAX directly with RxJS:

```
Rx.Observable.ajax(query)
```

Or, if your AJAX function uses Promises or a promise-like (deferred) interface (like jQuery's popular $.get()), then you can also use

```
Rx.Observable.fromPromise(ajax(query))
```

Using Promises to wrap these types of operations is the more functional approach because it provides an abstraction over the factor of time, which is a form of side effect. Also, many third-party libraries are wrapping their APIs with promises. Let's discuss this a bit more.

9.2.2 *Working with Promises*

In this section, we'll continue with our running example of invoking the ajax() function, except this time using Promises. As stated before, a Promise is a functional, continuation data type that allows you wrap any long-running operation, so that you can map functions via then() to the eventually created value. It's proven to be so successful that Mocha includes support for working natively with Promises through a Chai extension called chai-as-promised.js and the should.js fluent API (setup information available in appendix A).

Let's start by refactoring ajax() to use Promises. This is simple; just wrap the body of the function within the Promise and delegate the success and error conditions to the Promise's resolve and reject callbacks:

```
const ajax = url => new Promise((resolve, reject) => {
    let req = new XMLHttpRequest();
    req.responseType = 'json';
    req.open('GET', url);
    req.onload = () => {
      if(req.status == 200) {
        let data = JSON.parse(req.responseText);
        resolve(data);
      }
      else {
        reject(new Error(req.statusText));
      }
    };
    req.onerror = () => {
      reject(new Error('IO Error'));
    };
    req.send();
});
```

Now you're going to tell Chai to use the Promise extensions and load the should.js APIs into your tests. This is a quick setup at the top of the file:

```
chai.use(chaiAsPromised);
const should = chai.should();
```
To use Chai in environments that don't support Node.js-like CommonJS modules (like the browser), you'll need to use Browserify to create the compatible bundle. We've done that for you in the GitHub repo accompanying this book.

You can see that the test in listing 9.3 is similar to listing 9.2. The abstraction provided by the Promise allows the test framework to instrument the result of the test much better. Using the should.js APIs, you can wire up semantically meaningful expectations for Promises such as should.be.fulfilled to assert the call completed and should.eventually.have to inspect the results. Also, instead of passing done, Mocha expects you to return the Promise object under test to the engine to run the specified expectations.

Listing 9.3   Asynchronous testing with `Promises`

Instead of using the done() function, you return the Promise to Mocha so
that it knows to fulfill the Promise and run the necessary assertions.

```
describe('Ajax with promises', function () {
    it('Should fetch Wikipedia pages for search term +
      `"reactive programming"', function () {

    const searchTerm = 'reactive+programming';
    const url = `https://en.wikipedia.org/w/api.php?action=query& +
                `format=json&list=search&utf8=1&srsearch=${searchTerm}`;

    return ajax(url)                                          Uses the should.js
        .should.be.fulfilled              <————————————————|  support with Promises
        .should.eventually.have.property('query')    <——┐
          .with.property('search')                       |  Asserts the eventual
          .with.length(10);                              |  value resolved through
    });                                                  |  the Promise
});
```

Nothing much changes with this test compared to the previous one, except that you can work directly with the Promise returned from ajax(). It's incredible to see how descriptive and fluent tests can be using Mocha. Now that you've asserted ajax() works as expected, let's see how this function is used within the observable pipeline. The following listing shows a snippet of the search$ observable again.

Listing 9.4   Search stream used in the smart search component

```
const search$ = Rx.Observable.fromEvent(inputText, 'keyup')
  .debounceTime(500)
  .pluck('target','value')
  .filter(notEmpty)
  .do(term => console.log(`Searching with term ${term}`))
  .map(query => URL + query)
  .switchMap(query =>                         Your main area of focus
     Rx.Observable.fromPromise(ajax(query))   when testing this program
          .pluck('query', 'search')     <——┘
          .defaultIfEmpty([]))
  .do(result => {
    count.innerHTML = `${result.length} results`;
  })
  .subscribe(arr => {
    clearResults(results);
    appendResults(results, arr);
  });
```

Pay attention to how the code branches off in the call to switchMap(). This additional flow will make your tests complex. Because most of the data flow logic is handled by the observable itself, which you trust has already been tested extensively, all you need to worry about is testing that your own functions work as expected. In this case, you've tested that notEmpty() and ajax() work, and now you can test that this entire code block integrated with your functions works as well. Before you can do this, in the next sections, you'll try to split the AJAX stream into its own observable and test that independently. This will drastically simplify your tests and allow your code to be more modular and reusable.

Because observables are also pure functions (you can translate the black box analogy of inputs and output to be producer and consumer, respectively), you should be able to test them with some confidence. You'll need this for the stream projected into search$ as well. In the next section, you'll explore how to test reactive streams.

9.3 *Testing reactive streams*

Reactive testing follows a similar format to how you normally test functional programs as described earlier. Because observables are pure functional data types, the transitive property of purity applies, which states that if an observable is made up solely of pure functions, the entire observable sequence is itself pure. Let's begin with a cold observable that synchronously adds the numbers in an array.

Listing 9.5 Testing a stream that adds up all numbers of an array

```
describe('Adding numbers', function () {
  it('Should add numbers together', function () {

    const adder = (total, delta) => total + delta;

    Rx.Observable.from([1, 2, 3, 4, 5, 6, 7, 8, 9])
      .reduce(adder)
      .subscribe(total => {
          expect(total).to.equal(45);
      });
  });
});
```

Notice that because the semantics of observables are designed for asynchronicity with the producer/consumer model, you're able to place all the assertions into the downstream observer, which is intuitive because that's where the outcome of the stream is. Again, this works only with synchronous functions. Here's a similar program using generators:

```
it('Should add numbers from a generator', function () {
  const adder = (total, delta) => total + delta;

  function* numbers() {
      let start = 0;
      while(true) {
        yield start++;
      }
  }
```

```
    Rx.Observable.from(numbers)
      .take(10)
      .reduce(adder)
      .subscribe(total => {
          expect(total).to.equal(45);
      });
  });
```

And you obtain the same results. It's clear that testing synchronous observables is as simple as testing regular pure functions—you expect cold observables to behave like this. Let's mix it up a bit by injecting a time delay into your tests:

```
it('Should add numbers together with delay', function () {
    Rx.Observable.from([1, 2, 3, 4, 5, 6, 7, 8, 9])
        .reduce((total, delta) => total + delta)
        .delay(1000)
        .subscribe(total => {
            expect(total).to.equal(45);
        });
});
```

Running this code prints out the following:

```
✓ Should add numbers together with delay
```

It worked! But there's a red herring. Although you get the impression the test is passing, the subscribe() block or the observer isn't actually executing; it runs after a whole second has passed, and the result is ignored. Try failing the test case by changing the result to some nonsense value:

```
Rx.Observable.from([1, 2, 3, 4, 5, 6, 7, 8, 9])
  .reduce((total, delta) => total + delta)
  .delay(1000)
  .subscribe(total => {
    expect(total).to.equal('non-sense!');
  });
```

Now, instead of passing the test, you expect that Mocha will throw an error and fail. But you see the same outcome as in your test report. What happened? The obvious culprit seems to be that the delay operator introduces something into the test mixture that isn't properly handled by the test. This intuition is correct, and it's at the heart of what you're trying to accomplish with reactive testing. Because you've added an asynchronous time element that isn't being handled by the test, the test reports completion before the asynchronous block has completed running and you get a false positive. You were deceived by RxJS's abstraction over time. Observables make working with latency and time so simple that it seemed as though the operators were executing synchronously to the test. Of course, this isn't the case.

No fear, grab a cup of Mocha and get to it. Here, you'll need to come back to using done() with the it() callback. Do you recall how similar Mocha's concept of done() is to the observer's complete()? Try making them the same, as in the following listing.

Listing 9.6 Testing an observable with a delay

```
it('Should add numbers together with delay', function (done) {
    Rx.Observable.from([1, 2, 3, 4, 5, 6, 7, 8, 9])
        .reduce((total, delta) => total + delta)
        .delay(1000)
        .subscribe(total => {
            expect(total).to.equal(45);
        }, null, done);
});
```

Changing this output to anything other than 45 will break the test.

Uses done to signal the completion of the stream and hence the test. Because this code will never produce errors, you skip it by passing null.

Running it now prints this:

```
✓ Should add numbers together with delay (1008ms)
```

The time label in milliseconds next to the output should hint to you that Mocha waited for this test to complete and actually ran the expectations. Armed with the knowledge of how to test asynchronous observables, let's go back to the search stream search$ in listing 9.4. You can recognize that most of the observable pipeline in this code is synchronous, until this:

```
.switchMap(query =>
    Rx.Observable.fromPromise(ajax(query))
        .pluck('query', 'search').defaultIfEmpty([]))
```

This segment spawns an AJAX request against Wikipedia for search results that match the user's input, which is actually its own observable stream. You can test this function that's being mapped to the source observable and apply the same technique as you did in listing 9.6. The stream function under test this time is

```
query => Rx.Observable.fromPromise(ajax(query))
            .pluck('query', 'search').defaultIfEmpty([])
```

The next listing shows how to test your asynchronous, Promise-based observable mapped to the source observable.

Listing 9.7 Testing a promise AJAX call within an observable

Uses done to notify Mocha this will be an asynchronous test

Defines the function under test

```
it('Should fetch Wikipedia pages for search term "reactive programming" +
    `using an observable + promise', function (done) {

    const searchTerm = 'reactive+programming';
    const url = `https://en.wikipedia.org/w/api.php?action=query& +
            `format=json&list=search&utf8=1&srsearch=${searchTerm}`;

    const testFn = query => Rx.Observable.fromPromise(ajax(query))
        .subscribe(data => {
            expect(data).to.have.property('query')
```

```
                  .with.property('search')
                  .with.length(10);
              }, null, done);
    testFn(url);
});
```

Passes done in place of the completed observer method to signal the end of this observable sequence and hence the end of the test

Calls the function being tested

So far, you've covered lots of ground by testing all the functions that make up your business logic as well as the asynchronous branch of the search component, in isolation. This is certainly the right direction, but you shouldn't have to rebuild or copy and paste a testable version of your observable sequence into your unit tests; that duplicates your efforts. Instead, it's convenient to split these concerns so as not to mix browser-specific details like emitting a DOM event and rendering to the screen with actual data transformation and event processing. Let's refactor the existing observable to be testable, and we'll show how to write reactive code with testing in mind.

9.4 *Making streams testable*

As visually pleasant as long observable sequences are (at least for two of us), for matters of testability and even sometimes reusability, it's important to separate the observer from the pipeline and the subscription. Decoupling these main parts will allow you to inject any assertions that you need to make, depending on the stream under test. The goal is to not have to modify or rebuild the observable sequence in the application as well as in the unit test and have code duplicated in both areas. Continuing with the same mindset with which you started the chapter, to make this code more testable, you'll split up your functions so that they can be tested independently from the stream, as well as decompose the stream into its three main parts: producer, pipeline, and consumer. This will allow you to separate the pure (testable) part of the stream from the impure. The impure sections involve writing to a database, making actual AJAX calls, or writing to the DOM, all of which should be outside of your scope of test.

Start out with this simple program that generates 10 consecutive numbers every second and performs the sum of all the even numbers:

```
Rx.Observable.interval(1000)
    .take(10)
    .filter(num => num % 2 === 0)
    .map(num => num * num)
    .reduce((total, delta) => total + delta)
    .subscribe(console.log);
```

In order to make this program testable you need to do a few things:

1 Split out the business logic from the observable pipeline.
2 Decouple the consumer and producer and isolate the stream pipeline. This will allow you to inject your assertion code.
3 Wrap the stream into a function that you can call with the proper observer.

By applying these steps to the previous code, this program becomes a more generic set of functions that you can test thoroughly:

```
const isEven = num => num % 2 === 0;
const square = num => num * num;
const add = (a, b) => a + b;

const runInterval = (source$) =>
  source$
    .take(10)
    .filter(isEven)
    .map(square)
    .reduce(add);
```

←─┐ **Separates producer (source) and
   subscriber from the business
   logic by making an argument**

Notice how you also wrap the stream into a function that can be called from within your test with whatever event producer you want. It could be a literal sequence of numbers, an array, a generator, and others. The function allows you to pass in test input arguments. Without refactoring it this way, if all these functions were embedded into the observable itself as in the original version, you wouldn't have the flexibility to cover all the possible use cases required to run through all paths of this code. This is also much more efficient because you don't need to execute the entire sequence every time. Now, with a more testable version of this stream, let's proceed.

The functions isEven(), square(), and add() are straightforward to test. We'll leave those as an exercise for you and focus on the observable. Because observables are feed-forward, unidirectional flows that rely on side effect–free functions, you can just as easily consider the entire stream as being pure.

Instead of rewriting another version of the same stream in your test, just call it from within your test, provide a producer into it, and place your assertions into the subscribe block:

```
it('Should square and add even numbers', function (done) {
    this.timeout(20000);
    runInterval(Rx.Observable.interval(1000))
      .subscribe({
          next: total => expect(total).to.equal(120),
          err:  err  => assert.fail(err.message),
          complete: done
      });
});
```

**Increases Mocha's
timeout setting to
allow the stream
to complete**

←─ **The expectations are
wired up in the test,
decoupled from the
stream code.**

The producer and the subscriber are the boundaries of this pure stream. Figure 9.2 highlights the sections of code that got decoupled from the observable pipeline. By ensuring your functions work and trusting in RxJS to do the right thing, you can be confident in your expectations. Also, parameterizing the observer gives you the extra flexibility of directing the output of the stream toward a set of assertions (as in this case), the console, a filesystem, an HTML page, a database, and others.

Running this code prints the following:

```
✓ Should square and add even numbers (10032ms)
```

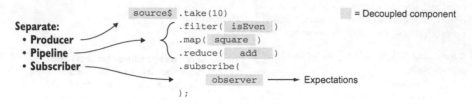

Figure 9.2   The areas from the stream that need to be decoupled in order to gain the maximum test coverage of the entire stream

This single unit test took 10 seconds to run, so you needed to tell Mocha that this test will surpass the default (two-second) timeout. Imagine having test suites with hundreds of these types of tests; it would easily render your CI pipeline useless. Unit tests should be quick; the culprit here is the `interval()` operator (the same would be true for `timer()`). How can you speed up tests of code that has explicit time values? The main reason for adding physical time into your stream is to create the illusion of movement for the user. For example, a panel slides to the right, a counter winds down, a color fades out, and so on. But this isn't important or relevant when running it as a unit test, so instead of refactoring your streams to use a synchronous producer or temporarily commenting out the timers, the proper way to solve this is to add a virtual timer or scheduler.

9.5   *Scheduling values in RxJS*

If you're dealing with observable sequences that publish values over an extended period of time, unit testing them can be time consuming. As you know, Mocha will run all your tests serially by design, so it's wasteful for Mocha to be sitting idle waiting for long intervals to complete. In RxJS, time is internally managed using an artifact called a *scheduler*. In this section, we'll briefly introduce this topic and then show how you can apply it to speed up the runtime of your tests. After we've finished introducing schedulers, we'll go back and fix our long-running unit test that uses a delay.

Schedulers control when a subscription starts and when notifications are published. This abstraction allows work to run immediately or in the future without the calling code being aware of it. Remember that RxJS is used to abstract the notion of time? At the heart of all this is a scheduler.

Generally speaking, a scheduler consists of three main parts:

- A data structure that stores all the actions queued to be executed.
- An execution context that knows where the action will be executed: timer, interval, immediately, callback, a different thread (for server-side Rx frameworks), and so on.
- A virtual clock that provides a notion of time for itself. This point will become very important for testing.

RxJS has different types of schedulers, but all abide by the same interface:

Returns a number that represents
current time as managed internally
by its own clock

Schedules new work to be
executed, specifying optional
delay and state fields that are
used for future execution and
state management, respectively

```
interface Scheduler {
    now(): number;
    schedule(work, delay?, state?): Subscription;
    flush(): void;
    active: boolean;
    actions: Action[];
    scheduledId: number;
}
```

Executes all actions and clears the queue

Indicates whether the queue is
currently executing a set of actions

Queue of
actions to
schedule

Here's how you can use it to schedule a set of actions to run synchronously and then flush as a series of notifications:

Temporarily stores the
scheduled actions so that
you can compare them to
what the scheduler remits.
Every time an action runs,
it stores its value into the
stored array.

```
it('Should schedule things in order', function () {
    let stored = [];

    let store = state => () => stored.push(state);

    let scheduler = Rx.Scheduler.queue;

    scheduler.schedule(store(1));
    scheduler.schedule(store(2));
    scheduler.schedule(store(3));
    scheduler.schedule(store(4));
    scheduler.schedule(store(5));

    scheduler.flush();

    expect(stored).to.deep.equal([1, 2, 3, 4, 5]);
});
```

Uses a simple scheduler that
queues the actions to run

Schedules actions to run immediately
(delay, the second parameter of
scheduler.schedule(), defaults to 0)

Runs all
the
actions

Performs a deep comparison of both data structures; looks at
the values contained within it. In later code samples, you'll be
using deep.equal as the basis for your assertions.

Just like observables, schedulers have a similar behavior in that you can push a set of actions that are internally queued or buffered. Every call to schedule returns a Subscription object that you can use to cancel the subscription if you wish to do so.

Up to this point, we haven't explicitly called out the fact that many of the RxJS factory operators you've seen in this book—from(), generate(), range(), delay(), debounceTime(), interval(), timer(), of(), and others—have an extra parameter for you to supply a scheduler. All operators make use of a single scheduler, if available. For synchronous data sources, typically a value of null is used so that notifications are delivered instantly. On the other hand, two often-used schedulers in RxJS are the AsapScheduler and the AsyncScheduler, which apply to delayed (async) actions (internally RxJS executes and manages these actions in the event loop through setTimeout() and setInterval(), respectively).

Let's spend some time looking at the effect of having a scheduler control the stream. In the same spirit as the previous code snippet, consider this simple range observable that pushes the values emitted into an external array:

```
it('Emits values synchronously on default scheduler', function () {
    let temp = [];
    Rx.Observable.range(1, 5)
    .do([].push.bind(temp))                ◄─── Side effect that pushes value into
    .subscribe(value => {                       array temp that lives outside the
        expect(temp).to.have.length(value);     context of your observable
        expect(temp).to.contain(value);
    });
});
```

This stream uses the default scheduler, so this test asserts that each value emitted by range() is pushed into temp and immediately propagated down to the subscriber. Your expectations check that the size of the array increases with every value and the array contains that value. This stream is fairly simple, and it's behavior that you're accustomed to. Now you're going to change the scheduler used to publish the value to an AsyncScheduler, and in the case of most factory operators, you can do this by passing an additional scheduler parameter. By doing so, as shown in the next listing, you change how the stream publishes the values produced by range() from synchronous to asynchronous. Let's introduce this new parameter and change your assertions to match this new behavior.

Listing 9.8   Publishing values on an `async` scheduler

Configures the stream to use an async scheduler to proxy the
values emitted by the producer. This additional proxying will
cause all values to be emitted before the subscription block.

```
it('Emits values on an asynchronous scheduler', function (done) {
    let temp = [];
    Rx.Observable.range(1, 5, Rx.Scheduler.async)
    .do([].push.bind(temp))                            Asserts that the array is
    .subscribe(value => {                              growing at every
        expect(temp).to.have.length(value)◄─          asynchronous emitted value
        expect(temp).to.contain(value);
    }, done, done);                ◄─
});                                      You can also pass an error handler to done() to
                                         indicate an exception condition (the test failed).
```

Notice that, because it's asynchronous, you need to use the done() resolution callback to let Mocha know to wait for all values to be emitted. In sum, just by using a scheduler, you can manipulate how time flows through the stream and control how the events are published. In this case, you overrode the default synchronous event-publishing mechanism to emit asynchronously.

The observeOn() operator

Aside from passing schedulers into the observable factory operations to control how producers emit events, you can also use the `observeOn()` instance operator to transform the emission of events midstream:

```
Rx.Observable.range(1, 5)
    .do([].push.bind(temp))
    .observeOn(Rx.Scheduler.async)
    .subscribe(...)
```

It's important to note that configuring the scheduler midway controls the emission of events downstream only from the point of `observeOn()`, not before. In other words, in this code the execution of `range()` and `do()` still happens synchronously, and the results of those events are then emitted asynchronously to the subscriber. For the examples in this chapter, however, we'll keep it simple and apply schedulers at the factory operator level, just like in listing 9.8.

It's important to note that in server-side implementations of the Rx family, like Rx.Net or RxJava, schedulers can be extremely important to offload heavy processing onto different threads while keeping the active UI thread idle to react to user actions. In the single-threaded world of JavaScript, you'd normally use the default schedulers, and it's rare to choose otherwise. For this reason, in this book we don't cover schedulers in regular application-level code; here's a good resource to start with if you're interested: http://reactivex.io/rxjs/manual/overview.html#using-schedulers. But given their ability to control time, schedulers are very useful, if not necessary, for unit testing asynchronous streams. Let's begin writing some unit tests in virtual time with `Rx.TestScheduler`.

9.6 *Augmenting virtual reality*

Now that you know what schedulers are, let's circle back to our long-running unit test that used `delay()` and where you also had to set an arbitrarily long timeout value—you want to avoid doing that at all costs! The root of the problem here is that the unit test was using physical time. We mentioned recently that by using schedulers, you could manipulate how these values were emitted, so a physical delay could become a virtual (fake) delay and your tests could run instantly. You can use the `Rx.TestScheduler` class, which is derived from `VirtualTimeScheduler`. This almighty artifact can actually create time!

```
it('Create time from a marble diagram', function () {
    let scheduler = new Rx.TestScheduler();
    let time = scheduler.createTime('-----|');
    expect(time).to.equal(50);
});
```

An empty marble diagram with five time frames

Each time frame counts as 10 units of time (usually milliseconds), so 5 units amounts to 50.

Instead of passing in a set of notification objects or actions, you probably recognize the "-----" notation as segments of a marble diagram. In this section, you'll learn how to use the virtual scheduler provided in RxJS and how it's intimately related to the marble diagrams you've seen all along.

9.6.1   *Playing with marbles*

The `TestScheduler` is driven by the RxJS language of marbles, which, among other characters, primarily contains frames and notifications. In Rx parlance, you use marble diagrams to communicate how a particular operator works with respect to time. Every event that's pushed onto the stream is internally wrapped using a `Notification` object, which transports all of the necessary metadata for a particular event. They're more useful as testing artifacts because they make it easier to represent events that you can extend to add more behavior, such as timestamps or numerical ordering, that you'd want to assert. Here's a simple example of how you'd use notifications directly in your tests:

> The dashes represent frames and the letters events (or notifications) that the stream will publish. Every dash represents 10 frames.

> The mapping comparisons used in your assertions

```
it('Should parse a marble string into a series of notifications',
    function () {
        let result = Rx.TestScheduler.parseMarbles(
            '--a---b---|',                        <----
            { a: 'A', b: 'B' });
        expect(result).deep.equal([
            { frame: 20, notification: Rx.Notification.createNext('A') },
            { frame: 60, notification: Rx.Notification.createNext('B') },
            { frame: 100, notification: Rx.Notification.createComplete() }
        ]);
    });
```

The marble diagrams are a convenience method of creating expectations and events. Under the hood, the test scheduler parses out the ASCII text, and from this it generates and queues the actions to perform, which then get published as notifications. The notification is an abstraction of the emission mechanism within RxJS. As you can see from this code, you have three types of emitted events in RxJS: a value, an error, and a completion—yes, this is the observer's API. Even though each type is fundamentally different, you can think of each one more generically as an event, similar to how all DOM events are an abstraction of a single base event type. In other words, you can create a data type to encapsulate an event type regardless of its underlying kind.

Luckily, this internal mechanism can also be abstracted even further by the test scheduler, which uses the high-level Marbles language, kind of like a DSL, to make testing even easier. Consider the `map()` operator we've been using extensively throughout the book. Representing a simple stream that uses it as a marble diagram in ASCII form looks like this:

```
source   --1--2--3--4--5--6--7--8--9--|
map            square => a  *  a
subs     --1--4--9--16--25--36--49--64--81--|
```

Let's use the `TestScheduler` to verify that this diagram holds, literally. This class has a rich set of features that helps you create and wire expectations onto observables. Here's a unit test of `map()` using the `square()` function.

Listing 9.9 Testing the `map()` operator

```
function square(x) {
  return x * x;
}

function assertDeepEqual(actual, expected) {
  expect(actual).to.deep.equal(expected);
}

describe('Map operator', function () {
    it('Should map multiple values', function () {
        let scheduler = new Rx.TestScheduler(assertDeepEqual);

        let source = scheduler.createColdObservable(
            '--1--2--3--4--5--6--7--8--9--|');

        let expected = '--a--b--c--d--e--f--g--h--i--|';

        let r = source.map(square);

        scheduler.expectObservable(r).toBe(expected,
            { 'a': 1, 'b': 4, 'c': 9, 'd': 16, 'e': 25,
              'f': 36, 'g':49, 'h': 64, 'i': 81});

        scheduler.flush();
    });
});
```

Helper function that uses Chai to perform a deep.equal assertion of its arguments

Creates an instance of the TestScheduler and passes the comparison function to use

Creates a cold observable from the ASCII diagram

Creates the assertion value placeholders

Source stream with square operation

Uses the scheduler to wire expectations

Flushes the stream, which causes the cold observable to emit its values

In this example, you use two marble diagrams to set up your test case. The first is used to create a source input that behaves like a cold observable. Like the normal diagrams that you saw earlier in the book, each number indicates an event, and each dash indicates a single unit of time. What a single unit of time means for your application is something you'll need to determine. Again, this comes down to how you dilate time in a stream, whether a dash means 1 ms or 1 minute. These marble diagrams carry a lot more meaning than just lines and letters. It turns out that each line segment "-" represents 10 frames of a time period. So, "-----" is a total of 50 frames of the unit of time (typically, each frame represents 10 ms).

The second stream is the expected stream. In order to clarify what's happening, you use a simple associative array that maps the expected values for each notification emitted through the stream.

The test scheduler is extremely powerful because it allows you to test your streams visually. In addition, you're able to test the entire range of observable behaviors, from the construction of the stream, to the emission of events, all the way to the teardown of the stream on completion.

But, admittedly, there are easier ways to test `map()` using a plain Mocha test because it's a synchronous operation and doesn't use time for anything. Remember, time is what makes asynchronous programming difficult, and that's the problem you're trying to solve.

> **MARBLE SYNTAX**   You can find the meaning of all the ASCII symbols of the marble language here: https://github.com/ReactiveX/RxJS/blob/master/doc/writing-marble-tests.md.

These frames are meaningful for operations that are based on time. Let's use the virtual scheduler to test a stream with `debounceTime()`, which would otherwise be complicated and brittle to test because you'd have to rely on adding your own timestamps to emitted notification objects. Let RxJS do this for you.

Listing 9.10   Testing the `debounceTime` operator

```
describe('Marble test with debounceTime', function () {
    it('Should delay all element by the specified time', function () {
        let scheduler = new Rx.TestScheduler(assertDeepEqual);

        let source = scheduler.createHotObservable(
            '-a--------b------c----|');          ◄——— Creates a stream with
                                                        the first element on
        let expected = '------a--------b------(s|)';  ◄—  the second frame

        let r = source.debounceTime(50, scheduler);  ◄—
        scheduler.expectObservable(r).toBe(expected);     You debounce with 50 ms
        scheduler.flush();                                (5 frames), the first input
    });                    Passes in the virtual scheduler after the fifth frame.
});                        into debounceTime()
```

Running this test creates a stream that simulates (fakes) the effect of `debounceTime()` with a behavior that matches the expected number of frames. As you can see from the diagram, the first notification as a result of emitting a should appear after the fifth frame in `debounceTime(50)`. Now that you know how to fake time, you can speed up that long-running unit test based on `interval()`.

9.6.2   *Fake it 'til you make it*

Removing time from the stream means that you shift to using the virtual timer's internal clock, which you can wind up by using the time units "-" in the marble diagrams. The `interval(1000)` operator emits consecutive integers every second and is an example of code you might use in production. So in order to simulate your one-second interval, you'll use a 10 ms mocked interval. Now, you know that a scheduler is what's controlling this behavior behind the scenes, so let's take advantage of it to create the mock source as well as the correct expectation.

Listing 9.11   Speeding up `runInterval()` with the virtual time scheduler

```
it('Should square and add even numbers', function () {
    let scheduler = new Rx.TestScheduler(assertDeepEqual);
    let source = scheduler.createColdObservable(  ◄——
```

Creates an observable that emits values every unit of time (10 ms)

```
        '-1-2-3-4-5-6-7-8-9-|');
    let expected = '-------------------(s-|';   ◁───  The expected output is a stream
                                                       with a single result at the end,
    let r = runInterval(source);                       given by the reduce operation.

    scheduler.expectObservable(r).toBe(expected, {'s': 120});  ◁─────
                                                         Asserts the end
    scheduler.flush();                                   value to be 120
});
```

Certainly, refactoring the `runInterval()` stream to make it more testable paid off. You were able to easily inject a virtual cold observable as the producer of events, and everything worked exactly as expected.

9.6.3 *Refactoring your search stream for testability*

As you've seen in this chapter, RxJS's notion of time is much more sophisticated than a simple callback, and your test cases must reflect that. The simple fact that you can incorporate delays or debouncing into a stream means that the test cases must also understand how time flows and, perhaps more important, must be able to manipulate it when necessary.

Let's finally circle back to the example of your search component, which used a `debounceTime()` operation to prevent flooding the Wikipedia servers with unnecessary search queries. This stream is a bit longer and more complex, but now you have everything you need to properly test it.

If you used a realistic time of 250–500 ms to handle this scenario, it would mean that your test case would likely need to run for at least a second. Although that may not seem like a lot, as we mentioned previously, in a large test suite with several hundred test cases, that could mean minutes to run, which throws continuous integration right out the window. You definitely want to do better than this for your tests if you plan to test as you develop. Now, let's apply what you learned and refactor your existing search stream with an eye for testability.

Testing this in its original state is somewhat difficult. Thus, one of the benefits of plugging this into the RxJS tests is that you can refactor the code based on best practices. So how would you test this?

As before, the focus should be on decoupling the producer, the pipeline, and the subscription so that you can test that your functions are working correctly as integrated into the stream without worrying about how the DOM emits events (producer) and gets updated (observer). You're interested in testing the actual business logic and not the interaction with any other technology.

Just like before, refactoring your stream into a function changes the stream from the hardcoded

```
const search$ = Rx.Observable.fromEvent(inputText, 'keyup')
  .pluck('target','value')
  .debounceTime(500)
  .filter(notEmpty)
  .do(term => console.log(`Searching with term ${term}`))
```

```
.map(query => URL + query)
.switchMap(query =>
    Rx.Observable.fromPromise(ajax(query)).pluck('query',
        'search').defaultIfEmpty([]))
.subscribe(arr => {
  count.innerHTML = `${result.length} results`;
  if(arr.length === 0) {
    clearResults(results);
  }
  else {
    appendResults(results, arr);
  }
});
```

to a more modular stream composed of a source$ to which you can pass a virtual observable stream and a search stream fetchResult$ in charge of making the AJAX call to fetch results from Wikipedia (which you already tested in listing 9.3). By mocking both of these parameters, you can execute the entire stream without worrying about asynchronous callbacks, how the data is produced, and how it's affected by debounceTime(). Here's the refactored search$ function, as implemented in application code:

```
const search$ = (source$, fetchResult$, url = '', scheduler = null) =>
    source$
        .debounceTime(500, scheduler)
        .filter(notEmpty)
        .do(term => console.log(`Searching with term ${term}`))
        .map(query => url + query)
        .switchMap(fetchResult$);
```

This way of encapsulating an observable sequence into its own function is known as an *epic*. Epics will become important in chapter 10, because they will allow you to easily embed RxJS into an overall reactive architecture.

To use the reactive architecture, just call the function with the source and AJAX streams:

```
search$(

    Rx.Observable.fromEvent(inputText, 'keyup')
      .pluck('target','value'),

    query =>
      Rx.Observable.fromPromise(ajax(query))
      .pluck('query', 'search')
      .defaultIfEmpty([])

).subscribe(arr => {
    if(arr.length === 0) {
      clearResults(results);
    }
    else {
      appendResults(results, arr);
    }
});
```

Furthermore, parameterizing the dependent streams keeps your tests from making outbound calls to the Wikipedia APIs. This is desirable because you don't want your unit test to be compromised by a third-party dependency. In other words, in place of `fetchResults$`, you'll provide an observable with a compatible return type.

This second version doesn't look as fluent as the original, but it's now a lot easier to test, as shown in the next listing. Using the virtual scheduler, you're also able to test how the debouncing works in the stream. Because your debouncing extends to half a second, you use a simple function `frame()` to easily inline any number of time units into your marble diagrams.

Listing 9.12   Unit test main search logic

```
function frames(n = 1, unit = '-') {          ◁──── Helper function to embed any number
    return (n === 1) ? unit :                        of time units "-"into a marble diagram
        unit + frames(n - 1, unit);
}

describe('Search component', function () {
    const results_1 = [                       ◁──── Dummy data for first search action
        'rxmarbles.com',
        'https://www.manning.com/books/rxjs-in-action'
    ];

    const results_2 =                         ◁──── Dummy data for second search action
        ['https://www.manning.com/books/rxjs-in-action'
    ];

    const searchFn = term => {                ◁──── Stub search stream that will be
        let r = [];                                  projected onto the source
        if(term.toLowerCase() === 'rx') {            observable as part of the search
            r = results_1;
        }
        else if (term.toLowerCase() === 'rxjs') {
            r =  results_2;
        }
        return Rx.Observable.of(r);
    };

    it('Should test the search stream with debouncing', function () {

        let searchTerms = {                   ◁──── User input into search stream
            a: 'r',
            b: 'rx',                                 Observable that describes the debounce
            c: 'rxjs',                               effect. Helper function frames(50) is used
        };                                           to emulate a debounceTime of 500 ms.

        let scheduler = new Rx.TestScheduler(assertDeepEqual);
        let source = scheduler.createHotObservable(
            '-(ab)-' + frames(50) +'-c|', searchTerms);
        let r = search$(source, searchFn, '', scheduler);

        let expected = frames(50) + '-f------(s|)';

        scheduler.expectObservable(r).toBe(expected,
            {
```

Invokes the search stream with all necessary pieces ──▷ (points to `let r = search$(source, searchFn, '', scheduler);`)

Creates expectations for the first and second result sets ──▷ (points to `scheduler.expectObservable(r).toBe(expected,`)

```
              'f': results_1,
              's': results_2
          });

      scheduler.flush();
   });
});
```

This unit test attempts to simulate a user entering the letters *rx* quickly, producing two results. The stream gets debounced with 500 ms, and finally the third and fourth letters are entered to make *rxjs*. At this moment, the dummy AJAX observable returns only one result to simulate the result set being filtered down. Finally, you've thoroughly unit tested the entire search component.

As Einstein postulated in the early 1900s, all time is relative to the observer. In RxJS, we can transpile this expression to "all time is relative to the scheduler used." In this chapter, we explored how to use the tools provided by RxJS to test reactive applications. In doing so, we also unpacked some concepts surrounding time and its relationship with streams and the RxJS internal notification publishing mechanism. These concepts are important to support the future maintainability of your code. In the next chapter, we'll take reactive programming to new heights. We'll put everything together to create a simple web application that mixes the power of RxJS with a UI component library known as React.

9.7   Summary

- Functional programs are easy to test, given that all functions are pure and have clear signatures.
- Testing asynchronous code can be challenging, and you need to leverage async-aware unit-testing frameworks like Mocha.
- You can combine Mocha with powerful assertion interfaces like Chai.js to create elegant and fluent tests.
- Testing synchronous observables follows the same procedures as testing any pure function.
- Testing asynchronous behavior as well as streams that bend time can be done effectively using the virtual scheduler.
- It's best to make your streams testable and modular. Attempt to keep your business logic separate, as a set of functions, and to decouple a stream from its producer and observer; this will allow you to manipulate its test boundaries to suit the different use cases you want to test.

RxJS in the wild

10

This chapter covers

- Integrating RxJS with other popular JavaScript libraries
- Introducing React and Redux
- Compartmentalizing UI components using React
- Feed-forward state propagation using Redux
- Rolling your own functional, asynchronous middleware using RxJS subjects
- Building a banking application using only reactive frameworks

The moment is finally here to answer a question you may have asked yourself a few times along this journey: "I can use RxJS to solve all of my asynchronous programming needs, but how can I use it in the context of an entire application?" This is a valid question and one that you'll answer by getting your hands dirty and seeing how RxJS plays out in the "Wild Wild Web."

This chapter is structured slightly differently from the previous ones, because we expect you to know most of the techniques from the earlier lessons by now. Given that you have a good understanding of Rx, we take the opportunity to introduce you to other technologies under the reactive umbrella called React and Redux. You can use these frameworks in conjunction with RxJS, and we think they're well worth your time learning about, especially if you're looking to scale the reactive paradigm to large JavaScript applications.

Arguably, you could use RxJS in conjunction with any competent web framework of your choosing, such as Backbone, Angular, or Ember, to name a few. But these frameworks promote paradigms (mostly object-oriented) that are very different from the functional and reactive paradigms you've learned about in this book. Although it's true that both can coexist, your aim is to create fully FRP applications, so you should prefer using frameworks that share similar principles.

Fortunately, the most difficult hurdle is the mental leap of changing paradigms, and you've successfully done that because you're here now. At a high level, the goal of this chapter is to teach you the components of an RxJS + React + Redux (what we call *the 3R*) architecture. Understanding how 3R works can be overwhelming at first, and a basic understanding of React and Redux would help you going through this chapter, but it's certainly not necessary. To make all this content easier to digest, we've laid out the following roadmap:

1 You'll explore the basic parts of React and Redux with simple examples (if you have previous experience with these technologies, feel free to skip these beginning sections and jump directly into section 10.4).

2 After rendering the UI using plain React components, you'll create a state management controller that allows you to communicate or pass state among these components. For this, you'll use Redux to dispatch actions that carry information as to how your state and corresponding UI changes.

3 You can implement simple synchronous state changes purely with Redux and simple functions, but asynchronous changes are much more complex (the story of our lives). Finally, you'll build a simple Redux middleware layer from scratch based entirely on RxJS. This middleware will allow you to dispatch asynchronous actions that can help you cope with asynchronous APIs like PouchDB.

We'll go through all these steps as you put together a simple banking site used to simulate the action of withdrawing money from a user's account and creating corresponding transactions.

Where can I find this code?

In some places in this chapter, we'll provide roadmap cues to guide you along with this code. It's all available on GitHub for you to play with and manipulate at your leisure (https://github.com/RxJSInAction/banking-in-action). Instructions on how to set up and run it are available in the README and appendix A.

Let's begin by briefly talking about the application in question and why we chose these technologies.

10.1 Building a basic banking application

Before we begin, we should first set the scene. Our goal for the chapter is to build a basic banking application that can handle various aspects of a user's finances. In this case, we'll focus on the actions that occur when a user attempts to withdraw money from their account and all the actions that happen behind the scenes, like making sure every transaction is captured and stored.

Informally, this application has a few functional requirements that serve as the basis for our implementation decisions:

- It must track a user's current balance and update it based on transactions, which can either add (credit) or subtract (debit) from the balance.
- It must allow the user to change the specifics of a transaction, such as which account to access and how much money to add or subtract.
- It must not allow transactions that would create a negative balance for the user.

As with all applications, it's important to have an idea of the overall structure before diving into the specifics of it. In figure 10.1, we present the UI of the component you're about to implement.

The architecture we're about to present fulfills four key requirements:

- Unidirectional state flow to go along with RxJS
- Immutable and side effect–free, or functional
- Unopinionated and lightweight
- Decoupled state and UI effects so that the business logic is agnostic to the view technology

The first two constraints (unidirectional state flow and immutable and side effect–free) should be obvious in light of the fact that this book is about functional, reactive programming using RxJS. The third requirement, to implement a lightweight architecture, is more about hitting as large a cross section of today's web developers as possible. Certainly, we could target older libraries or build from the ground up in vanilla JavaScript, but the reality is that, by and large, the JavaScript community has embraced various frameworks. Thus, in addition to showing how RxJS can stand alone, as we have for most of the book, we want to show off its use when other libraries are at play and

Figure 10.1 Screenshot of the component that handles user transactions related to withdrawal and deposit

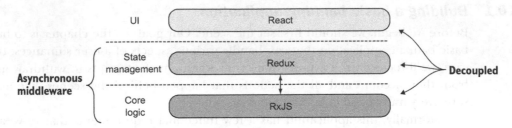

Figure 10.2   Layered diagram of the 3R architecture that shows the hierarchy of the different layers of the system and the purpose each serves

how you can use it to extend your reactive architecture. The final point, about decoupling state changes and UI effects from the main logic, is in line with RxJS's theme of decoupling the production of the event from the logic that consumes it; now, we take this principle to heart and apply it globally to the entire application.

For those reasons, we decided to present to you a lightweight RxJS architecture based on React and Redux. At a high level, these frameworks will layer in the manner illustrated in figure 10.2. With this simple picture in mind, our first stop in this journey is to introduce React and Redux.

10.2   *Introduction to React and Redux*

In order to understand why we chose React and Redux, you must first understand a little about them. First, what are they not? Neither React nor Redux is a complete framework compared to, say, AngularJS. We like this quality because we wanted to implement a lightweight architecture that includes RxJS. Unlike Angular, which is highly opinionated in its application design, React and Redux target single areas of concern and attempt to address them as well as they can.

> **TERMINOLOGY**   An opinionated framework is one that makes assumptions as to how you should organize and implement the components of your application. Redux has a minimal footprint and relies largely on using simple functions, thereby qualifying as an unopinionated framework.

Let's begin by learning more deeply about React.

10.2.1   *Rendering UI components with React*

React focuses on rendering the visible components that users interact with. React is all about controlling how (and if) components render on the screen. What sets it aside from other rendering technologies is how efficiently it decides to make updates and how decoupled it is from the logic leading up to the UI updates.

MEET REACT

React UIs are built compositionally, which means that a single HTML element can result from the composition of multiple (smaller) React components. Updating React state triggers the component to rerender itself recursively, like a nested DOM, checking at each step if a change is needed to a given section.

Other contenders in the reactive web space are Cycle.js and Yolk. One reason for choosing React over these alternatives is that we wanted to give you a chance to see how RxJS works with a framework that doesn't directly use RxJS from the ground up. Although React and Redux certainly have properties that make using them with RxJS relatively straightforward, they were not designed explicitly to use it, thus making it a more interesting integration problem when it comes to understanding how to design around interfaces that don't quite fit—this is what RxJS in the wild is all about!

REACT COMPONENTS

React components are the main unit of modularity and are remarkably simple. Most React components need only a `render()` method, which tells the React subsystem what to do when a component must be rerendered or drawn on the page. You'll need to know about only a couple of functions of the top-level API in this chapter. The first one is called `React.createElement()`; this is the method that's called when you want React to instantiate a particular element, like a `<span>` or a `<div>`. Here's what the top-level API looks like for this method:

```
React.createElement(
  type,
  [props],
  [...children]
)
```

It effectively creates a virtual version of a DOM (also known as a *shadow DOM*) element, which is used by React to render your application on the screen. Now, this call on its own doesn't draw anything onscreen; that's the job of the particular renderer that you're using, like ReactDOM, for example. Aside from `render()`, ReactDOM offers other APIs for removing or unmounting elements and finding DOM nodes in the HTML tree. These aren't used that often. Here's a simple "Hello RxJS!" application with empty properties:

```
const element = ReactDOM.render(
  React.createElement('div', {}, 'Hello RxJS!'),   ⟵ Passes an empty props object (this component is essentially stateless)
  document.getElementById('root')
);
```

This type of static rendering isn't particularly interesting, however; after all, you could have done this entirely with HTML in far fewer lines:

```
const element = '<div>Hello RxJS!</div>';
```

The next step is to build components that can actually do something. For instance, what if you want to change the language of your greeting? To do that you'll need a new approach. In React, you can think of all components as functions; they receive an input and output a visual. The important argument to understand about these functions is the `props` object, which is the mechanism by which you can transfer state into the React component and its inner children—the input argument. Thus, when defining components, it makes sense that the simplest type of component would be a function. You can define a localized Hello RxJS component by creating a function like so:

```
const HelloWorld = props =>
  React.createElement('div', {}, `${props.greeting} RxJS!`);
```

By convention, it's typical to initial cap the function name to denote this is a React component function.

React components are analogous to treating UI updates like functions as well—they take an input and emit some output. In the previous example, you take the input properties in an object called `props` and use them to render a single element—a *component function*. Now, you can create it whenever you want with different parameters:

```
ReactDOM.render(
  React.createElement(HelloWorld, {greeting: 'Hola'}),
  document.getElementById('root')
);
```

It's as simple as that. It's important to mention the close connection between React and FP in that all React components must act like pure functions with respect to their `props`. This means that a React component renders the exact same HTML output for the same `props`. This functional quality is known as referential transparency and it's the secret to why these components are so easy to compose and reuse.

Let's move on to a more interesting case. Imagine that instead of static data, you now want your data to change and update. A simple scenario for your banking application is an account balance component, which shows the current balance in a user's account. Remember the RxJS `interval()` factory operator? You can easily apply that here as well, given a simple `AccountBalance` component definition:

```
const AccountBalance = props =>
  React.createElement('div', {}, `Checking: ${props.checking} USD
     Savings: ${props.savings}`);
```

Next, you could invoke the `render` method each second to update the UI, mixing RxJS with some React to create a simple widget that updates account balances every second:

```
Rx.Observable.interval(1000)
  .map(value => ({checking: value, savings: value}))
  .subscribe(props =>
    ReactDOM.render(
      React.createElement(AccountBalance, props),
      document.getElementById('root')
    )
  );
```

As we mentioned earlier, React components are just plain functions that get invoked with parameters and return React (virtual HTML) elements, making them pure functions. Sometimes, however, this route is insufficient because you may want to also add event handlers, listen for when a component becomes mounted or attached to the DOM, or apply customizations to the state that's being passed in; then, you'd end up with very complex function bodies, which defeats the ES6 purpose. It's sometimes necessary for the developer to have more fine-grained control over a component's lifecycle as well as how it manages its state. React also exposes a mechanism for creating new components that offers more capabilities than a trivial function provides.

REACT CLASSES

The `React.createClass()` method is used for building more-advanced components where a function isn't enough. This static function takes an object bag as its argument, which contains definitions of the methods used during the lifetime of a component. The most important among these is, again, the `render()` method, which must be defined in order for the component to be used.

Try rewriting the account balances component to make use of this new approach:

```
const AccountBalance = React.createClass({
    render() {                              ⟵——— Uses ES6 class syntax
      return React.createElement('div', {},
          `Checking: ${this.props.checking} USD
          Savings: ${this.props.savings} USD`)
    }
});
```

Because this component is syntactically closer to a JavaScript class, notice that we're now reading props from the `this` object. The `this` keyword refers to the current context of a component, so it gives you access only to the component's state.

> **THE USE OF "THIS"** The use of `this` isn't common in functional programs because it implies you're accessing a scope outside the function or method, as the case may be. Nevertheless, considering that React is doing a good job of confining data access and mutations to the scope of the component itself (called the component's *context*) while you render data on the screen, it's a good trade-off to make. For the sake of making it easy to use, React relaxes the scope of data access from strictly local function scope in pure functional programs to the entire scope of a component.

So far, the previous component still isn't showing any new behavior, so let's add the next twist. The object bag passed to `React.createClass()` takes another method called `componentDidMount()`. It's called once by the React framework internally when a component instance has been initialized and has rendered on the page. So it's a good place to set up any initial logic and add some state into your UI. A React class lets you access this state through a property called `this.state` and allows you to update it through a method called `this.setState()`.

props vs. state

Earlier, we mentioned that props carries a React component's input. So what exactly is the difference between the `props` and `state` attributes? They're similar in concept but play different roles. First, both `props` and `state` make up the totality of a component's state. The former is used to configure the component—its options. It's received from its parent or the root, and it's immutable. Just like a pure function's input, `props` are not meant to change. On the other hand, `state` is meant to store data that will suffer mutations in time throughout the lifetime of a component.

But doesn't the thought of components exposing a window for other code to make changes to them violate the core functional principle of immutable objects? If we've done our job right, the very notion of sharing and changing state should be sending shivers down your spine. After all, state mutation is the root of all evil and what you're trying so hard to avoid!

Although all those reasons for disliking state mutation are valid (you'll be thankful for Redux later on), React minimizes its effect in a couple of ways and protects you from the normal cesspool of state management:

- *All mutation is done through the `setState()` method.* This means that the state variable isn't directly accessed and changed; there's some intelligence behind it. In fact, as you'll see, the local context of `state` is always safe when calling `setState()`.
- *React protects the individual state of components and contains it locally.* All state propagation is done through the `props` object that is then passed on to child states, meaning the parent component is responsible for initializing the `props` of a child component, which the child should never change thereafter. Remember, all components must act like pure functions with respect to their `props`, and this applies to all levels of the React element (DOM) tree.

With that said, let's move the interval logic into the `componentDidMount()` of `AccountBalances` so that it initiates with the component and localizes the effects of mutation to the component's context. You'll notice as well that instead of `this.props`, you're now effectively using `this.state` and `this.setState()` to read and write the current state of the component, respectively; the following listing shows these changes.

Listing 10.1 A React account balances that updates every second

```
const AccountBalances = React.createClass({
  getInitialState() {
    return {checking: 0, savings: 0};   ⟵── Sets the initial state for the component
  },
  componentDidMount() {                 ⟵── Uses JavaScript ES6 class syntax
    Rx.Observable.interval(1000)
      .map(value => ({checking: value, savings: value}))
```

```
      .subscribe(state => this.setState(state))
  },
  render() {
    return React.createElement('div', {},
      `Checking: ${this.state.checking} USD
      Savings: ${this.state.savings} USD`
    );
  }
});
```

Because you're using an arrow function, the keyword "this" in this case refers to the component instance rather than the observable.

> **NOTE** It's imperative that you understand to never mutate `this.state` directly; it should be treated as immutable, and you should allow only React to manage these mutations. `setState()` doesn't directly or immediately cause the mutation to occur; instead, it creates a pending transition state that also gives you hooks to control whether the state should occur and which portions of it are allowed to change.

You can plug this back into the original render component, and voila! Self-rendering components that change every second!

```
ReactDOM.render(
  React.createElement(AccountBalances, {}),
  document.getElementById('root')
);
```

This is the extent to which we'll cover core React in this book. The reason for this is that, for simplicity, we won't go into is JSX notation. A JSX preprocessor allows you to elegantly embed HTML directly into React components. We suggest you seek out materials devoted specifically to the topic in case you'd like to continue exploring it. And we honestly recommend you do. You can start with Manning's *React in Action* (www.manning.com/books/react-in-action) by Mark Thomas.

MANAGING THE STATE OF A REACT COMPONENT

Now that you can render React components, how can they communicate? A core philosophy of React is that every component feeds its state forward, just as you've become accustomed to with streams. In this case, it's propagated down to its children and not back up to its parent or out to any other component. This is very important to understand, because it will become the main reason why you'll use Redux later to dispatch state changes from one component to another.

For instance, in your banking app, suppose you want to show the account balances of checking and savings accounts independently. For this, you'd create two balance components to handle each and possibly wrap over them a parent component that would receive the data and send it down to each child. Listing 10.2 shows a simple `AccountBalance` function that you call to render for checking and savings and then a wrapping `Balances` React class that sends data down to each. Another concept shown here is injecting an observable sequence as `props` of `Balances`, which will produce the required state dynamically to simulate a steady stream of cash flow (if it were only that easy).

Listing 10.2   Communicating to child components using a single parent

```
const AccountBalance = props =>
  React.createElement('div', {}, `${props.name}: ${props.value} USD`);

const checking$ = Rx.Observable.timer(0, 1000);
const savings$ = Rx.Observable.timer(0, 1000 * 5);

const balance$ = Rx.Observable.combineLatest(checking$, savings$);

const Balances = React.createClass({
  getInitialState() {
    return {checking: 0, savings: 0};
  },
  componentDidMount() {
    this.props.balance$
      .subscribe(([checking, savings]) =>
          this.setState({checking, savings})
      );
  },
  render() {
    const { checking, savings } = this.state;
    return (
      React.createElement('div', {},
          React.createElement(AccountBalance,
            {name: 'Checking', value: checking}),
          React.createElement(AccountBalance,
            {name: 'Savings', value: savings}))
    );
  }
});

ReactDOM.render(
  React.createElement(Balances, {balance$}),
  document.getElementById('root')
);
```

- **Creates a simple subcomponent that formats its input**
- **Updates savings every 5 seconds**
- **Updates checking every second**
- **Creates a composite class for both accounts**
- **Combines the two inputs into a single stream**
- **Initializes the balances to zero**
- **Subscribes to updates on the balances**
- **Renders the component as the composition of two subcomponents**
- **Renders the balances component to the DOM and passes the balance$ stream as props to populate the UI with the illusion of constant cash flow into both accounts**

Obviously, there are a number of ways that you could implement a seemingly simple text field. So, for those of you who are new to React, this may seem a bit of a round-about way to render such a simple system. But what you've seen is the basis of a powerful concept. By combining RxJS streams with React components, you can create components that not only update in real time but also largely separate the concerns of the application. You achieve this separation by isolating UI changes and letting React efficiently manage the process, so that none of the components need to have an awareness of any others. This separation of the concerns and immutability of the data structures also prevents new features from interfering with existing ones.

So far, you've seen how to render DOM components and how to change them. But most of the dynamic interaction with rich state UIs originates from handling user input. User interfaces that use React that need to both handle user input and then render some output *on another component* based on those interactions present a slight challenge to RxJS's unidirectional flow (producers to consumers). The challenge is that these observables are then inextricably linked to the state of a single component but need to make changes somewhere else.

Take the standard search engine example you implemented in chapter 5. You learned that standard inputs can be used as event sources for data that comes from, say, keyup events. In the DOM, you could use a query to get the search bar element, attach the corresponding event handlers, and begin listening for events. After the stream is set up, you could begin subscribing to it from other parts of the application. If you were to implement the input box and the output list as React components, then the search results list, located somewhere else on the page, could subscribe to those events and update as new results arrive. But this becomes an issue in a feed-forward (unidirectional) model like React. Why? Remember that state flows smoothest when it's travelling to child components and not so well when it's going back upstream and into another isolated component, as shown in figure 10.3.

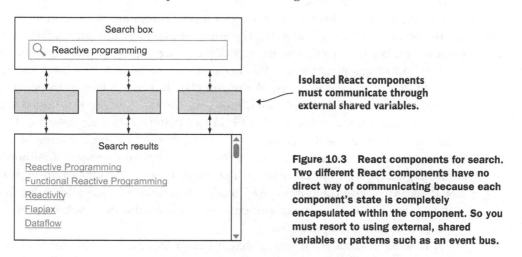

Figure 10.3   React components for search. Two different React components have no direct way of communicating because each component's state is completely encapsulated within the component. So you must resort to using external, shared variables or patterns such as an event bus.

When two isolated components need to communicate, this inevitably leads to sharing state variables, and you end up losing all the benefits of encapsulating state changes into a single downstream pipeline. This is important to understand. As you can see from figure 10.3, React components are good about keeping state to themselves, and it's meant to flow only downward. Therefore, if you modeled the search bar and the search results widgets as React components, there wouldn't be a direct way of sharing the data that originates in one with the other. This is a philosophical decision of React that states that components should never know (or care) whether another component is stateless or stateful.

In React, because components are composed hierarchically, it's difficult for one state to update another if those components don't have a direct parent/child relationship (as we did with the AccountBalance earlier), as shown in figure 10.4.

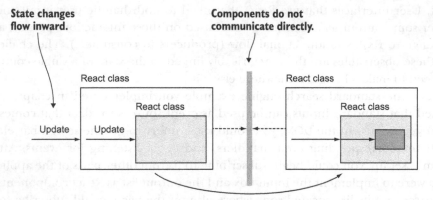

Figure 10.4   React components are walled off from each other, so that state changes can be propagated only from the parent component down to its children but never in isolation.

In this figure, there isn't a clear way for these components to communicate. Of course, you could think of wrapping the entire search page into an overarching React component. But then you'd run the risk of the entire page rerendering instead of just the bits and pieces that change. Another common solution might be to use two-way data binding of models to views, like in Angular. But this is known to become challenging as the size of the application grows. In the same way as decoupled architectures, you could use a variation of the observer pattern called an *event bus*. Using an event bus, several isolated components could subscribe to a single source of information and receive messages pertaining to the topics they're listening to. Although this would arguably work, the downside is that event buses are multicast and omnidirectional because events can flow in any direction; this can lead to problems that are hard to troubleshoot once many components loaded onto the page subscribe to receive messages, as shown in figure 10.5.

A downside to an event bus is that it's hard to picture what information flows through an event bus at any given time, and it clearly breaks the desired pattern of having information flow in a single direction. Also, it places the responsibility of writing the business logic of handling events of interest on the component itself.

What can you do to fix this issue, and how can you transform this unwieldy web of events into a single-direction flow of events? Again, it's the same mindset at play. And here we reveal the key to reactive applications. As it turns out, while you're tempted to look at unidirectional flow in the context of a line, *you could also visualize it as a circle* (a line that ties back to itself). Say what? In its path, this circle has multiple components that have different responsibilities. Consider the diagram in figure 10.6.

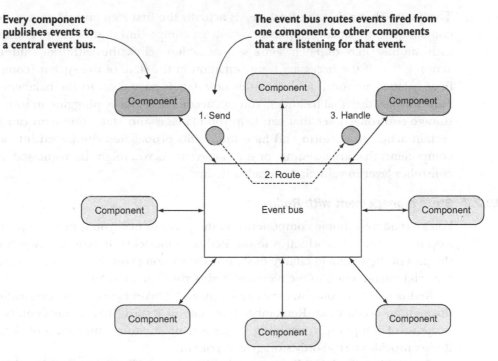

Every component publishes events to a central event bus.

The event bus routes events fired from one component to other components that are listening for that event.

Figure 10.5 A central event bus sends information from one component to another. These components can be React components or any other UI-rendering technology.

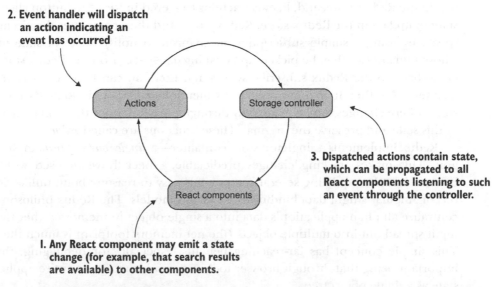

2. Event handler will dispatch an action indicating an event has occurred

3. Dispatched actions contain state, which can be propagated to all React components listening to such an event through the controller.

I. Any React component may emit a state change (for example, that search results are available) to other components.

Figure 10.6 The flow of states among different React components needs to be managed using actions and a controller that can dispatch such state changes and propagate them down to all components.

This figure shows that the final step is actually the first step and vice versa. So in the context of your banking application, a React component that needs to communicate with another may dispatch some sort of action (click the withdraw button). This action kicks off the necessary transformation in the state of the system (compute the final balance amount), and then this new data is passed on to the balances component (display the final balance). You can accomplish this by plugging in some type of storage controller layer that can help you manage your state, one than can act on a certain action to perform and have the results propagated downward into all React components that are listening for such an event. As you might have guessed, this state controller layer in your circle is called Redux!

10.2.2 *State management with Redux*

You've rendered simple components on the page, so now you'll move to your second stop on the roadmap, which is to use Redux to model your state management layer, the part of the system in charge of sharing data among your components. This section is a brief introduction to the pieces of Redux you'll need to know.

Redux is a state container for JavaScript, and it takes care of how information flows through an application. Remember that state in RxJS is always transient, so for the purpose of temporarily retaining it, instead of creating mutable, global variables, Redux provides a read-only storage component.

In addition, Redux follows several principles of FP that you explored in earlier chapters. Primary among these features is the use of single-directional flow to eliminate the side effects of sharing global data between components on the page. In a typical React/Redux application, data flows to a React component whenever it's changed within the Redux store, and, likewise, actions triggered in React (a button click) cause state to update in the Redux store. Redux stores and then completes the circuit, so to speak, by using a simple subscription mechanism to notify React of state updates. Those updates can then be picked up by calling `getState()` on the Redux store (we'll circle back to the Redux subscribe system and how you can build on it later in the chapter). Another functional dogma, as mentioned earlier, is Redux's immutable store, where changes can be made only through pure functions that create new copies of this state and preserve the original. These functions are called *reducers.*

Redux implements a singleton store container—a *single source of truth* in Redux jargon. This makes tracking changes predictable, especially when used with React, because it makes updating several components easy to reason about, unlike an event bus or Angular's tight data binding of views and models. The Redux philosophy is to centralize all of an application's data into a single object in memory rather than having it spread out into multiple objects (the net memory footprint is much the same). This simple concept has far-reaching benefits, especially for debugging, the most important being that through browser tools you can inspect your entire application's state as a single object tree.

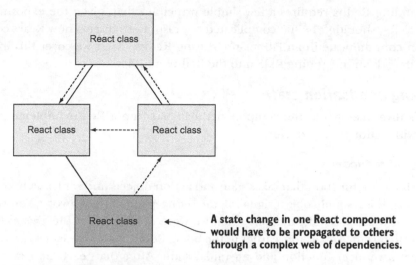

Figure 10.7 State changes should be done directly, because they create a dependency web that's too difficult to reason about.

Visually, with Redux you can turn a complex update graph of connected components, like in figure 10.7, into a simple graph where arrows move from a centralized object out to each component as needed. Then, every React component decides whether to accept the change and how it should be made in the most efficient fashion (figure 10.8).

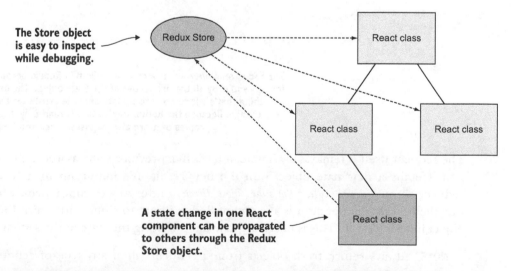

Figure 10.8 The Redux `Store` object becomes the storage controller that, upon receiving an event (action), can dispatch and cause state to propagate down to all subscribed React components.

Understanding Redux requires a few simple principles that, given the exposure you just had to Rx, shouldn't be too complicated to grasp. Let's discuss how React components can communicate in an FRP manner using Redux. After we cover this integration, we'll work on integrating RxJS into the Redux middleware.

10.3   *Redux-ing application state*

Now let's dive deeply into the components that make up a Redux implementation, starting with actions and reducers.

10.3.1   *Actions and reducers*

A *reducer* is a pure function that takes state and action objects and returns a brand-new state. An *action* is a simple object signaling the reducer function to invoke. You've seen instances of these sorts of functions when we were talking about the `reduce()` and `scan()` RxJS instance operators earlier in the book. Recall that you pass two arguments to `reduce`: a reducer function and an initial state. After that, each new event that arrives is subjected to this function and a new state is returned. The same concept happens in Redux. Reducers are similar to the simple React components that you saw earlier in that you can describe them as pure functions. Here's a simple reducer that can perform addition or subtraction, depending on the type of action that's being invoked:

```
const mathReducer = (state = {
  result: 0
}, action) => {
  switch(action.type) {
    case 'ADD':
    return {
      ...state, result: state.result + action.value
    };
    case 'SUBTRACT':
    return {
      ...state, result: state.result - action.value
    };
    default:
      return state;
  }
};
```

Reducers always key off of a type of operation to perform, and using string constants is the best approach and best practice in Redux.

The ES6 spread operator is a common idiom in Redux, because it helps you copy all the properties of the state object. The only thing that's left to do is to update only the attributes that change. Because the Redux single state is read-only, fresh copies of it are always passed back and forth.

The reducer itself is remarkably simple; it takes in a previous state, as well as an action, and it emits a new state object with the new result. It's important to note that a reducer should *never mutate the state object directly* under any circumstances, which is why the ES6 spread operator is a common Redux idiom to clone and return the state object in a single call. This is necessary to avoid polluting the state of the system.

> **NOTE**   Always return fresh objects from a reducer when any type of action takes place.

The next step is to apply that reducer to a piece of state and allow that state to change over time. This is critical if you expect to have the application respond to changes during the lifetime of a session.

10.3.2 *Redux store*

To begin, you use createStore(), which creates a Redux store that holds the complete state tree of your application. createStore() takes a given reducer function and matches it with a persistent state. It can optionally take in an initial state so that it has somewhere to start.

```
const store = createStore(mathReducer, 0);
```
◂——┘ **Stores points to your centralized Redux store object**

You can see how this works with an example. In the example of bank accounts, you had a simple object with two balances, one for each of your accounts:

```
const accounts = {
  checking: 100,
  savings: 100
};
```

You could build a reducer analogous to the mathReducer that updates the account balances like so:

```
const updateAccounts(state = {
    checking: 0,              ◂—— Initial (default) state
    savings : 0
}, action) => {
  switch (action.type) {
    case 'WITHDRAW':
      return { //#B
      ...state,
      [action.account]: state[action.account] -
          parseFloat(action.amount)
    };
    case 'DEPOSIT':
      return {                                      ◂——————
        ...state,
        [action.account]: state[action.account] +
          parseFloat(action.amount)
    };
    default:
      return state;
  }
});
```

Clones the shape of the state object, and overrides only the checking and savings amounts with the new values in the action's payload

This code creates a reducer that returns an updated balance for the accounts after a withdrawal or a deposit has occurred. Thus, you can use it like so:

```
const withdraw = {
    type: 'WITHDRAW',
    amount: 50,
    account: 'checking'
};

const newAccounts = updateAccounts(accounts, withdraw);
```

Actions have a type and a data (payload) property. The type of the action is what invokes the appropriate reducer.

Invokes the reducer with the current state and the action

The value returned from `updateAccounts()` would be the new balance state for the accounts. Plug that reducer into your app to get started:

```
const store = createStore(updateAccounts, accounts);
```

This store comes with the additional logic to break down actions and create a new state based on those actions. This means that instead of manually calling `update-Accounts()`, you now update accounts through the store using `store.dispatch (action)`. Redux will manage invoking the proper reducer depending on the action. This goes back to our previous discussion about not making changes directly but using the frameworks to dispatch and manage such changes. Figure 10.9 shows this interaction.

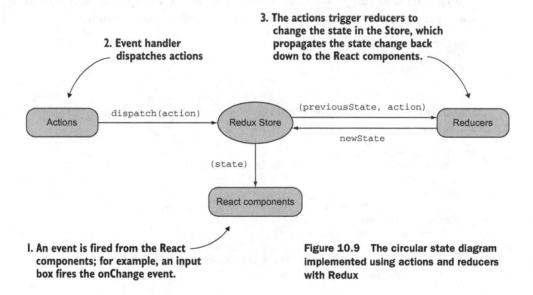

3. The actions trigger reducers to change the state in the Store, which propagates the state change back down to the React components.

2. Event handler dispatches actions

`dispatch(action)`   `(previousState, action)`   `newState`   `(state)`

Actions   Redux Store   Reducers   React components

I. An event is fired from the React components; for example, an input box fires the onChange event.

Figure 10.9   The circular state diagram implemented using actions and reducers with Redux

A simple interaction between React and Redux, shown in figure 10.9, works in the following manner. The event originates from the React component and fires its event handlers, for instance, a button click or text box change. Then, the handler instantiates the corresponding action to take and uses Redux to dispatch the action, which in turn modifies the state in the centralized store. Lastly, this store gets propagated down to all React components, which then decide how best to react to this change.

Let's move into implementing the pieces of this interaction and see how you can begin to include RxJS in the mix. The store executes all the reducers, and the type of the action represents how parts of the state need to be updated. Instead of just instantiating action objects, the best practice is to use action factories (functions that return action objects). Then, you can create actions at will and avoid having to type them in all the time. You can see this in our next snippet:

```
function withdraw(payload) {
  return {type: 'WITHDRAW', ...payload};
}
```
⟵ **Action factory that creates an action object**

```
const action = withdraw({amount: 50, account: 'checking'});
store.dispatch(action);
store.getState(); //-> {checking: 50, savings: 100}
```

As you can see, actions are easy to create. The only required element in Redux is the type property. Any other logic that you want to perform in the action body is up to you. We say Redux is an unopinionated framework because it applies few assumptions about the way you write your logic. Now, if you were to access the state of the store by calling store.getState(), you'd see that it had been updated by the withdraw() action. Now let's tie this into React. The dispatch() method of the store can then be used in your React components to send out events without worrying about their consumers or tightly coupling them to each other. For instance, to begin implementing your withdraw functionality in your simple banking form, you can use dispatch() in place of event handlers, as shown in the following listing.

Listing 10.3 Simple banking form with checking text field and withdraw button

Computes the result of a withdraw synchronously and emits an action to update the balances in the store

Updates the accounts if the transaction is allowed to occur

```
function handleClick (amount) {
    const { checking, savings} = store.getState();

    if(checking > amount) {
        store.dispatch(withdraw({amount, account: 'checking'}));  ⟵
    }
    else {
        throw 'Overdraft error!';          ⟵ Otherwise, fires an overdraft error
    }
}

React.DOM.button({id: 'withdraw',
    onClick: () =>
        handleClick(document.getElementById('amount').value)},
'Withdraw');                   ⟵ Reads the value from the text
                                  box and attempts a withdraw
```

This code allows you to send events to the store, but how would you then access those events? Remember, your application needs to be reactive, which means that ideally you should be able to listen for changes in the application state about the store you created.

As it turns out, there is a mechanism for this behavior. The store is already an observable or is "observable-like" with a much narrower observable specification and doesn't have all of the fancy bells and whistles that you've come to expect from your RxJS streams. That being said, it does feature a subscribe() method (it's a "subscribable" object), so you can convert it into an RxJS stream with little difficulty. Because

Redux deviates from what you'd consider your normal observable pattern, you'll need to do a bit of adaptation to make it fit. Here's where RxJS fits into the mix.

10.4   *Building a hot RxJS and Redux store adapter*

Integrating RxJS into your React/Redux architecture is easy. It's important to mention that a lot of the code you'll see in the next sections used to integrate RxJS and Redux has already been implemented in a third-party, open source library called redux-observable (https://github.com/redux-observable/redux-observable), which makes this integration seamless using a higher level of abstraction. But because this book is devoted to RxJS, we didn't want to just glance over this feature and thought it would be nice to implement this integration ourselves using pure RxJS constructs. It would also give us the chance to introduce another cool feature called Subject, which you're bound to come across as you explore more RxJS.

Although RxJS and Redux are designed to solve different problems, you have amazing leverage in the fact that Redux stores are observable-like and so you can cross over framework lines with a simple adaption.

The first thing you always should do is run down the list of normal factory methods that you could use for this purpose. The best option is to use the from() operator. This operator is special and very intelligent because it takes any observable-like objects and converts them into real observables. These include arrays and generators, as you've seen all along, but also objects that conform to the ES7 Observable specification, which Redux stores do to enough extent. Let's see how this works:

```
function createStreamFromStore(store) {
  return Rx.Observable.from(store)
    .map(() => store.getState())
    .publishBehavior(store.getState())
    .refCount();
}
```

store.getState() is called twice, so that subscribers always receive the latest state changes.

publishBehavior() is a flavor of a multicast (hot) operator that emits the latest value to all subscribers.

Makes this stream go live as soon as the first observer subscribes

As you can see, Redux's observable-like behavior is somewhat primitive compared to what you've dealt with in this book. Internally, Redux has been passed a next callback, which it invokes on each state change. But each time the next callback is invoked, it's only notifying observers of available data, not emitting it. Observers are required to explicitly call store.getState() in order to see the current state of the world. To amend this, you can use the map operator to call the getState method on every update and forward that state downstream.

It's important to note that in createStreamFromStore, the first call to store.get-State() is equivalent to the initial state. If there are no changes between the creation of the stream and its first subscribers' subscribe(), then they'll all receive that state. If a change occurs before a subscriber subscribes, then that change is now stored in publishBehavior(), and all new subscribers will receive the new state instead. This function is trivial but very powerful when used to build the bridge connecting Redux with Rx. Here, you've simply lifted the store into an RxJS observable and then mapped each next value onto the current state of the store's state. This simple mapping makes the Redux store seamlessly work like a normal RxJS observable. Internally, RxJS is subscribing to the store. The last part of this function converts the stream into a hot one. This is to optimize the stream and serve many subscribers at once. The `publishBehavior()` operator is a special flavor of the `publish()` operators from chapter 8, which store and emit the most recent value shared with all subscribers. This is useful if components will be hooking up at different times, which may or may not be before the observable emits. This way, you make sure that subscribers always get the latest state when they subscribe.

Earlier, we showed how you can create dynamic behavior using RxJS to update React components. Now, you'll use `createStreamFromStore()` to add asynchronous data flows, so that you can use async APIs like PouchDB, for example, to persist your withdrawal transactions.

10.5 *Asynchronous middleware with RxJS Subject*

Finally, you've arrived at the last stop of our roadmap before we show you all the pieces of your 3R architecture: building your Rx-based asynchronous middleware. What's the benefit of integrating RxJS into Redux? The issue is that, by design, everything in the eyes of Redux happens synchronously: dispatch an action, execute the reducers, and modify the state; all steps occur one after the other. Suppose you needed to perform some asynchronous action. How can you introduce wait times, or the latency of making an AJAX call to fetch data, or perhaps invoke a PouchDB call to persist a record in local storage? In this case, you want to be able to track every transaction (withdrawal or deposit) in the local store. You can examine the interaction diagram in figure 10.10 in order to understand where the challenge is.

Notice how the linear flow is broken in step 2 in an effort to accommodate asynchronous logic. The issue is that, to account for latency, your middleware actions need to invoke multiple subactions or subflows to signal when the long-running operation has completed (the normal Redux idiom is to dispatch actions with status flags like DONE). One of the canons of reactive architectures is that the application must always be responsive. Hence, the first action that needs to get dispatched is the one signaling that the asynchronous call began (DONE, false). You place that flag into the store, so that your application knows not to fire another action simultaneously.

> **TIP** For those with experience in concurrent processing, this is similar to using a semaphore.

Once the call completes, a second subflow is dispatched, signaling the completion of the event (DONE, true). Finally, the processing status is reset in the store, and the application is free to spawn subsequent actions.

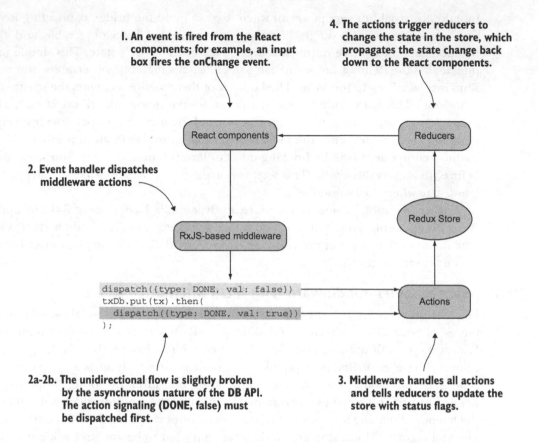

1. An event is fired from the React
   components; for example, an input
   box fires the onChange event.

4. The actions trigger reducers to
   change the state in the store, which
   propagates the state change back
   down to the React components.

2. Event handler dispatches
   middleware actions

2a-2b. The unidirectional flow is slightly broken
       by the asynchronous nature of the DB API.
       The action signaling (DONE, false) must
       be dispatched first.

3. Middleware handles all actions
   and tells reducers to update the
   store with status flags.

```
dispatch({type: DONE, val: false})
txDb.put(tx).then(
    dispatch({type: DONE, val: true})
);
```

**Figure 10.10 Async actions introduce the complicated state management needed to keep track of
the progress of the action from the moment the action starts processing to when it eventually returns.
In this case, an async flow is used to call the PouchDB APIs to retrieve initialization data.**

For brevity, we won't show you the full code, but you can imagine your withdraw
action being conditioned like so:

```
function shouldWithdraw(payload) {
  function (dispatch) => {
    if (payload.done) {
      return dispatch(withdraw(payload));
    }
  }
}

store.dispatch(shouldWithdraw({amount: 50, account: 'checking'}));
```

This form of action definition
is also supported by Redux.

Checking for additional flags in your actions clutters up all of your code. As you know
by now very well, RxJS is the perfect tool to model asynchronous logic as a single unidirectional line. In other words, you can build an observable pipeline through which
actions that can execute all sorts of asynchronous behavior can flow serially. Thus, you

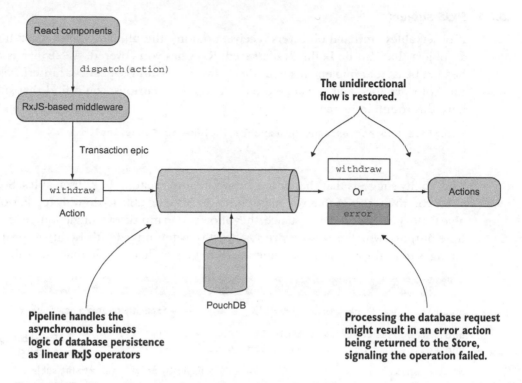

Figure 10.11 **Observables can string together actions and model them as a single downstream flow. The business logic encoded in the observable pipeline might produce an exception, which the withdraw action transforms into an error action sent back to the store. This logic will live in a function called an epic.**

can refactor step 2 to spawn asynchronous requests linearly as RxJS operators so that you can regain that logical unidirectional data flow and keep everything serial, as if it all happened synchronously. Remember the main goal of RxJS that you began learning about in chapter 1: Treat asynchronous code as though it was synchronous.

For simplicity, we'll zoom in on just that part of the interaction in step 2, as shown in figure 10.11.

Using RxJS in the middleware means that every action that passes through gets wrapped within an observable, processed through the pipeline, and emitted as an event. That means that you can eliminate the use of callbacks from your action logic. Also, you unlock all the power of RxJS to, say, throttle the withdraw action as the user repeatedly clicks the withdraw button. This will be implemented in a component called an epic, which we'll come back to after you build your asynchronous middleware.

To build your asynchronous middleware, you need to learn about one last core RxJS feature. Let's take a brief pause from Redux to discuss another cool feature of RxJS called a Subject. We'll look at a couple of simple examples using subjects, and then we'll circle back (no pun intended) to wrap up our discussion of reactive architecture.

10.5.1 *RxJS subjects*

If observables emit and observers receive, wouldn't the ultimate monster mash-up be an object that can do both? Rest assured; RxJS has you covered. A `Subject` is a two-headed beast that implements both the `Observable` and the `Observer` interfaces, so it can both produce and consume events. If you were curious, you'd find that subjects have this rough interface:

```
interface Subject extends Observable implements Subscription {

}
```

This ability suggests that they're the brains behind creating hot observables. Subjects allow you to do things that you might not otherwise be able to do with regular observable factory operators. For instance, they allow you to multicast a single source into multiple outputs, which is why they're so attractive when mixed with Redux to propagate changes to multiple React components. Here's a simple example that uses subjects.

Listing 10.4 Multiple subscriptions with subjects

```
const subject = new Rx.Subject();              ◁──── Explicitly creates a new Subject

subject.subscribe(x => console.log(`Source 1: ${x}`));   ◁──┐ First subscription
subject.subscribe(x => console.log(`Source 2: ${x}`));      │ to subject

subject.next(0);                    ◁──────── Explicitly passes a value to the subject

Rx.Observable.from([1, 2, 3, 4, 5])   ◁──┐
  .map(x => x * x)                         Uses another observable to
  .subscribe(subject);              ◁──┘  pass values to the Subject
```

Second subscription to subject (points to `subject.subscribe(x => console.log(`Source 2: ${x}`));` and `subject.next(0);`)

Running this code emits the values 0, 1, 4, 9, 16, 25 to all subscribers, just like `publish()`. In fact, `publish()` is just a façade that uses `Rx.Subject` to carry out its work. The publish family of operators that you learned about in chapter 8 leverages this ability to allow multiple subscribers to listen to the same source. This is possible because the subject won't notify the upstream when it gets new subscribers; thus, the only time that the source is subscribed to is when the subject initially subscribes. In general terms, this operation is described by an even more generic operator, aptly named `multicast()`, of which the set of overloaded `publish*()` operators is just calls to `multicast()` with different types of subjects. We show this in figure 10.12.

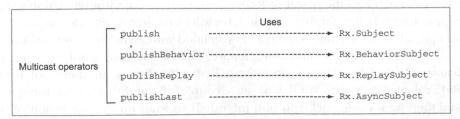

Figure 10.12 Multicast overloaded operators

`multicast()` accepts a subject (or subject variant) as its first argument and returns a `ConnectableObservable`. Downstream subscribers will always be subscribing to the subject, but the subject itself won't subscribe until `connect()` is called. Embedding subjects in a controlled and encapsulated manner can be extremely powerful; you'll use subjects to receive, process, and further propagate events to implement your business logic into the middleware of your banking application (more on this in the next section).

> **A WORD OF CAUTION**   For all their power, subjects can also be dangerous. For many newcomers to Rx, they're a panacea of possibility because they allow developers to use observables without all the baggage of FP. Unfortunately, this kind of usage often leads to overexposure of state, so we recommend them only when you really need this feature.

The case for subjects comes down to a limited set of behaviors that need to be tightly constrained. For instance, you could emulate standard promise functionality natively in Rx using the `Subject` derivation called `AsyncSubject`.

The async subject behaves just like the vanilla subject when it comes to accepting values and then reemitting them. But it has an additional constraint; it holds onto only a single value and emits only that one value to all current and future subscribers once the subject has been completed. So it shouldn't surprise you that the `publish-Last()` specialization is really just an async subject behind the scenes. In the following listing, we show a simple promise implementation using an async subject internally.

Listing 10.5   Build a promise-like operator with subjects

```
Rx.Observable.promiseLike = function(fn) {
  let subject = new Rx.AsyncSubject();          ⟵── Creates a new Subject

  let resolve = x => {                  ⟵┐  Simulates a promise's resolve method by delegating
    subject.next(x);                      │  to the subject's next method to emit a value and then
    subject.complete();                   │  immediately completing the stream (one value only)
  };

  let reject = e => {                  ⟵┐  Simulates a promise's reject method by delegating
    subject.error(e);                    │  to the async subject's error observer method
  };

  fn(resolve, reject);              ⟵── Invokes the function with the callbacks
  return subject.asObservable();         ⟵┐  Returns the Subject disguised
};                                         │  as a regular Observable
```

This code creates a naïve promise-like interface that returns an observable instead. Using a random number function, we'll prove to you that this observable behaves like a promise:

```
const randomInt = (min, max) => Math.floor(Math.random() * (max - min)) + min;

const random$ = Rx.Observable.promiseLike((resolve, reject) => {
  resolve(randomInt(0, 1000));
});
```

```
random$.subscribe(console.log);  //744
random$.subscribe(console.log);  //744
random$.subscribe(console.log);  //744
random$.subscribe(console.log);  //744
random$.subscribe(console.log);  //744
```

All subscribers will receive the same value, in this case 744 (because it's a random function, results will vary).

In this code, you can see that we've addressed two of the issues that we highlighted earlier. First, we constrained the subject to a highly restricted scope and we do not expose references to the subject in the return value. And second, we have a defined lifetime for the subject. These two solutions tend to be good rules of thumb when explicitly including a subject in your code. Having learned subjects, you can build your middleware layer.

10.5.2 *Building epic, reactive middleware*

Generally speaking, middleware is a component or set of components, usually based on some plugin architecture, that can be injected between certain chunks of logic without impacting other parts of the system. Middleware allows for clean, noninvasive code that doesn't clutter your actions, reducers, or the UI. Because Redux is agnostic to whether state changes need to happen synchronously or not, you need some way of injecting this additional waiting logic where actions are generated and before they're consumed by a reducer. Let's see how you can accomplish this.

Redux is small but supports injecting asynchronous plugins like redux-thunk (https://github.com/gaearon/redux-thunk), redux-promise-middleware (https://github.com/pburtchaell/redux-promise-middleware), and others. Figure 10.13 shows the flow of actions through the system when we plug in an RxJS-based middleware component that has actions flowing through observable streams that trigger a corresponding reducer on the Redux store.

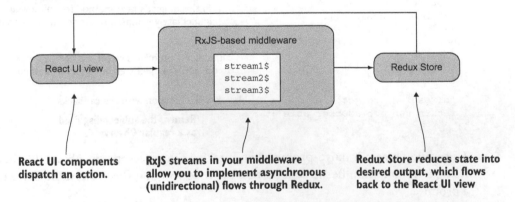

Figure 10.13 A flow diagram of how actions and state move in the application. Actions flow from React/UI events to the Redux/React component after being processed by middleware and are then sent back to the UI as state updates.

This figure shows that any actions dispatched by the UI components can flow through your middleware component (implemented using RxJS), which carries all of your business logic and is ideal to handle your asynchronous needs while keeping the feed-forward flow intact. This is where you could write to your PouchDB database or invoke an AJAX call to fetch search results. When the data is available, it flows through a set of reducers before being propagated out (multicast) to all React components through `setState()`. RxJS brings you this advantage by encoding your asynchronous business logic into a set of operators—hence, reactive middleware.

The objective of using RxJS in the middleware is to create a layer that can consume an observable action sequence and then asynchronously emit potentially different actions that will be consumed by the store that resulted from the logic flowing through the observable. That's the purpose of the middleware: to receive actions, do some processing, and return similar or different actions. The actions to process are contained in a set of epics (we borrow the term from redux-observable).

Epics are nothing more than functions that have access to the state as well as incoming actions that are dispatched from your UI components. You can think of them as functions that take a stream of actions and return a stream of actions—actions in, actions out. Say, for instance, that you wanted to create an epic to handle persisting every transaction to local storage as withdraw (or deposit) actions are dispatched. For this, you can create a `transactionLogEpic()` function, as shown in the next listing.

Listing 10.6 Plugging into the middleware

```
const txDb = new PouchDB('transactions');

class Transaction {                                       ← Slightly simplified version
  constructor(account, amount, balance, timestamp) {         of the Transaction class
    this.account = account;                                  from chapter 6
    this.amount = amount;
    this.balance = balance;                        Epic middleware function
    this.timestamp = timestamp;
  }
}                                                  Convenient new operator
                                                   implemented to filter incoming
                                                   actions based on type (analogous to
function transactionLogEpic(action$, store) {   ← how reducers work on action.type).
  return action$.ofType('WITHDRAW', 'DEPOSIT')  ← We'll show it in the next listing.
    .timestamp()
    .map(obj => ({...obj.value, timestamp: obj.timestamp}))
    .map(action => ({
      ...action,
      balance: store.getState()[action.account] - action.amount   ←
    }))
    .map(datedAction => (                          Gets a snapshot of the
      new Transaction(                             current state of the store and
        datedAction.account,                       updates the targeted account
        datedAction.amount,
        datedAction.balance,
        datedAction.timestamp
      )
```

```
    ))
.mergeMap(datedTx =>
  Rx.Observable.fromPromise(txDb.post(datedTx))
    .mapTo({payload: {...datedTx}, type: 'LOG'})
    .catch(() =>
      Rx.Observable.of({type: 'LOG', payload: 'TX WRITE FAILURE!'})
    )
  );
}
```

Dispatches instead an error action to the store to signal to the user that an error has occurred

---

ES 7 Object.assign()

For most of this book, we've been strictly sticking to ES 6 (ECMAScript 6) syntax. For this chapter, for the purposes of both brevity and popularity, we'll be using ES 7 `Object.assign` syntax. This syntax appears as `{...oldState, prop: 'VALUE'}`, where this block would normally be written `Object.assign({}, oldState, {prop: 'VALUE'})`. As of this writing, most browsers do not yet support this syntax, so if you wish to use it in your project, you'll need to use a transpiler like Babel (https://babeljs.io/).

With this change, your middleware will intercept any action of type WITHDRAW or DEPOSIT and create the proper transaction to store it. Functions like the one in listing 10.6 are the foundation of your observable-based middleware component. In order to make these functions come together, you need one more piece that you'll build yourself. You need to merge the resulting streams so that you can feed all the results into the Redux store. Consider the wiring where you define several such functions and add them to an array. Because these are functions that create new observables, we've taken to naming them "factories." You'll add your only epic function now; at the end of this chapter, we'll show you how to inject additional functionality by adding another epic to this array:

```
const epics = [
  transactionLogEpic,

  /* Add more epics for more functionality */
];
```

Just as you're used to switching on action types in reducers, you'll see that it's typical of the middleware to selectively process certain actions. For this, it's useful to extend the Observable type with an additional operator, ofType(). As you implement more epic functions, bringing this concept along as a first-class citizen will make your code much more succinct. The next listing shows how you can easily augment the Observable prototype with this new operator.

Listing 10.7 Implementing custom ofType operator

```
Rx.Observable.prototype.ofType = function (...types) {
  return this.filter(({ type }) => {
    const len = types.length;
    switch (len) {
      case 0:
        throw new Error('Must specify at least one type! ');
      case 1:
        return type --- types[0];
      default:
        return types.indexOf(type) > -1;
    }
  });
}
```

Now that you understand what epics are, you need to connect them to Redux so that the processing of dispatching an action begins to flow through the observable sequence. This connective tissue is implemented entirely with RxJS using Subjects.

A Subject is a key ingredient for building your middleware layer and dispatching actions that flow through Redux from React components. As far as your banking application is concerned, it's recommended to reduce subjects to the smallest possible scope to avoid abuse. In this case, you'll use them to dispatch and proxy changes along the middleware layer with code like this:

```
const action$ = new Rx.Subject();
const dispatch = action => action$.next(action);
```

This creates a Subject and wraps the next function in a lambda, which is what you'll expose to the rest of the application instead of the reference to the Subject itself. The logic is not that simple; you still need to do a bit of work. To make this all portable, you'll wrap the proxy mechanism into a function called createMiddleware() that knows how to mimic Redux's interface and glue observables into your middleware layer, as shown in this listing.

Listing 10.8 Building your middleware

At the top level, the middleware accepts a store and a set of epics

Creates a new private Subject instance used to emit actions to both the store and the epics

```
function createMiddleware(store, epics) {
  const input$ = new Rx.Subject();

  const actions =
    epics.map(epic =>
      epic(input$, store));

  const combinedActions$ = Rx.Observable
    .merge(...actions)
    .publish();
```

Invokes all the factories and stores their outputs as your middleware streams

Each factory takes the actions (input$) and state (store) to create a new stream.

Merges all the resulting streams into a single output

Converts that stream into a hot observable, so it's shared

Feeds the output of the epic functions (action streams) so that they can get handled by subsequent middleware in the chain

Simultaneously sends all events to the store as well, in case it can handle them

```
        combinedActions$.subscribe(input$);

        combinedActions$.subscribe(action => store.dispatch(action));

          const sub = combinedActions$.connect();

        return {
          dispatch:    (action) => input$.next(action),
          unsubscribe: () => sub.unsubscribe()
        };
      }
```

Returns a proxied version of dispatch that invokes next on the subject (thus sending actions to the middleware)

Connects the stream (makes it hot); this prevents the stream from emitting before both subscribers are subscribed

Puts the user in control of disposing the observable middleware

Listing 10.8 is probably a bit of a mind bender. So here's a quick, isolated example that shows the chain of commands as actions flowing into the middleware and out to the reducers:

```
function simpleReducer(state, action) {
    switch(action.type) {
        case 'LOG':
            return {...state, messages: [...action.payload, 'in Redux!']};
        default:
            return state;
    }
}

const store = createStreamFromStore(
    createStore(simpleReducer, {messages: []}));
const observableStore = createStreamFromStore(store);

observableStore.subscribe(({messages}) => console.log(messages.join('=>')));

function simpleEpic(action$, store) {
    return action$.ofType('LOG')
        .delay(1000)
        .map(action => {...action, payload: [...action.payload, 'in Rx!']});
}

const disposableDispatcher = createMiddleware(store, [simpleEpic]);

disposableDispatcher.dispatch({
    type:    'LOG',
    payload: ['Hello']
});
```

This code snippet shows a simple epic and a simple reducer. It's meant to illustrate the chain of commands. When the action is dispatched, it first reaches the middleware, and then the reducer. The middleware epic pipes the action through the observable and defers propagating it by a second. Afterward, you process the action and append "in Rx!" to the payload. The action finally makes it to the reducers, where it's modified once more to append "in Redux!" Hence, the output would look like the following:

```
(...after 1 second)
    Hello=>in Rx!=>in Redux!
```

Figure 10.14 illustrates the sequence of actions in this data flow roller coaster.

You astute readers should notice that the `Subject`, which you instantiated in the listing, is subscribing to *its own downstream*, in what would seem to violate the very laws of time and space! As the saying goes, this is not a bug; it's a feature. The reasoning behind this cycle (or feedback loop for those in the AI field) is simple; often, you'll need epics to work together. The epics themselves, as you'll see in the next section, are independent silos of logic (read "streams"), which will transform a stream of actions into another stream of actions; in other words: actions in, actions out. For a complex middleware layer, you may well want those output actions to become the input actions of another epic. Thus, the `input$` `Subject` is a means by which to convert those output actions into potential input actions for other epics.

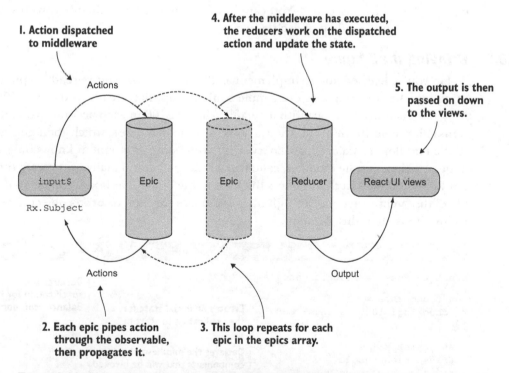

1. **Action dispatched to middleware**

4. **After the middleware has executed, the reducers work on the dispatched action and update the state.**

5. **The output is then passed on down to the views.**

Actions

input$

Rx.Subject

Epic

Epic

Reducer

React UI views

Actions

Output

2. **Each epic pipes action through the observable, then propagates it.**

3. **This loop repeats for each epic in the epics array.**

Figure 10.14 This diagram shows the flow of actions within `createMiddleware()`. The `input$` subject is in charge of injecting the world of Redux into RxJS. After the action is wrapped in a `Subject` observable, it flows through each of the epics in the array in order. Finally, the actions resulting from executing this series of epics are dispatched further into the Redux reducers.

The loopback logic is only one part of the code, though; in the second half of listing 10.8, you're also subscribing to the combined output of actions and dispatching all output actions to the store. In effect, this means that an action is evaluated at two points: first, by the epics, to determine if it can be further processed; and second, by the reducer itself, to see if the store must be updated and a new state emitted. To optimize this process, you utilized the publish/connect operators, which were discussed in chapter 8. Recall that by publishing the stream, you share it between all subscribers so that new pipelines aren't created for each subscriber. Finally, you `connect()` the parent stream so that the two subscribers (the `Subject` and the store) can begin receiving events when they're emitted. You allow the user to shut down the system by exposing the unsubscribe logic to the user through a method. This allows the user of your library to instigate a controlled shutdown of the application and switch off the streams when they're finished with them.

The result is an interface that more or less resembles that of the original store but that transparently handles asynchronous actions without changes to the Redux store. This is important, as you'll see in the next section, because of how the middleware will fit into the overall system. Now that you finally have all of your components and have seen how you might use them, let's hook them up so that your banking application can handle user transactions. You can do this in any order; remember, your components are all independent of each other.

10.6   *Bringing it all home*

So far, you've learned how to implement all the pieces. Now, you're ready to put everything together to complete your simple banking app that's ready to receive withdraw or deposit actions. You start with a default value of $100 in each account. You add the transaction epic (to insert all transactions into the database), which then gets added to the middleware via `createMiddleware()`. Your store component knows only about a single reducer at the moment, called `updateAccounts()`. Finally, you create the parent React component that renders the UI into the document body. You make it capable of dispatching actions through the middleware through its `props` object. The next listing shows all of this wired up.

Listing 10.9   Building the application

```
const Balances = React.createClass({/**/});          ◁── Declares the
                                                          specification for the
const accounts =                      ◁──                 Balances component
   checking: 100, savings: 100    │ Creates an initial state for
};                                 │ the application to start in
                                  ◁──

const epics = [                   ◁── Declares the middleware
  transactionLogEpic                │ components that will be invoked
  /*  add more epics here */        │
];                                                    Creates an instance of
                                                      a Redux store to house
const store = createStore(updateAccounts, accounts);  ◁── state changes
```

```
const state$ = createStreamFromStore(store);

const middleware = createMiddleware(store, epics);
ReactDOM.render(
  React.createElement(Balances,
    {appState$: state$, dispatch: middleware.dispatch}),
  document.getElementById('root')
);
```

Combines the store with the middleware to build the application

Creates an instance of the Balances component powered by the application

Uses the method defined earlier to convert the store into an Rx Stream (you can do this because the store is a subscribable object)

There are several major advantages to organizing your code as you have. For one, you've virtually removed coupling between components. You have streams, reducers, and React components, all tied together loosely by the types of events they create and consume. This means that you can add more components to your application unobtrusively. Note as well that this is superior to a standard event bus, typical of this kind of architecture, because the single direction that events follow means that you avoid race conditions. Further, the compartmentalization of the handlers and reducers means that you can test each of them in isolation. Finally, by using immutable state throughout the application, you prevent new features from unexpectedly creating changes to other components in the system and polluting your system-wide state, which is always problematic for JavaScript developers.

Lastly, to demonstrate how easy the task of adding new features is, you can add another quick feature. For instance, consider a task to calculate interest payments periodically. These payments would be some fraction of the overall balance that's applied over a fixed period of time. How would you add such a feature to your system?

The first question to ask is, where does this logic actually reside? In this case, you could think of automated transactions just like any user transaction that you've seen so far. But with interest, there's no user interaction. Remember as well that your transaction management is done without knowing who initiated a transaction. This means that you'll likely need to create a new handler:

```
const computeInterest = p => 0.1 / 365 * p;

function interestEpic(action$, store) {
  return Rx.Observable.interval(15000)
    .map(() => store.getState())
    .map(({savings}) => {type: 'DEPOSIT',
      account: 'savings', amount: computeInterest(savings)}))
}
```

Then, you need to add that handler to your initial stream list:

```
const epics = [
  transactionLogEpic,
  interestEpic
];
```

Voila! You now have new functionality enabling interest payments. We should point out as well that at this point, you're dealing almost exclusively with streams, which is exactly what you want. What you've seen here is merely a small sample of what you could do with this pattern. We invite you to also check out and run the sample application that was built using this architecture (https://github.com/RxJSInAction/rxjs-in-action). We've included several more examples with varying degrees of complexity.

10.7   Parting words

This journey through RxJS has taken you to some new places: from the fundamentals of reactive programming, all the way to a full-fledged web application. Along the way, you've explored how observables are created and destroyed. You looked at how you can merge and split observables, injecting or extracting the information you need. You experimented with notions of time, which surround and interweave with observables, and you used that understanding to build purer, more testable functions. As we said at the outset, this book wasn't meant as a definitive guide to all things RxJS; instead, by focusing on a variety of topics and how they pertain to your real applications, we've hopefully given you both a taste and a hunger for more, because the lessons here are merely the beginning of what you can do with RxJS. Also, remember that the principles we covered in the previous chapters are not confined to JavaScript. You can utilize them across the stack in a variety of languages. Finally, we hope that this book has encouraged you not just to use RxJS in your projects (and we really do hope you do!) but also to examine your code with a more critical eye toward many of the concepts covered in the book, namely, purity, immutability, composability, testability, and laziness. These are valuable ideas that can be applied even without fancy frameworks (though they do tend to make it easier).

10.8   Summary

- Understanding how data is transformed and moved will inform decisions on how to include RxJS in your project.
- Keep events moving in a single direction by looping streams in order to create complex UI interactions that are easy to reason about.
- Manage state immutably and keep all components separate. This will ensure a clear separation of concerns that will allow you to scale your architecture to support new features without linearly increasing the complexity of your application.
- You can use `Subjects` to implement advanced middleware or stream-proxying solutions. While powerful, `Subjects` can be hard to troubleshoot given that they can act as both observables and observers. We recommend you keep `Subjects` to a minimum and well encapsulated.
- You can use RxJS to create middleware that handles asynchronous data flows so that actions dispatched from the UI can flow through an observable pipeline to be translated into a separate action that flows out of an epic.
- RxJS in an intricate part of the Redux/React architecture, which we call 3R.

appendix A
Installation of libraries
used in this book

Installing the example projects

To help you better understand the text, we've made two code repositories available to download and run so as to better see *RxJS in Action*.

The primary repository we use throughout the text contains the runnable code samples.

URL: https://github.com/RxJSInAction/rxjs-in-action

Node	`git clone https://github.com/RxJSInAction/rxjs-in-action.git`
	`cd rxjs-in-action`
	`npm install`
	`npm start`
	`<Open browser to localhost:8080>`

The second repository, which is used only for chapter 10, contains a standalone application that can be accessed and run via the following.

URL: https://github.com/RxJSInAction/banking-in-action

Node	`git clone https://github.com/RxJSInAction/banking-in-action.git`
	`cd banking-in-action`
	`npm install`
	`npm start`
	`<Open browser to localhost:8080>`

You can also find all the installation instructions on the respective repositories.

Installing RxJS

This book uses the latest release of RxJS. RxJS 5 is a complete overhaul/redesign of the previous RxJS 4 version. The main factor driving this project is a focus on performance and simplicity. Re-architected under the Lift architecture by Paul Taylor, RxJS 5 features a significant reduction in the use of function closures, thereby lessening its runtime footprint. RxJS 5 was simplified to allow easier debugging and stack trace reports.

Furthermore, the new `Observable` data type was redesigned to be more conformant to the upcoming ES-observable-spec slated for JavaScript ES7. Finally, there's a focus on modularity so that users can now download and use only the parts of RxJS they need instead of having to install a single monolithic library.

Version: 5.0.2
Homepage: https://github.com/ReactiveX/rxjs
Installation details follow.

Browser	https://unpkg.com/rxjs/bundles/Rx.min.js
Node	npm install rxjs

In ES6 environments, you can load the Rx library in the following ways:

```
import Rx from 'rxjs/Rx';

const Rx = require('rxjs/Rx');
```

Installing Ramda.js

This utility library was designed specifically for functional programming, which facilitates the creation of function pipelines. All of Ramda's functions are immutable and side effect–free. In addition, all the functions have automatic currying, and their parameters are arranged to make it convenient for currying and composition. Ramda also contains property lenses, which are used in this book to read/write the properties of objects in an immutable manner.

Version: 0.18.0
Homepage: http://ramdajs.com/
Installation details follow.

Browser	<script src="ramda.js"></script>
Node	npm install ramda

Installing PouchDB

PouchDB is an open source JavaScript database inspired by Apache CouchDB that's designed to run well within the browser. PouchDB was created to help web developers build applications that work as well offline as they do online.

Version: 5.3.2
Homepage: https://pouchdb.com/
Installation details follow.

Browser	`<script src="` `https://cdn.jsdelivr.net/pouchdb/5.3.2/pouchdb.min.js"></script>`
Node	`npm install pouchdb`

Installing Moment.js

Moment.js was designed to parse, validate, manipulate, and display dates in JavaScript.

Version: 2.13.0
Homepage: http://momentjs.com/
Installation details follow.

Browser	`<script src="https://cdnjs.cloudflare.com/ajax/libs/moment.js/` `2.13.0/moment.min.js"></script>`
Node	`npm install moment`

Installing Google client APIs

The Google client library unlocks the power to access all of Google's web APIs, including the URL shortener used in chapter 9. The only requirement to use the library is to have an active Google account and to generate the OAuth2 token for that API, which you can do through the Google APIs console.

Version: 14.0.0
Homepage: https://www.npmjs.com/package/googleapis
Installation details follow.

Browser	`<script src="https://apis.google.com/js/api.js"></script>`
Node	`npm install googleapis`

Using the Bitly Web API

Bitly exposes a web service used to shorten URLs. You need to have an active Bitly account and use the login and token information in your profile settings.

Homepage: https://app.bitly.com
Installation details follow.

Browser	Make AJAX calls to `https://api-ssl.bitly.com`
Node	`npm install bitly`

Installing Mocha

Mocha is a feature-rich unit-testing framework for JavaScript that runs on both Node.js and in the browser. It uses a serial test runner to support both synchronous and asynchronous unit tests.

Version: 3.1.0
Homepage: https://mochajs.org/
Installation details follow.

Browser	`<script src="https://cdnjs.cloudflare.com/ajax/libs/mocha/3.0.2/mocha.min.js"></script>`
Node	`npm install mocha`

Installing Chai.js

Chai.js is a test-framework-agnostic library for BDD/TDD types of assertions. In this book, we used Chai to enhance the assertion capabilities of Mocha.

Version: 3.5.0
Homepage: https://www.npmjs.com/package/chai
Installation details follow.

Browser	`<script src="https://cdnjs.cloudflare.com/ajax/libs/chai/3.5.0/chai.min.js"></script>`
Node	`npm install chai`

Installing React.js

React is a lightweight component UI library for creating fast, reactive, and modular UI frontends. It uses a unidirectional flow and a fast diffing mechanism to reduce side effects and improve performance.

Version: 15.3.1
Homepage: https://facebook.github.io/react/
Installation details follow.

Browser	`<script src="https://unpkg.com/react@15.3.1/dist/react.js"></script>` `<script src="https://unpkg.com/react@15.3.1/dist/react-dom.js"></script>`
Node	`npm install react react-dom`

Installing React-Bootstrap

React-Bootstrap is a small extension library of React that allows you to use bootstrap components in React.

Version: 0.30.0
Homepage: https://react-bootstrap.github.io/
Installation details follow.

Browser	`<script src=" https://cdnjs.cloudflare.com/ajax/libs/` `react-bootstrap/<version>/react-bootstrap.min.js"></script>`
Node	`npm install react-bootstrap`

Installing Redux.js

Redux is a small application state library that provides a functional interface to managing state change in an application without mutation and the associated side effects.

Version: 3.6.0
Homepage: http://redux.js.org/
Installation details follow.

Browser	`<script src="https://unpkg.com/redux@3.6.0/dist/redux.min.js">` `</script>`
Node	`npm install redux`

appendix B
Choosing an operator

The following is a list of operators and a description of when to use them. We cover the operators (static and instance) used in this book. Some operators can act as both static and instance, and we indicate which ones. For a more complete list, please visit http://reactivex.io/rxjs/manual/overview.html#choose-an-operator.

All factory operators are called as static methods of the `Rx.Observable` type. See table B.1.

Table B.1   Static scope operators

Situation	Purpose	Operator

Creating a new instance	With custom logic
	From a given value
		`create`
		
		`of`

	From an observable-like object	`from`
	From a range of numbers	`range`
	With an exception	`catch`

	From an ES6 promise
	From any event originated by an event emitter like WebSockets or the DOM
		`fromPromise`
		
		`fromEvent`

	Wrapping a callback	`bindCallback`

	Attach some recourse dependent on the lifecycle of an observable
	Spawn an AJAX request and merge the result into the observable sequence
	Conditionally create a stream with an if-then-else approach
		`using`
		
		`ajax`
		
		`if`

Table B.1 Static scope operators *(continued)*

Situation	Purpose	Operator

Creating a time-based instance	Single timed interval
	Multiple timed intervals
	Run all observable sequences in parallel and collect their last elements
		`timer`
		`interval`
		`forkJoin`

All instance operators are called through an observable instance (`Rx.Observable
.prototype`). See table B.2.

Table B.2 Instance scope operators

Situation	Purpose	Operator
Transforming a sequence	Delaying or offsetting the entire emission of an event sequence	`delay`
	Prepend an element onto the stream	`startWith`
	Transform elements one-to-one	`map`
	Fold entire event sequence into a single value	`reduce`
	Just like `reduce`, but emit each subsequent fold as an event	`scan`
	Extract object properties from emitted data	`pluck`
	Buffer a certain amount of data and emit all at once	`bufferCount`
	Buffer for a specific period of time and emit all at once	`bufferTime`
	Buffer at the pace of when a subordinate observable emits a value	`buffer`
	Like `buffer`, but use a function that creates a new observable to indicate when to close the buffer	`bufferWhen`
Filtering sequences	Remove events according to a predicate function	`filter`
	Skip a certain number of events	`skip`
	Grab the first *N* number of events	`take`
	Emit the values of an observable until a subordinate observable emits; emit events until some other observable tells you not to.	`takeUntil`
	Emit only the first event of a sequence	`first`
	Emit only the last event of a sequence	`last`

Table B.2   Instance scope operators *(continued)*

Situation	Purpose	Operator
Filtering sequences *(continued)*	Emit values only after a particular time span given by another observable has passed	`debounce`
	Debounce for a fixed period of time	`debounceTime`
	Emit event at most once every time period	`throttleTime`
	Emit only items that are distinct by comparison (given by you) from the previous item	`distinctUntilChanged`
	Like the previous operator, except now you compare the keys of the emitted items	`distinctUntilKeyChanged`
Utilities	Perform any sort of necessary side effect such as logging to the screen; useful for debugging purposes	`do`
	Embellish the event object with the interval duration span; useful for computing time deltas between emission	`timeInterval`
Error handling	Catch an exception produced from any operator and replace it with a continuing observable	`catch`
	Allow the sequence to halt and terminate into the observer's error handlers	`throw`
	Retry an operation for a certain amount of time	`retry`
	Implement additional logic such as a backoff retry strategy	`retryWhen`
	Call function when an observable completes or finishes with errors; good for cleanup tasks	`finally`
Coordinating sequences	Combine the latest values from a collection of streams when all of them have emitted; can be used as a static factory operator as well	`combineLatest`
	Like the previous operator, except this will emit the latest values from each observable when the source observable emits	`withLatestFrom`
Joining events of multiple observable sequences	Forward events from multiple sequences in order of arrival; can be used in static form as well	`merge`
	Append the events of one observable sequence after another (in order); can be used in static form as well	`concat`
	Cancel a source observable midstream and replace it with a new one	`switch`

Table B.2   Instance scope operators *(continued)*

Situation	Purpose	Operator
Joining events of multiple observable sequences *(continued)*	Merge a collection of observables using a selector function and emit when all the observable sequences have emitted at a corresponding index; useful for keeping a map of corresponding events. Can be used in static form as well	`zip`
Projecting or branching other observables, making AJAX requests, DB lookups, and so on	Merge an observable object into the source observable; flatten the result into a single observable (alias: `flatMap`)	`mergeMap`
	Like `mergeMap()`, but dispose the source observable when it's no longer needed (alias: `flatMapLatest`)	`switchMap`
	Project and flatten a source observable but maintain order of events	`concatMap`
Broadcasting the outcome of an observable sequence to multiple subscribers	Create a lazy observable that you manage that multiple subscribers can connect to; use it to control when you want to let events flow with `connect`	`publish`
	Create an observable that shares the outcome with multiple subscribers. RxJS manages the lifecycle of this observable internally through `refCount`.	`share`
	Share the last *N* number of events with all subscribers	`publishReplay`
	Share the last observable event with all subscribers	`publishLast`
Cancel/dispose of the stream	Unsubscribe from the stream	`unsubscribe()`

index

Symbols

. (dot) notation 70

A

absolute time 91
abstracting over time 21–23
Account class 178
accumulator function 75–76
actions, Redux 286–287
add() function 259
addEventListener() function 216
addListener() method 12
aggregate data, scanning 76–77
aggregate operators 82
aggregates, sequencing operator pipelines with 77–84
  performance advantages of sequencing with RxJS 80–84
  referential transparency 77–80
  self-contained pipelines 77–80
aggregating results with reduce 75–76
ajax operator 310
AJAX, testing requests 250–253
ajax() function 7, 13, 159, 166, 184
allocation
  allocating objects 62

eager, disadvantages of 62–64
  lazy 64–65
appendResults() function 104
array extras 18
Array object 35
Array.map() method 35
ArrayList 41
arrow functions 7
AsapScheduler 261
asynchronous code, testing 250–255
  AJAX requests 250–253
  working with Promises 253–255
asynchronous computing, vs. synchronous computing
  event emitters 11–12
  issues with blocking code 5–6
  non-blocking code with callback functions 6–7
  understanding time 7–9
  using callbacks 9–10
asynchronous data sources
  multi-value 48–49
  single-value 47–48
asynchronous middleware 291–302
  building 296–302
  with RxJS subjects 294–296
asynchronous streams 141–146
asynchronous timing, with JavaScript 88–94
  explicit 88–90

implicit 88
  JavaScript interfaces 90–94
AsyncScheduler 261–262
AsyncSubject 295
augmenting virtual reality 263–270
  refactoring search streams for testability 267–270
  with marbles 264–266
  with virtual time scheduler 266–267

B

bare observables, creating 55–56
bindCallback operator 310
Bitly Web API 307
bitly$ stream 166
blocking code, issues with 5–6
boundary conditions 246–247
bounded context 78
buffer() function 112, 175, 311
bufferCount() function 113, 311
buffering 111–117
BufferIterator function 39
bufferTime operator 311
bufferWhen() function 113, 177, 311
bulk data, writing 175–177
bulkDocs() function 175
business processes, coordinating
  building reactive database 170–181

315

business processes, coordinating *(continued)*
   hooking into observable
      lifecycle 151–152
   joining parallel streams with
      combineLatest 159–162
   joining parallel streams with
      forkJoin 159–162

C

callbacks
   delegating errors to 184–186
   non-blocking code with 6–7
   overview 7
   using 9–10
   with Promises 12–14
cancelling
   streams 62–68
      cancellation mismatch
        between RxJS and other
        APIs 67–68
      disadvantages of eager
        allocation 62–64
      explicitly cancelling
        subscriptions 65–67
      lazy allocation 64–65
      subscribing to observables
        64–65
      subscriptions, explicitly
        65–67
catch block 184
catch() operator 187, 195, 197,
   206, 310, 312
Chai.js, installing 308
classes, React 277–279
clearInterval() function 67
clearResults() function 104
clearTimeout() function 105
clients, WS (WebSockets)
   220–221
closing observable 112
code
   issues with blocking 5–6
   non-blocking with callback
      functions 6–7
code bases
   functional 188–189
   reactive 188–189
cold observables 212–217
   making from hot observables
      228–230
   making into hot observables
      230–232

cold resubscribe 222
combinatorial operators 170
combineLatest() function 115,
   121, 159, 162–163, 165,
   312
complete() function 58, 155,
   251
components
   React 275–277, 279–284
   user interface, rendering
      with React 274–284
composing functions 9
computing, synchronous vs.
   asynchronous 5–12
   event emitters 11–12
   issues with blocking code
      5–6
   non-blocking code with call-
      back functions 6–7
   understanding time 7–9
   using callbacks 9–10
concat() function 130, 312
concatenating streams
   overview 124
   preserving event order by
      130–133
concatMap operator
   dragging and dropping with
      146–150
   overview 313
ConcurrentLinkedList 41
conformance 152
connect() method 238–239,
   295
ConnectableObservable 238
connecting one observable to
   many observers
   237–244
   publish 237–240
   publish last 242–244
   publish with replay 240–241
consumers 23–24
consuming data with observers
   53–60
   creating bare observables
      55–56
   observable modules 57–60
   Observer API 53–54
containerizing data 140
continuation 12
coordinating business processes
   building reactive database
      170–181
   hooking into observable
      lifecycle 151–152

   joining parallel streams with
      combineLatest 159–162
   joining parallel streams with
      forkJoin 159–162
CORS (cross-origin resource
   sharing) 34, 138, 251
CPS (continuation-passing
   style) 12
create() method 56, 310
createMiddleware() function
   299
createStore() method 287
createStreamFromStore 290
CSV (comma-separated value)
   array 72
custom observables 67

D

data
   aggregate, scanning 76–77
   consuming with observers
      53–60
      creating bare observables
        55–56
      observable modules 57–60
      Observer API 53–54
   generated 44
   observable, switching to
      latest 133–135
   sources of
      identifying 43–44
      multi-value, asynchronous
        48–49
      multi-value, synchronous
        46–47
      single-value, asynchronous
        47–48
      single-value, synchronous
        46
   static 44
   wrapping sources with
      Rx.Observable 43–52
      creating RxJS observables
        44–45
      identifying different
        sources of data 43–44
      pull-based semantics
        49–52
      push-based semantics
        49–52
      when and where to use
        RxJS 46–49
data flows 17–18
data pipelines 24

data streams. *See* streams
databases
  joining related operations
    177–180
  populating reactively
    172–175
  reactive 180–181
data-driven programming
  41–43
Date.now() function 87
Date() function 91
deallocating objects 62
debounce operator 312
debounce() method 106
debounceTime() function 101,
  107, 266–267, 312
debouncing 101–108
delay operator 311
delay() function 97
delegating errors, to callbacks
  184–186
design document 177
discriminant function 73
dispatch() method 289
DisposableResource object 156
distinctUntilChanged operator
  144, 312
distinctUntilKeyChanged
  operator 312
do operator 205, 312
DONE status flag 291
dot (.) notation 70
DoublyLinkedList 41
downstream compartmentalization 152
dragging and dropping, with
  concatMap 146–150
DSL (domain-specific
  language) 249
dynamic data sources 21

E

eager allocation, disadvantages
  of 62–64
effectful computations 83
emitters. *See* event emitters
endofunctor 44
error handling 182–208
  common techniques
    183–188
    delegating errors to
      callbacks 184–186
    with Promise 186–188
    with try/catch 183–184

dealing with failure 193–208
  catching errors 195–196
  propagating errors down-
    stream to observers
    193–194
  reacting to errors 195–196
  reacting to failed
    retries 199–208
  retrying failed streams for
    fixed number of
    times 197–199
functional approach
  189–192
imperative techniques
  188–189
error() function 194
errors
  catching 195–196
  delegating to callbacks
    184–186
  Promises and 186–188
  propagating downstream to
    observers 193–194
  reacting to 195–196
evaluating streams 62–68
  cancellation mismatch
    between RxJS and other
    APIs 67–68
  disadvantages of eager
    allocation 62–64
  explicitly cancelling
    subscriptions 65–67
  lazy allocation 64–65
  subscribing to observables
    64–65
event bus 282
event emitters 11–12
event hooks 153
EventEmitter class 11, 48, 153
events
  filtering out unwanted 72–74
  interleaving by merging
    streams 124–129
  preserving order by concate-
    nating streams 130–133
example projects, installing 305
explicit cancellation, of
  subscriptions 65–67
explicit timing 88–90

F

factory functions 155
failure
  catching errors 195–196

propagating errors down-
  stream to observers
  193–194
reacting to errors 195–196
reacting to failed retries
  199–208
retrying failed streams for
  fixed number of times
  197–199
Failure type 190
falsy value 74
fetchDataInterval$ stream 199
fetchResult$ stream 268
filter() function 73, 77, 311
filtering unwanted events
  72–74
finally() operator 155, 205–206
findRecordById() function
  189
first operator 311
flattening data 122, 139
fluent programming 77
forkJoin operator
  joining parallel streams with
    159–162
  overview 311
FP (functional programming)
  as pillar of RP 29–40
  overview 30–37
frame() function 269
from operator 226, 290, 310
fromEvent operator 310
fromPromise operator 223, 310
FRP (functional reactive
  programming) 4
function chaining 30
functional code bases 188–189
functional programs, testing
  inherently built into
  246–250
functional sequences of events
  4
functor 35, 44

G

generated data 44
getOrElse() function 192
getState() method 284, 290
Google client APIs,
  installing 307

H

handling errors 182–208
  common techniques
    183–188
    delegating errors to
      callbacks 184–186
    with Promise 186–188
    with try/catch 183–184
  dealing with failure 193–208
    catching errors 195–196
    propagating errors down-
      stream to observers
      193–194
    reacting to failed retries
      199–208
    retrying failed streams for
      fixed number of times
      197–199
  functional approach
    189–192
  imperative techniques
    188–189
higher-order observable 135
hooks. *See* web hooks
hot observables
  making from cold
    observables 230–232
  making into cold
    observables 228–230
  overview 212, 215, 217
hot RxJS, building 290–291

I

if operator 310
immutable function 30–31
imperative error-handling
  techniques 188–189
implicit timing 88
IndexedDB 171
input, from users 101–110
  debouncing 101–108
  throttling 108–110
installing
  Chai.js 308
  example projects 305
  Google client APIs 307
  Mocha 308
  Moment.js 307
  PouchDB 306–307
  Ramda.js 306
  React.js 308
  React-Bootstrap 309
  Redux.js 309
  RxJS 306
instance methods 102
interfaces, timing JavaScript
  90, 94
interleaving events by merging
  streams 124–129
interval() operator 94, 214,
  260, 276, 311
inversion of control 7
isEven() function 259
iterator patterns 38–40

J

JavaScript
  asynchronous timing with
    88–94
    explicit 88–90
    implicit 88
    timing interfaces 90–94
      setInterval 93–94
      setTimeout 91–92

K

keyCode property 73

L

last operator 311
latency 4
lazy allocation 64–65
lazy data source 63
lazy data types 20
lazy evaluation 30, 36–37
lifecycle, of observables
  152–154
LinkedList 41
logic of streams, replaying
  222–223

M

managing
  state of React components
    279–284
  state with Redux 284–286
manual debouncing 105
map() function 71, 264–265,
  311
mapped observable 125
mapping operations on
  observables 70–72
marbles 264–266
Math.random() function 87
mathReducer 287
merge() function 125–126,
  162, 312
mergeMap operator 135–141,
  313
merging operations 151
merging streams, interleaving
  events by 124–129
middleware, asynchronous
  291–302
  building 296–302
  with RxJS subjects 294–296
mismatch, of cancellation
  between RxJS and other
  APIs 67–68
Mocha
  installing 308
  overview 250
modules, observable 57–60
Moment.js, installing 307
monads 141
mousedown event 123
mousemove event 123, 147
mouseup event 123, 147–148
mouseUp$ stream 124, 133
multicast() function 228, 237,
  294
multicasting operators 237
multiple streams 122–135
  interleaving events by
    merging 124–129
  preserving event order by
    concatenating 130–133
  switching to latest observable
    data 133–135
multi-value data sources
  asynchronous 48–49
  synchronous 46–47
MVC (model-view-
  controller) 20

N

nested observables, unwinding
  135–141
next() method 39, 51, 53, 56
Node.js, simple WS (Web-
  Socket) servers in
  219–220
non-blocking code, with callback functions 6–7
notEmpty function 248

O

object-oriented programming.
    See OOP
object-oriented. *See* OO
Observable class 79
Observable data type 29
observable instance methods
    102
Observable interface 294
observable methods 102
observable operators 69–77
  aggregating results with
    reduce 75–76
  filtering out unwanted
    events 72–74
  mapping operations on
    observables 70–72
  scanning aggregate data
    76–77
observable pipeline 193
observables 23, 154, 211–244
  bare, creating 55–56
  changing temperature of
    226–237
    creating hot-by-operator
      streams 232–237
    making cold observable
      hot 230–232
    making hot observable
      cold 228–230
    producers as
      thermometers 227–228
  cold 212–217
    making from hot 228–230
    making into hot 230–232
  connecting to many
    observers 237–244
    publish 237–240
    publish last 242–244
    publish with replay
      240–241
  creating 44–45
  hot 212, 215–217
    making from cold
      230–232
    making into cold 228–230
  impact of side effects on
    replay 221–226
    replay vs. resubscribe 222
    replaying logic of stream
      222–223
  impact of side effects on
    resubscribe 221–226
    replay vs. resubscribe 222

    resubscribing to stream
      224–226
  lifecycle 152–159
    hooked on 154–159
    observer patterns 153–154
    web hooks 153–154
  mapping operations on
    70–72
  modules 57–60
  subscribing to 64–65
  switching to latest data
    133–135
  unwinding nested, with
    mergeMap operator
    135–141
  WS (WebSockets) 217–221
    clients 220–221
    overview 218–219
    simple servers in Node.js
      219–220
observeOn() operator 263
Observer API 53–54
Observer interface 294
observer patterns 20, 153
observers
  connecting one observable to
    many 237–244
    publish 237–240
    publish last 242–244
    publish with replay
      240–241
  consuming data with 53–60
    creating bare observables
      55–56
    observable modules 57–60
    Observer API 53–54
observers, propagating errors
    downstream to 193–194
of operator 310
offset time 91
ofType() operator 298
OO (object-oriented) 28
OOP (object-oriented
    programming) 26
operations
  database, joining related
    177–180
  mapping on observables
    70–72
operator chaining 77
operators 61–94, 101
  cancelling streams 62–68
    cancellation mismatch
      between RxJS and other
      APIs 67–68

    disadvantages of eager
      allocation 62–64
    explicitly cancelling
      subscriptions 65–67
    lazy allocation 64–65
    subscribing to observables
      64–65
  choosing 310–313
  evaluating streams 62–68
    cancellation mismatch
      between RxJS and other
      APIs 67–68
    disadvantages of eager
      allocation 62–64
    explicitly cancelling
      subscriptions 65–67
    lazy allocation 64–65
    subscribing to observables
      64–65
  observable 69–77
    aggregating results with
      reduce 75–76
    filtering out unwanted
      events 72–74
    mapping operations on
      observables 70–72
    scanning aggregate
      data 76–77
  pipelines, sequencing with
    aggregates 77–84
  propagation 98–99
  sequential time 99, 101
opinionated framework 274

P

paradigms, programming
    26–27
parallel streams
  joining with combineLatest
    159–162
  joining with forkJoin
    159–162
passive resources 212
patterns
  iterator 38–40
  observer 153
pipelines
  operator, sequencing with
    aggregates 77–84
  self-contained 77–80
pluck operator 311
pointerup event 129
populating databases,
    reactively 172–175

post() method 174
PouchDB
  installing 306–307
  overview 171, 177, 180
predicate function 73
processes. *See* business processes
producers
  as thermometers 227–228
  overview 23
programming
  data-driven 41–43
  functional 29–40
  reactive, functional program-
    ming as pillar of 29–40
  without loops 34
programming paradigms
  26–27
progressive loading 171
projected observable 125
Promise data type 13, 48
Promise.catch() operator 186
Promises
  errors and 186–188
  improving callbacks with
    12–14
  limitations of 162
  testing 250, 253–255
propagating errors, down-
    stream to observers
    193–194
propagation 17–99
props attribute 278
publish
  last 242–244
  with replay 240–241
publish operator 294, 313
publishBehavior() method 290
publishLast operator 313
publishReplay operator 313
pull-based semantics 49–52
pure functions 8, 247
pure observables 213
push-based collections 50
push-based semantics 49–52

R

Ramda.js, installing 306
range operator 310
range() function 63, 263
React
  classes 277–279
  components 275–277,
    279–284

rendering UI components
    with 274–284
  overview 274–275
  state management with
    Redux 284–286
React.createElement()
    function 275
React.js, installing 308
React-Bootstrap, installing 309
reactive code bases 188–189
reactive databases, building
    170–180
  joining related database
    operations 177–180
  populating database
    reactively 172–175
  writing bulk data 175–177
Reactive Extensions for Java-
    Script. *See* RxJS
Reactive Manifesto 123
reactive programming. *See* RP
reactive programs, testing
    245–270
  asynchronous code 250–255
  augmenting virtual
    reality 263–270
  inherently built into func-
    tional programs
    246–250
  making streams testable
    258–260
  Promises 250–255
  reactive streams 255–258
  scheduling values in RxJS
    260–263
reactive streams 121–150
  asynchronous 141–146
  dragging and dropping with
    concatMap 146–150
  multiple 122–135
    interleaving events by
      merging 124–129
    preserving event order by
      concatenating 130–133
    switching to latest observ-
      able data 133–135
  testing 255–258
  unwinding nested observ-
    ables, with mergeMap
    operator 135–141
reduce operator
  aggregating results with
    75–76
  overview 82, 311

reducers
  overview 284
  Redux 286–287
reduction operation 75
Redux 286–290
  actions 286–287
  reducers 286–287
  state management with
    284–286
  store 287–290
  store adapter 290–291
Redux.js, installing 309
refactoring search streams for
    testability 267–270
refCount() method 239
reference counting 239
referential transparency 77–80
relative time 91
render() method 275, 277
rendering UI components with
    React 274–284
  managing state of React
    components 279–284
  overview 274–275
  React classes 277–279
  React components 275–277
  state management with
    Redux 284–286
resubscribing
  impact of side effects on
    221–226
    replay vs. resubscribe 222
    resubscribing to stream
      224–226
  to streams 224–226
  versus replaying 222
results, aggregating with reduce
    75–76
retry() operator 198, 312
retrying
  failed streams for fixed num-
    ber of times 197–199
  reacting to failure when
    199–208
retryWhen() operator 199, 312
RP (reactive programming),
    functional program-
    ming as pillar of 29–40
runInterval() function 267
Rx.Observable, wrapping data
    sources with 43–52
  creating RxJS observables
    44–45
  identifying different sources
    of data 43–44

Rx.Observable, wrapping data sources with *(continued)*
   pull-based semantics 49–52
   push-based semantics 49–52
   when and where to use RxJS 46–49
Rx.Observable.ajax() operator 250
Rx.Observable.create() method 66
Rx.Observable.fromEvent() operator 180
Rx.TestScheduler class 263
RxJS (Reactive Extensions for JavaScript)
   abstracting over time 21–23
   advantages of using 14–16
   creating observables 44–45
   data flows 17–18
   installing 306
   introduction to 18–19
   other APIs and 67–68
   propagation 17–18
   scheduling values in 260–263
   sequencing with 80–84
   streams 17, 19–25
   subjects 294–296
   when and where to use 46–49
      multi-value, asynchronous data sources 48–49
      multi-value, synchronous data sources 46–47
      single-value, asynchronous data sources 47–48
      single-value, synchronous data sources 46

S

scalability 4
scan() function 77, 286, 311
scanning aggregate data 76–77
scheduler 260
scheduling values in RxJS 260–263
search streams, refactoring for testability 267–270
search$ stream 137
self-contained pipelines 77–80
semantics
   pull-based 49–52
   push-based 49–52
sendRequest() function 107, 136

sequencing, operator pipelines with aggregates 77–84
   performance advantages of sequencing with RxJS 80–84
   referential transparency 77–80
   self-contained pipelines 77–80
sequential time 99, 101
servers, WS (WebSockets) 219–220
SessionDisposable object 157–158
setInterval() function 42, 44–94
setState() method 278
setTimeout() function 42, 44–92
shadow DOM 275
share() operator 234, 239, 313
shareReplay() operator 240
side effects 8, 31, 224
   impact on replaying 221–226
      replay vs. resubscribe 222
      replaying logic of stream 222–223
   impact on resubscribing 221–226
      replay vs. resubscribe 222
      resubscribing to stream 224–226
sinceLast variable 78
single-value data sources
   asynchronous 47–48
   synchronous 46
skip operator 311
slice() method 63
sources of data
   identifying 43–44
   multi-value, asynchronous 48–49
   multi-value, synchronous 46–47
   single-value, asynchronous 47–48
   single-value, synchronous 46
   wrapping with Rx.Observable 43–52
square() function 259
startWith operator 154, 311
state
   managing with Redux 284–286
   of React components 279–284

state attribute 278
stateful functions 246
static data 44
static methods 102
stock ticker 231
streams 17, 19–25
   asynchronous 141–146
   cancelling 62–68
      cancellation mismatch between RxJS and other APIs 67–68
      disadvantages of eager allocation 62–64
      explicitly cancelling subscriptions 65–67
      lazy allocation 64–65
      subscribing to observables 64–65
   components of 23–25
      consumers 23–24
      data pipelines 24
      producers 23
      time 24–25
   creating hot-by-operator 232–237
   evaluating 62–68
      cancellation mismatch between RxJS and other APIs 67–68
      disadvantages of eager allocation 62–64
      explicitly cancelling subscriptions 65–67
      lazy allocation 64–65
      subscribing to observables 64–65
   failed, retrying for fixed number of times 197–199
   interleaving events by merging 124–129
   joining parallel with combineLatest 159–170
   making testable 258–260
   multiple 122–135
   preserving event order by concatenating 130–133
   reactive 121–150
      asynchronous streams 141–146
      dragging and dropping with concatMap 146–150
      multiple 122–135

streams, reactive *(continued)*
    testing 255–258
    unwinding nested
        observables 135–141
    replaying logic of 222–223
    resubscribing to 224–226
    search 267–270
Streams data type 35
sub.unsubscribe() function 56
subactions 291
subflows 291
subjects, RxJS 294–296
subscribe() function 49, 53, 64,
    79, 289
subscriptions
    explicitly cancelling 65–67
    to observables 64–65
Success type 190
switch blocks 128
switch() function 135, 312
switchMap operator 313
synchronizing streams 163
synchronous computing, vs.
    asynchronous
    computing 5–12
    event emitters 11–12
    issues with blocking code
        5–6
    non-blocking code with call-
        back functions 6–7
    understanding time 7–9
    using callbacks 9–10
synchronous data sources
    multi-value 46–47
    single-value 46

T

take operator 311
takeUntil() function 148, 311
temperature, of observables
    226–237
temporal dependency 9
testing
    AJAX requests 250–253
    asynchronous code 250–255
        testing AJAX requests
            250–253
        working with Promises
            253–255
    Promises 250–255
        testing AJAX
            requests 250–253
        working with 253–255

reactive programs 245–270
    augmenting virtual
        reality 263–270
    inherently built into func-
        tional programs
        246–250
    making streams testable
        258–260
    scheduling values in RxJS
        260–263
reactive streams 255–258
refactoring search streams
    for 267–270
thenable function 43
this keyword 7, 277
throttleTime operator 312
throttling 108, 110
throw operator 312
tick$ observable 206, 235
time
    abstracting over 21–23
    understanding 7–9
    virtual scheduler 266–267
time coupling 9
timeInterval operator 96, 312
timer operator 311
timestamping events 127
timing 85–117
    asynchronous with JavaScript
        88–94
        explicit 88–90
        implicit 88
        interfaces 90–94
    buffering 111–117
    explicit 88–90
    handling user input 101–110
        debouncing 101–108
        throttling 108–110
    implicit 88
    importance of 87
    JavaScript interfaces 90–94
        setInterval 93–94
        setTimeout 91–92
    operators 94–101
        propagation 98–99
        sequential time 99–101
touchend event 123
touchEnd$ stream 124
touchmove event 123
touchstart event 123
transactionLogEpic() function
    297
transformational operations 70
transient 26

transparency, referential 77–80
truthy value 74
try block 190
try/catch, error handling with
    183–184

U

UI (user interface), rendering
        components with React
        274–284
    managing state of React
        components 279–284
    overview 274–275
    React classes 277–279
    React components 275–277
    state management with
        Redux 284–286
unicast transmission 227
unopinionated framework 26,
    274, 289
unsubscribe operator 66, 155,
    157–158, 313
unwinding nested observables,
        with mergeMap
        operator 135–141
upstream compartmentaliz-
    ation 152
user input 101–110
    debouncing 101–108
    throttling 108–110
user interface. *See* UI
using operator 159, 310
UX (user experience) 5, 87

V

value object 96
values, scheduling values in
    RxJS 260–263
virtual reality, augmenting
    263–270
    refactoring search streams
        for testability 267–270
    with marbles 264–266
    with virtual time scheduler
        266–267
virtual time scheduler 266–267

W

web hooks 153–154
withdraw function 179
withLatestFrom operator 312

wrapping data sources with
Rx.Observable 43–52
creating RxJS observables
44–45
identifying different sources
of data 43–44
pull-based semantics 49–52
push-based semantics 49–52

when and where to use RxJS
46–49
WS (WebSockets) 217–221
clients 220–221
overview 218–219
simple servers in Node.js
219–220

X

XmlHttpRequest object 14, 250

Z

zip() operator 202, 205, 313

MORE TITLES FROM MANNING

Secrets of the JavaScript Ninja,
Second Edition
by John Resig, Bear Bibeault, and Josip Maras

ISBN: 9781617292859
464 pages
$44.99
August 2016

Functional Programming in JavaScript
How to improve your JavaScript programs using
functional techniques
by Luis Atencio

ISBN: 9781617292828
272 pages
$44.99
June 2016

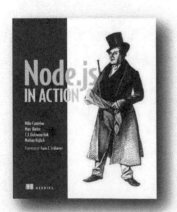

Node.js in Action
by Mike Cantelon, Marc Harter, T.J. Holowaychuk,
and Nathan Rajlich

ISBN: 9781617290572
416 pages
$44.99
October 2013